NORTHROP FRYE

NEW DIRECTIONS FROM OLD

NORTHROP FRYE

NEW DIRECTIONS FROM OLD

Edited by

David Rampton

uOttawa

The University of Ottawa Press acknowledges with gratitude the support extended to its publishing list by Heritage Canada through its Book Publishing Industry Development Program, by the Canada Council for the Arts, by the Canadian Federation for the Humanities and Social Sciences through its Aid to Scholarly Publications Program, by the Social Sciences and Humanities Research Council, and by the University of Ottawa.

We also gratefully acknowledge the Faculty of Arts at the University of Ottawa whose financial support has contributed to the publication of this book.

LIBRARY AND ARCHIVES CANADA CATALOGUING IN PUBLICATION

Northrop Frye : new directions from old / edited by
David Rampton.

(Reappraisals, Canadian writers 1189-6787 ; 33)
Includes bibliographical references and index.
ISBN 978-0-7766-0695-8

1. Frye, Northrop, 1912-1991--Criticism and
interpretation. 1. Rampton, David, 1950-
11. Series: Reappraisals, Canadian writers ; 33

PN75.F7N673 2009   801'.95092   C2009-901836-5

∞

PRINTED AND BOUND IN CANADA

CONTENTS

PART V

NEW APPROACHES

Contributors

John Ayre, Frye Biographer
D. M. R. Bentley, University of Western Ontario
Robert Denham, Roanoke College
Michael Dolzani, Baldwin-Wallace College
Jeffery Donaldson, McMaster University
Troni Grande, University of Regina
David Jarraway, University of Ottawa
Alvin Lee, McMaster University
Jean O'Grady, Editor, Collected Works of Northrop Frye
J. Russell Perkin, Saint Mary's University
Garry Sherbert, University of Regina
Michael Sinding, Justus Liebig University (Germany)
Reverend Ian Sloan, United Church Minister
Robert David Stacey, University of Ottawa
Sára Tóth, Károli Gáspár University, Hungary
Thomas Willard, University of Arizona

Abbreviations

Standard Abbreviations for Northrop Frye's Works and Collections

AC	Anatomy of Criticism 1957
BG	The Bush Garden 1971
CP	The Critical Path 1971
CR	Creation and Recreation 1980
DG	Divisions on a Ground 1982
DV	The Double Vision 1991
EAC	The Eternal Act of Creation 1993
EI	The Educated Imagination 1963
FI	Fables of Identity 1963
FS	Fearful Symmetry 1947
FT	Fools of Time 1967
GC	The Great Code 1982
MC	The Modern Century 1967
MD	The Myth of Deliverance 1983
MM	Myth and Metaphor 1990
NFCL	Northrop Frye on Culture and Literature 1978
NFF	Northrop Frye Fonds
NFS	Northrop Frye on Shakespeare 1986
NP	A Natural Perspective 1965
OE	On Education 1988
RCLI	Reflections on the Canadian Literary Imagination 1991
RE	The Return of Eden 1965
RW	Reading the World: Selected Writings 1935–1976. 1990

SES	The Secular Scripture 1976	
SM	Spiritus Mundi 1976	
STS	The Stubborn Structure 1970	
SER	A Study of English Romanticism 1968	
TSE	T.S. Eliot 1963	
WGS	A World in a Grain of Sand 1991	
WP	Words With Power 1990	
WTC	The Well-Tempered Critic 1963	

Volumes in The Collected Works of Northrop Frye

1–2	NFHK	The Correspondence of Northrop Frye and Helen Kemp
3	SE	Northrop Frye's Student Essays
4	NFR	Northrop Frye on Religion
5–6	LN	Northrop Frye's Late Notebooks, 1982–1990: Architecture of the Spiritual World
7	WE	Northrop Frye's Writings on Education
8	Diaries	The Diaries of Northrop Frye, 1942–1955
9	TBN	The "Third Book" Notebooks of Northrop Frye, 1964–1972
10	LS	Northrop Frye on Literature and Society, 1936–1989
11	NFMC	Northrop Frye on Modern Culture
12	NFC	Northrop Frye on Canada
13	RT	Northrop Frye's Notebooks and Lectures on the Bible and Other Religious Texts
14	FS2	Fearful Symmetry: A Study of William Blake
15	NR	Northrop Frye's Notebooks on Romance
16	M&B	Northrop Frye on Milton and Blake
17	ENC	Northrop Frye's Writings on the Eighteenth and Nineteenth Centuries

VOLUMES OF THE COLLECTED WORKS OF
NORTHROP FRYE AND OF FRYE STUDIES

(University of Toronto Press)

Vols. 1–2. *The Correspondence of Northrop Frye and Helen Kemp*, ed. Robert D. Denham (1996). Also *A Glorious and Terrible Life with You: Selected Correspondence of Northrop Frye and Helen Kemp, 1932–1939*, selected and ed. Margaret Burgess (2007).

Vol. 3. *Northrop Frye's Student Essays*, ed. Robert D. Denham (1997).

Vol. 4. *Northrop Frye on Religion*, ed. Alvin A. Lee and Jean O'Grady (2000).

Vols. 5–6. *Northrop Frye's Late Notebooks, 1982–1990: Architecture of the Spiritual World*, ed. Robert D. Denham (2000).

Vol. 7. *Northrop Frye's Writings on Education*, ed. Jean O'Grady and Goldwin French (2000).

Vol. 8. *The Diaries of Northrop Frye, 1942–1955*, ed. Robert D. Denham (2001).

Vol. 9. *The "Third Book" Notebooks of Northrop Frye, 1964–1972*, ed. Michael Dolzani (2002).

Vol. 10. *Northrop Frye on Literature and Society, 1936–1989*, ed. Robert D. Denham (2002).

Vol. 11. *Northrop Frye on Modern Culture*, ed. Jan Gorak (2003).

Vol. 12. *Northrop Frye on Canada*, ed. Jean O'Grady and David Staines (2003).

Vol. 13. *Northrop Frye's Notebooks and Lectures on the Bible and Other Religious Texts*, ed. Robert D. Denham (2003). The lectures on the Bible edited by Denham are also in *Biblical and Classical Myths: The*

Vol. 30. *Index to The Collected Works of Northrop Frye, Volumes 1–29*, comp. Jean O'Grady (2010).

Frye Studies

Lee, Alvin A., and Robert D. Denham, eds. 1994. *The Legacy of Northrop Frye*.

Boyd, David, and Imre Salusinszky, eds. 1999. *Rereading Frye: the Published and Unpublished Works*.

Cotrupi, Caterina Nella. 2000. *Northrop Frye and the Poetics of Process*.

O'Grady, Jean, and Wang Ning, eds. 2003. *Northrop Frye: Eastern and Western Perspectives*.

Donaldson, Jeffery, and Alan Mendelson, eds. 2004. *Frye and the Word: Religious Contexts in the Writings of Northrop Frye*.

Gill, Glen Robert. 2006. *Northrop Frye and the Phenomenology of Myth*.

Introduction

David Rampton

"ASCENT MAY be to the new: when it is, descent is the recovery of the old that was excluded by repression, forgetting, or lack of awareness. It's a harrowing of hell or rather limbo: a redemption of the dead, a recalling of past to present. Similarly new formulations of myth recapture lost and neglected implications. The Grail stories are profounder than cauldrons-of-plenty myths, and my reading of them is profounder than they are."[1]

Northrop Frye, the curious universal scholar who wrote this confident and prophetic account, liked to use the short paragraph as a mode for his extemporized formulations. This one posits links between essential notions in psychology, religion, and literature and suggests innumerable others to the receptive reader. His mind works fast and makes ours work faster. Both the originality of such an approach and the cool assessment of the value he added in the process of articulating it help explain the perennial interest in his work. When Frye's oeuvre was made the subject for the annual Canadian Literature symposium at the University of Ottawa, the date seemed auspicious: 2007 was the fiftieth anniversary of the publication of *Anatomy of Criticism* and various people had been thinking that a conference should be held to celebrate the event. Contributors were therefore invited to draw on any aspect of Frye's work, to range as widely as possible and to work at bringing seemingly disparate things together. With a rubric as non-specific as "New Directions from Old," the contributions themselves ended up determining the focus, since much of what is new in Frye studies is dedicated to the old in a chronological sense, namely, the correspondence, diaries, and early essays recently published in the Collected Works series. And much of what is old seems new to those who have come to literary criticism long after *Anatomy of Criticism* ceased to be the vade mecum for graduate students that it was in the years immediately following its publication.

The idea of making this tribute a sort of omnium-gatherum was also inspired in part by the astonishing range of Frye's interests, about which we have learned a great deal since his death in 1991. The energy with which he pursued them and the audacity of the imaginative leaps he made in asserting their conjunction have become that much more apparent as we read the entries in the diaries he wrote as his career was taking shape and the notebooks in which he wrestled with his daimons. He once defined the object of his search as the "grammar of poetic language that would bring all of literature together," and one feels that only someone with Frye's erudition and single-mindedness could have attempted it. When he asks (in *The Critical Path*), "What is the total subject of study of which criticism forms a part?" the answer is still far from clear to him, but on the basis of the early diaries, the late notebooks, the volumes that made his reputation, and the clutch of articles that have been described as "pure gold," we can perceive its outlines more clearly.

The overwhelming impression of these new materials is a sense of what a busy guy Frye was, from his undergraduate years to his hectic retirement, recovering the past, redeeming the dead, and searching for the Grail. If one looks, for example, at Volume 8 of the Collected Works, the one devoted to the 1942–1955 diaries, one gets a vivid sense of an impossibly energetic purveyor of literary insights, endlessly positing original ways of reading an astonishing variety of texts, whirling up data from literature and contiguous disciplines and working it into bold new configurations. The start of the winter term in 1950 is typical (*Diaries* 223–230). On Monday, 9 January, Frye described in his diary how his graduate seminar at Victoria College that day had gone:

> I started to try to work out the progressive & regressive characters of romance: virgin or heroine-anima against the harlot, wise old man against the malignant old man, and so on. I must realize that, as the monster usually contains the old man, so the hero is supported by the bearing animal (horse), in which, as Jung showed, there's some suggestion of a progressive mother. It also occurred to me that the hero-monster antithesis is always a victim-tyrant one. The hero is always in a revolutionary role: he releases the victim from the tyrant, which is why the giant is usually an enemy. Feudal or chivalric aristocracy owed its power to its militant struggle for order against rapacity: its decline began with the regularizing of the crusading impulse on which it was founded into an external war, & so a defence of the senex order in Christendom. Also, if the bearing animal can become a machine, the old-man monster could too—the labyrinth is a machine, & so is the mill with its revolving wheels.

Again, when one counts up the disciplines evoked and thinks about the energy and inspired guesswork that bring them together, one is left with the impression of a mind that is different in kind. There's a sense of urgency too—"I must realize"—that gives the passage a hortatory feel, a sense of things out there waiting to be discovered.

The next day's entry included a summary of a lecture on John Henry Newman: "In the middle of it I got a strong vision of the identity of the

Roman law and the Roman Church, and of both, especially the law, as intimately connected with the Aristotelian entelechy or law of the organized being, a biological conception that seems to permeate all our thinking." On Wednesday, it was Hooker's turn:

> I gave them the idea of law spread out over the chain of being. Man halfway between the angelic & the animal, hence a three-fold law; the law of the church, which is "intuitive," a symbol or [Joseph] Butlerian "analogy" of Eternal law; the law of society, which is rational and distinctively human, & the law of instinct, which produces the army of Caesar (I added this for completeness). How law begins as external & arbitrary command, then becomes the inner discipline of reason, then the reconstructed accuracy of instinct, via ceremonial & ritual, on the higher level.

That was in the morning. At noon it was Newman again, a lecture that linked his "genetic & pragmatic ('skeptical,' he calls it) view of probability with his choice of the genetic confession form and his primarily historical cast of mind." In the Thursday lecture on Milton, Frye identified sin and death with Scylla and Charybdis, tried to work out the symbolic significance of Eden's topography, and mused about the importance of olfactory imagery in *Paradise Lost* ("the 'myopic' visualization is in Book IV shifted to perfumes, smell being the most languorous & least critical of the senses"). That would have to suffice that day, for his noon-hour lecture on Job "had nothing new in it."

To round out the week it was *Paradise Lost* again. Frye used "He for God only" as his text:

> Humanity is descended from Eve in its natural form & needs a mediator with God who can only be a new Adam. More on the dream as the revolt of the egocentric libido, the principle of pride, against a law which it regards as an external censor—this clicks with an old hunch I've had that Freud describes the man under

the law—it's not an accident that he wrote a book on Moses and regards the conquest of the Promised Land as the "future of an illusion." Then how Satan in the temptation communicates directly with the proud libido in Eve, a parody of the way the Holy [S]pirit in man answers to the Word. The problem of the ultimate externality of both libido & Spirit remains unsolved. Also of the fact that unfallen Eve is the "passion" part of Adam's own body, whereas the fallen Eve is the entering wedge of an external "nature."

On the sixth and seventh days, he rested—or at least tried to. Though he intended to deal with the correspondence he'd been neglecting, Frye worked instead on Dante's *Inferno*, instructively comparing it to Milton's epic and Orwell's *1984*, and ending up contradicting one of his own essential tenets about literature:

> I can't help feeling that there is some development in literature, for all I say to the contrary. George Orwell's *1984* presents a real hell, not just one we happen to be more scared of, & his book is morally an infinitely better book than the *Inferno*. Surely this moral superiority has some relevance to critical standards.

Frye also noted he didn't have to read Dante's great poem in the original because he had already memorized most of it in the original.

The diaries also make clear that he fitted all this thinking into days made very full by other things. During the same week, Frye marked dozens of student essays, met with his Tuesday creative writing group (an informal weekly gathering he volunteered to coordinate), dedicated a couple of evenings to Canadian Forum business, ministered to his wife when she suddenly fell ill, discussed the prospect of a series of Renaissance lectures for later in the year, attended lectures on Bacon and Francis Thompson, mused about the possibility of a job offer from Princeton, and attended to all the other business associated with a new term. And all of this frenetic activity took place in the depths of a Canadian winter, a still point of the year that often has academics dreaming of a long hibernation.

Two more things: anyone who thinks I have loaded the dice by choosing a particularly charged week is welcome to look at the entries for the next one, 16–22 January 1950, which feature a set of equally suggestive musings on Browne's *Religio Medici*, rationalist readings of history, Arnold, Bentham, Carlyle, and Marx on class in the 19th century, and Gnosticism, along with more detailed accounts of Canadian Forum work, *Paradise Lost*, Dante, administrative affairs, and so on. The other thing to note is that during that first week, when one of his early classes was cancelled, Frye lamented having "dawdled" away the morning and called himself a "lazy bastard."

These entries and hundreds of others like them are the essence of what makes Frye so special. Such dazzling combinations so confidently asserted remind us of just how difficult it is to explain adequately the extent to which Frye revolutionized literary criticism in the 1950s. Reading these thumbnail sketches of how Frye thought, musing about what the actual hour-long lectures must have been like—the details noted above are just the barest of bare outlines, after all—conjuring with the leaps of synthetic imagination recorded in such matter-of-fact detail, one is struck most perhaps by the extraordinary restlessness of Frye's mind, the originality of his formulations, the eclectic nature of the resources he drew on, the indivisibility of his teaching and scholarship, the dialogic nature of his imagination, and the startling combination of the intuitive and the schematic that characterizes his critical endeavours in general. True, all of these things were well known, amply documented, and much discussed when Frye was the best-known literary critic in the English-speaking world. Yet it is rapidly becoming obvious that the publication of the Collected Works has launched an important new stage in Frye criticism. It has provided readers with detailed accounts of the context and background for the work to come, the multiple points of departure, the sense of Frye feeling his way, a better understanding of how crucial guesses and hunches are in this sort of work and of how arbitrary he has to be while starting to work things out ("I added this for completeness"), and, finally, a clearer grasp of the almost infinite series of vistas and possibilities that presented themselves to him. For anyone interested in language, metaphor, narrative, myth, society, politics, religion, the visionary, or simply the interpenetration of literature and life on a daily basis, here is God's plenty.

In his introduction to a collection of essays on Frye and religion, Jeffery Donaldson notes, "We are only just beginning to appreciate the rhetorical impact and function of Frye's assembling of evidence, his avoidance of strict narrative argument in favour of non-linear metaphoric juxtapositions of observed details, his emphasis on showing rather than telling" (17). In other words, the man whose name rapidly became a household word for his ability to engage in ultra-arcane mental operations ("He's no Northrop Frye" was a standard putdown for a long time) is someone who can instruct us in the importance of non-linear ways of thinking as well.

The first section of this book features three essays on Frye's status in the academy, the different ways his contributions to how we talk about literature have been assessed, and what it is that makes him distinctive.

We begin with Alvin Lee's account of the publishing history of the Collected Works. Involved in the project from its inception and currently general editor of the series, Lee is in an ideal position to give readers an overview of how Frye's posthumous publications have taken shape. He makes three essential points: First, that a scholarly edition of Frye's works represented an almost inevitable next step in a sequence of events designed to ensure some sort of permanent status for Frye studies. Because Frye had already been the centre of critical attention for a number of decades, because critics and readers had for so long wanted to apply his insights, imitate his methods, argue over his propositions, or just get together to talk about him, when the subject of the Collected

Works was first broached the University of Toronto was already collecting material by and about Frye, and the centre named after him was fully operational. Although Lee doesn't say it, the names of critics whose work has been commemorated in such a way would make a very short list indeed. Second, the actual encounter with the material in the diaries, notebooks, and correspondence obviously made it clear to the editorial committee just what an unpublished treasure trove Frye had left behind. Negotiating the terms of publication with lawyers and administrators, publishers and granting agencies, Lee and his committee were unwavering in their conviction that Frye's work should be made available to as large a readership as possible. Finally, there is the clear sense that those at work on the project knew from the beginning that, despite the range of Frye's interests and the different modes in which he articulated them, his work constituted a unity, and their labours would help reveal both that unity and the extraordinary mix of materials of which it was composed. The quality of the works published thus far and their public reception have amply confirmed Lee's determination to see the project through to its end.

Robert Denham's account of Frye's current status begins with a series of epitaphs on his demise, collected from a range of critics who insist that Frye's work is now obsolescent. Such a reaction was perhaps the inevitable result of Frye's conviction that the study of literature in and of itself was a supremely important thing. Many of those who came after Frye have been deeply suspicious of such claims, hence the impatience with his work felt by feminists, postmodernists and political critics of various stripes, and what is perceived as the démodé quality of his totalizing vision. For Denham, who knows more about Frye's reception than anyone, such claims must be measured against a lot of contradictory evidence: the fact that his name figures on reading lists at all sorts of universities in North America and Europe, that the number of students writing dissertations on his work continues to grow, that since 1980 translations of it have appeared in a startling array of tongues, and that the way Frye's ideas "have been applied by philosophers, historians, geographers, an-thropologists, political scientists, and by writers in the fields of advertis-ing, communication studies, nursing, political economy, legal theory, organization science, and consumer research" shows just how relevant he still is for readers in the 21st century.

One of the most interesting things about the evidence Denham as-sembles is that it shows Frye as one of those critics dedicated to creating a new kind of canon by putting the old and the new, the literary and the non-literary, in conversation with each other. In suggesting that readers might profit from thinking about why so much work is still being done on Frye, Denham implicitly posits the existence of something larger and more all-encompassing than a sequence of critical trends. For Denham, Frye's ideas about literature represent a perpetual renewal of possibil-ities, which will in turn continue to make him an important guide for those in search of innovative ways of reading.

Thomas Willard tackles the question of Frye's extraordinary critical gifts in a different way, by meditating on how we should interpret Frye's description of himself as a genius in an anticipatory obituary he wrote. Willard distinguishes between the Classical and the Romantic inflec-tions of this particular word and muses about whether there is some identifiable quality that distinguishes Frye's work from that of his con-temporaries, something that makes it different in kind. Genius can also mean "guide" or "tutelary spirit" or "guardian angel," something one has rather than something one is. The mention of Socrates's daimon in this context leads to a discussion of Frye's ideas concerning education and the importance of the visionary in his work. Then there is the impersonal form of genius, the genius of an imaginative space or genre. The ideal or-der of words that is literature, decisions about what constitutes the can-on, the recognition of the power of tradition in determining the forces that shape readers and critics—all of these are related to this impersonal idea on which Willard rightly focuses. The final context for his inquiry into Frye's use of the word "genius" is the religious one. In a Christian sense, genius is related to the presence of a power in which we move and have our being, something shared that connects us with the spiritual world, something we aspire to rather than possess. Willard builds on this notion to conclude that "the genius that guided Frye *through* his writing and teaching, and guided us *to* the writing, is one that remains to be found *in* the writing," and invites us to contemplate the implications of that process for Frye's continued relevance.

Part II treats Frye and Canadian literature. For a substantial part of his career, Frye was a central figure in Canadian Studies. His essays and reviews made important contributions to its development, but he is a more marginal figure in this area now. Frye was always convinced that Canadian literature was somehow belated, and the early texts that fascinate many critics these days were often the objects of his scorn. In one diary entry, he wrote, "We hear a lot about the wonderful respect for the humanities everybody had around 1900. Well, what did they do with it? Was Canada, in 1900, turning out poets & novelists worth a shit in a cow barn? Was it turning out real scholars who could write important & lasting books? Nonsense" (*Diaries* 226). This view, bracing as it is, is no longer widely shared. The essays included in this section focus on Frye's conviction that Canadian literature was best seen as part of a historical rather than literary tradition, and they come to intriguingly different conclusions about his most famous discussion of the topic, namely, the "Conclusion to a *Literary History of Canada*."

David Bentley uses Frye's "Conclusion" as a means of assessing his overall usefulness as a critic of Canadian literature. Bentley begins by pointing out how significant Frye's contribution has been in this regard, and the critics he cites show how influential certain ideas Frye articulated came to be for a whole generation of Canadian writers. Frye's intense dislike of physical nature, amply documented by his comments on Canadian landscapes and topography in the notebooks and diaries, is crucial for understanding his response to its literature. The "ghastly nightmares, Gothic dread, and a sense of personal disintegration" he finds there are, suggests Bentley, the product of Frye's own "psycho-physical reaction to the unhumanized and non-human aspects of the Canadian environment." Even as he praises Frye as a cartographer of the spaces created by the mythic imagination, Bentley points out how mis-leading his attempts to mythologize parts of the Canadian experience actually are, as when Frye argues that the lack of an Atlantic seaboard and the consequent journey up the St. Lawrence River led to the cre-ation of an image of a country that swallows its early immigrants by in-volving them in a sort of slow-motion disappearing act. As Bentley dem-onstrates, not only does this run counter to the testimony of all kinds of people whose first port of call was in the Maritimes, but it also fails to take into account the descriptions of writers who recorded their reac-tions on their arrival from Europe by sea. Bentley submits Frye's famous "garrison mentality" trope to similar scrutiny and finds it wanting, al-though he does see it as important for understanding the desire to con-trol the environment as an essential tenet of Frye's thinking. In Bentley's view, Frye's great contribution to Canadian culture turns out to be not his writings on Canadian literature but the exercise in self-creation that made him an iconic figure and a literary theorist whose name became as-sociated with his country's most important literary achievements.

Robert David Stacey tackles the "Conclusion" to the *Literary History of Canada* from a rather different perspective. In "History, Tradition, and the Work of the Pastoral," he takes up Bentley's point about the im-portance of the "Conclusion's" influence, describing its primary func-tion as "not to present a coherent theory of Canadian literature ... but to construct a coherent *critic* who might preside over a single unified (and unifying) critical approach." Stacey supports this contention by focusing on the discussion of the pastoral in the "Conclusion," seeing it as "a generic trope of origin and identity, of communal belonging and spiritual immanence" that helps explain Frye's seemingly contradictory statements on the status of Canadian literature and brings his local cul-tural and international theoretical projects together. Stacey notes that the champion of literary continuity argues for the discontinuity of Canadian literature as early as 1943 and notes that "environment" for Frye is both physical and socio-cultural. He also invites us to think of the "garrison mentality" as one of Fredric Jameson's "ideologemes" and suggests "displacement" as a useful term for understanding the Canadian writer's relation to the European tradition. In addition, Stacey points out that for Frye's Canadian writer "meaning is never simply present" but "exists in a dialectic between the pre-existing forms and the social and historical circumstances of their production and use." Frye's emphasis on displacement and belatedness in the "Conclusion" confirms this take on Canadian literature, and his focus on the pastoral brings together Canadian literature and its traditional mythological framework. All of this proves that even Frye's refuted claims possess a suggestiveness that makes them a rich source of new syntheses and provocative reconsiderations.

The next section comprises three essays on Frye and the sacred. Long before he published his studies on the Bible, critics had noticed just how interested Frye was in religious ideas, and we know that his knowledge of the esoteric tradition was extensive. Add to that his readings on mysticism and the visionary, Buddhism, the I Ching, and even subjects as arcane as astrology and numerology, and the importance of this aspect of Frye's work becomes clearer.

Ian Sloan's essay discusses Frye's importance as a theologian. He points out that when Frye was ordained as a minister of the United Church in 1936, he joined a church that not only brought together Methodists, Congregationalists, and Presbyterians but also sought to unite other Christian communions that shared its ideals. Sloan sees an important link between Frye's adherence to a church founded by such a unifying movement and characterized by its theological pragmatism and its inclusivity, on the one hand, and his idea about the autonomy of the critic and one's desire to become what one identifies with, something most clearly associated with his totalizing approach to literary criticism, on the other. Sloan also reminds us that Frye's critique of organized religion is bound up with its being a mere analogy "of the imaginative universe of the individual in community." Sloan develops his argument by using Blake's theory of contraries, noting that for both Blake and Frye the idea of throwing off imaginative passivity in the face of abstract authoritarian structures is especially important. This in turn leads to a discussion of the importance of the sacraments to any Christian and Frye's ambiguous attitudes toward them. Sloan points out how a better understanding of Blake's attack on organized religion can help us make sense of the choice Frye made in deciding to remain a minister of the church while seeking refuge in the university, staying away from church, and teaching students how literature contributes to what he called the architecture of the spiritual world.

Sára Tóth takes as her point of departure the description of God as "a spiritual Other" (in Frye's posthumously published *Double Vision*) and sets out to determine how Frye's views on religion led him to such a formulation. This is a subject that has received considerable attention of late, most notably in the book of essays edited by Donaldson and Mendelson (2004) and Denham's 2003 study of Frye the religious thinker. Tóth follows Denham by claiming that what's at stake in such questions is inextricably bound up with Frye's take on our literary experience. As she points out, without Frye's vision of a shared imaginative community shaped by something more than human, the very possibility of being moved by what we read is undermined. If otherness involves in some sense the text itself, then a sustained encounter with it bespeaks some genuine attempt at identification. In the process of making her case, Tóth shows how Lacan's narrative of alienation was important for Frye, and how it enabled him to see in Buber a sort of comic reversal of that narrative, one that replaces the mystic's self-abnegation with the idea of interpenetration. Tóth also examines Frye's translation of the dialogic principle into Christian terms, his identification of Narcissus as a type of the fall of Adam, his reading of the book of Job as a manifestation of the paradoxes of divine power and human incomprehension, and the crucial role otherness plays in the human relations informed by this matrix of notions.

Garry Sherbert is also interested in the relation between the sacred and the secular in Frye. In his exploration of this subject, he repeatedly shows how useful Derrida's thoughts on religion as a discourse can be in piecing together what Frye thinks about the "word within the Word." Late Derrida is full of evocative formulations that attempt to define the sacred, and Sherbert uses them skilfully to support the series of rapprochements on which his argument depends. He shows how interested Frye was in "pure speech" throughout his career, from *Fearful Symmetry* to *The Critical Path* to *Words With Power*. He links Frye's fascination with Heidegger to their mutual interest in the limits of language and points out the ways Frye's interest in myth is related to "the suspension of reference in both literature and religious writing." For Frye, Mallarmé is a figure who looms almost as large as Blake, and Sherbert illustrates the analogy between religion and literature by citing an apposite comment by Mallarmé on the need that both religion and literature have for mystery. Using this as a springboard for his claim that Mallarmé "exemplifies the literary version" of negative theology, Sherbert goes on to analyze how important this notion is in Frye's own work. This leads to a discussion of the parable and the aphorism and Frye's suggestive comments about them. In the rest of the essay Sherbert explores Frye's comparison of literary discourse to the visionary language of the mystics and quotes him to show that the social function of the poet, such as it is, is bound up with Eliot's notion of purifying the language of the tribe. Sherbert also invokes Frye's comments on Foucault to fill in a tentative definition of what "God" might mean and concludes by showing how for Frye the secrets at the heart of literature and religion are bound up with the nature of the creative imagination itself. Reading Tóth on Frye and Lacan or Sherbert on Frye and Heidegger, one is struck by how potentially useful such connections could finally prove to be, not only because they compel us to revise our views on the secular and the sacred but also because they enable us to see as figures on a continuum a range of writers who are often discussed as if they lived on different planets.

The next group of essays "recapture[s] lost and neglected implications," to use Frye's term, in ways that show how much mileage there still is in new studies of the old.

Frye's biographer John Ayre begins by musing on the relative lack of tables, diagrams, and visual aids generally in English studies, and the resistance schematic formulations often create. When Frye encountered such resistance after submitting his book to Princeton, he removed several diagrams, and they were not published until the Collected Works edition of 2006. Ayre contends that the impulse to downplay this aspect of Frye's work is understandable but unfortunate, since it deprives us of important assumptions he makes about the ways in which his subject can be represented. As Ayre explains, the structure of the mandala Frye used for *Anatomy of Criticism* is actually quite simple and incorporates traditional associations with the vertical and the horizontal, with the positive and exalted things at the top of the circle and the degraded and destructive ones that figure at the bottom. Of course Frye encountered such diagrams in Blake, but Ayre adduces as evidence other sources he must have drawn on, including Dante, Milton, and Dickens. The contemporary critical figure he focuses on is Wilson Knight, Frye's colleague at the University of Toronto in the 1930s, who in his study of Shakespeare argued that "a Shakespearian tragedy is set spatially as well as temporally in the mind." Ayre quotes Frye to very similar effect and goes on to suggest how important such schemata were to Frye in his teaching as well as his writing. Like Einstein in his search for a unified field theory, Frye hoped to find what he called "the kind of diagrammatic basis of poetry that haunts the occults & others." Heraclitus's double gyre, the Four Zoas, the evolution of cosmologies in the Romantic period, Spengler, Frazer, and Hesse—all of these are useful as Ayre plots the course of the battle that Frye fought with himself to "reinvent the wheel." In offering us the outlines of this struggle, Ayre manages to tell the story of an intellectual and spiritual quest of great interest.

Michael Dolzani's essay treats one of Frye's most persistent preoccupations, the utopia. Dolzani links it to the mandala patterns that Ayre sees as central to *Anatomy of Criticism* and to Frye's thinking more generally. Dolzani then surveys works in which the utopian theme prominently figures, ranging from *The Odyssey* to *The Tempest* to utopias in our own time. This in turn leads to a meditation on why the genre seems to be so limited. Dolzani notes, "With the exception of William Morris's *News from Nowhere*, it is hard to think of another utopia that qualifies as a major work of literature." For Dolzani, this speaks to the primacy of ideology in utopian fiction, which makes it a genre characterized by attempts to describe possible worlds governed by all-too-human limitations. Offering his own typology of utopias, Dolzani suggests that "the varieties of utopian experience" involve healing "particular modes of alienation." He goes on to cite different examples: "The ego can be alienated (1) even from itself, as in various states of split consciousness; (2) from the body; (3) from the refractory instrument of language; (4) from lovers; (5) from society; (6) from nature; and (7) ultimately from God." The subsequent examination of these categories leads Dolzani into a discussion of subjects as various as B.F. Skinner, Herbert Marcuse, Aldous Huxley, courtly love, the Co-operative Commonwealth Federation, Thoreau's *Walden*, Milton's *Areopagitica*, Rousseau's notion of the general will, and Jameson's study of utopia, *Archeologies of the Future*. In other words, Dolzani ranges as widely and synthesizes as effortlessly as Frye himself. In the process, he reminds us that yet another reason for asserting Frye's topicality is how endlessly interesting his topics are. The ideas that swirl around utopian visions are the ones that have found their way into every sort of human dream, and this makes Frye's work seem timeless. The critic who participated so actively in the debates that shaped his century and his country keeps on forcing us to enlarge our perspective.

Russell Perkin considers Frye's complex relations with Victorian writers in an essay that seeks to build on various conceptions of realism. He starts by reminding his readers how at home in the 19th century Frye was, both in terms of his upbringing and his early literary interests. Frye read Ruskin as part of the tradition of biblical typology, and Perkin notes how helpful it is to think of them in conjunction. He compares their definitions of myth, the role of anagogy in their vision, their pedagogical interests, and their importance as "secular preachers." The heart of the essay is the discussion of Frye's attitude to realism. Why, for example, is he more interested in William Morris than George Eliot, in James's *The Other House* than *Portrait of a Lady*, in Trollope's plots rather than his depiction of Victorian mores, and so on? Perkin suggests that in reacting against the influence of F.R. Leavis, Frye's work constitutes a veiled critique of a criticism that focuses on estimations of value based on notions of maturity and verisimilitude. This leads to a concluding section on the links between Frye and Wilde, in which the latter's notion of the centrality of creativity in criticism, his attack on Victorian naïve realism, the emphasis he puts on the liberating power of the creative imagination, and his interest in the anagogic and the archetypal all make him an intriguing precursor for the 20th-century critic who admired him so much.

Jean O'Grady takes up Frye's stance on value judgments in her essay with a view to exploring its implications for a range of things in which he was interested. Having surveyed the deprecatory claims he made about such judgments in *Anatomy*, O'Grady notes how often Frye resorted to them in his reviews. In invoking criteria such as sincerity or genuineness, says O'Grady, Frye is engaging in an experienced reader's "intuitive evaluations of the author's commitment." She goes on to track another criterion by which Frye is prone to judge works of art—that is, its capacity for leading us to what he calls "the centre of our imaginative experience." O'Grady wants to argue for a shift in emphasis toward this valuation of the visionary, one that occurs over the last two decades of Frye's life. It corresponds in her view with Frye's increasing emphasis on the links between literature and society, a new interest in the role of the reader, and a conviction that literature and works of art more generally constitute what he describes as "ways of cultivating, focusing and ordering one's mental processes." This involves O'Grady in a discussion of the importance and complexity of Frye's notion of the kerygmatic, one that enables her to say penetrating things about Frye and the Bible, Arnold's touchstone theory, Longinus's treatise *On the Sublime*, the prophetic quality in literature, the responsibilities of the critic, canon formation, and the idea of criticism as prophecy. The essay illustrates just how richly significant the idea of value is when thinking about Frye's work, and how many contiguous areas it opens up for those interested in revisiting it.

This final section is comprised of essays in which Frye's work is used to shed light on issues or approaches that have not been part of mainstream Frye studies. The essays in this section show just how helpfully his work can be adapted to the most disparate sorts of inquiry and how much light it has to shed on them.

Troni Grande chooses to explore how feminists can use Frye's criticism in new and interesting ways. She argues that "feminist critics have not attended to the ways in which the woman in Frye time and again becomes a crucial vehicle of divine inspiration and resurrection, moving society to a new order," and sets out to show how a more attentive reading of Frye demonstrates how "the woman comes to occupy the centre as an absent presence." Her paper focuses on the image of the silent Beatrice in Frye's reading of Dante, and on the way women are characterized in his notebooks and diaries. Grande claims that, for Frye, Beatrice is a beatific symbol of the maternal, a manifestation of divine grace, and Dante's means of escape from sin: she is both Virgin Mary and scolding mother, at once immanent and embodied. Grande goes on to examine Frye's interest in female sacrality, in the character of the earth mother and Graves's Triple White Goddess, noting his early interest

DAVID RAMPTON

in fertility cults and his conception of the death-rebirth archetype as "feminine or maternal." In support of these arguments she touches on Shakespearean comedy and romance, the Cinderella archetype, gender exclusive language, and the fact that female scholars have been responsible for so much of the important work done on ritual and archetype. In the last section, Grande writes movingly about Frye's discussion of the death of his wife Helen, the "silent Beatrice" who served as his guide and companion for so many years, concluding that "Frye's search for renewal takes place in and through the woman whose body, now absent, still marks the site of plenitude."

In his essay on Frye and film, David Jarraway begins by citing Frye who quotes Plato on the subject of art as "a dream for awakened minds," a formulation that neatly sets up the investigation of Frye and film that follows. Before designating film noir as the particular area in which he is interested, Jarraway speculates about what an encyclopaedic account of film along the lines of *Anatomy of Criticism* might look like, and one is instantly struck by a dozen different ways that this vast array of material might be re-contextualized from Frye's critical perspective. The ways in which Frye's work on the romance alone sheds light on all those westerns, comedies, and musicals his generation grew up with have often been remarked on but never comprehensively dealt with. Here Jarraway limits himself to an exploration of the ironies in Hitchcock's early films in light of Frye's comments about "the communicative arts' sense of critical or ironic detachment." This insight leads him to an account of the complex ways in which identity functions in the murder mystery and in Hitchcock's work more generally, with some intriguing detours into Lacan on the "corps morcelé," Deleuze on embryology, the queer subtext in Hitchcock's film, the usefulness of seeing ways of maintaining a sense of ironic detachment as attempts to protect identity, "the organic reification of American culture in economic terms," Frye's distinction (following Coleridge) between "stupid" and "prophetic" realism, and American sexual politics in the postwar era. Putting Frye into conversation with so many different interlocutors should help readers come up with other ways of discussing film that show how much he has to offer those interested in studying this particular aspect of culture.

Michael Sinding's "Reframing Frye" is an exploration of what Frye's work has in common with two recent critical movements, namely, Cultural Studies and Cognitive Linguistics. In this essay Sinding confines his analysis to how such movements approach the question of "how cultural meaning creates political common sense." The example he chooses to concentrate on involves the linguistic choices made in arguments between liberals and conservatives. Here Sinding focuses on George Lakoff's cognitive studies of politics, particularly his explanations of the frames used in political arguments that imply certain ways of seeing the world and work at forcing voters to accept them. Lakoff distinguishes the political world view that ensues by breaking it down to reveal its moral coherence. Frye's work, Sinding argues, can tell us important things about the literary aspects of these political visions. Drawing on Frye's account in *The Critical Path* of the myth of freedom and the myth of concern, Sinding shows how Frye's equation of the conservative with the social contract and the liberal with the utopia complements Lakoff's account. The narratives implicit in Lakoff's frames constitute the myths Frye sees as organizing the verbal universe. By using Frye's work to explore the extent to which metaphor, narrative, and conceptual reasoning come together, Sinding illustrates how relevant that work still is for those intent on understanding how the words we use and the stories we tell create ideology and cultural meaning. He suggests that, in reminding us of the literary dimensions of ordinary discourse, Frye can help us escape the potential insularity of semiological approaches to culture.

The last of the new directions, proposed by Jeffery Donaldson, involves comparing Daniel Dennett's approach to consciousness and Frye's commentary on the book of Job. Donaldson's intention is to show how useful Frye's work can be for those interested in science and theories of language. In Dennett's recent book on the origins of religion, he examines the evolutionary advantages of the religious attitude but goes on to suggest that it is now time to move beyond religion itself. Reversing Dennett's terms of reference, Donaldson invites us to consider "tying spirit to the advent of consciousness and metaphoric thinking," with a view to understanding better how the contiguity that he sees "between neuronal synapses and spirit might manifest itself in our understanding of imaginative and scientific thinking." Donaldson uses Frye's commentary on the Book of Job as his text, comparing the series of events that instruct Job to the way consciousness developed in the human species, in order to show how the biblical story can offer insights into a scientific process. Along the way, he manages to touch on subjects as diverse as Dennett's metaphors for consciousness, the nature of "unconscious neurological inputs and outputs," the links between these and Frye's mythopoeic worlds, and the ones between consciousness of self and consciousness of God. Donaldson goes on to note that the latter phrase means God as both an object of conscious thought (e.g., scientific enquiry) and the object of the search for the spiritual (looking beyond the facts provided by such enquiry). He concludes that Dennett's description of how we learn about the world is strikingly similar to Frye's own, and using the Book of Job as an example of a text that can help us define what ultimately constitutes the self, he brings together Frye's and Dennett's versions of how human beings cope with their environment.

There is a special tone that characterizes the conclusions of many of Frye's essays and books (O'Grady and Perkin both comment interestingly on this), which makes it tempting to try to imitate him here. That tone hints at first and last things, interpenetrating worlds and their implications, great aspirations and dying falls, and the implication that posterity will have to be the final judge of all these enquiries into the mysteries of how literary structures organize themselves. This is the meditative counterpart of the sprightly, confident tone of the excerpt I quoted at the outset. In the conclusion to an essay called "Criticism

Visible and Invisible," for example, Frye writes, "All the poet or critic can do is to hope that somehow, somewhere, and for someone, the struggle to unify and to relate, because it is an honest struggle and not because of any success in what it does, may be touched with a radiance not its own" (*StS* 89). Such wistful cadences quickly disabused the first generation of Frye's readers of any preconceptions they might have had about Frye as a bloodless taxonomist or gloomy systematiser. As we can see by this collection, his struggle to synthesize and move beyond conventional approaches continues to inspire all sorts of readers and thinkers to make their own attempts "to unify and to relate."

ENDNOTES

1   Robert D. Denham, ed., *Northrop Frye's Late Notebooks 1982–1990: Architecture of the Spiritual World*, The Collected Works of Northrop Frye. Vol. 5 (Toronto: University of Toronto Press, 2000), 12.

WORKS CITED

Donaldson, Jeffery, and Alan Mendelson, eds. 2004. *Frye and the Word: Religious Contexts in the Writings of Northrop Frye*. Toronto: University of Toronto Press.

Frye, Northrop. 2001. *The Diaries of Northrop Frye, 1942–1955*. The Collected Works of Northrop Frye. Vol. 8. Ed. Robert D. Denham. Toronto: University of Toronto Press.

———. 1970. *The Stubborn Structure: Essays on Criticism and Society* London: Methuen.

FRYE'S LEGACY

PART I

THE COLLECTED WORKS OF NORTHROP FRYE

The Project and the Edition

Alvin Lee

THE INITIAL idea of a collected edition of Frye's writings and speeches first surfaced on 2 May 1991, a little more than three months after Frye's death. James Carscallen, a colleague and former student of Frye, made the suggestion in a conversation with Eva Kushner, President of Victoria University, who then asked him to put the case for such an undertaking in the form of a letter to her. Later that day Carscallen did so, in a two-page single-spaced letter in which he recognized something of the complexity of what he was proposing and the large body of Frye's productions, including many repetitions, but made this comment: "... I've never read or heard anything from him that didn't give me the feeling of newness—a sense that I had to open my mind in a way I'd never done before."[1]

The first two volumes, with the title *The Correspondence of Northrop Frye and Helen Kemp 1932–1939*, edited by Robert D. Denham, appeared

in late 1996, "in memory of John M. Robson." A good deal had happened
in the almost six intervening years. I shall tell that story briefly, concentrating on the defining points and the individuals and groups involved,
and then move on to the more recent part of the narrative, bringing us
to May 2008, at which time twenty-five volumes of a thirty-volume collected edition were in print. One is imminent, three are in press, and the
final volume, a cumulative index, is building steadily. With the synoptic
story of those thirty volumes before us, we can proceed to examine what
it is that Frye has done and how his works might still be used.

Kushner readily saw the appropriateness of Carscallen's suggestion
that Victoria University should sponsor a scholarly edition of Frye's
works. In the latter half of the twentieth century, Frye had been the most
influential thinker in Canada about human cultures and works of the
human imagination. He had enjoyed a broad global impact. But he had
chosen to stay at Victoria College in Toronto, in spite of numerous blan-
dishments to move elsewhere. A reliable collected edition of his works
would make it possible for him to become the object of serious scholarship.

Kushner's respect for Frye's achievements and her collegial relation
with him had begun in 1965, when he went to Carleton University to
help inaugurate the Comparative Literature program she was founding there. Frye and his wife, Helen, had also gone with Kushner to
Islamabad to take part in an international conference on Comparative
Literature. He had been chancellor of Victoria University during her
time as president and vice-chancellor, and in that period she had established the Northrop Frye Centre (in 1988). Its purposes were to encourage and sustain research on the writings and thought of Frye as well as
humanities research projects compatible with Frye's intellectual and
cultural achievement. For some years, extending a little after Kushner's
presidency (which ended in June 1994), the centre thrived, with a series of fellowships, visitors, and lectures, under the encouragement of an
honorary board of prestigious individuals and a smaller management

board. For the past decade, aside from a few visiting scholars, the only major activity in the centre has been the editorial project.

An additional responsibility shared by Frye and Kushner had been the University of Toronto Graduate Centre for Comparative Literature, in which she played a leading role and he had accepted appointment as the first chair, largely because the centre was having difficulty getting established in the midst of jurisdictional disagreements. The commitment of someone of Frye's eminence let it happen.

The crucial first move now for Kushner in 1991 was to choose someone to help define the editorial project and start the administrative and scholarly process of putting it together. A year earlier, John M. Robson, a long-time faculty member at Victoria, had brought to a conclusion the editorial project The Collected Works of John Stuart Mill, which had produced thirty-three volumes from the University of Toronto Press. That work had taken most of Robson's professional life, thirty years, and he certainly would have been justified in asking his president to look elsewhere when she asked him to front the Frye project. The Mill edition had established levels of editorial excellence and scholarly production that will stand for a long time as one of Toronto's major academic achievements.

In spite of the scope of this new large project, Robson did agree to take it on. By November 1992 he had produced for Kushner a set of proposals that would lead to the first definition of the work to be done and the kind of organization he thought desirable.[2] Robson recommended that the president appoint a ten-member editorial committee whose chair would be the general editor, someone from Victoria University. The general editor would have authority over all editorial decisions once a protocol covering editorial principles and practices had been agreed on. Several of the members, he suggested, should be from Victoria or the University of Toronto. Robson foresaw that in the first year the committee would be busy and meet frequently while working out details, but gradually would have "only a supervisory role except in special circumstances." He asked that the Collected Works project be given a workroom in conjunction with the Frye Centre, which is on the second floor of the old Vic Library building on Charles Street West.

Work to be done in the short term included (a) the committee surveying all of Frye's published works to determine which of them were still in print and which were not and where copyright lay (b) surveying all unpublished manuscript materials (including notebooks and letters) to determine which merited consideration for publication and what arrangements (tentative or otherwise) had been made about them, and on that basis (c) drawing up a tentative publication program. These tasks having been carried out, the committee should then approach a publisher and try to sign an advance contract for the series and for the first volumes, the editors of the volumes to be chosen from Canadian universities and elsewhere. And finally, at this last stage of the first phase of the Works of Frye editorial project, applications for funding should be made.

Robson's proposals in November 1992 were the basis for action over the next three years, and in some respects for the project to this day, fifteen years later, but there were serious obstacles and progress was slow. By March 1993, he had assembled an editorial committee of fourteen people (larger than he had contemplated), with himself as chair. The inaugural meeting was held on 11 March 1993. The purpose of the project was sharpened, making clear that the goal was to produce a scholarly collected edition, not a complete works.

Beginning in November 1990, two months before Frye's death, Robert Denham of Roanoke College and Michael Dolzani of Baldwin-Wallace College had agreed to work together on editing Frye correspondence, permission having been given for this through Jane Widdicombe, former secretary to Frye and executrix of the Frye estate. With the initial discovery in 1991 of the riches in the unpublished notebooks and diaries, the realization was growing that there was much more to the unknown story of Frye's life and works than the letters. It was agreed at the 11 March 1993 meeting that the first volumes should include at least some of the unpublished papers. By 1992 Denham and Dolzani had obtained permission from the executors to edit and publish all the unpublished papers, though each of the contracts had to go through the executors for approval. Those at the meeting discussed the long time it might take to finish the project. Robson reported that he had applied to the Social Sciences and Humanities Research Council (SSHRC) with a letter of intent under the Major Collaborative Research Initiatives Program and that the council's response would be available shortly. The committee agreed the project would proceed regardless of the SSHRC decision, it being recognized that such first inquiries were frequently unsuccessful but still could be useful in later applications. By agreement between the general editor and the executors of the Frye estate, Widdicombe approached three presses—Harcourt Brace Jovanovich, Princeton, and the University of Toronto—to ascertain possible interest in publishing the edition. Harcourt showed polite interest and asked to be kept advised of developments. Princeton was cautious, concerned that the project might reduce their profits from the sales of *Fearful Symmetry* and *Anatomy of Criticism*. The University of Toronto Press was enthusiastic.[3]

Assembling the materials of the Frye oeuvre and sorting them into lists of possible subject areas was the first major editorial challenge. Finances had to be seen to. An agreement had to be made with a publisher.

Kushner was strongly supportive, and committed space, equipment, and secretarial help in the Frye Centre. She undertook to help find funds from Victoria University's Board of Regents and from external bodies, including not only SSHRC but also foundations. In the meantime the committee, through two sub-committees, one concerned with previously published works and the other with the unpublished materials, would formulate a publishing plan once Robson, Denham, and Widdicombe had done the preliminary sorting and arranging of materials.

The Frye estate, with Widdicombe, Denham, and Frye's tax account-
ant Roger Ball as trustees, still had not been settled at this point, early in
1993. Until it was, the executors were responsible for all decisions about
publication. It was known that all Frye's books and papers, unpublished
and published, were willed to Victoria University, along with a substantial cash legacy, but Victoria still did not have permission from the executors to publish.

The Northrop Frye Fonds at Victoria University Library had been
started much earlier, during Canada's centennial year 1967, with the
acquisition of the typescripts of *The Well-Tempered Critic* and *Fools of
Time: Studies in Shakespearean Tragedy*. Later additions during the next
twenty-five years included a partial typescript of a draft of the introduction and three chapters of *Fearful Symmetry*. There are typescripts,
sometimes annotated with corrections, of most of Frye's articles from
the 1960s on, including those published in collections such as *The Bush
Garden, Divisions on a Ground, The Stubborn Structure*, and so on. The
additions in the early 1990s included a large body of writing not published during Frye's lifetime. These are: eighty-five notebooks ranging in
size from 2 to 270 pages and dating from 1942 to 1990, a total of about a
million words; correspondence with Helen Kemp, whom he later married; diaries; essays written while a student; and something like 20,000
leaves of professional correspondence. The collection also includes the
annotated volumes in Frye's personal library (there is interesting sleuth-
ing still to be done in these) and his published works. These last are extensive. At the time of Frye's death in January 1991 he was the author
of twenty-eight books, followed posthumously that year by *The Double
Vision*. He had edited or co-edited thirteen books, been general editor
of a series of Shakespeare's plays, and served as supervisory editor of thirteen volumes of *Literature: Uses of the Imagination*. His essays and chapters appeared in more than sixty books. His separately published mono-
graphs, journal articles, introductions, and reviews are many. As well,
along the way there were miscellaneous writings and a host of utterances

in interviews, dialogues, radio talks, television programs, and film documentaries. Much of the work that was unpublished until the new collected edition is of prime intellectual and autobiographical interest. A good deal of the previously published work was out of print or scattered in relatively obscure places. All these intellectual products, published and unpublished, had to be brought together and considered as a whole to make the Collected Works edition possible.[4]

In the period after the first meeting of the editorial committee, serious problems began to emerge. Robson had a period of illness. That year, from the ninety that had sent letters of intent, SSHRC chose twenty-one research teams to proceed to the second stage of evaluation. Ours was not one of the chosen. It was becoming clear that the settlement of the estate was going to drag on and that there were unresolved questions between the executors and the people at Victoria about the choice of press and the nature of the edition. Still, in 1993 and early 1994, using Widdicombe's records and Denham's bibliographic work on Frye's writings, and assisted generously by both individuals, Robson was able to provide the committee with three important things (1) a two-page set of editorial principles (2) a survey of existing copyrights, and (3) the first of what was to become a series of lists of Frye's works, the first list being his writings on Canada. The committee agreed that editors would be selected for each category of materials or title and that the responsibility for determining the text would be theirs, while the general editor would be responsible for coherence throughout the edition. An editorial manual would be needed. The two main divisions of the materials would be "previously published works" and "unpublished writings."

The contents of the volumes of previously published works would be decided on as follows: titles by Frye of whole-volume size would be treated as discrete volumes and retain their original titles (e.g., *Fearful Symmetry, The Great Code*); collections of essays, chapters, forewords, and so on would be reorganized according to subject and grouped when appropriate into thematic series. The division into volumes would also be partly generic, with letters and interviews in particular volumes. As time went on, this theoretical definition of collections volumes was to involve many shuffles in the placing of individual items, sometimes leading to fairly arbitrary decisions—any number of texts could belong in more than one of the volumes—but the intention was that each volume would be coherent in subject matter and the items would be chronologically arranged within the volume. Moreover, each title was to have a critical/historical introduction, a short textual description, annotation, and an index. The texts were to be collated with all authorially approved exempla in English, the copy-text being the latest approved by Frye. The Collected Works was not to be a "critical" or variorum edition publishing all variants, but the record of the text's development was to be described. Annotation was to be used but with restraint. Frye's notes and quotations were to be checked and corrections indicated.

By this time Denham and Dolzani had made major progress on the previously unpublished materials. Denham was the major bibliographer of Frye's works, author of the first book about his criticism, and an editor of several collections of Frye papers. Dolzani had been Frye's graduate student and then research associate during the last decade of Frye's life. The initial task was to transcribe about a million words, mostly from Frye's difficult handwriting but some from typescripts. This new revolutionary material in the understanding of Frye was being made available in electronic form to members of the project. Initially, two types of writings were recognized, notebooks and diaries and then correspondence, the former being intellectually more important. For these materials it was agreed to produce a diplomatic text but with considerable annotation, since the detail is specific to time and place and much of it is closely related to published works and Frye's public career. The editorial apparatus for these new materials was to be like that planned for the previously published works. The correspondence between Helen Kemp and Frye was chosen by Denham, the committee, and the University of Toronto Press to be the first publication in the project.[5] It was agreed that the mass of professional correspondence would probably not be published in the foreseeable future.

In the fall of 1993, Robson appointed three additional area editors (to join Denham, who was doing the unpublished materials): David Staines for the writings on Canada; A.C. Hamilton for those on criticism; and me, to cover Frye on the Bible and religion. In early 1994, Jean O'Grady, who had worked with Robson on the Mill project and had expertise as a textual editor, joined the team and became a central strength of the whole project. Progress accelerated on the creating of thematic lists and in defining a policy on annotation and other editing practices. Denham was steadily working on his two-volume edition of the Frye-Kemp correspondence. Because a small grant had been received from the Lilly Foundation, work also started on what was to become volume 4, *Northrop Frye on Religion*, which O'Grady and I co-edited with the help of a part-time student assistant.

But in March 1995, Robson wrote an understandably gloomy report. Two major difficulties were seriously threatening to undermine the project. There was almost no money—a bit from the Department of English, a bit from Victoria University's block grant from SSHRC, and the designated Lilly grant—a total of about CA$9,000. It was not feasible to go back to SSHRC until the second problem had been solved, which was this: Victoria and the University of Toronto Press had not succeeded in getting the cooperation of Roger Ball, one of the executors of the estate, and a contract for the edition could therefore not be drawn up. His objections, interspersed with long delays, stemmed in part from his ignorance of the culturally significant nature of the materials he was dealing with. Ball knew little about matters of publication. His approach to Frye's works was to treat them as financial commodities and to tender his bills while prolonging the process of decision-making. Until a contract existed, no new approach to SSHRC could be made, and it was possible to proceed only in a piecemeal way, title by title, hiring even part-time assistants only on an occasional basis. At one point, thoroughly frustrated, Robson sent a letter of resignation to the president. In brief, he and the editorial team had defined an excellent project, one with large cultural significance and ideal for Victoria University and the University of Toronto Press, but things had almost reached an impasse. Robson's untimely death in the summer of 1995 made a fairly dire situation worse.

Late in 1995, matters began to improve. Brian Merrilees, a professor of French and by then the director of the Frye Centre, convened and chaired a committee to propose to the president of Victoria, Roseanne Runte (since July 1994), a successor as general editor of the Collected Works.[6] At the end of the year I was asked to take over.

If I had realized fully at the time the bleak financial situation the project was in, the continuing obduracy of one of the executors, and the sheer size of the intellectual task, I might well have turned away. On the other hand, my years as a senior administrator at McMaster University, including ten years as president, had prepared me to take on large tasks. Most importantly, from the time of my first year as a university student (1949–50), in Frye's course called The English Bible, I had been fascinated by his mind and imagination and his learning. The freshman course, in which we saw set out before us the imaginative interconnecting identities and typological patterns of the Bible as a supreme work of the human/divine imagination, was the beginning of intellectual and cultural consciousness for me. Later in a third year course on the drama, I heard Frye articulate his theory of comedy, and started to realize, literally for the first time, something of what literary structure is. Still later in a graduate course, Frye's chalkboard delineation of centripetal and centrifugal meaning (a circle inside a circle and with arrows) started a mental process I'm still working on.

The publication of *Anatomy of Criticism* in 1957, with its large patterns and hundreds of penetrating observations on works of literature, came at the right time for me as I was working my way through the old general examinations reading list for doctoral candidates in English at the University of Toronto, in all the periods of English literature. Years later, after three decades of intense work at McMaster, I was asked, on Frye's recommendation, to be Frye Professor of Literary Theory at the University of Toronto for 1991–1992. In accepting that invitation I had hoped at long last to have more frequent conversations with him. But he died before the appointment took effect and I ended up instead chairing a major international conference on his legacy, at Victoria University in 1992. This event was to have been a celebration of Frye's eightieth birthday. Because of all these things, and more, I knew when Victoria approached me that Frye's works had to be made fully available in reliable reading texts for our generation as well as future ones, and I was caught.

With the help of Jean O'Grady—if she had not been on staff, with her extensive experience as an editor and a textual editor, I'd definitely not have signed on—we moved forward on the complex matter of the lists and the divisions into volumes, and on several other detailed editorial matters. For the first time, we printed out and put to use a thematic outline of the whole edition with projections of the number of volumes in each section.[7] The outline pointed to a possible nineteen volumes but to date there will be sixteen of the previously published works, accompanied by and interspersed with thirteen volumes of the unpublished works edited by Denham and Dolzani, plus a cumulative index, for a thirty-volume collected edition. We also agreed with the University of Toronto Press on volume numbering: each title would be numbered in the order in which it was ready for publication.

There remained the crucial matter of appointing editors for unassigned volumes. By the fall of 1997, with advice from the principal editors and soundings elsewhere, we had editors or co-editors for most of the volumes, one in Australia, three in the United States, and the others in Canada. It is a mark of the cultural importance and intellectual excitement of the project that each scholar invited to serve said yes. Over the years since, there have been a few changes, including O'Grady stepping in as co-editor to bring to completion volumes that were lagging and Denham and Dolzani each taking on an additional volume when the first assignees had to be replaced, but in the main the first roster has completed or is doing the job. In late 1996, Denham's fine edition of the Frye-Kemp letters, meticulously annotated, appeared. By then he had also submitted to the centre and the University of Toronto Press what was to become volume 3, *Northrop Frye's Student Essays 1932–1938,* which appeared in 1997. Denham and Dolzani had by then completed transcription of the unpublished materials and these were now fully available, most of them of course still unedited, to workers in the project. Staines, Hamilton, O'Grady, and I agreed that the concept of "area editors" had ceased to be useful and that Adamson, Denham, Dolzani, Hamilton, Lee, O'Grady, and Staines would instead function as a team of principal editors. The other members of the original editorial committee, in 1997 already six years in existence, would remain as advisors, and have been called on from time to time.

While all this fundamental work was occurring, I was intent on trying to find real money for the pathetically underfunded project. I quickly learned that although it is not easy for a university president to raise large sums of money, it is a piece of cake compared to a private scholar searching on behalf of an editorial project in the humanities. Throughout 1996, with some help from Roseanne Runte, by then the president of Victoria University, I had got a CA$7,000 grant from the Gelber Foundation, but received a string of refusals elsewhere. Jean O'Grady was working as half-time assistant editor for an embarrassing pittance and we had a minuscule part-time staff. Mr. Ball was still stalling. Early in 1997, however, there was a breakthrough. I persuaded a friend, a wealthy businessman and former neighbour in West Flamborough, Michael G. DeGroote, to have his family donate through McMaster University CA$1 million to the project. This was put into a designated trust fund with expendable capital at McMaster University and has been the main financial base of the project for the last eleven years. To date, the investment income from the unspent capital has brought the original gift to well over the original million, about $1.4 million, from which we spend as needed. It was the DeGroote donation, plus strong pressure from Roseanne Runte and Victoria University, that finally induced Mr. Ball to settle and withdraw from the scene. At last, in early 1997, Victoria University and the University of Toronto Press were clear to move forward.

As co-investigators, Jean O'Grady and I have received CA$348,897 in the form of three successive three-year standard grants from SSHRC. At the time of the last grant we were told that the selection committee had made this statement: "The record of research achievement and the proposed program of research were judged to be of exceptional quality." They recommended that our proposal be funded at the level requested. We were told that the particular selection committee had considered 120 applications and had ranked ours number one. The DeGroote and the SSHRC money together have freed us to carry almost to completion this large, culturally important project. We have had a properly paid associate editor, Jean O'Grady, a half-time editorial assistant, Margaret Burgess, who once co-taught with Frye and is a knowledgeable and meticulous worker on his texts, and also, since 2001, a second editorial assistant, Ward McBurney (now succeeded by Erin Reynold), and a reliable succession of graduate student assistants. From 1998 to 2001 we had assistant editor Nicholas Halmi, who was in a tenure-stream position at McMaster and who edited *Fearful Symmetry* as well as doing important work in obtaining permissions from publishers. Finally, on the financial front, the Board of Regents of Victoria University have provided since 2001 a subvention for each volume to the University of Toronto Press, this decision having been made on the recommendation of Roseanne Runte in one of her last acts as president before taking up an appointment in the United States, and confirmed since by President Paul Gooch.

We're not all the way yet to completion of the project but the end is in sight. We calculate that about two or three more years will see The Collected Works of Northrop Frye in print in those handsome teal-coloured volumes now familiar to most of you. The index, volume 30, may take a little longer, but it is steadily taking shape as each of the other titles comes into print. What the world will have available in this edition is a treasure trove, the collected works of a great modern humanist, one of

13

the most brilliant, erudite, and accessible minds of the 20th century. It has been an exciting journey, travelling and interrelating with that mind, and I am grateful for the privilege.

ENDNOTES

1 The Carscallen letter is in the files of the Northrop Frye Centre at Victoria University.

2 The Robson recommendations are in the form of a letter to Kushner, now in the Frye Centre files, dated 18 November 1992.

3 The replies to J. Widdicombe from Harcourt and Princeton are in the Frye Centre files. The vice-president of publishing (W. Harnum) and the editor-in-chief (R. Schoeffel) of the University of Toronto Press, both of whom were to become major strengths of the project, had met with Widdicombe.

4 For a detailed guide to the Frye Fonds see *Guide to the Northrop Frye Papers*, comp. Dolores A. Signori (Toronto: Victoria University Library, 1993).

5 Given the widespread interest in the Collected Works edition of the Frye-Kemp correspondence, we have subsequently published *A Glorious and Terrible Life with You: Selected Correspondence of Northrop Frye and Helen Kemp, 1932–1939*, selected and edited by Margaret Burgess (Toronto: University of Toronto Press, 2007).

6 The committee was Brian Merrilees (chair), William Callahan (principal, Victoria College), William Harnum (University of Toronto Press), A.C. Hamilton (Queen's University), Eva Kushner (Frye Centre), Robin de J. Jackson (Victoria College), and Jane Millgate (Victoria College).

7 Writings on the Bible and Literature (three volumes); Writings on Canada (two, which later became one); Writings on Critical Theory and Mythology (reference to mythology later dropped, four volumes); Writings on Shakespeare and the Renaissance (two volumes, now becoming one); *Fearful Symmetry* (one volume); Writings on Milton and Blake (one volume); Writings on the Eighteenth and Nineteenth Centuries (one volume); Writings on Twentieth-Century Literature (one volume); Writings on Modern Civilization (later changed to Modern Culture, one volume); Writings on Education (one volume); Interviews (two volumes, later one).

"Pity the Northrop Frye Scholar"?

Anatomy of Criticism Fifty Years After

Robert Denham

I HAVE a relatively clear memory of my first encounter with *Anatomy of Criticism*. Browsing the shelves of the University of Chicago bookstore in the early 1960s, I picked up a copy of the book, not because anyone had recommended it but because it looked interesting. I had decided by then that I would be doing my degree in the history and theory of criticism, and leafing through this book made me think it worth looking into, though I did not actually read it until a couple of years later. That was after I was jerked out of my graduate studies in 1964 to serve in the army. I headed off with my wife and two-year-old son to the Air Defense School at Fort Bliss, Texas, where I was trained to be a battery commander for the Nike Hercules missile defence system. As it turned out, I received orders to remain at the school to edit training manuals— a rather cushy job. The editing work took about a half hour per week, so I more or less hid out in my office and read books.

One of the first ones I turned to was the *Anatomy*, which had been staring at me from my shelves for a couple of years. Well, I read it and remember thinking, "This is a real book." I was more or less transported by its expansive scope, its structural ingenuity, its rhetorical power, and its authoritative voice. Why hadn't they told me about this guy Frye in graduate school? I scurried over to the library at Texas Western University to see if I could turn up anything on him. I naturally ran across a good deal. I photocopied two reviews of the *Anatomy*, now dog-eared, one by Frank Kermode in *Review of English Studies* and the other by M.H. Abrams in *University of Toronto Quarterly*. Because Kermode has just written *The Romantic Image*—it was also published in 1957—he had the symbolist aesthetic on his mind, and so he read the *Anatomy* through that lens. He ended up calling the book a work of "sixth-phase Symbolism." The *Anatomy*, he said, was "a work of criticism which has turned into literature" (23). Like Kermode, Abrams praised the book, but he had his own misgivings. He concluded that the *Anatomy* was an example of wit criticism. It illustrated the free play of a richly stored mind, but its principles could not be confirmed. Kermode and Abrams were clearly very smart people, but I later came to see that they had mistaken the means for the end. At the time, all I realized was that the views of Kermode and Abrams did not conform to my own view of the book, which was that it taught me a great deal about literary conventions.

In any event, that encounter with the *Anatomy* in the deserts of Texas was what began a long odyssey. Who knows what my professional career would have turned out to be had they given me a real job in the army, or had I come to Frye by way of *Fearful Symmetry*, the path followed by my friend Michael Dolzani. In the years that followed, I spent a considerable amount of time trying to figure out the ends and means of the *Anatomy*, its arguments and taxonomies, its language and assumptions, and I eventually convinced Wayne Booth to let me write a dissertation on Frye's critical method. My initial encounter with the *Anatomy* goes back, then, more than forty years. I was, as I say, at Fort Bliss, Texas,

where we would quip, "Ignorance is Bliss. Welcome to Fort Ignorance."
I was very ignorant at the time, but I had a clear sense that by reading
Frye's book I might become less so.

Anatomy of Criticism went to press in February 1957 and was released
three months later, in May. The same month, Frye was granted the first
of his thirty-nine honorary degrees, a doctorate of laws awarded by
Carleton, which had just been elevated from a college to a university.
A month after the conferring of this degree, in June 1957, Frye travelled
to Ottawa from Harvard, where he was teaching for the term, to deliver
a speech, "The Study of English in Canada," at the inauguration of the
Association of Canadian University Teachers of English. That same year
Lester Pearson, also a Victoria College graduate, won the Nobel Peace
Prize, Queen Elizabeth II opened the Canadian Parliament (the first
monarch to have done so), and the Canada Council was established. So
2007 was a jubilee year on several counts, including the golden anniversary of another archetypal book, *The Cat in the Hat*. The jubilee celebration goes back a long way. In the Book of Leviticus (25:9–12) we are told
that every fifty years there was to be a celebration marking the freeing of
slaves and prisoners, the forgiveness of debts, and the outpouring of the
mercies of God. There were plenty of reasons for celebrating the jubilee
year, among them the facts that *Anatomy of Criticism* has been continuously in print for more than fifty years and has sold over 150,000 copies.
But I want to begin by noting that, fifty years after, not everyone agrees
there is anything to celebrate:

· Marcia Kahan, writing in *Books in Canada* in 1985, reports on a debate between Frank Kermode and Terry Eagleton. "About the only subject on which they could agree," she says, "was Frye's obsolescence," adding that Eagleton asked what was a decidedly rhetorical question, "Who
now reads Frye?" (3–4). That was twenty-three years ago.

· Graham Good writes in 2004, "This is a wintry season for Frye's
work in the West"; "the once-great repute of the Wizard of the North is
now maintained only by a few Keepers of the Flame" (186), the Keepers

of the Flame being, apparently, the editors of the Collected Works volumes and a handful of others scattered here and there.

· William Kerrigan remarks, "More than any critic of his day, Frye exercised the literary canon. No one, not even his great rival, M.H. Abrams, seemed able to touch the great works of many periods and languages with such omni-competent authority. But Frye is gone now. The feminists, postmodernists, new historians, and neo-Marxists have buried him in a mass grave marked White Male Liberal Humanism" (198).

· Joseph Epstein, writing in *Commentary* three years ago, includes Northrop Frye in a group of critics who for some time, Epstein claims, have been "fading from prominence and [are] now beginning to fade from memory" (53).

· Denis Donoghue writes in a review of *The Double Vision*, "For about fifteen years—say from 1957 to 1972—Frye was the most influential critic in the English-speaking world.... [He] went out of phase if not out of sight when readers lost interest in 'first and last things' and set about a political program of one kind or another under the guise of reading and teaching literature." That was sixteen years ago.

· In a 2006 interview Frank Kermode, now Sir Frank Kermode, expresses a similar opinion: "Looking back at the study of English in universities over the years the first thing that occurs to me is how very important the subject once seemed. In America the New Criticism—a school led by Cleanth Brooks and Robert Penn Warren—argued that the close study of poetry was a supremely valuable thing. This was a view that was then accepted generally. And the leading academic literary critics were, in those days, very famous people. Think, for example, of Northrop Frye. Frye's is now a name that you never hear mentioned but which was then everywhere" (Sutherland).

· Also writing in 2006, Richard Lane declares, "The overarching project of the *Anatomy of Criticism* reveals why Frye's approach is now out of favour: he attempts to account for the entire field of literary criticism in a totalizing gesture that is now read as deluded" (112).

· In a review of Ford Russell's book on Frye, Warren Moore puts a similar sentiment like this: "Pity the Northrop Frye scholar. While the broad heading of literary theory seems to offer room for a virtual pantechnicon of ideas, the Canadian theorist's works have been marginalized to the point of being considered something like alchemy—possibly of historical interest but really of no use in a post/modern world. The reasons for this fall from grace range from the lack of immediately apparent political usefulness ... to the currently fashionable pluralistic worldview that rejects 'synoptic theories' by definition" (87).

Others have expressed sentiments similar to those in these eight points—that Frye is obsolescent, that he has been buried with other dead white males in a mass grave, that no one today reads him, that he is fading from memory if not from sight, that those deluded few who do read him are to be pitied, that his name is never mentioned nowadays, and so on. Several years back I heard a bit of gossip about a poor student at the University of Toronto who wanted to write a dissertation on Frye but who was told that Frye was out of fashion and that he should choose another topic if he wanted to preserve his career in the academy from irreparable damage. Such attitudes go back more than twenty-five years.

In 1980 Frank Lentricchia located the *Anatomy* at the head of a line of "-ologies" and "-isms" that marched onto the scene "after the new criticism"—that is, existentialism, phenomenology, structuralism, and post-structuralism. Lentricchia worried about Frye's attack on subjectivity, individuation, and the romantic conception of the self, and he noted that Frye's conception of the centre of the order of words "anticipates and, then, crucially rejects" Derrida's notion that such metaphors of centre, origin, and structure close off the possibility of "freeplay" (13–14). Moreover, Frye is said to have privileged spatial over temporal conceptions, centripetal over the centrifugal movements, the romantic over the ironic modes of literature, and utopian desire over contingent, historical reality. Lentricchia's assumption here is that it is self-evident in each case that the latter idea in each of these oppositions is to be preferred to the former. Years later he claimed that his essay "tried to point up the structuralist and poststructuralist moment in Frye" (Salusinszky 186), but that is a caricature of the aim of his chapter, which is to debunk all Frygean assumptions that do not conform to his armchair view of historical consciousness and anti-foundational awareness.

Lentricchia maintains that Frye continued to "water down"—his phrase—the positions taken in the *Anatomy* through a series of books (30), but he gives no evidence of having read, say, *The Critical Path* (1971), in which Frye addresses the forms of ideology that underlie the program for criticism that Lentricchia prefers. He concludes that by the mid-1960s "Frye ... was unceremoniously tossed 'on the dump' ... with other useless relics" (30). This is the claim I would like to examine: that Frye has been decaying in the critical garbage dump since the mid-1960s. It's a claim that was made, as I say, in 1980, twenty-eight years ago and twenty-three years after the *Anatomy* was published.

How might one go about testing the truth of Lentricchia's claims? One could point, first of all, to counter claims. It was in the mid-sixties that the English Institute devoted its session to Frye, and Murray Krieger's bold opinion delivered on that occasion was that because of the *Anatomy*, Frye

has had an influence—indeed an absolute hold—on a generation of developing literary critics greater and more exclusive than that of any one theorist in recent critical history. One thinks of other movements that have held sway, but these seem not to have developed so completely on a single critic—nay, on a single work—as has the criticism in the work of Frye and his *Anatomy*. (1–2)

This claim was echoed by Lawrence Lipking six years later: "More than any other modern critic, [Frye] stands at the center of critical activity" (180). In 1976, eleven years after Frye was declared a "useless relic," Harold Bloom remarked that Frye had "earned the reputation of being the leading theoretician of literary criticism among all those writing in English today" ("Northrop Frye"). A decade later, Bloom had not changed his opinion: Frye, he wrote, "is the foremost living student of Western literature" and "surely the major literary critic in the English language" (Salusinszky 58, 62). The judgments of these surveyors of the critical scene from the mid-1960s until the late 1980s are about as far as one can get from the "useless relic" declaration. And what would Lentricchia do with the fact that at the very time he was engaged in his debunking antics, the *Anatomy* was the most frequently cited book by a writer born in the 20ᵗʰ century?[1]

In his foreword to the reissue of the *Anatomy* in 2000, Harold Bloom remarks that he is "not so fond of the *Anatomy* now" as he was when he reviewed it in his very first publication forty-three years earlier (vii). Bloom's ambivalence springs from his conviction that there is no place in Frye's myth of concern for a theory of the anxiety of influence, Frye's view of influence being a matter of "temperament and circumstances" (vii). However, Bloom's foreword is not chiefly devoted to the *Anatomy* but, rather, to his own anxieties about Frye's influence, presented in the context of his well-known disquiet about what he calls the School of Resentment—the various forms of "cultural criticism" that take their cues from identity politics. In the 1950s, Bloom says, Frye provided an alternative to the New Criticism, especially Eliot's High Church variety, but today he is powerless to free us from the critical wilderness. Because Frye saw literature as a "benignly cooperative enterprise," he is of little help with its agonistic traditions. His schematisms will fall away: what will remain is the rhapsodic quality of his criticism. According to Bloom, in the extraordinary proliferation of texts today, Frye will provide "little comfort and assistance": if he is to afford any sustenance, it will be outside the universities. Still, Bloom believes that Frye's criticism will survive not because of the system outlined in the *Anatomy* but "because it is serious, spiritual, and comprehensive" (xi).

There is no denying the importance of the post-structural moment. Frye's late work clearly illustrates that he was quite aware of the dominant modes of inquiry during the last two or three decades of the 20ᵗʰ century. One runs across occasional comments in his notebooks about his being "old hat," "a member of an aging chorus" (*LN* 1:23, 175), and the like. At times he even seems anxious about his position in the contemporary critical world. This is not an anxiety of influence but an anxiety of displacement:

> I am told that the structure of the Anatomy is impressive but futile, because it would make every other critic a Gauleiter of Frye. People don't realize that I'm building temples to—well, "the gods" will do. There's an outer court for casual tourists, an inner court for those who want to stay for communion (incidentally, the rewards of doing so are very considerable). But I've left a space where neither they nor I belong. It's not a tower of Babel: that tries to reach something above itself: I want to contain what, with a shift of perspective, contains it. Why am I so respected and yet so isolated? Is it only because I take criticism more seriously than any other living critic? (*LN* 1:120)

In a notebook entry from the early 1980s, Frye wrote, "My function as a critic right now is to reverse the whole 'deconstruction' procedure, which leads eventually to the total extinction of both literature and criticism: people are naturally attracted first, and most, by the suicidal and destructive" (NRL 302). Well, of course Frye was not able to reverse the "whole 'deconstruction' procedure." But if we take a somewhat longer view of things, it seems clear that if Frye is no longer at "the center of critical activity," as he was in the mid-1960s, he still remains very much a containing presence at the circumference. While it is true that graduate courses in critical theory often exclude his work, it is no less true, as a glance at current university catalogues and course descriptions reveal, that both undergraduate and graduate students continue to read his works at a number of major universities. A couple of years ago I did an online survey of course descriptions, and I discovered that

Frye was on the reading list in English and comparative literature cours-
es at a large number of universities, including Harvard, Yale, Berkeley,
Stanford, Chicago, Virginia, North Carolina, Vanderbilt, Pennsylvania,
Notre Dame, York, McMaster, Texas, and Concordia.[2] Outside of
North America, students were reading Frye at universities in Bucharest,
Oslo, Rome, Brussels, Budapest, Prague, Stuttgart, Venice, Lecce (Italy),
Syddansk (southern Denmark), Lisbon, Rennes (Brittany), Mainz,
Olomouc (the Czech Republic), Brazil, Aalborg (Denmark), Nanjing
and Heilongjiang (China), Freiburg, Copenhagen, Oviedo (Spain),
Toulouse, and Hohhot (Inner Mongolia). Bloom's prediction, then, that
Frye will disappear from the universities appears to have not yet begun.

We get similar evidence, at least at the graduate level, when we consider the relatively large number of people who continue to write dissertations in which Frye figures importantly. In 1963 Mary Curtis Tucker
wrote the first doctoral dissertation on Frye. The period between 1964
and 2003 saw another 192 doctoral dissertations devoted in whole or
part to Frye, "in part" meaning that "Frye" is indexed as a subject in
Dissertation Abstracts International. The number of dissertations for
each of the decades falls out as follows: 1960s = 5; 1970s = 28; 1980s =
63; 1990s = 68; and in the first four years of the present decade, 29.[3] These
data obviously indicate that during the twenty-year period following
the height of the post-structural moment, interest in Frye as a topic of
graduate research substantially increased. During the 1980s and 1990s,
he figured importantly in more than six dissertations per year, and in
2000 and 2003, in eight per year. In 2003, Frye was indexed as a subject
in fourteen doctoral dissertations, the highest number for any year, and
the majority of these have to do with topics treated in the *Anatomy*—
Menippean satire, romance, myth, genre theory, and typological imagery.[4] Glen Gill's recently published book on Frye and the phenomenology of myth emerged from a 2003 McMaster dissertation.

The point is that the interest in Frye in doctoral studies has not abat-
ed at all. Whether the almost geometric progression of this interest in

the 1970s and 1980s will level off in the current decade is not clear, but what is clear is that a large number of graduate students and their advisors have not been convinced by the "useless relic" hypothesis.

Other indicators also suggest increased academic attention to Frye. When *Northrop Frye: An Annotated Bibliography* was published in 1987, there were eight books devoted in their entirety to his work. Since that time another thirty-one have appeared.[5] The two most recent relate Frye's *Anatomy* to music and film. And I should not fail to mention the most ingenious application of the *Anatomy*—a literal appliqué. For their mid-term project in a fabric design class at the University of Georgia, students were asked to take an old piece of clothing and refurbish it with something unconventional in order to give the item a new life. For her project, Amy Brodnax, a sophomore, attached pages of Frye's *Anatomy* to the skirt of an old dress with mirrors and aluminum foil at the top (McWane).

Frye continues to wear well, one might say—figuratively and literal-

ly. I don't know what it is about Frye and Georgia. One of the reviews of the *Anatomy* I ran across some years ago was in Florence Hill Morris's 1976 column "Fireside Gardening" in the *Augusta* [Georgia] *Chronicle*. After advising her readers to "pore through books on the subject" of foliage and flower arrangement, she proceeded to annotate a list of such books. Included among them is, in a classic case of generic confusion, *Anatomy of Criticism*, the complete

annotation for which is this: "A difficult book to read, but with study the material is most helpful." I don't know how to explain this bizarre thirteen-word review. Perhaps Florence Hill Morris had remembered what Frye had said in the Second Essay of the *Anatomy* about books on gardening being an example of verbal structures in the descriptive phase of symbolism (72).

But to return to the counter evidence for the "useless relic" thesis: my 1987 bibliography recorded 588 essays or parts of books devoted to Frye, written over the course of forty years. Since that time, more than 950 additional entries (excluding the hundreds of news stories about Frye and reviews of his books) have been added to the bibliography. In other words, during the past two decades, about twice as much has been written about Frye than in the previous forty or so years. Of the nineteen symposia and conferences devoted to his work, which have taken place on four continents, sixteen have occurred since 1986: two have been held in China, two in Australia, two in the United States, seven in Canada, one in Italy, one in Korea, and one in Spain.

Almost all of what has been written about the *Anatomy* has been within the field of literary criticism. But a critic's reputation and status are also revealed by the extent to which his or her work has been appropriated by those outside the field. In this regard it is worth reminding the death-of-Frye prophets that his ideas have been applied by philosophers, historians, geographers, anthropologists, political scientists, and by writers in the fields of advertising, communication studies, nursing, political economy, legal theory, organization science, and consumer research.[6]

The *Anatomy* was the book that made Frye's international reputation. In 1964, about the time that, according to Lentricchia, Frye had become a "useless relic," the German translation of the *Anatomy* appeared. This was followed on the European continent by the French, Italian, Romanian, Portuguese, Spanish, and Greek translations. In Eastern Europe, one can read the *Anatomy* in Serbo-Croatian, Hungarian, and Czech; in the East, in Japanese, Korean, and Chinese. In 1991 two Arabic translations appeared, one in Libya and the other in Jordan. Altogether, the *Anatomy* has been translated into fifteen languages. Six of these have appeared since 1990. It appears, then, that there is no diminishing of the interest in the *Anatomy* outside the Anglo-American world. And to judge by the increasing number of translations of all of Frye's books, the interest in reading him in other languages has been steadily increasing: of the 104 translations into twenty languages, almost three-quarters (76) have appeared since 1980.

Finally, pockets of Frye scholars exist in what might at first seem unlikely places. From 1997 to 2004 the late Professor Wu Chizhe of Hohhot University in Inner Mongolia translated the *Anatomy* and five of Frye's other books into Chinese. In Hungary, Sára Tóth recently completed a dissertation on Frye, and in 2003, János Kenyeres published *Revolving around the Bible: A Study of Northrop Frye*. Péter Pásztor has translated *The Great Code* and *Words With Power* into Hungarian, and Tibor Fabiny, the dean of Hungarian Frygeans, continues to lecture and publish on Frye. In addition, courses on Frye have been recently offered at two universities in Budapest. In Italy, Korea, and China, Frye is frequently taught in Canadian Studies programs.

Earlier I noted Warren Moore's woeful observation that readers of Northrop Frye are to be pitied because his works are more or less like alchemical texts, possibly of some historical interest but of no use to the modern reader. However, pity is an emotion we feel in the presence of a fallen hero, like Oedipus. I see little evidence that we should be pitied for coming together in a recent conference on Frye: I have tried to suggest that the proper answer to Terry Eagleton's question, "Who now reads Frye?" is "A considerable number." Even a post-structuralist like Jonathan Culler, who had never been very friendly to Frye's enterprise, has lately come around to granting that Frye's vision of a coherent literary tradition is something to be devoutly wished for literary studies.

In 1988 the *Arts and Humanities Citation Index*, mentioned earlier, recognized the *Anatomy* as a "Citation Classic." Frye was asked to comment on the honour. Accordingly, in January 1989 there appeared in *Current Contents* a brief article under Frye's byline entitled, "Critical

Theory: Structure, Archetypes, and the Order of Words." I quote a short passage:

> In literary theory itself, the *Anatomy* seems most often regarded as a book of its time, a transitional successor to the New Criticism and precursor to later movements such as structuralism; in its "Polemical Introduction" and "Tentative Conclusion" the book in fact takes a rather similar view of itself.... Nevertheless, it is possible that its perspective is due for a return to fashion someday.

I said that this article appeared under Frye's byline, but you will not find it in the Adamson/Wilson edition of the criticism from Frye's last decade, nor will you find it in any of the other volumes of the Collected Works. The reason for its absence is that it was written by Michael Dolzani, who did a great deal of ghostwriting for Frye, mostly in the form of correspondence. This does not mean that Frye would not have agreed to the opinions expressed in the article. In fact, Dolzani has confided to me that Frye gave it his imprimatur. In any event, the point I want to make is that Frye was aware that he was out of fashion. In the mid-1980s he knew the ballpark in which the game was being played. But he also knew that the rules of the game remained constant. Thus he could write in one of his notebooks from the 1980s:

> If there's no real difference between creation & criticism, I have as much right to build palaces of criticism as Milton had to write epic poems. My whole and part interchange works here too: inside the Anatomy, everyone is a disciple & to some degree a captive of Frye—every writer has a captive audience—but surely one can finish the book & then do as one likes, with something of me inside him. If he doesn't have something of me inside him, he won't, at this time of history, have anything of much use to say as a critic. (*LN* 1:123)

I conclude with that passage of uncharacteristic immodesty, adding only my judgment that Frye has already entered into the tradition. We are in the same position as Eliot, looking back on Arnold's *Culture and Anarchy* a half century after it appeared. Eliot, who saw his own work as forming a radical break with the poetry and criticism of the 19th century, nevertheless says of Arnold that he "does still hold us ... by the power of his rhetoric and by representing a point of view which is particular" (382–383). All of the writing about Frye that I've briefly summarized convinces me that Frye also still holds us, and my guess is that as we begin inching now toward the centennial of the *Anatomy*, new readers, with the Collected Works at their disposal, will continue to find new directions from old.

ENDNOTES

1 Garfield's article lists the 100 most-cited authors in the *Arts & Humanities Citation Index* for 1977 and 1978. The list reveals that in the more than 900,000 entries in the *AHCI*, only Marx, Aristotle, Shakespeare, Lenin, Plato, Freud, and Barthes were more frequently cited than Frye. A second list published by Garfield in the same article shows that for 1978 and 1979 *Anatomy of Criticism* was the most frequently cited book written by an author born in the 20th century. Eight years after his initial survey, Garfield updated and expanded the list, publishing the results in "The 250 Most-Cited Authors in the *Arts & Humanities Citation Index, 1976–1983*," *Current Contents* 48 (1 December 1986): 3–10. Marx remained in first place, followed by Aristotle, Shakespeare, Lenin, Plato, Freud, Barthes, Kant, Cicero, Chomsky, Hegel, and Frye. At the time, then, Frye was the third most-cited author born in the 20th century.

2 My cursory search of recent catalogues and course descriptions turned up these courses in English (E), comparative literature (CL), and other fields in which Frye was being read: Harvard University (E193), Yale University (E463b), Berkeley (CL100, CL155), Stanford (E166/266A, E302A, CL369, C172), University of Chicago (E47200), University of Virginia (E255, E481), University of North Carolina (E027.003), Vanderbilt

University (E337a, E105W, CL312, CL314 [course on Frye's central texts]), University of Pennsylvania (CL360.401), University of Notre Dame (E510), York University (E4109), McMaster University (E798), University of Texas, Austin (E5360), and Concordia University (Religion 365). Similar courses can be found in numerous college catalogues.

3 These data include six Ed.D. and two DLS dissertations. While it is difficult to get an accurate count of MA theses, fifty-one have been recorded from 1967 to 2004.

4 Within the past dozen years the one hundred or so universities where students have completed dissertations in which Frye is a subject include Harvard, Yale, Princeton, Penn, Chicago, Toronto, Wisconsin, Indiana, Illinois, Ohio State, Virginia, NYU, McMaster, Oxford, and Stockholm.

5 For the books on Frye, see Appendix.

6 Some accounts that reveal the influence of Frye's ideas outside of literary criticism include James L. Peacock, Comment on M. Pluciennik's "Archaeological Narratives and Other Ways of Telling," *Current Anthropology* 40: 5 (December 1999), 670 ff.; G.V. Johar, Morris B. Holbrook, and Barbara B. Stern, "The Role of Myth in Creative Advertising Design: Theory, Process and Outcome," *Journal of Advertising* 30: 2 (Summer 2001), 1–25; Barbara B. Stern, "Consumer Myths: Frye's Taxonomy and the Structural Analysis of Consumption Text," *Journal of Consumer Research* 22 (September 1995), 165–185; Rebecca Hagey, "Codes and Coping: A Nursing Tribute to Northrop Frye," *Nursing Papers / Perspectives en nursing* 16 (Summer 1984), 13–39; Jonathan M. Smith, "Geographical Rhetoric: Modes and Tropes of Appeal", *Annals of the Association of American Geographers* 86: 1 (1996), 1–20; Robert Babe, "Foundations of Canadian Communication Thought," *Canadian Journal of Communication* 25: 1 (2000), 19–37; Metin M. Coşgel, "Metaphors, Stories, and the Entrepreneur in Economics," *History of Political Economy* 28: 1 (1996), 57–76; Lynn Hunt, *Politics, Culture, and Class in the French Revolution* (Berkeley: University of California Press, 1984); Douglas Long, "Northrop Frye: Liberal Humanism and the Critique of Ideology," *Journal of Canadian Studies / Revue d'études canadiennes* 34: 4 (Winter 2000), 27–51; David Cook, "'Double Vision': The Political Philosophy of Northrop Frye," *Ultimate Reality and Meaning* 15 (September 1992), 185–194; Don L.F. Nilsen, "Northrop Frye Meets Tweedledum and Tweedledee: Adolescent Literature as Comedy, Romance, Tragedy, and Irony," *Journal of Evolutionary Psychology* 19: 1–2 (March 1998), 10–20; Roy Schafer, "Language, Narrative, and

Psychoanalysis: An Interview with Roy Schafer," in *Criticism and Lacan: Essays and Dialogue on Language, Structure, and the Unconscious*, ed. Patrick Colm Hogan and Lalita Pandit (Athens: University of Georgia Press, 1990), 123–144; Robin West, "Jurisprudence as Narrative: An Aesthetic Analysis of Modern Legal Theory," *New York University Law Review* 60 (May 1985), 145–211; John Murphy, "Narrative and Social Action: The Making of a President 1960," paper presented at the 1989 annual meeting of the Speech Communication Association, San Francisco, 18–21 November; P. Baker, "'Night into Day': Patterns of Symbolism in Mozart's *The Magic Flute*," *University of Toronto Quarterly* 49: 2 (Winter 1979), 95–116; Kaj Sköldberg, "Tales of Change: Public Administration Reform and Narrative Mode," *Organization Science* 5 (May 1994), 219–238; Robert Nozick, *Philosophical Explanations* (Cambridge: Harvard University Press, 1981), 623; Hayden White, *Metahistory* (Baltimore: Johns Hopkins University Press, 1973).

APPENDIX: BOOKS ON FRYE (ALPHABETICAL BY AUTHOR)

Adamson, Joseph. 1993. *Northrop Frye: A Visionary Life*. Toronto: ECW Press.

Ayre, John. 1989. *Northrop Frye: A Biography*. Toronto: Random House of Canada.

Balfour, Ian. 1988. *Northrop Frye*. Boston: Twayne.

Bates, Ronald. 1971. *Northrop Frye*. Toronto: McClelland and Stewart.

Boyd, David, and Imre Salusinszky, eds. 1999. *Rereading Frye: The Published and Unpublished Works*. Toronto: University of Toronto Press.

Cayley, David. 1992. *Northrop Frye in Conversation*. Concord, ON: Anansi.

Cook, David. 1985. *Northrop Frye: A Vision of the New World*. New York: St. Martin's.

Cook, Eleanor, et al., eds. 1985. *Centre and Labyrinth: Essays in Honour of Northrop Frye*. Toronto: University of Toronto Press, in association with Victoria University.

Cotrupi, Caterina Nella. 2000. *Northrop Frye and the Poetics of Process*. Toronto: University of Toronto Press.

Denham, Robert D. 2004. *Northrop Frye: A Bibliography of His Published Writings, 1931–2004*. Emory, VA: Iron Mountain Press.

———. 2004. *Northrop Frye: Religious Visionary and Architect of the Spiritual World*. Charlottesville: University of Virginia Press.

———. 1987. *Northrop Frye: An Annotated Bibliography of Primary and Secondary Sources.* Toronto: University of Toronto Press.

———. 1978. *Northrop Frye and Critical Method.* University Park: Pennsylvania State University Press.

———. 1974. *Northrop Frye: An Enumerative Bibliography.* Metuchen, NJ: Scarecrow Press.

Denham, Robert D., and Thomas Willard, eds. 1991. *Visionary Poetics: Essays on Northrop Frye's Criticism.* New York: Peter Lang.

Donaldson, Jeffery, and Alan Mendelson, eds. 2003. *Frye and the Word: Religious Contexts in the Criticism of Northrop Frye.* Toronto: University of Toronto Press.

Dyrkjøb, Jan Ulrik. 1979. *Northrop Frye's litteraturteori.* Copenhagen: Berlinske Verlag.

Feltracco, Daniela. 2005. *Northrop Frye: Anatomia di un metodo critico.* Udine: Forum, Editrice Universitaria Udinese.

Gill, Glen Robert. 2006. *Northrop Frye and the Phenomenology of Myth.* Toronto: University of Toronto Press.

Gyalokay, Monique Anne. 1999. *Rousseau, Northrop Frye et la Bible: Essai de mythocritique.* Paris: Honoré Champion.

Hamilton, A.C. 1990. *Northrop Frye: Anatomy of His Criticism.* Toronto: University of Toronto Press.

Hamilton, Mark. 2006. *Categorizing Twentieth-Century Film Using Northrop Frye's Anatomy of Criticism: Relating Literature and Film.* Lewiston, ME: Edwin Mellen Press.

Hart, Jonathan. 1994. *Northrop Frye: The Theoretical Imagination.* London: Routledge.

Kee, James M., ed. 2002. *Northrop Frye and the Afterlife of the Word. Semeia* 89. Atlanta: Society of Biblical Literature.

Kenyeres, János. 2003. *Revolving around the Bible: A Study of Northrop Frye.* Budapest: Anonymus.

Kogan, Pauline. 1969. *Northrop Frye: The High Priest of Clerical Obscurantism.* Montreal: Progressive Books and Periodicals.

Krieger, Murray, ed. 1966. *Northrop Frye in Modern Criticism.* New York: Columbia University Press.

Krishnamoorthy, S., ed. 1993. *The Importance of Northrop Frye.* Kanpur, India: Humanities Research Centre.

Lee, Alvin, and Robert D. Denham, eds. 1994. *The Legacy of Northrop Frye*. Toronto: University of Toronto Press.

Lee, Sang Ran, ed. 1992. *The Legacy of Northrop Frye in the East and West: Proceedings of the Third Annual International Conference of Canadian Studies*. Seoul: Canadian Studies Center, Sookmyung Women's University.

Lemond, Ed, ed. 2005. *Verticals of Frye / Les verticales de Frye: The Northrop Frye Lectures and Related Talks Given at the Northrop Frye International Literary Festival*. Moncton, NB: Elbow Press.

Lombardo, Agostino, ed. 1989. *Ritratto de Northrop Frye*. Rome: Bulzoni Editore.

Ning, Wang, and Jean O'Grady, eds. 2001. *New Directions in Northrop Frye Studies*. Shanghai: Shanghai Foreign Language Education Press.

Ning, Wang, and Yen-hung Hsü, eds. 1996. *Fu-lai yen chiu: Chung-kuo yü hsi fang* [*Frye Studies: China and the West*]. Beijing: Social Sciences Press of China.

O'Grady, Jean, and Wang Ning, eds. 2003. *Northrop Frye: Eastern and Western Perspectives*. Toronto: University of Toronto Press.

Pandey, Santosh Kumar. 2005. *Contrapuntal Modes in Northrop Frye's Literary Theory: Continuities in Literary Structuralism*. Delhi: Adhyayan Publishers.

Ricciardi, Caterina. 1992. *Northrop Frye, o, delle finzioni supreme*. Rome: Empirìa.

Russell, Ford. *Northrop Frye on Myth: An Introduction*. New York: Garland, 1998; London: Routledge, 2000.

Signori, Dolorès A. 1993. *Guide to the Northrop Frye Papers*. Toronto: Victoria University Library.

WORKS CITED

Abrams, M.H. 1959 (January). "*Anatomy of Criticism*." *University of Toronto Quarterly* 28: 190–196.

Bloom, Harold. 2000. Foreword. *Anatomy of Criticism*. Princeton, NJ: Princeton University Press, vii–xi.

———. 1976 (18 April). "Northrop Frye Exalting the Designs of Romance," *New York Times Book Review* 23: 21.

Culler, Jonathan. 2003 (Winter). "Imagining the Coherence of the English Major." *ADE Bulletin*, 133: 6–10. Rpt. in *Profession 2003*, 1 (December 2003): 85–93.

Donoghue, Denis. 1992 (9 April). Review of *The Double Vision*. *New York Review of Books* 39: 25.

Eliot, T.S. 1950. "Arnold and Pater." *Selected Essays of T.S. Eliot*. New ed. New York: Harcourt, Brace, 382–393.

Epstein, Joseph. 2005 (1 December). "Forgetting Edmund Wilson." *Commentary* 120: 53–58.

Frye, Northrop. 2006. *Anatomy of Criticism: Four Essays*. The Collected Works of Northrop Frye. Vol. 22. Ed. Robert D. Denham. Toronto: University of Toronto Press.

———. 2006. *Northrop Frye's Notebooks on Renaissance Literature*. The Collected Works of Northrop Frye. Vol. 20. Ed. Michael Dolzani. Toronto: University of Toronto Press.

———. 2006. *"The Secular Scripture" and Other Writings on Critical Theory, 1976–1991*. The Collected Works of Northrop Frye. Vol. 18. Ed. Joseph Adamson and Jean Wilson. Toronto: University of Toronto Press.

———. 2000. *Northrop Frye's Late Notebooks, 1982–1990: Architecture of the Spiritual World*. The Collected Works of Northrop Frye. Vols. 5–6. Ed. Robert D. Denham. Toronto: University of Toronto Press.

———. 1989 (30 January). "Critical Theory: Structure, Archetypes, and the Order of Words." *Current Contents*, 14.

Garfield, Eugene. 1979 (6 August). "Most-Cited Authors in the Arts and Humanities, 197–1978." *Current Contents* 32: 5–10. Rpt. in Garfield, *Essays of an Information Scientist*. 15 vols. Philadelphia: ISI Press, 1981, 4:238–243.

Good, Graham. 2004 (Winter). "Frye in China." *Canadian Literature* 183: 156–158.

Kahan, Marcia. 1985 (April). "Pillow Talk." *Books in Canada* 14: 3–4.

Kermode, Frank. 1959 (August). Review of *Anatomy of Criticism*. *Review of English Studies* 10: 317–323.

Kerrigan, William. 1996 (Winter). "Bloom and the Great Ones." *Clio* 25: 196–206.

Krieger, Murray. 1966. "Northrop Frye and Contemporary Criticism: Ariel and the Spirit of Gravity." In *Northrop Frye in Modern Criticism: Selected Papers from the English Institute*, ed. Murray Krieger. New York: Columbia University Press. 1–30.

Lane, Richard. 2006. "Northrop Frye." In *Fifty Key Literary Theorists*, ed. Richard Lane. London: Routledge. 111–116.

Lentricchia, Frank. 1980. *After the New Criticism*. Chicago: University of Chicago Press.

Lipking, Lawrence I. 1972. "Northrop Frye." In *Modern Literary Criticism, 1900–1970*, ed. Lawrence I. Lipking and A. Walton Litz. New York: Atheneum, 180–188.

McWane, Katie. 2007 (6 March). "Fabric Design Students Flaunt Midterm Project" [online] redandblack.com. http://media.www.redandblack.com/media/storage/paper871/news/2007/03/06/Variety/Fabric.Design.Students.Flaunt.Midterm.Projects-2758432.shtml.

Moore, Warren S. III. 2001 (Autumn). Review of *Northrop Frye on Myth: An Introduction*, by Ford Russell. *Journal of the Midwest Modern Language Association* 34: 3, 87–89.

Morris, Florence Hill. 1967 (26 November). "Fireside Gardening." *Augusta Chronicle* (Georgia).

Salusinszky, Imre. 1987. *Criticism in Society: Interviews with Jacques Derrida, Northrop Frye, Harold Bloom, Geoffrey Hartman, Frank Kermode, Edward Said, Barbara Johnson, Frank Lentricchia, and J. Hillis Miller*. New York: Methuen.

Sutherland, John. 2006 (29 August). "The Ideas Interview: Frank Kermode." *The Guardian Unlimited* [online] http://books.guardian.co.uk/comment/story/0,,1860357,00.html.

THE GENIUS OF NORTHROP FRYE

Thomas Willard

THE CODA to *Northrop Frye's Late Notebooks* is a brief but memorable statement:

> STATEMENT FOR THE DAY OF MY DEATH: The twentieth century saw an amazing development of scholarship and criticism in the humanities, carried out by people who were more intelligent, better trained, had more languages, had a better sense of proportion, and were infinitely more accurate scholars and competent professional men than I. I had genius. No one else in the field known to me had quite that.[1]

Robert Denham, who edited the late notebooks, reports that the typewritten statement turned up among papers from the mid-1970s, when Frye was approaching the age of mandatory retirement and struggling with his first book on the Bible and literature. A statement written at this time would have been more for his own eyes than posterity's, more to cheer himself up than to shape his reputation. Frye was too modest personally to issue such a statement, but his notebooks make it clear that there was more to him than the public persona. There was also, in a word, genius.

The statement was bound to be provocative. The general public distrusts genius. Indeed, as Oscar Wilde pointed out, "It forgives everything except genius" (Wilde 3). And critics, like artists, hate to have their own genius overlooked. In his introduction to a posthumous reissue of Frye's *Anatomy of Criticism*, Harold Bloom called the statement "unfortunate" and asked whether Kenneth Burke and Wilson Knight, among others, did not have similar claims to genius (Bloom, "Introduction" viii). Anticipating such grumbles, one press reviewer wanted to have the statement cut from the published notebooks, Denham has told me, fearing that it would damage Frye's "modest, avuncular" image.[2] Denham insisted that it be kept, and his headnote explains why: "one can sense in the coda both the impishness of the Socratic ironist, jolting us with the unexpected, and the truth contained in the literal meaning of the word 'genius,' reminding us of what finally motivated this architect of the spiritual world." The irony is that Frye denies having "technical knowledge," in Denham's words, while "claiming something greater"—very much as Socrates said he knew nothing but demonstrated that people who thought they knew something actually knew less than nothing. Denham does not elaborate on the literal meaning of genius, though he suggests it has something to do with the spiritual world that so interested Frye.

I want to explore Frye's understanding of genius and his uses of the word—both in the late notebooks and in the "Polemical Introduction" to the *Anatomy*, where it has bearing on such key terms as "tradition," "canon," and "value judgment." In that discussion I shall return to Bloom as one of Frye's best early critics. Finally, I shall return to the "statement" and explain why it should not be read as a press release but may provide a key to Frye's enduring value as a critic.

Genius is a tricky word. The *Oxford English Dictionary* recognizes seven distinct definitions or "senses," and Frye uses all of them in the late notebooks alone, where the word appears more than two dozen times.[3] The various senses are sufficiently connected that one blends into the next, despite some clear differences. For present purposes, there are two main distinctions to be drawn. The first is between two varieties of personal genius, which may be called Classical and Romantic. The second, which we shall come to later, is between personal and impersonal genius.

The word *genius* came into the language in Chaucer's time with the same meaning that it had in Classical Latin. It referred originally to the tutelary spirit that guides the individual throughout life and into the afterlife. Over time, it became generalized to include any kind of spirit and also to refer to non-spiritual characteristics, as in a person's genius for satire or politics. Beginning in Milton's time and culminating in the Romantic period, this later sense of genius as attribution took on the further quality of innate intellectual power, often contrasted with mere talent. While all people have the Classical sort of genius, whether they know it or not, only a select few can have the Romantic sort. Such a person is said not only to *have* genius but to *be* a genius.

Frye's "statement" clearly invokes the Romantic variety of genius. Where others had formal training and linguistic skills, it seems to say, he had a special kind of intellect. Jean O'Grady has quoted the remark as an example of self-assessment on Frye's part, a reflection "on his own strengths and weaknesses" (O'Grady 24). As such it combines his characteristic modesty with a self-assurance usually left to implication. One might compare Frye's contribution to a special issue on research, prepared for *Daedalus: Journal of the American Academy of Arts and Sciences*, which opens with a disclaimer of any qualification to write on the subject but ends with a plan for improved communication among researchers in the humanities, similar to that offered in the *Anatomy* ("Search"). In the essay, Frye professed to nothing more than his Canadian identity; however, he demonstrated the genius he admired without ever naming it. This was typical. In a private letter to his fiancée he could joke about his genius or praise hers (*NFHK* 53, 210–11), but writing for publication he would call the quest for genius and personal greatness a "Romantic provincialism" (*AC* 62). If the "statement" had ended by saying, "I had my intellectual home in Toronto" or "a special attachment to Blake and Romanticism," it would have been entirely unexceptionable. It would not have been so revealing, though, let alone so interesting.

A notebook from the early 1980s—a few years later by Denham's reckoning—shows that genius was indeed part of Frye's self-assessment: "By the standards of conventional scholarship, *The Great Code* was a silly and sloppy book," he wrote. "It was also a work of very great genius. The point is that genius is not enough" (*LN* 160). In other words, genius needs to be complemented by the qualities that Frye said others possessed to a greater degree: intelligence, training, scholarly accuracy, professional competence. We may well ask, what is the proper relation of genius to scholarship?

When genius is not enough, it becomes disconnected from the "romantic ideology of genius" that Bloom detected in the statement—and for which he admitted a certain "sympathy." It ceases to be the possession of the isolated individual and moves toward the Classical conception of the spiritual guide that all people have, though few people heed it. Bloom sensed this when he went on to raise "an impish archaism: was the Magus of the North attended by a spirit?" He responded to his own question: "It seems likelier that Frye, a formidable ironist, would refer to his aspiration, more even than his natural endowment."[4] In other words, Frye could have been saying, "I had *a* genius," a guide in realms he first explored when writing about Blake.

Frye's late notebooks show that he often thought of genius as a tutelary spirit or daimon—indeed, more often than not. He noted "that a lot of people, from Heraclitus to Blake, have identified man's guardian angel with his own essential genius" (LN 78). He reflected on the daimon of Socrates, which the Loeb edition of the *Phaedo* has translated as "genius" (Plato 373; 108b), and remarked, "I must never forget that I'm a literary critic. Socrates' daimon, tutelary deities, angel guardians, may well be ourselves in a future stage of development" (LN 715). These were natural thoughts in notebooks where he was exploring and designing what he called "the spiritual world" (LN 414).

Several great authors in antiquity wrote essays on the daimon of Socrates. Each one emphasized the educative function. Plutarch wrote that the daimon brings mental images of higher ideas (337; 588e); Plotinus, that it connects us to the cosmos and generates "the energy of our own personal career" (168; 3.4.3); Apuleius, author of *The Golden Ass*, that it may be found in anyone, but was present in Socrates "in an eminent degree" (47). We might note that the two charges brought against Socrates at his trial—corrupting youth and introducing new gods—were closely connected. These gods were called *daimonia*, and the youth were corrupted by being advised to rely on their inner resources rather than external authority (Plato 90; *Apology* 24c).

In the preface to *The Great Code*, Frye wrote about the Socratic approach to education. Convinced that the teacher's job is not to inform students but to remind them, he suggested that "the best strategy in doing this is first of all to get the student to recognize what he already potentially knows, which includes breaking up the powers of repression in his mind that keep him from knowing what he knows" (xiv). Anyone who has taught a course in the Bible and literature has no doubt seen these "powers of repression" in full swing, but they can surface just as easily in a literature survey. Frye did not discuss genius in *The Great Code*, beyond saying that he never found it "a very useful word" (xvi). However, he wrote much about spirit and the spiritual world, to which the Bible connects readers through myth and metaphor. He wrote even more about vision. He had learned the word from Blake and Yeats and, of course, from the Bible itself. It was one of the strongest terms in his critical vocabulary; indeed, he has been called a visionary critic (Hamilton). It was also basic to his conception of literary education, in which the literary work provided a vision of the world as it could be and the teacher of literature helped students to a vision of the imaginative universe (Willard, "Visionary"). The teacher who can accomplish this is no doubt a genius in the Romantic sense, at least to his or her students, but also serves the function of a genius in the Classical sense. Such a teacher serves as a guide to the imaginative world, which, for Frye, is very close indeed to the spiritual world. But at this point another kind of genius enters the picture.

In addition to the two sorts of personal genius, the Classical and Romantic, there is also an impersonal genius. In the *Anatomy*, Frye wrote about the lyrical or satirical genius, not only in writers like Shelley or Swift but in literature itself (235, 246). He wrote about the genius of a genre in the sense of its distinguishing characteristic, and he suggested that this genius could be a sort of daimon when he observed, "The presiding genius of comedy is Eros, and Eros has to adapt himself to the moral facts of society" (*AC* 181). He later developed a whole series of presiding gods or spirits in the *"Third Book" Notebooks* and *Late Notebooks*, culminating in the "variations" that form the second half of *Words With Power*. He noted that Nietzsche and Jung would each serve as the "presiding genius" of an imaginative space, the *genius loci* or spirit of the place, much as Edward King in *Lycidas* became "a pagan genius," Milton's "Genius of the shore."[5]

The *OED* treats the impersonal form of genius as an extension of the first modern sense of genius as personal characteristic, an abstracted form applied to a language or culture or subject ("genius" *n.*1 7; see 3b–e). In the history of English, it occupies a transitional position between what we have been calling the Classical and Romantic genius. In this middle position, or *tertium quid,* there may be an explanation of how

Frye could at once "have genius" and "have a genius," how he could guide others in his criticism and be guided himself.

When Bloom suggested that Frye had a genius in the word's original sense of tutelary spirit, he opened an old sore. Twenty-five years earlier, Bloom had distanced himself from his early model and mentor in a highly tendentious essay on "The Dialectics of Poetic Tradition," written for a theoretical journal and included in the aptly titled *Map of Misreading*. He began with a backhanded compliment: Frye could be considered "the Proclus or Iamblichus of our day" (Bloom, *Map* 30). This was a compliment inasmuch as Proclus is largely responsible for introducing the concept of symbolism into philosophy, notably in his commentaries on the *Timaeus* and other dialogues of Plato, and Iamblichus was another key transmitter of Platonic tradition. But it rankled with Frye, who remarked testily that they were pagans, initiates of mystery religions, and rather nebulous writers (Frye, "Expanding" 117). Introducing the reissued *Anatomy*, Bloom changed the comparison "belatedly" to Plotinus (Bloom, "Introduction" x), a visionary essayist of great power, though one whom Frye compared unfavourably to Blake (*FS* 8). Frye's connection to the Gnostic authors admired by Bloom, like his connection to the avowedly Gnostic C.G. Jung, deserves to be reassessed.[6] In the present essay, however, it is possible only to consider the context of Bloom's original pronouncement.

Immediately after the backhanded compliment, Bloom likened Frye's understanding of literary tradition to Eliot's, calling it a "Low Church version of T.S. Eliot's Anglo-Catholic myth of Tradition and the Individual Talent." Bloom explained,

[T]he student discovers that he becomes something, and thus uncovers or demystifies himself, by first being persuaded that tradition is inclusive rather than exclusive, and so makes a place for him. The student is a cultural assimilator who *thinks* because he has *joined* a larger body of thought. Freedom, for Frye, like Eliot, is the change, however, slight, that any genuine single consciousness brings about in the order of literature simply by joining the simultaneity of such order.[7]

Bloom noted that Eliot's famous essay on tradition introduced the conception of literature as an ideal order, which Frye called a "very fundamental criticism" and tried "to annotate" in the *Anatomy* (18). He recognized that the *Anatomy* is a teaching book in that it guides the student into the ideal order. However, he questioned the very possibility of simultaneity in tradition and suggested that it was a "noble idealization," much needed in the radical sixties but a "lie against time" that could not survive. In truth, the difference between simultaneity and movement within literary traditions is much like that between continuity and discontinuity or structure and deconstruction: a matter of emphasis, a saying that the proverbial glass is half full or half empty. For Bloom, literary education means introducing students to "the presence of the past," but this presence is not concordant so much as discordant, not a vision so much as a revision, brought about by the struggle of each new reader or writer with all precursors. The struggle includes that of teacher and student.

Noting that the original conception of *litteratura*, in Quintilian's *Institutes*, included both reading and writing, Bloom suggested that the parallel between Eliot's talented writer and Frye's "A" student is more than superficial:

No teacher, however impartial he or she attempts to be, can avoid choosing among students, or being chosen by them, for this is the very nature of teaching. Literary teaching is precisely like literature itself; no strong writer can choose his precursors until first he is chosen by them, and no strong student can fail to be chosen by his teachers. Strong students, like strong writers, will find the sustenance they must have. And strong students, like strong writers, will rise in the most unexpected places and times, to wrestle with the internalized violence pressed upon them by their teachers and precursors. (39)

Students may resist the idea that they lack free choice and are in fact "chosen" by their teachers, but that is exactly what happens when a good student of literature comes into the presence of a genuine teacher. They may also feel that the teacher's lasting effect on them is something more benign than "internalized violence," especially if the teacher has tried to develop independent thinkers rather than disciples. Frye certainly promoted independence, and challenged students to think hard as they thought for themselves. One former student told me that, in Frye's classes, he "thought better, more deeply and quickly," than at any other time in his life. In the language of his day, he "found himself" as a student in Frye's lectures and seminars. In Bloom's word, he was "chosen."

Perhaps I should say "in Frye's word," for the central perception in Bloom's essay on "The Dialectics of Poetic Tradition" has an unacknowledged debt to Frye. Bloom writes that this dialectics boils down to a pair of questions: "do we choose a tradition or does it choose us, and why is it necessary that a choosing take place, or a being chosen?" (32). This choose-or-be-chosen motif strongly echoes the closing sentence of Frye's little book on Eliot: "The greatness of his achievement will finally be understood, not in the context of the tradition he chose, but in the context of the tradition that chose him" (*TSE* 99). This is a stunning chiasmus, and the effect is the reversal of reality that Frye so liked to contemplate.

Another former student, Angus Fletcher, has suggested that Frye's teaching of literary tradition was dominated by "the impulse toward the canonical" (Fletcher 750): the tendency "to seek the canonical divisions

43

and coherence of the 'body' ... of literature." Fletcher uses the word *canon* in the word's original sense of a "standard of judgement."[8] This may seem a curious claim, given Frye's well-known resistance to the view that criticism is centrally concerned with judgments of value. However, Frye uses canonical measures to place works within "literature as a whole" rather than decide which ones to include or exclude. For example, he uses "canons of probability" to determine whether a novel belongs to his low mimetic mode or his high mimetic (*AC* 34, 65, 95). His canons are rules for identifying, not the best works of literature, but the best or most salient features of literature as a whole.[9]

In mounting the famous case against value-judgments, Frye hoped to show that literary criticism, though necessarily concerned with matters of taste, could rise above the tastes of a given period or group (*AC* 3, 8–9). Here again, the Romantic genius proved itself a useful ally, for it was said to transcend taste as well as talent. Kant famously asserted that genius "gives the rule to art," meaning that it takes more than simple talent or taste to conceive, to create, or indeed to perceive the beautiful work of art (§46). It follows that the attempt to identify the best in literary art, and to describe it, requires genius of a sort parallel to the genius that creates that art—and not inferior to that genius. Frye recognizes that artistic genius can take a conservative bent, like Bach's, or a revolutionary one, like Beethoven's: it can concentrate on working within the rules of the art or on smashing through them (*RE* 90–93). With his commitment to Blake's "left-wing" vision, Frye would probably have considered himself the more revolutionary theorist of art, and Kant the more conservative, but their views of genius seem compatible. With them we come back to the third sense of genius as an impersonal characteristic.

Shortly after responding to Frye's "statement," Bloom had occasion to formulate his own definition of genius. Introducing one hundred rhapsodic sketches of people who showed genius in their creative work, he found that he could not improve on Emerson's sense of genius as "the god within, the Self of 'Self Reliance'"—an essay which, he says, "admonishes us to fall back upon our genius" (*Genius* 11, 337).[10] Unable and unwilling to arrive at a materialistic definition of genius, Bloom returned to the Classical sense as a connection to the spirit world. He used a Romantic essayist as his guide, but an essayist who identified the true genius of the individual human being in relation to something beyond the material, that is, to the spiritual world. Bloom's own sense of literary genius turns out to be not only late Romantic but expressly Gnostic; indeed, he defines Gosticism as "the religion of literature," the very excess of which Eliot had complained (*Genius* xviii).

Genius, then, is a key word for Frye and a remarkably fluid one. In its Classical form, it refers to a power potentially present in all. In its Romantic form, it refers to a power actually realized in a few. Meanwhile, it also refers to something outside any one person in a language or culture. It enables critics to identify the canons associated with a tradition and thus obviates the need of value judgments such as Frye dismisses. Literature demands all of these, and they are combined in Blake's principle that "The Poetic Genius is the true Man" (*Complete Writings* 98). Frye began his career by affirming with Blake, and against Locke, that genius was the proper condition of mankind, the highest common denominator.[11] His personal reflection on *The Great Code* as a flawed work, but one of genius, suggests he held fast to the truth of Blake's message.

To be sure, there is some tension between the individual and collective aspects of a tradition, but Frye suggests a step beyond the divide. When we realize that he complements the Classical and Romantic genius with the Christian Spirit that moves in all things, we can see how the several forms of genius are potentially brought together. What Paul terms "the Spirit in our hearts" (2 Corinthians 1:22) is the spirit in which we ideally read and write.[12] And when we are in the spirit, we are not alone; we are in the presence of something larger. As a Christian, Frye would call this the Word of God, which makes our words possible and gives them meaning. He pointed out, over and again, that the Bible's ideal reader is not the individual Christian but the Spirit working in her or him. Milton wrote of "a two-fold Scripture; one external which is the written word, and the other internal, which is the Holy Spirit, written in the hearts of believers according to the promise of God" (Milton 1041; Jeremiah 31:33). Frye condensed the phrase when he quoted Milton, approvingly, as suggesting "that the ultimate authority in the Christian religion is what he calls the Word of God in the heart" (*GC* 138). Here he returned to the threefold Word of God that he elaborated in *Fearful Symmetry* and summarized in the book's final paragraph (428).

I said earlier that Frye knew better than to write a publicity statement. There is one final reason to think so. In *Words With Power*, he wrote (what he often said in lecturing on the Book of Job), "There are certain contexts in which one can no longer speak of oneself as a subject. One cannot, for example, say, 'I am a wise and good man,' without suggesting that one is nothing of the kind because such predicates as wisdom and goodness will not fit into any sentence starting with 'I am'" (*WP* 81). The same applies to saying that one is a genius, or has genius. For genius, like wisdom or goodness, is larger than any flawed individual. It represents the true identity toward which the individual strives. The genius that guided Frye *through* his writing and teaching, and guided us *to* the writing, is one that remains to be found *in* the writing. And when we have found it, I think we can safely say that *he* had genius.

ENDNOTES

1 Frye, *LN* 725. The statement was originally published in *Northrop Frye Newsletter* 7.2 (Summer 1997): 31.

2 Personal communication, 11 July 2006. As the second press reviewer, I noted only how rare it was to have a writer's notebooks available to such a full extent so soon after his death. I suspect that this passage, like many others, will become less controversial with time.

3   *Oxford English Edition*, "genius"; hereafter *OED*. Frye does not use the second sense of genius as a demon or genie, but follows Blake in noting that the daimon has been corrupted into the demon; see Blake, *Complete Writings* 98 and note 10 below.

4   Bloom, "Introduction" vii. The term *Magus im Norden* was originally applied to the eighteenth-century philosopher Johann Georg Hamann.

5   Frye, *LN* 306–7 and 254, alluding to line 183 of Milton's *Lycidas*.

6   For some early discussions of their relations see Gill 45–72; Russell 116–23; Willard, "Alchemy in the Bible," and Willard, "Archetypes of the Imagination."

7   Bloom, *Map* 30; Bloom's emphasis. Bloom alludes to a statement in Eliot's "Tradition and the Individual Talent" (Eliot 38). Eliot quoted the statement in "The Function of Criticism" (Eliot 68), which responded to Matthew Arnold's essay on "The Function of Criticism at the Present Time." Frye used the statement as the starting point of his essay "The Function of Criticism at the Present Time," which formed the basis of his introduction to the *Anatomy*. Needless to say, none of these essays were concerned with church governance, though Eliot later distanced himself from the cultural authority that he thought Arnold had given to poetry, maintaining that culture is "the incarnation (so to speak) of the religion of the people" (Eliot 295). Frye's religious writings suggest he assumed a position between Arnold and Eliot.

8   *OED*, "canon" *n.¹*, 2c; *OED Online*, "canon" *n.¹*, draft addition a (Dec. 2002).

9   Further parting ways with Frye, Bloom adapted the concept of modern canon formation in Curtius 264–72 (*Map* 35). He conceded that Curtius thought it impossible to identify canonical authors more recent than Goethe, but has proceeded to offer canons for what he calls the Democratic and Chaotic Ages and even to venture "A Canonical Prophecy" (*Western Canon* viii).

10 Emerson writes of "that divine idea which each of us represents," an idea equated with "the aboriginal Self," and of "the divine fact" that "God is here within" ("Self-Reliance" 148, 156, 159).

11 Frye, *FS* 3–29. Frye's Blakean understanding of the creative genius, which was closely allied to his understanding of the Romantic imagination, had some influence on work with the psychology of genius in the 1960s and their aftermath. See, e.g., Pearce 112–20.

12 Paul's phrase echoes the words of Moses in Deuteronomy 30:14: "the word is very nigh unto thee, in thy mouth, and in thy heart, that thou mayest do it," the Hebrew *dabar*

having the dual meaning of "saying" and "commandment." See Smith 31: "In the Bible 'The Word of God' is not just another name for 'the Bible,' but generally means the word of God in the *heart* or on the *lips* of his servants."

WORKS CITED

Apuleius. 1993. *The God of Socrates*. Trans. Thomas Taylor. Reprint Gillette, NJ: Heptangle.

Blake, William. 1966. *The Complete Writings*. Ed. Geoffrey Keynes. Oxford: Oxford UP.

Bloom, Harold. 2000. "Foreword: Northrop Frye in Retrospect." *Anatomy of Criticism: Four Essays*. By Northrop Frye. Princeton: Princeton UP. vii–xi.

———. 2003. "The Dialectics of Poetic Tradition." Chap. 2 in *A Map of Misreading*. 2nd ed. New York: Oxford UP. First published in *Boundary* 2.3 (1974): 528–538.

———. 1994. *The Western Canon: The Books and School of the Ages*. New York: Harcourt.

———, ed. 2002. *Genius: A Mosaic of One Hundred Exemplary Creative Minds*. New York: Warner.

Curtius, Ernst Robert. 1953. *European Literature and the Latin Middle Ages*. Trans. Willard R. Trask. New York: Pantheon.

Denham, Robert D. 11 July, 2006. Personal communication.

Eliot, T.S. *Selected Prose*. 1975. Ed. Frank Kermode. New York: Farrar.

Emerson, Ralph Waldo. 1957. "Self-Reliance." In *Selections from Ralph Waldo Emerson: An Organic Anthology*. Ed. Stephen E. Whicher. Boston: Riverside. 147–168.

Fletcher, Angus. 1975. "Northrop Frye: The Critical Passion." *Critical Inquiry* 1.4 (June): 741–56.

Frye, Northrop. 1957. *Anatomy of Criticism: Four Essays*. Princeton: Princeton UP.

———. 1996. *The Correspondence of Northrop Frye and Helen Kemp, 1932–1939*. Ed. Robert D. Denham. 2 vols. continuously paginated. Toronto: University of Toronto Press.

———. 1976. "Expanding Eyes." In *Spiritus Mundi: Essays on Literature, Myth, and*

Society. Bloomington: Indiana UP. 99–122. First published in *Critical Inquiry* 2 (1975): 199–216.

———. 1947. *Fearful Symmetry: A Study of William Blake*. Princeton: Princeton UP.

———. 1949. "The Function of Criticism at the Present Time." *University of Toronto Quarterly* 19 (October): 3–29.

———. 1982. *The Great Code: The Bible and Literature*. New York: Harcourt.

———. 2000. *Northrop Frye's Late Notebooks, 1982–1990: Architecture of the Spiritual World*. Ed. Robert D. Denham. 2 vols. continuously paginated. Toronto: University of Toronto Press.

———. 1976. "The Search for Acceptable Words." In *Spiritus Mundi: Essays on Literature, Myth, and Society*. By Northrop Frye. Bloomington: Indiana UP. 3–26. First published in *Daedalus* 102 (Spring 1973): 11–26.

———. 2002. *The "Third Book" Notebooks of Northrop Frye, 1964–1972*. Ed. Michael Dolzani. Toronto: University of Toronto Press.

———. 1981. *T.S. Eliot: An Introduction*. 1963. University of Chicago Press.

———. 1990. *Words with Power: Being a Second Study of the Bible and Literature*. New York: Harcourt.

Gill, Glen Robert. 2006. *Northrop Frye and the Phenomenology of Myth*. Toronto: University of Toronto Press.

Hamilton, A.C. 1979. "Northrop Frye: The Visionary Critic." *CEA Critic* 42 (November): 2–6.

Immanuel Kant, *Critique of Judgement*, trans. J. E. Bernard (New York: Hafner, 1951), 150; section 46.

Milton, John. 1946. *The Student's Milton*. Ed. Frank Allen Patterson. 1930. New York: Appleton.

O'Grady, Jean. 1999. "Northrop Frye at Home and Abroad." *Northrop Frye Newsletter* 8.1 (Summer): 22–32.

Oxford English Dictionary. 2nd ed. 1989. Oxford: Oxford University Press.

Pearce, Joseph Chilton. 1981. *The Bond of Power*. New York: Dutton.

Plato. 2005. *Euthyphro, Apology, Crito, Phaedo, Phaedrus*. Trans. Harold North Fowler. Loeb Classical Library, 36. 1914. Rev. edn. Cambridge: Harvard University Press.

Plotinus. 1991. "Our Tutelary Spirit." *The Enneads*, trans. Stephen MacKenna, ed. John Dillon. London: Penguin. 166–173.

Plutarch. 1992. "On Socrates' Personal Deity." *Essays*. Trans. Robin Waterfield. London: Penguin. 308–358.

Russell, Ford. 1998. *Northrop Frye on Myth*. London: Routledge.

Smith, Richard M. 1894. "Beliefs of a Brother." *The Biblical World* 3.1 (January): 30–34.

Wilde, Oscar. 1991. "The Critic as Artist." *Prose Writings and Poems*. Everyman's Library 42. New York: Knopf. 1–65.

Willard, Thomas. 1982. "Alchemy in Literature." *Centre and Labyrinth: Essays in Honour of Northrop Frye*. Ed. Eleanor Cook et al. Toronto: University of Toronto Press. 115–127.

———.1994. "Archetypes of the Imagination." *The Legacy of Northrop Frye*. Ed. Alvin A. Lee and Robert D. Denham. Toronto: University of Toronto Press. 15–27.

———. 1991. "The Visionary Education." *Northrop Frye: Visionary Poetics*. Ed. Robert D. Denham and Thomas Willard. New York: Peter Lang. 11–39.

FRYE & CANADIAN LITERATURE

PART II

Jumping to Conclusions

Northrop Frye on Canadian Literature

D. M. R. Bentley

... I imagine it lies deep in my mind, just above the very lowest, or
Sherbrooke, layer of archetypes.
— Northrop Frye, *The Diaries of Northrop Frye, 1942–1955* (115)

"Do you get *The Forum*?" Duncan Campbell Scott asked E.K. Brown in December 1943. "If so you will have read the article in the Dec[ember] N[umber] on Canadian Poetry.... I suppose Northrop Frye is a nom de plume; if so who is he?" (McDougall 86). The article to which Scott refers is "Canada and Its Poetry," the lengthy review of A.J.M. Smith's *Book of Canadian Poetry: A Critical and Historical Anthology* (1943) in which Frye made his major public debut as a critic of Canadian literature and first enunciated his view that "the outstanding achievement of Canadian poetry is in the evocation of stark terror":

Not a coward's terror ... but a controlled vision of the causes of cowardice. The immediate source of this is obviously the frightening loneliness of a huge and thinly settled country. When all the intelligence, morality, reverence and simian cunning of man confronts a sphinx-like riddle of the indefinite like the Canadian winter, the man seems as helpless as a trapped mink and as lonely as a loon....

And the winter is only one symbol ... of the central theme of Canadian poetry ... [the] riddle of inexplicable death: the fact that life struggles and suffers in a nature which is blankly indifferent to it. (*BG* 138–139)

Twenty years later, this view would find its most influential expression in Frye's first "Conclusion to a *Literary History of Canada*" (1965), where "deep terror in regard to nature" is identified as the cause of a distinctively Canadian "garrison mentality," and the two help shape the question he sees at the heart of the Canadian perplex: not "Who am I?" but "Where is here?" (830, 826). It is not my intention to pursue yet again the elusive hares released by the second riddling question,[1] but, rather, to take a close and critical look at some of the most influential statements about Canada and Canadian literature, found in Frye's 1965 "Conclusion," with a phenomenological eye on the two other questions that have entered the discussion: Scott's puzzled "Who is he?" and Frye's own rejected "Who am I?"

Between the publication of "Canada and Its Poetry" in 1943 and the appearance of the *Literary History of Canada* in 1965, Frye published the books and essays that propelled him to international and national fame as a literary theorist and a commentator on Renaissance, Romantic, and modern literature: *Fearful Symmetry* (1947), *Anatomy of Criticism* (1957), *The Well-Tempered Critic* (1963), *The Educated Imagination* (1963), *T.S. Eliot* (1963), *Fables of Identity* (1963), *A Natural Perspective* (1965), *The Return of Eden* (1965), and—to name only his most famous essay of the same period—"Literary Criticism" (1963), a condensed and

almost immediately controversial statement of his Popperian contention that criticism should avoid the pseudo-science of evaluation or
judgment (and see *AC* 20–29). During these years, he also contributed
to and became an editor of the *Canadian Forum* (1948–1952),[2] served
as a member of the Executive Council of the Canadian Radio and
Television Commission (1958–1961), contributed an annual overview
of Canadian poetry to the "Letters in Canada" section of the *University
of Toronto Quarterly* (1950–1959),[3] and wrote three essays on Canadian
poetry: "The Narrative Tradition in English-Canadian Poetry" (1946),
"Preface to an Uncollected Anthology" (1957), and "Poetry" (1958).

As the dates and relative weights of these achievements and activities
suggest, the preponderance of Frye's efforts in the years prior to the writing of his "Conclusion" to the *Literary History of Canada* lay outside the
area of Canadian literature.[4] Frye's essays of 1946, 1957, and 1958 also
did not include either an extensive knowledge of Canadian literary materials or a sustained engagement with Canadian literary scholarship,
despite their sweeping titles.[5] In other words, the essays did not include
the sorts of achievements and activities that might be considered pre-
requisites for an editor of the *Literary History of Canada*, let alone for a
contributor to the volume. That Frye was the former is entirely understandable: he was a literary critic and theorist of enormous stature who
would bring commensurately immense kudos to the project. That he
was also the latter is due to a combination of the same reason and the
embarrassed realization on the part of his fellow editors that, with the
exception of Claude Bissell (who had his hands full with the presidency
of the University of Toronto), Frye was the only one who was not con-
tributing to the book's contents.[6] So it was that, in the words of the general editor, Carl F. Klinck, "after the manuscript for the rest of the book
was complete, " Frye was charged with the task of providing it with "a
critical Conclusion" (Introduction xii).

Since Frye played no part in the "six-year programme ... [of] basic
research" (Klinck, Introduction ix) embodied in the *Literary History
of Canada* but had spent the bulk of those six years elaborating and

applying the theories presented in the *Anatomy of Criticism*, it is scarcely, if at all, surprising that in many key respects his "Conclusion" is a projection of those theories onto, it must be said, a largely superficial and second-hand knowledge of Canadian writing. Nevertheless, the ingenuousness and panache of the opening paragraphs of the "Conclusion" are as breathtaking as what they imply about the value and use of "basic" or foundational research. When "the first tentative plans for th[e] book" were drawn up, Frye recalls, he expressed the hope that it would help "to broaden the inductive basis on which some writers on Canadian literature, " notably himself, "were making generalizations that bordered on guesswork, " adding, "I find, however, that this book tends to confirm me in most of my intuitions on the subject[,] the advantage for me ... [being] that this attempt at conclusion and summary can involve some self-plagiarism."[7] Seldom does the hermeneutic circle reveal its turnings so blatantly and with such confidence in the primacy of intuition: for the educated imagination of the well-tempered critic, greater knowledge based on six years of research and writing by more than two dozen scholars has not yielded fresh insights that might change perceptions or prompt new conclusions but merely confirmed the soundness of "generalizations" based on "intuition" and limited knowledge.[8] In short, the function of the *Literary History of Canada* was to confirm what was readily apparent to an intuitive critic on the basis of limited evidence.

What Frye means by "self-plagiarism" becomes quickly evident in the second and third paragraphs of the "Conclusion." From the "Literary Criticism" essay comes a compliment to "the maturity of Canadian scholarship" and his fellow editors for "hav[ing] completely outgrown the view that evaluation is the end of criticism" (821, 822).[9] From the *Anatomy of Criticism, The Educated Imagination,* and *The Well-Tempered Critic* comes the notion that literature constitutes an "autonomous" realm of "verbal relationships" that are best studied without reference to the actual world (*AC* 122, 350). The logical problems generated by these and similar forays into "self-plagiarism" (or self-adaptation) lead the kindly Linda Hutcheon to claim that Frye's "Canadian writing displays postmodern *both/and* thinking" (113). A less charitable view, however, is that his writings produce some very tortured rationalizations. In "Literary Criticism," the "metaphor of the judge" upon which evaluative or "judicial" criticism rests is relegated to the minor league of "reviewing, or surveying current literature and scholarship" (58), but in the context of Canadian literature the metaphor of "the critic as 'judge' hold[s]" because "Canada has produced no author who is classic in the sense of possessing a vision greater in kind than that of his best readers." Therefore, "the Canadian critic ... is never dealing with the kind of writer who judges him" (821). In addition, Frye continues, Canadian literature does not qualify as literature, for by failing even in "the orthodox genres of poetry and fiction" to transcend its authors' "social and historical setting" (821–822), it falls short of the goal of being "independent of real experience" (*WTC* 149) and "as unlike life as possible" (*EI* 35). It is therefore "more significantly studied as a part of Canadian life" than as a part of "literary experience itself," which should be "stud[ied] ... as a coherent and unified order of words" (821–822; "Literary Criticism" 68). Perhaps the slippery phrase "more significantly studied" reflects the logic of "*both/and*," but in all important respects the argument rests on an either/or distinction that leaves Canadian literature out in the cold, exiled from the "autonomous" realm of "verbal relationships," and beneath serious consideration.[10] It is telling that later in his "Conclusion" Frye refers to the historical context of Canadian literature as a "seminal fact ... that we have *stumbled over* already (835; emphasis added).

Given that it is inextricably and lamentably mired in Canadian life, history, and, possibly worst of all, the nature for which literature and myth provide release, Canadian writing was perhaps doomed by its very character to elicit from Frye comparisons and analogies with aspects of the natural world. With his "simian cunning" and other mental resources exhausted by the Canadian landscape and climate, the unfortunate "man" of "Canada and Its Poetry" "seems as helpless as a trapped mink and as lonely as a loon." The most remarkable aspect of Edward Hicks's *The Peaceable Kingdom* (ca. 1830), one of the "two famous primitive American paintings" to which Frye somewhat surprisingly resorts to "sum up the ... argument [of the 'Conclusion'] emblematically," is not the "Quaker settlers" or the Native peoples with whom they are treating, but the "group of animals"— "lions, tigers, bears, oxen"— that "illustrate the prophecy of Isaiah about the recovery of innocence in nature" and "stare past us with a serenity that transcends consciousness" (846, 848). To suggest that a Canadian painting—say Tom Thomson's *The Jack Pine* (1916–1917) or, reaching back to the colonial period, Ebenezer Birrell's *Good Friends* (ca. 1834)—might have been a more fitting choice than *The Peaceable Kingdom* to represent "the Canadian tradition" (848) would of course be beside Frye's point that Hicks's painting represents the pastoral management of nature (and, incidentally, the Native peoples) in the interests of achieving a level of social organization akin to the transcendence of history and geography in the "universe ... of verbal relationships" that is literature (*AC* 122). Little wonder that in the paragraphs preceding and following his elevation of *The Peaceable Kingdom* to the status of a Canadian icon, Frye first argues through E.J. Pratt's "The Truant" that "the sinister and terrible ... in nature" are identical with "the death-wish in man" and then identifies the same poem as a "foreshadow[ing] of the poetry of the future, when physical nature has retreated to outer space and only individuals and society are left as effective factors in the imagination" (845, 848). Not everyone would agree that such abjection — indeed, ejection — of "physical nature" would be possible or desirable, let alone utopian.

That Frye draws the "Conclusion" to the *Literary History of Canada* to a close by eagerly envisaging a time when "only individuals and society are ... effective factors in the imagination" has little or nothing to do with Canadian literature and much, perhaps everything, to do with a dislike amounting to fearful loathing of "physical nature" on the part of Frye himself. A number of comments concerning nature and animals in Frye's notebooks and diaries reflect this psychophysical disposition,[11] as does the pejorative use of the word "simian" in the phrase "simian cunning," and the analogy he employs in an essay called "Canadian and Colonial Painting" in the March 1940 issue of the *Canadian Forum* to illustrate the "process of material and imaginative *digestion*" that for him characterizes the relationship of "all communities" to their "bodily" and "mental" environments:

> A large tract of vacant land may well affect the people living near it as too much cake does a small boy: an unknown but quite possibly horrible Something stares at them in the dark: hide under the bedclothes long as they will, sooner or later they must stare back. Explorers, tormented by a sense of the unreality of the unseen, are first: pioneers and traders follow. But the land is still not imaginatively absorbed, and the incubus moves on to haunt the artists. (*BG* 199)[12]

Like "too much cake," this passage implies, "large" and "vacant"—extensive and undomesticated—nature is best avoided, for to ingest and internalize it through contemplation is to invite a degree of physical discomfort and psychological distress that leads to the creation of phobic fantasies. That this was so for Frye himself is strongly suggested by George Woodcock's recollection of Frye's reaction to the mountains he had been invited to admire during a visit to Vancouver in the 1950s: he "grew visibly paler as he stood for an instant looking out. Then he turned ... [and] hurried indoors, saying 'Those mountains make my blood run cold'" (71). "I wish I knew where I get this terrific agoraphobia that besets me when I travel alone," runs Frye's entry in his diary for 27 April 1949, which then proceeds to psychoanalyze the anxiety disorder primarily as a response to landscape and environment:

It has something to do with an introverted attitude combined with a withdrawal of the persona, to use Jungian terms. My thinking apparatus seems to go all to pieces in unfamiliar territory; there's a profound disturbance in what I should guess was the sympathetic nervous system.... [E]xploring, finding new experiences & surroundings constipates my brains, & all my observations are superficial and out of perspective.... A profound resentment of change, linked to an intense desire to root my thinking organically in a home, wells up in me & makes me deliberately create fears. (*Diaries* 194)

These reactions, coupled with the passage in "Canadian and Colonial Painting" and a closely related passage in "Canada and Its Poetry" in which he characterizes "Canadian poetry ... at its best" as "a poetry of incubus and *cauchemar*" whose "source is the unusually exposed contact of the poet with nature which Canada provides" (BG 141), points to a phobic psychophysical response to extensive, "unfamiliar, " and undomesticated space as essential to Frye's relationship to Canada and Canadian literature. Sandra Djwa is substantially correct in observing that "[t]oday's reader—or yesterday's reader—browsing through *The Book of Canadian Poetry* will not find 'stark terror.'" (135). Frye did because what he saw there and in other texts was an all-too-natural body of writing whose failure to properly digest Canada's "large, " "vacant, " "new," and "unfamiliar" "tract[s] of ... land" and "territory" produced ghastly nightmares, Gothic dread, and a sense of personal disintegration rather than the peaceful dreams, utopian visions, and sense of unified identity that would come with the transcendent literature of the future.[13]

In the case of "Canada and Its Poetry" and his discussion of *The Peaceable Kingdom*, Frye's references to animals are enlivening and innocuous, but in the adaptively self-plagiarized paragraphs at the beginning of the "Conclusion" they serve quite complex rhetorical and polemical purposes. When the contributors to the *Literary History* are praised in the second paragraph for rejecting evaluation because to have adopted it as a "guiding principle" would "have been only a huge debunking project, leaving Canadian literature a poor naked *alouette* plucked of every feather of decency and dignity" (821), the amusing metaphor of the "*alouette*" combines with a rush of alliteration to occlude the tendentiousness of the argument and to encourage the reader to forget that several contributions to the book—not least the immediately preceding essays on modern poetry by Munro Beattie—are astringently evaluative without leaving the corpus of Canadian literature "plucked of every feather of decency and dignity."

In his notorious attack on Frye's non-evaluative stance, in "Northrop Frye: Criticism as Myth," W.K. Wimsatt briefly suspends his withering barrage to praise the refreshing "liveliness, the moments of vivid wit and charm ... the freedom and swash and slash" of Frye's style (84). This is a well-deserved compliment and as applicable to the "Conclusion" of the *Literary History* as to Frye's other works, but so too, unfortunately, is Wimsatt's observation that "the speed and energy of his style" sometimes "enable[s] ... [him] to get away with ... violations of logic and order" and, it must be added, accuracy (84).

Scarcely has the "poor naked *alouette*" faded from the mind's eye of the reader of the "Conclusion" than in the next paragraph, another and no less dazzlingly witty bird trope appears with the assertion that "[t]he literary, in Canada, is often only an incidental quality of writings which, like those of the early explorers, are as innocent of literary intention as a mating loon" (822). In this instance, an amusing comparison functions not as a source of insight or enlightenment but as an impediment to them, and, worse, raises questions about the extent of the knowledge on which it is based. What precisely is meant by "many of the early explorers"? As a category, whom does it exclude and whom does it include? Samuel Hearne spent years revising and expanding his journals for publication in a market hungry for Gothic fiction, and sensationalized the

Bloody Fall incident accordingly. Alexander Mackenzie employed the famous Dr. Syntax to assist him with the writing of his narrative; David Thompson never did succeed, despite prolonged effort, in subduing his diaries to a narrative structure. Were these writers and others, such as Alexander Henry and Simon Fraser, really "innocent of literary intention"? If not, then which explorers were? It may be protested that by raising such questions and prompting rebuttal, Frye's assertion and simile were critically productive goads to scholarly work. This does not appear to have been their intent, however, and, like the "*alouette*" trope, the figure of the "mating loon" has the feel of a condescending quip based not on extensive knowledge of the butt of its humour but on unexamined stereotypes of Canadian writing, Canadian history, and Canadian nature.

While Frye's "*alouette*" and "loon" are distinctively Canadian animals, his amusing and diverting use of them has a long lineage and profound implications. Writing of the Stoics in the 2003 Tanner Lectures in Human Values, Martha S. Nussbaum observes that "[p]ejorative remarks about animals frequently substitute for argument in their accounts of human nature and human dignity," a rhetorical manoeuvre that assumes a "sharp split, not only between humans and other animals, but also between human life when moral rationality gets going and human life at other times (including ... childhood up to adolescence)" (130). Taken "even further" by Immanuel Kant, this separation of "human dignity and ... moral capacity ... from the natural world" rests on a number of troubling occlusions and assumptions, not least a failure to recognize that human dignity is merely the "dignity of a certain kind of animal," a denial that "animality can itself have dignity, and a pretense that "the core of ourselves ... [is] atemporal ... and utterly removed, in its dignity, from material events" (132). Each of these points loudly resonates with aspects of Frye's treatment of Canadian literature, none more so than the last, for imbricated with "stark terror" in the face of nature in his analysis is a distinctly temporal fear of materiality and all that it implies in terms of mutability and mortality—a fear whose manifestation in another register is the rejection of history that Marxian commentators on Frye find so repugnant and the flight to an autonomous verbal universe whose mapping is one of the great achievements of the *Anatomy of Criticism*. There may be a lot more truth than initially meets the eye in Frye's assertion in the preface to *The Bush Garden* that his "writing career," mainly concerned though it was with "world literature and ... an international reading public," drew "its essential characteristics" from Canada, specifically, the evidence now placed on view suggests, from a psychophysical reaction to the unhumanized and non-human aspects of the Canadian environment. Ironically, the dislike of "physical nature" that made Frye a nervous and misleading commentator on Canadian literature may have helped make him the 20th century's great cartographer, not to say creator, of the verbal universe of myth and literature.

Toward the end of a review of the *Anatomy of Criticism,* one that is more restrained in its criticisms than the piece by Wimsatt quoted a few moments ago, M.H. Abrams identifies the "particular achievement" of Frye's magisterial synopsis as its "wit"— that is, its "'combination of dissimilar images, or discovery of occult resemblances in things apparently unlike'"(196). In its lowest form, Frye's "wit criticism" (as Abrams calls it) is evident in the animal tropes of the "Conclusion" but it is more elaborately obvious in the discussion of *The Peaceable Kingdom* and in the following passage, in which Frye, inspired by William Blake's use of the biblical monster Leviathan to represent the material world[14] and Donald Creighton's Laurentian thesis of Canadian economic and political development,[15] asserts that in contrast to the United States,

> Canada has, for all practical purposes, no Atlantic seaboard. The traveller from Europe edges into it like a tiny Jonah entering an inconceivably large whale, slipping past the Straits of Belle Isle into the Gulf of St. Lawrence, where five Canadian provinces surround him for the most part invisible. Then he goes up the St.

Lawrence and the uninhabited country comes into view, mainly a French speaking country, with its own cultural traditions. To enter the United States is a matter of crossing an ocean; to enter Canada is a matter of being silently swallowed by an alien continent. (824)

It is a testament to the suggestive force of this yoking together by force of myth and geography that it helped inspire the opening section of Margaret Atwood's *Journals of Susanna Moodie* (1970) (and, in so doing, received retrospective validation to the extent that Atwood's Moodie became the lens through which readers saw the historical Moodie).[16] Yet to judge by their writings, Moodie, Catharine Parr Traill, Samuel Strickland, and countless other immigrants to Canada in the 18th, 19th, and 20th centuries experienced the journey up the St. Lawrence as a blessed and exciting relief after a monotonous and sometimes dangerous ocean voyage, and took varying degrees of pleasure in the sublime scenery of the estuary and the picturesque sights of Quebec. The tropes of Canada as "whale" and the "traveller" as Jonah and the contingent notion of being "silently swallowed by an alien continent" are both striking, fanciful, and utterly belied by the facts, as is the assertion that "for all practical purposes" (or for other than mythopoeic purposes) "Canada has ... no Atlantic seaboard." Travellers and immigrants who landed at Halifax and other ports would beg to differ, as would all Maritimers and anyone who has visited the Maritime provinces. As Janice Kulyk Keefer observes in *Under Eastern Eyes: A Critical Reading of Maritime Fiction* (1987, 27), an "incidental result" of Frye's adoption and adaptation of the "Laurentian paradigm ... is [a] demolition of the Maritimes." The realities of both history and geography are in this instance forfeited to an apparent determination to connect a portion of Canadian experience to a mythological pattern, one that horrifyingly inverts the process of imaginative ingestion that produces literature to figure Canada as a monstrous consumer and—for the Jonah story continues—disgorger of human beings.

The confirmatory effect of the *Literary History* on his intuitions that Frye describes in the opening paragraph of the "Conclusion" is most evident in the passage alluded to at the outset of this essay, where he coins the term "garrison mentality" to "characteriz[e] the way in which the Canadian imagination has developed in its literature" (830). Preceding the passage in question is a rehearsal of the central aperçu of "Canada and Its Poetry," with none of the anxious hesitancy of the original:[17]

> I have long been impressed in Canadian poetry by a tone of deep terror in regard to nature.... It is not a terror of the dangers or discomforts or even the mysteries of nature, but a terror of the soul at something that these things manifest. The human mind has nothing but human and moral values to cling to if it is to preserve its integrity or even its sanity, yet the vast unconsciousness of nature in front of it seems an unanswerable denial of these values. (830)

Bracketing this passage and confirming its "intuition" are two brief quotations from the *Literary History*, one citing a description of "mosquitoes" as "mementos of the fall" and the other citing a Methodist preacher on "the loneliness of the forests" as a "'shutting out of the whole moral creation.'" (830) It might be thought that is slim evidence in comparison with the vast quantity of poetry and prose from every period of Canadian writing in which no "terror" whatsoever is to be found and what "terror" does exist more often than not comes mingled with sublime awe at the manifestations of divine power in the immensities of Canadian nature. Nevertheless, and now—as perhaps not in 1943—armed with a Vichian conception of mythology and literature as responses to the loneliness and fear that humans experience in the face of natural phenomena that

lack "a human shape or a human meaning"(*EI* 3), Frye proceeds to describe the origin of the Canadian "garrison mentality":

> Small and isolated communities surrounded with a physical or
> psychological "frontier, " separated from one another and from
> their American and British cultural sources: communities that
> provide all that their members have in the way of distinctively
> human values, and that are compelled to feel a great respect for
> the law and order that holds them together, yet confronted with
> a huge, unthinking, menacing, and formidable physical setting—
> such communities are bound to develop what we may provision-
> ally call a garrison mentality. (830)

As evidence of the pervasiveness of this Heimlich manoeuvre, Frye declares that "[i]n the earliest maps of the country the only inhabited centres are forts, and that remains true of the cultural maps for a much later
time." In *The History of Emily Montague* (1769), Frances Brooke "wrote
of what was literally a garrison; novelists of our day studying the impact of Montreal on Westmount write of a psychological one" (830). "As
the centre of Canadian life moves from the fortress to the metropolis,
the garrison changes correspondingly," Frye adds by way of introducing
one of several further convolutions of the thesis. The garrison "begins
as an expression of the moral values generally accepted by the group as a
whole, and then, as society gets more complicated and more in control
of the environment, it becomes more of a revolutionary garrison within
a cosmopolitan society" (834).[18] "*Control of the environment*": that this
is the "physical ... [and] psychological" raison d'être for the "garrison
mentality" and a great deal more in Frye's work seems indisputable and,
indeed, was so recognized by Woodcock when Frye fled from a sight to
which "most people respond ... with delight": "he created huge critical
schemata because he wanted literature to appear as a construct apart

from the nature he feared; he used the garrison as a metaphor ... because he dreaded the wilderness" (71).

Although a combination of his own psychophysical reactions to unhumanized nature and a Freudian as well as a Vichian conception of reaction-formation may be sufficient to explain Frye's notion of the "garrison mentality," a third factor may have contributed to its formulation: the Conradian observations of Oscar Handlin in *Race and Nationality in America* (1950) on the reactions of American settlers to the wilderness:[19]

> The receding ships left them at the edge of an impenetrable wilderness; they moved up the river and the dark jungle [!] closed in behind them.... [I]n their aloneness there was one pre-eminent danger, the emptiness of the land about them. The world of familiar objects in their place had disappeared; the wilderness remained. No church, no town or village, no judge! Where was religion or law or morality?
>
> There was only the dark forest, the secret home of unknown beings.... The awesome thought came to those who were alone: no reckoning of right or wrong could find them out here.... Mostly, however, they refused to give way and insisted on living in clearings in the dark. Within a circumscribed area at least they made the effort to recapture the order that had gone out of life at their departure. In the spaces in the forest the old God could look down, the old church be re-established, and the old forms of dress and behavior imitated—if only they could keep out the wilderness that ever threatened to break in upon them. (114–115)

Whatever their textual and psychophysical sources, and even if there were such an entity as "*the* Canadian imagination" (which seems unlikely in such a culturally and geographically diverse country as Canada), Frye's "stark terror" and "garrison mentality" are by turns too narrow and too broad to adequately characterize it, but their influence on Canadian criticism was for a time very great. They will always remain for Canadian scholars two of the most intriguing reflections—indeed, symptoms—of the profoundly complex and brilliant being from whose body and mind they emanated.[20]

The back cover of *The Bush Garden* carries the usual paeans of praise for the merits of the book and its author. Peter Buitenhuis calls the publication of the collection a "literary event ... of the highest importance to Canadian literature"; George Woodcock proclaims that "in *The Bush Garden*, Frye shows himself as good a field critic as he is a theoretical one"; Robert Weaver suggests that Frye's essays are "still relevant, partly because ... [he] is such a good critic and partly because ... [they] embrace ... such a wide range of poetry"; John Robert Colombo confesses that he cannot "imagine a more perceptive book being written about the Canadian poetic imagination"; and Kildare Dobbs opines that "[p]erhaps the most remarkable thing about *The Bush Garden* is that it reveals ... Frye as a practical critic, " adding that "[h]e does not try to fit everything he reads into preconceived theories" and that "the range of his sympathies is admirably wide." Today, none of these statements can be easily read without a quizzical furrowing of the brow, an amused crinkling of the eyes, or a dismayed shaking of the head. However, there is surely more truth than Buitenhuis knew in his observation that "[t]ethered in its own backyard, as it were, " in the narrowly focused essays of *The Bush Garden*, the "formidable creature" that is Northrop Frye "can be observed more closely than it can be when it roams the far reaches of the literary world."

For various reasons and on different counts, this essay has been sharply critical of Frye's views of Canadian literature. Not merely because of the event for which it was written but, more important, because I greatly admire Frye's work and have benefitted greatly both as a teacher and as a scholar from his writings, I wish to end on an unmitigatedly positive note. Frye was an acute observer of Canada who regarded engagement with Canadian culture and literature as a serious responsibility. He contributed immeasurably to Canada's cultural and literary life in the second half of the 20th century and his writings continue to do so, and not just because of the publications of the Northrop Frye project. He was and remains a literary theorist of international stature whose work stands almost alone in roundly disproving his contention that "Canada" has produced no author who is "a classic in the sense of possessing a vision greater in kind than that of his best readers" (821).

ENDNOTES

1 See the opening chapter of my *Canadian Architexts: Literature and Architecture in Canada, 1759–2005* for Frye's question as the point of departure for a phenomenological discussion of Canadian literature and architecture. This essay has its distant beginnings in "Some Different Conclusions" to the *Literary History of Canada*, a seminar delivered at the invitation of Robert Lecker and Brian Trehearne at McGill University in October 1982. Lecker's chapter on Frye in *Making It Real: The Canonization of English-Canadian Literature* (Concord, ON: Anansi, 1995) is to date the fullest published discussion of his commentaries on Canadian literature and their impact on Canadian literary studies, but see also the essays of Linda Hutcheon, Sandra Djwa, David Staines, and others in the "Imagined Community: Frye and Canada" section of *The Legacy of Northrop Frye*, ed. Alvin A. Lee and Robert D. Denham (Toronto: University of Toronto Press, 1994), 105–173. The earliest extended response to "Canada and Its Poetry" appears to be John Sutherland's "Old Dog Trait: An Extended Analysis," *Contemporary Verse* 29 (Fall 1949): 17–23, which faults Frye for "mistakenly ignor[ing] the vitality of Canadian poetry" and makes a number of telling points about its assertions, such as, "It is ... clear that Frye's brief illustrations, although persuasive and frequently brilliant, cannot indicate the actual value of his argument in the absence of any detailed application of its terms to individual writers," and "[l]ogically we have to conclude that the sense of fear and the

preoccupation with evil which are in some way characteristic of Canadian poetry are in some way characteristic of Canadians, but Frye makes no attempt to establish such a relationship" (22, 19, 21).

2   Frye's impact on such writers as Al Purdy, whose work he critiqued as part of the editorial process, remains to be recognized and discussed, as does his unfashionable admiration for at least some of the work of the truculently anti-modern Wilson MacDonald (see *BG* 172 and Betty Lee).

3   "What a job," wrote Frye in January 1952 of his annual review. "If I can get through ... [it] without outraging either the people who write Canadian poetry or the people who read it, if any, I'm going to apply for the honorary degree of ... Doctor of Canadian Literature" *(Diaries* 482–483).

4   When, in January 1950, John Sutherland sent him a copy of "Old Dog Trait: An Extended Analysis," a largely positive response to "Canada and Its Poetry," Frye responded by advising Sutherland "to develop his ideas himself, as ... [he] [Frye] would never have time to write much more on Canadian literature" *(Diaries* 240).

5   That Frye continued to rely on Smith's anthology is suggested by a number of observations in his essays and reviews of the late 1940s and 1950s, not least his remark in "The Narrative Tradition in English-Canadian Poetry" that Standish O'Grady's *The Emigrant* (1840, 1841) is "brilliant" (*BG* 150). In 1948–1949, Frye was involved with a Canadian Literature Club ("that very naive organization ... that practically strangled me to death last year" he wrote of it in 1949) and in 1954–1955 he gave talks to "a small Canadian Literature group on Thomas Chandler Haliburton's *The Clockmaker*, John Richardson's *Wacousta*, Susanna Moodie's *Roughing It in the Bush*, and the poetry of Archibald Lampman" (see *Diaries* 187, 596–604, 616).

6   In *Giving Canada a Literary History: A Memoir* (McGill-Queen's University Press, 1991), Klinck cites Bissell's "deep ... involve[ment] in the affairs of a great university" as the reason for the paucity of references to him in the chapter on the inception and creation of the *Literary History* (119), but draws a veil over the circumstances leading to the commission of Frye's "Conclusion, " which he communicated to me in a conversation in the mid-1980s.

7   This and subsequent page references to Frye's "Conclusion" are from the text in the *Literary History of Canada*, since the text subsequently published in *The Bush Garden:*

Essays on Canadian Literature (1971) differs significantly in its opening paragraphs. For example, the *Bush Garden* version of the final sentence quoted above reads, "I find, however, that more evidence has in fact tended to confirm most of my intuitions on the subject," and entirely omits the statement about the "advantage" that this affords in the form of "self-plagiarism" (213). The text of the "Conclusion" in *Northrop Frye on Canada*, the splendid compendium of Frye's writings about Canada edited by Jean O'Grady and David Staines, is properly based on the text in the *Literary History of Canada*.

8   In 1942, Frye had regarded "'[i]ntuition' as generally understood ... [as] a mental short cut employed by the unintelligent, who are no doubt pleased to be told that it's superior to intelligence, " but by 1949, when he had come under the increasing influence of Carl Jung, he saw "intuitive apprehension" as a property of the "unconscious" and "intuition" or "literal apprehension" as the "begin[ning] [of] all creative activity" (*Diaries* 31, 60).

9   Other instances of "self-plagiarism" include the idea that "[t]he forms of literature are autonomous: they exist within literature itself, and cannot be derived from any experience outside literature. What the Canadian writer finds in his experience and environment may be new, but it will be new only in content: the form of his expression of it can take shape only from what he has read, not from what he has experienced"— a process characterized as "pour[ing] the new wine of content into old bottles of form" (835; and see *EI* 13–18).

10   "[T]he study of mediocre works of art remains a random and peripheral form of critical experience," writes Frye in one of many portions of *Anatomy of Criticism* that does not eschew evaluation, "whereas the profound masterpiece draws us to a point at which we seem to see an enormous number of converging patterns of significance" (170; and see 20–29 for his dismissal of literary value judgments).

11   "I don't know why I have such a horror of animals," wrote Frye in his diary on 24 July 1942; "[a] recurrent nightmare is badly hurting an animal and stomping it furiously into a battered wreck in a paroxysm of cowardly mercy. And that is to some extent what I'm like. Any intimate contact with an animal I dislike, & their convulsive movements give me panic. If I go to hell, Satan will probably give me a wet bird to hold. For one thing, they're afraid, & fear is something I'm an abnormal conductor of. There's a pigeon sitting outside my window now giving me pigeon-flesh" (*Diaries* 14). Subsequent remarks about animals in Frye's diaries include: "The city is the community become conscious:

it is to the country what man is to animals. Animals live; man knows that he lives".... "I recently saw a spaniel sniffing with great concentration at a little girl's wet diapers, & reflected on the fact that ... we regard that type of experience with nausea, & the nausea must be (as I think nausea always is, from Sartrean existentialism to sea sickness) the result of panic" ... and "[a]nimals' minds are still an unexplored mystery of nature, & hence become a hideout for superstition of all kinds, from anti-vivisection to the popular (because anti-intellectual) beliefs in the mysterious accuracy and insight of animal instinct" (99, 376, 459; and see 24, 38, 138, 153, 193, 279, 469).

12   This passage recalls the famous "something nasty in the woodshed" that haunts Aunt Ada Doom in Stella Gibbons's *Cold Comfort Farm* (1932) and brings to mind Charles Dickens's response to the frescoes of martyrdoms in Santa Stefano Rotondo in Rome: "Such a panorama of horror and butchery no man could imagine in his sleep, though he were to eat a whole pig, raw, for supper" (qtd. in Kahn 213). The tone of Frye's analysis does not suggest either that it was intended to be humorous or, such being case, that it is an instance of anxiety transformed into humour. His diaries from 1942 to 1953 contain numerous references to constipation and several comments on the relationship between digestive and mental/emotional activities, including the statement that, in his view, "nightmares ... represent a kind of emotional excretion" (*Diaries* 272).

13   In "'Monckton Did You Know?' Northrop Frye's Early Years," Robert D. Denham quotes a passage from an early notebook in which Frye relates his agoraphobia to an early dream: "When I was about seven I had a passion to live in a cave, which lasted a surprisingly long time, & if I'd been born in Tibet or early Christian Egypt I suppose I'd have become an anchorite. At eleven I had an equally strong passion for a private study, which I still have. This may be an underground current that breaks out in the form of my recurrent agoraphobia. A psychoanalyst would talk about wombs & foetuses & mothers & of course the everlasting Oedipus: I see it as the necessity for a Beulah or a place of intellectual seed" (77).

14   In her portion of the introduction to *Northrop Frye on Canada*, Jean O'Grady observes that the "distrust of nature" apparent in Frye's review of Smith's *Book of Canadian Poetry* is also evident in *Fearful Symmetry*, where he "first used the Jonah's-whale figure, " adding that, "[s]ince th[e] Leviathan image is his Blake- and Bible-derived figure for 'the monster of indefinite time and space' ... from which humankind needs to be delivered,

Canadian nature acquires even more negative, and typically Frygian, overtones" (xxx-vii). Grady also observes of the "stark terror" that Frye found in Canadian poetry that "he was predisposed to find it there."

15 Creighton's rhapsodic personification of the St. Lawrence in the opening chapter of *The Empire of the St. Lawrence* (Toronto: University of Toronto Press, 1956) stands in stark contrast to the passage about to be quoted above: "It was the one great river which led from the eastern shore into the heart of the continent. It possessed a geographical monopoly; and it shouted its uniqueness to adventurers. The river meant mobility and distance; it invited journeyings; it promised immense expanses, unfolding, flowing away into remote and changing horizons. The whole west, with all its riches, was the dominion of the river. To the unfettered and ambitious, it offered a pathway to the central mysteries of the continent.... [F]rom the river there rose, like an exhalation, the dream of western commercial empire.... This was the faith of successive generations of northerners.... The river was not only a great actuality: it was the central truth of a religion. Men lived by it, at once consoled and inspired by its promises, its whispered suggestions, and its shouted commands; and it was a force in history, not merely because of its accomplishments, but because of its shining, ever-receding possibilities" (6–7).

16 The title of *The Bush Garden* is of course taken from *The Journals of Susanna Moodie*, which Frye describes in the preface to the collection as "a book unusually rich in suggestive phrases defining a Canadian sensibility" (x). The mutually reinforcing relationship between Frye's and Atwood's conceptions of Canada and Canadian culture is further evident in their identification of "schizophrenia" as a characteristic of the Canadian psyche (*BG* 133, *Journals* 62; and see "Conclusion" 825 and elsewhere).

17 In the final paragraph of "Canada and Its Poetry," Frye writes of the idea that "[n]ature is consistently sinister and menacing in Canadian poetry: "[t]his is not, I hope, a pattern of thought I have arbitrarily forced upon Canadian poetry: judging from Mr. Smith's book and what other reading I have done this seems to be its underlying meaning, and the better the poem[,] [the] more clearly it expresses it. Mr. Smith has brought out this inner unity quite unconsciously because it is really there...." (*BG* 143).

18 Subsequent iterations and variations of the "garrison mentality" appear in the "Conclusion" to a *Literary History of Canada* (838) (where it is attributed to "officers") and in several of the later pieces collected in *Northrop Frye on Canada*; see, for example,

470–471: in the 19ᵗʰ century "[t]he garrison mentality ... [was] defensive and separatist" but by the late 20ᵗʰ century it reflected in Canadians' "sense of occupying our particular garrison on our part of the globe"; 569–570: "the garrison encapsulates a great deal of imaginative feeling in Canada, even down to the twentieth century" and is manifested in various "enclave cultures" within the country; and 647: "a ... typical garrison attitude survived psychologically in the rural and small-town phase of Canadian life, with its heavy pressures of moral and conventional anxieties. Canadians are now, however, one of the most highly urbanized people in the world, and the garrison mentality, which was social but not creative, has been replaced by the condominium mentality, which is neither social nor creative, and which forces the cultural energies of the country into forming a kind of counter-environment."

19 Frye was both widely read and keenly interested in American literature and appears to have taught all or part of a course in the field sometime before the summer of 1950 (see *Diaries* 420 and elsewhere).

20 After observing that "a 'garrison mentality' is not unique to Canadian poetry," Djwa briefly discusses similar patterns in the work of such writers as Thomas Hardy and D.H. Lawrence, adding that the "attitude to nature" of Pratt, the poet who, in her view, most influenced Frye in this respect, is "atypical of Canadian poetry as a whole" (139–140). From comments in "Canada and Its Poetry," it would seem that Pratt's "Silences" (1937) and Earle Birney's "David" (1942), both of which are reprinted in *The Book of Canadian Poetry*, played a considerable part in nourishing Frye's "terror" thesis: in the former, he found "civilized life ... seen geographically as merely one clock tick in eons of ferocity" and in the latter a "glacier" that is subject to "no 'pathetic fallacy' about ... [its] cruelty or that of whatever gods may be in charge of it" (*BG* 141, 139); and see "Conclusion" (845–846).

WORKS CITED

Abrams, M.H. 1959 (January). "Anatomy of Criticism." Review of *Anatomy of Criticism*, by Northrop Frye. *University of Toronto Quarterly* 28: 190–196.

Atwood, Margaret. 1970. *The Journals of Susanna Moodie*. Toronto: Oxford University Press.

Bentley, D. M. R. 2006. *Canadian Architects: Essays on Literature and Architecture in Canada, 1759 – 2005*. www.canadianpoetry.ca

Colombo, John Robert. 1974. *Canadian Quotations*. Edmonton: Hurtig.

Creighton, Donald. 1970. *The Empire of the St. Lawrence*. 1956. Toronto: Macmillan.

Denham, Robert D. 2004 (Summer). "'Moncton Did You Know?' Northrop Frye's Early Years." *Antigonish Review* 138: 67–82.

Djwa, Sandra. 1994. "Forays in the Bush Garden: Frye and Canadian Poetry." In *The Legacy of Northrop Frye*, ed. Alvin A. Lee and Robert D. Denham. Toronto: University of Toronto Press, 130–145.

Frye, Northrop. 2003. *Northrop Frye on Canada*. The Collected Works of Northrop Frye. Vol. 12. Ed. Jean O'Grady and David Staines. Toronto: University of Toronto Press.

———. 2001. *The Diaries of Northrop Frye, 1942–1955*. The Collected Works of Northrop Frye. Vol. 8. Ed. Robert D. Denham. Toronto: University of Toronto Press.

———. 1973. *The Critical Path: An Essay on the Social Context of Literary Criticism*. Bloomington and London: Indiana University Press.

———. 1973. Conclusion. *Literary History of Canada: Canadian Literature in English*, ed. Carl F. Klinck et al. 1965. Toronto: University of Toronto Press.

———. 1971. *The Bush Garden: Essays on the Canadian Imagination*. [Toronto]: House of Anansi Press.

———. 1963. *The Educated Imagination*. Toronto: CBC Publications.

———. 1963. "Literary Criticism." In *The Aims and Methods of Scholarship in Modern Languages and Literatures*, ed. James Thorpe. New York: Modern Language Association of America, 57–69.

———. 1963. *The Well-Tempered Critic*. Bloomington and London: Indiana University Press.

———. 1957. *Anatomy of Criticism: Four Essays*. Princeton: Princeton University Press.

Handlin, Oscar. 1957. *Race and Nationality in American Life*. 1950. New York: Doubleday.

Hutcheon, Linda. 1994. "Frye Recoded: Postmodernity and the Conclusions." In *The Legacy of Northrop Frye*, ed. Alvin A. Lee and Robert D. Denham. Toronto: University of Toronto Press, 105–121.

Kahn, Robert, ed. 1999. *City Secrets: Rome*. New York: The Little Bookroom.

Keefer, Janice Kulyk. 1987. *Under Eastern Eyes: A Critical Reading of Maritime Fiction*. Toronto: University of Toronto Press.

Klinck, Carl F. 1991. *Giving Canada a Literary History: A Memoir*, ed. Sandra Djwa. Ottawa: Carleton University.

———. 1973. Introduction. *Literary History of Canada: Canadian Literature in English*, ed. Carl F. Klinck et al. 1963. Toronto: University of Toronto Press, ix–xiv.

Lecker, Robert. 1995. *Making It Real: The Canonization of English-Canadian Literature*. Concord, ON: Anansi.

Lee, Alvin A., and Robert D. Denham. 1994. *The Legacy of Northrop Frye*. Toronto: University of Toronto Press.

Lee, Betty. 1958 (18 January). "MacDonald: The Self-Admitted Genius of Canadian Poetry." *Globe Magazine* (Toronto): 8–11.

McDougall, Robert L., ed. 1983. *The Poet and the Critic: A Literary Correspondence between D.C. Scott and E.K. Brown*. Ottawa: Carleton University Press.

Nussbaum, Martha C. 2006. *Frontiers of Justice: Disability, Nationality, Species Membership*. Cambridge, MA, and London: Belknap Press of Harvard University Press.

O'Grady, Jean, and David Staines. 2003. Introduction. *Northrop Frye on Canada*. The Collected Works of Northrop Frye. Vol. 12. Ed. Jean O'Grady and David Staines. Toronto: University of Toronto Press, xxi–xlviii.

Smith, A.J.M, ed. 1943. *The Book of Canadian Poetry: A Critical and Historical Anthology*. Chicago: University of Chicago Press.

Staines, David. 1994. "Frye: Canadian Critic/Writer." In *The Legacy of Northrop Frye*, ed. Alvin A. Lee and Robert D. Denham. Toronto: University of Toronto Press, 155–163.

Sutherland, John. 1949 (Fall). "Old Dog Trait: An Extended Analysis." *Contemporary Verse: A Canadian Quarterly* 29: 17–23.

Wimsatt, W.K. 1966. "Northrop Frye: Criticism as Myth." In *Northrop Frye in Modern Criticism: Selected Papers from the English Institute*, ed. Murray Krieger. New York and London: Columbia University Press, 75–107.

Woodcock, George. 1947. *Beyond the Blue Mountains: An Autobiography.* Markham, ON: Fitzhenry and Whiteside.

HISTORY, TRADITION, AND THE WORK OF PASTORAL:

Frye's "*Conclusion to a Literary History of Canada*"

Robert David Stacey

IT WOULD be difficult to exaggerate the impact Frye's 1965 "Conclusion to a *Literary History of Canada*" has had on the theory and practice of Canadian literary criticism. Republished in 1971 as the conclusion to yet another landmark text, Frye's own *The Bush Garden: Essays on the Canadian Imagination*, which collected the author's Canadian criticism written over the previous twenty-five years, the essay has exerted a tremendous influence—registered with varying degrees of anxiety—on successive generations of Canadian critics. For Robert Lecker writing in 1993, the ideas expressed in the "Conclusion" "form the primary basis of how most Canadian critics of the past two decades have envisioned and evaluated their literature" (284). While it no longer occupies quite the dominant position Lecker could attribute to it, the essay continues to function as an essential touchstone for thinking about Canadian cultural production and its criticism, especially among post-colonial critics for whom the essay represents an early attempt to account for the effect of Canada's colonial history on its literatures.

But if the "Conclusion" has remained relevant and compelling, it is partly due to an awareness of its inadequacies and fallacies, an awareness that has generated and, indeed, continues to generate theoretical adjustments and alternatives: to be sure, it has become a fairly typical pattern in writing about the "Conclusion" to begin by invoking its current or one-time hegemony before proceeding to an enumeration of its various heresies. And so it is that Lecker, after echoing previous critics who, like him, can find no single work of Canadian criticism "more influential than Northrop Frye's 'Conclusion'" (284), turns to expose its biases and omissions. The "Conclusion," he writes, is "characteristically mythopoeic, formal, centralist, Protestant, male-centred, and overwhelmingly English. As a history, it appears to be fundamentally untroubled by the dual linguistic and cultural heritages that both define Canada and threaten its stability as a nation" (284). Though I am not insensitive to these criticisms, I am more interested here in questions concerning the *form* of the "Conclusion" and the mediating role it plays between Frye's previous Canadian criticism and as his broader critical project as outlined in the *Anatomy of Criticism* (1957) and subsequent writings.

In fact, the great strength of Lecker's article is that it endeavours to explain the "plot" of Frye's essay. Significantly entitled "'A Quest for the Peaceable Kingdom': The Narrative in Northrop Frye's 'Conclusion to the *Literary History of Canada*,'" the article reads the "Conclusion" in the context of Frye's "major" internationalist criticism, arguing that the essay builds on the *Anatomy* and anticipates *The Secular Scripture* by describing Canadian literary history in terms of romance. Importantly, for Lecker the "Conclusion" itself exhibits the tropes and structure of a romance and operates like romance insofar as it presents a transcendent narrative of Canadian cultural origin. A "meditation on poetic genesis" (286), the "Conclusion," says Lecker, "glosses the romantic myth of fall and redemption" (284), which "construct[s] Canada as an apotheosis of metaphor, while reconstructing the criticism attached to Canada ... as a romance, a fiction, a myth" (285).

While I have deep misgivings regarding Lecker's suggestion that the shape of the "Conclusion" is motivated by Frye's own desire to figure himself the hero of his own national romance,[1] the article is convincing in its depiction of Frye actively constructing a history of Canadian literature that conforms to or is made intelligible by his broader theoretical project, a project for which romance is very nearly emblematic, embodying, as it does for Frye, the goal of fictional narrative itself. "Romance," Frye observes in an oft-quoted passage from *The Secular Scripture*, "is the structural core of all fiction ... it brings us closer than any other aspect of literature to the sense of fiction, considered as a whole, as the epic of the creature, man's vision of his own life as quest" (*SeS* 15). In fact, so strongly does romance speak to the utopian desire at the heart of Frye's critical project that Ian Balfour can describe that project as Frye's "romance with romance" (in Lecker 61).

That the "Conclusion" should rehearse the plot and emphasize the values of Frye's basic approach hardly seems shocking, except that in arguing for this kind of consistency Lecker rejects what has come to be seen by many as its greatest legacy (and heaviest burden) for the Canadian critic, namely, a disconcerting awareness of the basic *incommensurability* of Frye's Canadian criticism and his major internationalist work. Such a view, it is pointed out, is openly encouraged in the "Conclusion" by Frye's insistence that a national literature such as Canada's that has produced no genuine literary "classic[s]" demands a sociological and historically contextualized approach, unlike the English tradition more generally:

> If no Canadian author pulls us away from the Canadian context toward the centre of literary experience itself, then at every point we remain aware of his social and historical setting. The conception of what is literary has to be greatly broadened for such a literature.... Even when it is literature in its orthodox genres of poetry

and fiction, it is more significantly studied as a part of Canadian life than as part of an autonomous world of literature. (216)

Necessarily "studied as part of Canadian life," Canadian literature is properly the object of what Frye calls "cultural history" (217), the final goal of which is to delineate what is variously termed "the Canadian imagination" (217), the Canadian "social imagination" (217), or "Canadian consciousness" (223). Opposed to this is "literary criticism" that takes "the autonomous world of literature" as its object of study. In an early essay, "The Function of Criticism at the Present Time" (1949), Frye speaks of the need for a theory of literature (one that could account for its forms, symbols, and themes) whose terms were derived from an inductive analysis of the tradition itself. Needless to say, he would eventually provide this theory himself in the landmark *Anatomy of Criticism,* for which the earlier essay formed the basis of its "Polemical Introduction" and whose basic principles Frye would reaffirm throughout his career, most notably in *The Educated Imagination* (1963) and *The Critical Path* (1971). Corresponding to the disinterestedness of literary language itself, such criticism, Frye insists, must likewise be disinterested. Consequently, "there can be no such thing as a sociological 'approach' to literature" (66) taken as *literature,* just as true literary criticism, like the literature it addresses, must transcend "the tyranny of historical categories" (76).[2] And yet it is as a social critic and literary historian that Frye wishes to address Canadian literature—precisely because it fails to draw us into the "centre of literary experience itself."

In "Reading for Contradiction of the Literature of Colonial Space," Heather Murray may understandably therefore speak of the "Frye dilemma," whereby the Canadian critic is faced with a troubling distinction:

As Frye construes it, there is on the one hand a literature which is Canadian, contextualized, connected someone to life: it is unorthodox, slightly failed or fallen short. On the other hand is a

Literature which is general and autonomous, the term 'Literature' signifying both the realm of 'literary experience itself' and the fully achieved 'classics' which belong there. (73)

"To determine what is the relationship" between these distinct usages, writes Murray, "has been the job of English-Canadian literary criticism, and this is not an easy task" (73). Linda Hutcheon, writing in her introduction to the 1995 reissue of *The Bush Garden* identifies a similar problem but locates it within the Canadian criticism itself: "What many have seen as a major contradiction in Frye's work—between theories of general mythic patterns in literature and assertions of specifically Canadian culture—is indeed a real tension in his writing about Canada" (xv).

It is my contention that far from retrenching this contradiction, the "Conclusion," taken as a whole, rather works to reduce the tension between these two aspects of his work. Read in the context of *The Bush Garden*, it stands less as a summation of his thinking about Canadian literature than as a corrective to it. Its primary function is not to present a coherent theory of Canadian literature (which it could never hope to achieve) but to construct a coherent *critic* who might preside over a single unified (and unifying) critical approach. If there is an anxiety at the heart of the "Conclusion" it does not, as Lecker suggests, concern Frye's position as a father or hero of Canadian literature, but rather the contradictory and possibly negating role that his Canadian criticism plays vis-à-vis his other career-defining critical project. As Murray recognizes (but does not pursue), "If Canadian literature does not measure up to Frye's notion of literature, neither does his concept of literature measure up to Canadian writing" (73). This essay therefore takes direction from Murray's suspicion that "his theoretical containment of Canadian literature serves to protect his 'other' theoretical system from the challenge posed by colonial and post-colonial writings" (n. 2, 81). Playing a crucial role in this operation is the pastoral, whose archetypes are at the heart of his theory of romance. Indeed, it is precisely a discussion of the Canadian pastoral vision—a discussion Frye launches somewhat precipitously in the final section of the "Conclusion"—that differentiates the "Conclusion" from the rest of *The Bush Garden*, where the focus is almost exclusively on the tendency toward terror, "incubus and *cauchemar*" ("Canada and Its Poetry" 143) in the Canadian imagination. In all respects a generic trope of origin and identity, of communal belonging and spiritual immanence, the pastoral works in the "Conclusion" to erase the differences between the two "literatures" identified by Murray, to integrate Frye's Canadian and international work, and to assert a final harmony between "cultural history" and "literary criticism" proper.

But because Frye's Canadian criticism up to but not including the final section of the "Conclusion" is, as Murray observes, a grounded one, rooted in the writer's social and historical context, it—for all its bogeymen, lacunae, and unsupportable generalizations—amounts to a genuinely dialectical and materialist theory of literature. Latent in the Canadian criticism is a *critical* theory of literature one wishes Frye had given himself greater permission to explore and develop, and which I attempt to draw out here in the hope of reclaiming Frye's work for politically aware (and therefore inescapably *interested*) reading of Canadian literature.

Such a reading must begin with an awareness—or rather Frye's awareness—of the "difference" of Canadian literature. Whereas continuity and universality are the essential hallmarks of an archetypal or mythopoeic literary criticism for which "tradition," despite its implications of a diachronic view of literature as a collection of literary works in time, continually collapses into a synchronic understanding of literature as an "always-already" completed *system*,[3] Frye's Canadian criticism (or cultural history) is dominated by an awareness of the dissonance between its local tradition(s) and the so-called order of words. In one of his earliest published works on Canadian literature, a 1943 review essay of A.J.M. Smith's *The Book of Canadian Poetry*, Frye outlined his view of the Canadian writer's alienation from "the" literary tradition:

To an English poet, the tradition of his own country and language proceeds in a direct chronological line down to himself, and that in its turn is part of a gigantic funnel of tradition extending back to Homer and the Old Testament. But to a Canadian, broken off from this linear sequence and having none of his own, the traditions of Europe appear as a kaleidoscopic whirl with no definite shape or meaning, but with a profound irony lurking in its varied and conflicting patterns. ("Canada and Its Poetry" 138)

Thus, the pre-eminent critic of literary universality and generic continuity begins his exploration of the imaginative underpinnings of Canadian literature by acknowledging the discontinuity that marks its usage of European literary forms and conventions and makes it somehow problematic. Bearing in mind that Fredric Jameson's chief complaint about Frye's mythopoeic criticism is that it "proposes an unbroken continuity between the social relations and narrative forms" of diverse social groups separated in time and space (*Political Unconscious* 69), we can already see how Frye's Canadian criticism presents an alternative approach perhaps more congenial to a materialist criticism where literary meaning is always produced "in situation."

Given this attention to the context of literary production, it is perhaps not surprising that "environment" should emerge as a crucial term in Frye's Canadian criticism beginning with "Canada and Its Poetry." By environment, or more precisely, the writer's "imaginative environment," Frye means both his physical place as well as what poet Denis Lee (himself a student of Frye's) would later call "civil space." Frye argues that in both its dimensions the Canadian writer's environment separates him, "breaks him off," from the imaginative continuum of the Old World. In physical terms, the Canadian environment differs from that of Europe insofar as it is "consistently sinister and menacing" ("Canada and Its Poetry" 143). (For our purposes, it does not matter if this is actually the case.) Socially and politically, the Canadian imagination takes root in a place that is "pure colony, colonial in psychology as well as in mercantile economics" (Foreword xxiii).[4] The first situation, says Frye, leads to the development of social structures productive of the now infamous "garrison mentality" that itself produces a pattern in the literature repeated so often we may wish to call it an archetype, except that its origin is local and historically conditioned rather than universal and transhistorical. The second dimension of the Canadian "imaginative environment," its colonialism, constitutes a

> frostbite at the roots of the Canadian imagination, and it produces a disease for which I think the best name is prudery. By this I do not mean reticence in sexual matters: I mean the instinct to seek a conventional or commonplace expression of an idea. Prudery that keeps the orthodox poet from making a personal recreation of his orthodoxy: prudery that prevents the heretic from forming an articulate heresy that will shock: prudery that makes a radical stutter and gargle over all realities that are not physical: prudery that chokes off social criticism for fear some other group of Canadians will take advantage of it. ("Canada and Its Poetry" 136)

In short, as Frye explains in his foreword to *The Bush Garden,* "most of the imaginative factors common to the country as a whole are negative influences" (xiii). Consequently, his various discussions of Canadian literature are, with only a few exceptions, dominated by an exploration of the *inauthenticity* of Canadian writing, and the various historical and environmental factors blocking the Canadian writer from producing a genuine literary work, one that might take its proper place in the literary tradition.

Such discussions, of course, provided the theoretical and political impetus for a great deal of the so-called thematic criticism that followed on the heels of the "Conclusion," of which Margaret Atwood's *Survival* (1972) is likely the best known and most vilified.[5] But crucially such comments reveal Frye in the act of performing a kind of critical reading of Canadian literature, exactly the kind of contextualized, situated "reading for contradiction" that Heather Murray would call for in the late 1980s. Frye's "garrison mentality," for instance, constitutes what Jameson would call an "ideologeme," "a historically determinate conceptual or semic complex which can project itself variously in the form of a 'value system' or 'philosophical concept,' or in the form of a protonarrative" (*Political Unconscious* 115). Of course, for Jameson *all* of Frye's archetypes are, in actuality, ideologemes, though unbeknownst to him. The "garrison mentality" is notable, however, insofar as it reveals Frye, operating under the aegis of "cultural history," articulating his own version of a "historically determinate" literary pattern. More important, though, is Frye's general sense of the "irony" of the Canadian writer's relationship to tradition and its failure to wholly partake in the tradition. For if Canadian literature fails in this respect, it can only be because it embodies the social contradictions arising from its environment, contradictions that prevent it from properly inhabiting its inherited forms.

The question here concerns the process by which a particular (social) content makes itself available to a given form. Indeed, the biggest task facing the Canadian writer, Frye says, is figuring out how "to pour the new wine of content into the old bottles of form" ("Conclusion" 234) and to "adjust [his] language to an environment which is foreign to it, if not foreign to himself" ("Narrative Tradition" 147). In the *Anatomy* Frye calls this form of "adjustment" "displacement"—principally, the process by which an earlier literary pattern or unit is accommodated, or made usable, within a later historical context. Expanding on this definition in *The Secular Scripture*, he writes,

> The imagination has to adapt its formulaic units to the demands of [the] world to produce what Aristotle calls the probable impossibility. The fundamental technique used is what I call displacement, the adjusting of formulaic structures to a roughly credible context. (36)

Though he does not use the word in his Canadian criticism, he neverthe-less repeatedly describes the process of displacement, though here the distance from a generic origin or centre is less temporal than it is *spatial*, stemming from the geographical dislocation of the Canadian writer, cut off from Europe and its more nourishing "imaginative environment."

Yet this spatial problem has a temporal dimension as well insofar as the Canadian environment is an overwhelming primitive one. In his 1946 essay "The Narrative Tradition in Canadian Poetry," Frye writes, "What the poet sees in Canada" is

> different ... from what his European contemporaries see. He may
> be a younger man than Yeats or Eliot, but he has to deal with a
> poetic and imaginative environment for which, to find any paral-
> lel in England, we should have to go back to a period earlier than
> Chaucer. In certain Old English poems, notably "The Wanderer"
> and "The Seafarer," there is a feeling which seems to a modern
> reader more Canadian than English: a feeling of the melancholy
> of a thinly settled country under a bleak northern sky, of the ter-
> rible isolation of the creative mind in such a country. (148)

Hence, the roots of Canadian "difference" are both geographical and temporal, Canada exhibiting—at the imaginative level at least—what Imre Szeman, following Johannes Fabian, calls "allochronism," the ex-perience of a different historical texture from that of other societies shar-ing the same moment in time. Because he is allochronic, the Canadian poet, to the extent that he is true to his materials and "imaginative en-vironment," is inevitably out of sync with the prevailing forms and styles the age demands. To explain this disharmony, Frye employs the follow-ing analogy:

> If we can imagine a contemporary of the Beowulf poet, with equal
> genius and an equally strong urge to write an archaic epic of the
> defeat of a monster of darkness by a hero of immense strength and

endurance ... yet writing for the same public as Ovid and Catullus, and forced to adapt their sophisticated witticisms and emotional refinements to his own work, we shall begin to get some idea of what the Canadian poet is up against. (149)

This idea is repeated in "Preface to an Uncollected Anthology" (1956) when Frye notes that "the imaginative content of Canadian poetry, which is often primitive, frequently makes extraordinary demands on forms derived from romantic or later traditions" (176).

Over and over again, Frye finds the Canadian writer is faced with a "problem of form" (176) she can never fully resolve. Most often, says Frye, the only way that writer can reconcile her content to the existing forms of literature is by way of "some kind of erudite parody, using that term, as many critics now do, to mean adaptation in general rather than simply a lampoon" (176). As parodist, the Canadian writer, regardless of the form in which she writes, thus finds herself facing an extreme version of the dilemma of the modern realistic writer for whom "the require-ments of literary form and plausible content always fight against each other" ("Myth, Fiction, and Displacement" 417). But it's not a fair fight. Whereas for a Marxist critic like Jameson literary change is always "es-sentially a function of content seeking its adequate expression in form" (*Marxism and Form* 328), Frye is steadfast in maintaining throughout his Canadian criticism, as elsewhere, the autonomy of literary forms:

> When a poet is confronted by a new life or environment, the new life may suggest a new content, but obviously cannot provide him with a new form. The forms of poetry can only be derived from other poems, the forms of novels from other novels.[6] ("Preface" 176)

The problem, as should now be clear, is not that the Canadian writer is obliged to invent new forms but precisely that she *can't* invent new forms, even though the content would seem to demand it.

At some basic level, then, Frye must read Canadian literature as problematic in order to maintain his belief in the autonomy of forms—or, to put it less polemically, Canadian literature will always seem at odds with "the" tradition as long as that tradition remains essentially fixed, unaffected by content or social context. However, at what point does the extremity of the "problem of form" for the Canadian writer—and specifically the Canadian writer—begin to raise doubts about the transhistorical nature of literary form itself? At which point does it become a problem not of form but *for* it, a difference of degree transformed into a difference in kind? The more emphatically Frye insists in these early essays that it's possible for content to be inadequate to a given form, the closer he also comes to asking whether the form may not itself be inadequate to a given content. To admit this much, however, would be to open up form to a process of displacement, resulting in a radical historicization of the literary system everywhere imagined as "responding to but not determined in its form by an external historical process" (*CP* 24).

Even so, insofar as it acknowledges that changes in the social sphere—the "demands of the world"—determine the range of the literarily acceptable, displacement already manifests itself as an historicized sphere of operations within Frye's general system of generic universality and permanence. And so, while the forms of literature are autonomous, displacement's necessarily expanded role in his reading of Canadian literature finally begins to crowd out the principle of autonomy and, indeed, raises some serious questions about how, exactly, literary forms function *in Canada*. Whereas it is generally accepted that for Frye generic meaning is universal and inherent in the forms themselves, which possess their own particular semantic values, his insistence that the Canadian writer is obliged but largely unable to harmonize form and content suggests that meaning is never simply present, never "in" the bottle, but rather exists in a dialectic between the pre-existing forms and the social and historical circumstances of their production and use—in the bottling process, we might say.

In fact, throughout *The Bush Garden*, Frye repeatedly reads the Canadian "problem of form" symptomatically, in the process very nearly anticipating Jameson's claim in *Marxism and Form* (located in the chapter significantly entitled "Towards a Dialectical Criticism") that for any given text "the adequation of content to form there realized, or not realized, or realized according to determinate proportions, is in the long run one of the most precious indices to its realization in the historical moment itself" (329). Because for Jameson literary forms are ideological matrixes, conflicts between form and content "are [to be] taken as the signs of some deeper corresponding social and historical configuration which it is the task of criticism to explore" (331). By linking the dissociation of form and content in the texts of Canadian writers to the geographical, cultural, and historical specifics of the writing situation, Frye, unlikely as it may seem, performs that task. In light of this, Frye's disparaging remarks concerning the quality of Canadian literature—remarks he will repeat in the "Conclusion"—which have been regarded by some as elitist, even colonial insofar as they deny Canadian literature the universal significance he sees in other national traditions, take on a very different meaning. However disappointed with Canadian literature Frye may be, his disappointment speaks directly to an acute awareness of the material and historical foundations of literary signification.

Though far more comprehensive and ambitious than the other essays collected in *The Bush Garden*, the "Conclusion" repeats much of what we've just seen. Certainly, as in those other essays, there is the strong suggestion that the traditional forms are subtly transformed in Canada: unable to mean the same thing, or mean the same way, when employed by a Canadian writer. So while a "writer who feels removed from his literary tradition tends rather to take over forms already in existence" (234), it is also true that

> in surveying Canadian poetry and fiction, we feel constantly that all the energy has been absorbed in meeting a standard, a self-

defeating enterprise because real standards can only be established, not met. Such writing is academic in the pejorative sense of the term, an imitation of a prescribed model, second-rate in conception, not merely in execution. (224)

From this we see that the Canadian writer is not only "removed" but also tragically *belated*: second as well as second rate. This fact might be taken as a variation on the allochronism Frye had previously identified with Canadian culture. Whereas the great works of literature share in and are therefore identifiable with the tradition, Canadian works are works after the fact, mere "imitations." In *The Critical Path*, Frye speaks of tradition as both a body of texts produced over time as well as a "pattern of analogous structures" exemplified by those texts. "When we follow this pattern of analogous structures," he writes, "we find that it leads, not to similarity, but to identity. Similarity implies uniformity and monotony.... It is identity that makes individuality possible: poems are made of the *same* image, just as poems in English are all made out of the same language" (23). In this sense, Canadian writing, though availing itself of the same forms and images, is at best only "similar" to the tradition, related to it the way a copy relates to the original.[7] The "academic" character of Canadian literature—like its "prudery" and formal contradictions—therefore marks the distance between the Canadian imagination and the nourishment and continuity of that literary horn of plenty, "the gigantic funnel of tradition," contact with which guarantees a kind of priority and immanence for which overall quality is just the sign.

Disjunction, displacement, and belatedness are the overarching themes of the first three sections of Frye's "Conclusion." Adopting the terminology of Romantic philosopher Friedrich von Schiller, we can see the essay as a mediation on "the sentimental" in Canadian literature—its consciousness and internalization of a "spiritual" separation from both a redemptive nature and a literary tradition typified by its embodiment of a correspondence between the poet and his place, the world, or nature. It is precisely because the Canadian writer is alienated from his natural environment and perennially *out* of place—Frye, after all, makes "where is here?" (222) the defining question of Canadian litera-ture —that he has access to the forms but not the informing spirit of tradition. And it is because he is deprived of this generative and regener-ative power that he can never be "at home" in the works of his own im-agination. Poets, writes Schiller, "will either *be* nature, or they will *seek* lost nature" (106):

> Once man has passed into the state of civilization and art has laid her hand upon him, that *sensuous* harmony in him is withdrawn, and he can now express himself only as a *moral* unity, i.e., as striving after unity. The correspondence between his feeling and thought which in his first condition *actually* took place, exists now only *ideally*; it is no longer within him, but outside of him, as an idea still to be realized, no longer as a fact of his life. (111)

Born of loss, sentimentality manifests itself as the literary expression of historical rupture and cultural displacement from an origin that cannot be genuinely recaptured or recreated except in the most abstract terms. The "academic" Canadian writer is therefore analogous to Schiller's modern sentimental poet whose use of the "naïve" forms of classical art must always be self-conscious and ironic because they are severed from the original conditions that spawned them.

Thus Frye—whose indebtedness to Schiller is elsewhere made ex-plicit[8]—discovers in its *fallen* condition the peculiar modernity of all Canadian writing, which, in his now famous phrase, "was established on a basis not of myth, but of history" (233). Inspired by the historical phil-osophy of Giambattista Vico, who demonstrated "how a society, in its earliest phase, sets up a framework of mythology, out of which all verbal culture grows, including its literature" (*CP* 34), Frye finds that no such framework has been available to the Canadian writer "down to the be-ginning of the twentieth century, at least" (235). "[W]hen a mythology crystallizes in the centre of a culture, a *temenos* or magic circle is drawn around that culture, and a literature develops historically within a limited orbit of language, reference, allusion, belief, transmitted and shared tradition" (35). Historically deprived of a mythology of his own, and working in a colonial situation in which he is actively encouraged to align himself with an English tradition whose *temenos* could only ever fence him out, the Canadian writer lacks—in literary terms, at least—a centre, a home, an origin.[9] Paradoxically, if Canadian literature is fallen, it is not fallen *from*, having never enjoyed the luxury of an original state of identity—symbolized in Schiller's work by Greek antiquity—from which to have lapsed.

How this particular local discovery (or discovery of local particularity) might be accommodated within a theory of literary universality remains unclear. At the very least, though, we can see how the absence of a proper mythological framework for Canadian literature, no less than the myriad ways that history and environment continually revealed themselves to him as determinative constraints on the quality and meaning of Canadian writing, might make it necessary, practically and philosophically, for Frye to call this work "cultural history" as opposed to literary criticism. Yet we have also seen how the very practice of "cultural history" calls into question the premises of that other—and for Frye certainly more crucial—theoretical project. Surely, this double bind helps explain the surprising final section of the "Conclusion" where Frye, seemingly against all odds, discovers in Canadian writing a mythological and archetypal tradition that had been there all along. This discovery has the effect of redeeming Canadian literature, it is true, but redeeming it as a *literature* calling out for a proper literary criticism, one that Frye was fortunate enough to have on hand. At stake is not simply the possibility of Canadian literature becoming a legitimate object of literary criticism, but also the viability of an archetypal criticism.

So while Canadian literature is simply fallen in the Canadian criticism written before the "Conclusion" (and, indeed, before the *Anatomy*), in the "Conclusion," it falls only to be raised up. As Eli Mandel points out,

Frye's cultural history finally "turns out to be a version of the romantic fall into modern consciousness, the wilderness or labyrinth of space
and time, and the antithetical quest for a return to an integrated being"
(285). Presiding over that "return" is the pastoral, the dominant archetype of romance and the primary symbol of the drive toward apocalypse
that motivates literature as a whole.[10] Associated with the innocence
of childhood and the idyllic lives of shepherds, pastoral represents the
unity of man and nature, subject and object. It

> seems to represent something that carries us to a higher state of
> identity than the social and comic world does. The closer romance
> comes to a world of original identity, the more clearly something
> of the symbolism of the Garden of Eden reappears, with the social
> setting reduced to the love of individual men and women within
> an order of nature which has been reconciled to humanity. (*SeS*
> 149)

Accordingly, whereas Frye at first spoke of a prevailing "tone of deep
terror in regard to nature" (227), describing Canadian literature almost
exclusively in terms of its depiction of nature's ferocity or soul-negating
meaninglessness, at the end of the "Conclusion" he turns to proclaim
instead "the haunting vision of serenity that is both human and natural
which we have been struggling to identify in the Canadian tradition"
(251). (Struggling indeed!) Canadian writers, it turns out, do not live in
a land so "bleak and comfortless" that "even the mosquitoes have been
described as 'mementoes of the fall'" (227) but "in a land where empty
space and the pervasiveness of physical nature have impressed a pastoral
quality on their minds" (249). Most importantly, a "genuine" "pastoral
myth" has "found its influence in some of the best Canadian writers"
(243).

Opposed to the typical Canadian writer Frye had first described, a
writer whose work seemed always to register her alienation from the

natural world—thereby crippling it in some hard-to-define but critical way—the work of the "best" Canadian writers is "marked by the imminence of the natural world" (249). Indeed, "everything that is central in Canadian writing" is marked by this imminence (249)." Symbolizing an *identity* between man and nature, pastoral "suggests a life in which nature itself has become home, its animals and plants a rejoined part of our society" (*SeS* 154). Through the pastoral Frye arranges a kind of homecoming for the Canadian writer, who discovers in its form the means to imaginatively reconcile herself to her own environment. Or, given Frye's claim that there may not be another "national consciousness [that] has had so large an amount of the unknown, the unrealized, the humanly undigested so built into it" (222), we could put this another way and say that the pastoral allows the writer to finally "digest," to transform into *human* terms, her hitherto unassimilatable world.

Since literature as a whole likewise seeks to construct a "totally human world" (*EI* 9), we can see how the pastoral enables the Canadian writer to find a home at "the centre of the literary experience itself" as well. For not only does pastoral represent "[t]he elimination of irony from the poet's view of nature" (246), it also represents the elimination of an ironic relationship to tradition. Inasmuch as "the story of the loss and the regaining of identity is ... the framework of all literature" (*EI* 21), pastoral, as an archetype of identity, stands in more than a merely synecdochal relationship to that framework: it is its primary symbol, the very archetype of literary desire. If pastoral is "central" in Canadian writing, this can only be because it is "the most explicitly mythopoeic aspect of Canadian literature that we have to turn to (244). For Frye, the problem with Canadian literature had always been one of irony and self consciousness, of a distance from an origin variously identified as tradition, myth, or the world of autonomous forms. The presence of a pastoral myth in Canadian literature therefore stands for the reconciliation of Canadian literature and the mythological framework with which tradition is pretty well synonymous. Like the cities and villages of Canada that, as Frye repeatedly points out, "do not 'nestle'" but stand out in "garish and tasteless defiance" of their surroundings ("Narrative Tradition" 148), Canadian literature was initially regarded by Frye as similarly out of sorts with its literary environment. At the end of the "Conclusion," however, Canadian literature at last begins to "nestle" within its forms and, by extension, within the mythopoeic tradition itself.

It could not be otherwise. For as much as he seems to sometimes adopt the vocabulary and even postures of Schiller the lost sense of identity that defines the sentimental condition is, for Frye, ultimately recoverable in a way that it could not be for Schiller, for whom history constituted a genuine and untranscendable limit. In the final analysis, literature is always naïve, identifiable with myth and embodying the essential continuity of the "verbal imagination." In the end, the discovery of a pastoral vision in the Canadian imagination allows Frye to transform the history of Canadian literature into an allegory of the story of "all literature," of the verbal imagination as such, a move the reader will now realize was anticipated at the outset of the essay when Frye remarks that it is "much easier to see what literature is doing when we are studying a literature that has not quite done it" (216). The "Conclusion" is really about what "literature is doing" when it might have been, as seemed initially to be the case, about what *Canadian* literature was doing (or, more precisely, not doing). In this transformed history, pastoral both represents and helps achieve an elision of the local differences and historical contingencies that are made explicit when Canadian literature is treated as a special (because dysfunctional) case.

Once he has identified the workings of a pastoral myth in the Canadian tradition, Frye does not pursue it much further: "To go on with this absorbing subject," he writes, "would take us into another book: a *Literary* Criticism *of Canada*, let us say" (249; emphasis added). This is telling, as it makes clear his desire to harmonize his "cultural history"—inevitably, an exploration of Canadian difference—with "literary criticism," a system thoroughly grounded on principles of autonomy, continuity, and identity. What the "Conclusion" makes apparent is that he can do so only by assimilating the former to the latter. The tensions between these conflicting modes of literary understanding disappear only when "culture" and "history" are finally brought under the purview of "criticism." "Literature," says Frye in a memorable line from *The Educated Imagination*, "does not reflect life ... it swallows it" (33). The same, it seems, may be said of Frye's criticism, though perhaps without the note of triumph.

ENDNOTES

1   Lecker's point throughout is to link Frye's narration of the heroic emergence of Canadian literature with Frye's own desire to construct a triumphant self within that narrative. "Frye's conception of literary history making is simultaneously an act of culture making and self-making" (285), writes Lecker, who goes on to suggest that the narrative thrust of the "Conclusion" is motivated by a "male dream of potency." In the "Conclusion," we are told, Frye "gain[s] both potency and the means to self expression," and "can be seen as the romantic hero and, metaphorically, as the erotic quester whose journey into the country is an impregnating act" (287). The suggestion here is that Frye styles himself as a "father" of Canadian literary culture and, in an oedipal twist, fathers himself in the process.

2   In *The Critical Path* (which, not incidentally, was published the same year as *The Bush Garden*) Frye speaks at length about the need to recognize convention as "a force even stronger than history" (23). Consequently, the critic should see literature as "a coherent structure, historically conditioned but shaping its own history, responding to but not determined in its form by an external historical process. This total body of literature can be studied through its larger structural principles, which I have described as conventions, genres and recurrent image-groups or archetypes. These structural principles are largely ignored by most social critics" (24).

3   Whereas for a critic like Walter Benjamin "tradition" refers to an unofficial or subterranean history of politically unsanctioned and culturally devalued beliefs and practices (including literature) persisting in time and ever available to disrupt or even supplant

what he calls the "homogenous time" of the ruling elite, Frye's tradition *is* homogenous, a repeated "pattern of analogous structures" (*CP* 22). Literary tradition is therefore equatable with its "mythical framework" (50).

4   See Lee's "Cadence, Country, Silence," *Body Music: Essays* (Toronto: Anansi, 1998) for his discussion of the impact of a "contradictory" civil space on the writing of Canadian literature. Like Frye, Lee reads Canadian literature as inauthentic and similarly locates the roots of this condition in the country's colonial past.

5   See Frank Davey's "Surviving the Paraphrase," in *Surviving the Paraphrase: 11 Essays on Canadian Literature* (Winnipeg: Turnstone, 1983), Russell Brown's "The Practice and Theory of Canadian Thematic Criticism: A Reconsideration" (*University of Toronto Quarterly* 70:2 [Spring 2001], 653–689), and Paul Steuwe's *Clearing the Ground: English-Canadian Literature After Survival* (Toronto: Proper Tales Press, 1984) for discussions of the thematic tradition in Canadian criticism.

6   In "Myth, Fiction, and Displacement," Frye writes, "I call it displacement for many reasons, but one is that fidelity to the credible is a feature of literature that can affect only content.... Literary shape cannot come from life; it comes only from literary tradition, and so ultimately from myth" (417).

7   It is precisely in these terms that Imre Szeman, in his "Belated or Isochronic? Canadian Writing, Time, and Globalization," reads the "Conclusion" as an exploration of the sense of inauthenticity typical of many post-colonial societies.

8   When discussing his theory of displacement in the *Anatomy*, Frye directly invokes Schiller before going on to use his terms (see 35–36). Furthermore, "naïve" and "sentimental" are employed as terms in a number of other Frye works, including *The Secular Scripture* and, in a modified form, *The Critical Path*. Even in the "Conclusion" Frye differentiates between "sentimental" versions of a myth and more "genuine" ones. As I will demonstrate in a moment, however, there is a certain disingenuousness in Frye's use of Schiller, which tends to undermine or obscure the reasons why Schiller might be so valuable to a materialist criticism.

9   In a passage that both diagnoses and reflects a certain colonial bias, Frye addresses the question of Aboriginal myth: "We have been shown how the Indians began which included all the main elements of our own. It was, of course, impossible for Canadians to establish any real continuity with it: Indians like the rest of the country were seen as nineteenth-century literary conventions" (235).

10 Lecker likewise notes the importance of pastoral here, and the way it aligns the "Conclusion" with Frye's broader project so that it may "satisfy the utopian impulse informing much of Frye's extended poetics" (285). Consequently, there are several points of convergence between my reading of the end of the "Conclusion" and his own, though our views as to the essay's final purpose remain distinct. For Lecker, "Frye discovers a pastoral version of English Canadian literary history that transcends the divisiveness endangering his country. Assuming the role of narrator as reader and romantic quester, he moves from a distanced and innocent condition to a final harmonious state that merges innocence and experience, the objective and the subjective, the perceiver and the perceived" (284). On the other hand, I tend to locate that anxiety-causing divisiveness in his work rather than in the country it examines.

11 Compare this to Frye's claim in "Canada and Its Poetry" that "Canadian poetry is at its best a poetry of incubus and *cauchemar*" (143).

WORKS CITED

Frye, Northrop. 2006. "The Function of Criticism at the Present Time." 1949. In *The Educated Imagination and Other Writings on Critical Theory*: 1933–1963. The Collected Works of Northrop Frye. Vol. 21. Ed. Germaine Warkentin. Toronto: University of Toronto Press, 60–76.

———. 2006. "Myth, Fiction, and Displacement." In *The Educated Imagination and Other Writings on Critical Theory*: 1933–1963. The Collected Works of Northrop Frye. Vol. 21. Ed. Germaine Warkentin. Toronto: University of Toronto Press, 401–419.

———. 1995. "Canada and Its Poetry." 1943. *The Bush Garden: Essays on the Canadian Imagination*. Toronto: Anansi, 131–146.

———. 1995. "Conclusion to a *Literary History of Canada*." 1965. *The Bush Garden: Essays on the Canadian Imagination*. Toronto: Anansi, 215–253.

———. 1995. "The Narrative Tradition in Canadian Poetry." 1946. *The Bush Garden: Essays on the Canadian Imagination*. Toronto: Anansi, 147–157.

———. 1995. "Preface to an Uncollected Anthology." 1956. *The Bush Garden: Essays on the Canadian Imagination*. Toronto: Anansi, 165–182.

———. 1976. *The Secular Scripture: A Study of the Structure of Romance*. Cambridge, MA: Harvard University Press.

———. 1971. *The Critical Path: An Essay on the Social Context of Literary Criticism*. Bloomington: Indiana University Press.

———. 1963. *The Educated Imagination*. Toronto: Canadian Broadcasting Corporation.

———. 1957. *Anatomy of Criticism: Four Essays*. Princeton: Princeton University Press.

Hutcheon, Linda. 1995. Introduction. *The Bush Garden: Essays on the Canadian Imagination*. Toronto: Anansi, vii–xx.

Jameson, Fredric. 1981. *The Political Unconscious: Narrative as a Socially Symbolic Act*. Ithaca: Cornell University Press, 1981.

———. 1971. *Marxism and Form*. Princeton: Princeton University Press.

Lecker, Robert. 1993 (March). "'A Quest for the Peaceable Kingdom': The Narrative in Northrop Frye's 'Conclusion to the *Literary History of Canada*.'" *PLMA* 108:2, 283–293.

Lee, Dennis. 1998. "Cadence, Country, Silence." 1972. *Body Music: Essays*. Toronto: Anansi, 3–26.

Mandel, Eli. 1983. "Northrop Frye and the Canadian Literary Tradition." In *Centre and Labyrinth: Essays in Honour of Northrop Frye*, ed. Hosek Cook et al. Toronto: University of Toronto Press, 284–297.

Murray, Heather. 1987. "Reading for Contradiction of the Literature of Colonial Space." In *Future Indicative: Literary Theory and Canadian Literature*, ed. John Moss. Ottawa: University of Ottawa Press, 71–84.

von Schiller, Friedrich. 1966. *Naive and Sentimental Poetry and On the Sublime: Two Essays*. Trans. and ed. Julius Elias. New York: Frederick Ungar.

Szeman, Imre. 2000 (Fall). "Belated or Isochronic? Canadian Writing, Time, and Globalization." *Essays on Canadian Writing* 71: 186–194.

FRYE & THE SACRED

PART III

THE REVEREND H. NORTHROP FRYE

Ian Sloan

NORTHROP FRYE's original theological concept, the concept of the kerygmatic mode of language, emerged late in his thinking and writing. Before then, Frye is probably best seen as a profoundly able teacher of the liberal arts who, along with many others, transformed the liberal humanism arts curriculum of the late 19th century into a curriculum for his time. His debts as a teacher of literature to a liberal Christian religious tradition were always there to be seen (perhaps nowhere more explicitly than in *The Critical Path* [1972]). However, his exposition of the excluded initiative of the kerygmatic in his second book on the Bible, *Words With Power* (1990), shows Northrop Frye the theologian appearing in his own recognition scene.

Northrop Frye is the most complete United Church of Canada theologian that particular church has yet produced. He was a gifted and pioneering minister in a denomination whose formal existence was recognized in 1925 but whose union roots were already present in Canadian life well before Frye's own birth in 1912. Methodists, Presbyterians, and Congregationalists, for example, began formal union discussions in 1902. However, the first official union proposal was made in 1886 by the Anglican Church. (Overtures to join the discussions initiated in 1902 were soon made to Anglicans and Baptists.)[1] This broad based movement toward union provides a critical context for the story Frye related to his biographer John Ayre of casting off as a teenager the religion of sin and damnation.[2] His teenage insight occurred within a few years of the 1925 inauguration of the United Church. One of the United Church's organizational aims was to move personal relationships out of dogmatic straitjackets. Denominationalism in particular was thought by many religious leaders in Canada and abroad to be a highly discreditable straitjacket. Religiously speaking, Frye was a child of his times in Canada.

Frye was ordained by the United Church of Canada in 1936 after theological studies at Emmanuel College and before his MA studies at Oxford. The evidence is unequivocal that Frye identified with the ordination throughout his career. Copies of the routine paperwork through which a minister and the United Church of Canada keep an ordination in good standing when the minister is not in active congregational ministry are found carefully gathered together in Frye's professional papers.[3] In a letter written in 1984 he told his United Church correspondent,

After my graduation from Emmanuel, I was very hesitant about ordination because I knew by that time that I was unlikely to be engaged in conventional pastoral work and my belief in the priesthood of believers seemed to make it unnecessary. I consulted various friends: the general consensus was that I should take ordination, and having taken it, I regard it as permanent and wish to retain it.[4]

A few years later he wrote in one of his last notebooks, "Any biography would say that I dropped preaching for academic life: that's the opposite of what my spiritual biography would say, that I fled into academia for refuge and have ever since tried to peek out into the congregation and make a preacher of myself."[5] Frye thought his ordination a genuine vocational commitment, which helps us understand him. But Frye's excluded pastoral ministry is important because it helps to understand the United Church of Canada.

The United Church of Canada is an organic union of "denominations" of Christianity. "Organic" means that the union extinguishes the separate interests and polities of the uniting denominations. The first denominations to join the United Church of Canada were the Methodist, Presbyterian, and Congregationalist. A few others have since joined, but organic union between denominations did not become the norm for 20th-century Protestantism beyond Canada or, ultimately, within Canada. At present the United Church of Canada numbers about 650,000 members. This is a very small number indeed in comparison to worldwide Methodism and Presbyterianism and Anglicanism, not to mention other denominations established in Canada as well as elsewhere. Though the United Church sees itself as part of each of the worldwide "legacy" denominations from which the United Church was formed— especially the Presbyterian, Methodist, and Congregationalist—it cannot help but be something of a square peg in a round hole in each of these organizations because it is not organized exactly like any of them. Frye's affection and dry respect for this union denomination and its implicit capacity to skewer imperialistic tendencies of the religiously ambitious is demonstrated in a 1949 diary remark that he liked the denomination because it had effectively knocked three churches out of commission.[6]

The aim of this union church has been, and is, to make more unions. At its inauguration in 1925, the United Church of Canada committed itself to fostering a spirit of unity "in the hope that this sentiment of unity may in due time, so far as Canada is concerned, take shape in a Church which may fittingly be described as national."[7] An essay permanently part of the polity documents remarks, "The present Union, now consummated, is but another step toward the wider union of Evangelical Churches, not only in Canada, but throughout the world."[8] Ten years later, at the time Frye was engaged in theological studies at Emmanuel College, the United Church reaffirmed this commitment and expanded on it:

> In a renewed conviction of the worth of inclusive Christian fellow-ship, the United Church of Canada enters its second decade, pre-pared, as the opportunity may offer and as God may direct, to seek with other Christian communions further development of its ideals, whether by increased co-operation, organic union, or otherwise, and so fulfill its purpose of being not merely a united, but a uniting Church.[9]

A seminal characteristic in aid of its seeking "inclusive fellowship" is that neither United Church of Canada clergy nor laity are ever bound to subscribe to any dogmatic formulation of faith. To this day, those presenting themselves as candidates for ordination are examined for "essential agreement" to the articles of faith that serve as the theological basis for the union. The articles were formulated by an inter-denominational committee (Methodists, Congregationalists, and Presbyterians) in the first decade of the 1900s. It was recognized at the time that the theological basis that had been pulled together by the committee was full of inconsistencies, if not outright contradictions in doctrine between the three uniting denominations. The unionists, however, were not unnerved by this situation. On the one hand, they made much of what could be believed in common. On the other, the decision not to demand any form of subscription to doctrine was a concession by the Presbyterians to the Congregationalists.[10] The concession was made in the spirit of unity. "Essential unity" to this union church could and would mean a paradoxical absence of material unity. What held it all together was an underlying conviction that individual Christians within this denomination would seek rigour in dogma and doctrine out of a spirit of unity itself.

If theologies and doctrines are forms of ideology, then any sustained attempt to argue for any one of these three well-marked-out denominational theologies within the context of the United Church might have led to internecine or internal warfare. Over time some kind of systematic statement of doctrine might have emerged,[11] but two features of the union have prevented this, and a third actually promoted the kind of system Frye built. The first two features are ones I have just very briefly identified—the intellectual pragmatism that led to a religious union in the face of theological and doctrinal differences, and the commitment to a non-subscription basis for membership in the denomination.

The third feature that has promoted the kind of system Frye built is the union drive itself. The theologically pragmatic basis for the union created propitious conditions for a new church but was not a basis on which the union was to become whatever it was to become. The basis, as we have seen above, lay rather, and determinedly, in the spirit of unity. In the same 1949 diary entry in which Frye expressed his liking for a church that includes in itself a "church-destroying principle," Frye noted that an acquaintance of his in the United Church of Canada's national offices told him that he had "given the United Church up" because all it had going for it (in the acquaintance's words) was "the principle of union," and it had "no evangelical cutting edge" (this last phrase was Frye's). The acquaintance planned to look for a place in the American Presbyterian Church.[12] Frye chose not to leave Canada, and he took upon himself the task of developing an "evangelical cutting edge" for the union church of which he was a minister.

Frye's most substantive ground for literary criticism is the unity of the field of literature. As I see it, the way that he developed this ground, from his early assertion of the independence and autonomy of the critic to the concept of the excluded initiative of "becoming what one identifies with" of kerygmatic language, shows us that Frye was at work as a pioneering ordained minister within this union church, making up terms in which a national denomination created to advance a liberal religion for individuals could at once stay united within itself and reach out to seek to unite with others. To be successful in either endeavour, his system (or any, for that matter) would also have to be able to allow individuals to relate to other individuals in exactly the same way.

In short, I think that Frye was a theologian and a distinctively United Church of Canada theologian. In an unpublished review of Paul Tillich's *Systematic Theology, Volume 3* (1963), Frye wrote, "Christianity ... is a revolutionary dialectic which moves toward the obliteration of the distinction between theory and practice. Consequently its conceptual structure is not just a structure, but *the* structure which is to be realized in practice." The drive to unity can be felt in Frye's vital and imaginatively violent concept of "the obliteration of the distinction between theory and practice that is not just a structure, but *the* structure which is to be realized in practice." He goes on, however: "We want to know what [a theologian's] commitment is in advance, because we know that he is going to start rationalizing that commitment sooner or later." This is the sort of assertion made possible by the very processes that went into and continue to refresh the organic union of the United Church of Canada. There can be no final dogmatic resting place because all dogmas lead to a false notion of unity, and every false notion of unity is a present danger to the true, "essential" unity of the church. The false resting place of a rational sense of unity is thus opposed to *the* reasonable one that seeks to obliterate the distinction between theory and practice.

How, though, if one gives up the "rational" for the "reasonable," does one thwart an evil system of belief, the sort, for example, that has led and can lead again to the unspeakable actions of a Nazi Germany? Frye's approach is to say that belief itself as generally construed is unwise,[13] and then goes on to redefine the verbal, imaginative, and intellectual context in which belief has meaning to enable a redefinition of belief itself.[14] Again, this solution is consistent with historical United Church of Canada contingencies.

Within the theological framework of the United Church of Canada, one can be dogmatically precise about belief but the dogmatic point internal to the denomination is (in Frye's way of thinking) that belief is an expanding, developing, and imaginatively liberating obliteration of the distinction between theory and practice. This is what Frye means by kerygma, which he understands as a mode of language that reverses the usual direction of language. Humans usually direct language to God and to each other. In kerygma, the direction is turned inside out: kerygma is a "two way street, the interpenetrating of Word and Spirit, not the 'proclamation' of God to Man."[15]

The supple and integrating expression of key United Church of Canada concepts just observed gives context to statements about religion found in various places in Frye's notebooks and sometimes in his published writings. At one place in his notebooks he stated that a long-held ambition was "to write something in religion" that "[would] gain a new perspective on the subject."[16] At another he argued that Christianity has the virtues necessary for becoming a world religion, ahead of Judaism and Islam. Here, obviously, is an example of something that looks like hegemonic thought, but if we are going to let history be history, then we will note that the likely critical source for Frye's musings is the commitment of the United Church to lose itself in greater and greater unions, one logical extension of which would be a world union of the scope Frye was imagining; another, the United Church's apology to First Nations peoples of Canada (1986); another, the Church's conviction that God may call people of all sexual orientations to ordained ministry (1988).[17] Finally, Frye was convinced that in his approach to the apocalyptic elements of the Bible, he had found the way to advance the reformation of

the church begun in the 16th century, a reformation that in his view was
sandbagged by the Protestant scholasticism of the late 16th century and
after.[18] An energetic comment in the late notebooks depends upon this
conviction. When he said in the late notebooks that the vision "has traditionally been secular rather than Biblical, largely because the Bible has
been fucked up by theologians,"[19] he sounds angry, but this is simply a
sign of the intellectual effort to put into motion something inert.

Thus, Frye places himself in an antithetical relationship not to theology but to those who have practiced theology. His ordination in the
United Church of Canada helps explain how he could hold this position with integrity. The experience out of which the United Church of
Canada emerged was one in which genuine questions about the value
of any dogmatic assertion had to be asked, and the answers, in almost
every instance, postponed so that the denomination could achieve its
own ends.

To sum up so far: If Frye's ordination in the United Church of Canada
is not borne in mind by theologians (and it is specifically the ordination
in the United Church of Canada that is at issue, an ordination understood by the denominations of the magisterial reformation[20] to be an
ordination to the holy orders of the "catholic church"), then theologians may miss the central role of theology in Frye's thought. Similarly,
if Frye's ordination is not borne in mind by literary critics, then they may
not understand the central role Frye's hatred of value judgments plays
in his thought. For Frye, all theology and all value criticism in literature
perform the same rationalizing function that he sees as antithetical to
the advancement of religious and imaginative life. Frye dislikes the notion that assessing others' intellectual or aesthetic achievement is central to criticism precisely because intellectual engagements as a United
Church minister lie in unity and liberty.[21] So if it is said that Frye's work
does not materially advance theology as a discipline at all, then it must
also be said that his work does not materially advance literary criticism

as a discipline, either. Frye the minister brings a positive attitude to literary criticism to bear against a negative attitude to theology and makes of them contraries though which he forges contributions to both literary criticism and theology.

Frye's major critique of organized religion is that it is an analogy (at his most cutting, he would say a demonic parody) of the imaginative universe of the individual in community. Thus far I have developed an analogy of his criticism within the ideological framework of a religion to which I have made intellectual and emotional commitments and in which I seek to work productively and earn a living, and in which, for whatever reasons, he maintained his ordination. The argument of this essay could be said to rationalize my commitments to this ideology by seeking to make credible the idea that Frye would be in agreement with me about religion. What I really have to do to establish his theological credentials against his own public diffidence about church and theology, then, is to turn the analogy between his critical thought and his identity as a minister of the United Church of Canada inside out.

The literary critical battleground on which to engage Frye to gain the point that there is a theological significance to his work is William Blake's theory of contraries and negations. Let us start with negations. With our reason we abstract qualities from things. Blake calls these negations. Morality, says Frye, is based on determining which of these negations are good and which are bad (FS 189). If an egg is rotten, it must be a bad egg. "Rotten" becomes "bad" and is contrasted with "wholesome" and "good." However, though not good to eat, a rotten egg may be good to throw at someone. Relationship thus has a tremendous amount to say about value. Where the action in life really is, then, is in contraries, because contraries are not abstractions but rather relationships. To put Frye's dismissal of paraphrase as a critical principle in the same way, any paraphrase of something must be a negation because it is inevitably an abstraction. Theology in essence is all paraphrase, and therefore all negation, because it abstracts qualities from the stories of the Bible. Theology moralizes those negations into the mentally passive institutional church.

Bible study is one place in which a minister might practice a disciplined sort of open-ended questioning. Literary criticism provided Frye with the possibility of such an open-ended practice in Bible study. His first tour de force in criticism was his exposition of William Blake. Frye showed the poet saturated in the image universe of the Bible, and his poetry as a whole as a structure that made tremendous religious sense if it was approached with a unifying imagination.

In contrast, the tyrants who foster negations are people in leadership in the church—those who hold power—the ordained being the obvious suspects, though they are not alone. There are many interested in wielding the power of negation by controlling or influencing clergy. Against them, the poet and critic—Blake and Frye respectively—say nothing: rather than attack the tyrants, they attack the victims, whom the tyrants make victims by keeping them imaginatively passive. Freedom comes when the victim puts off the chains of imaginative passivity.

Then what happens? There would be an end of churches, to be sure. But then what? And to whose benefit? Frye himself had an axiom he employed with respect to these sorts of questions: "The initial test is cui bono? Whose cultural ascendancy is being preserved by this belief?" he writes in one of his notebooks as he follows through some logical consequences of his thinking about belief. "If it's anybody's [ascendancy]," he continues, "throw it away."[22] What is the point of creating a churchless society if that society is simply going to result in an ascendant secularism that is destructive of human rights and human environment? But there is no point in sustaining churches that accomplish exactly the same outcome.

This set of questions forms the outline of a program of expansionary union of churches. Let the first church in this expanding union be called "the United Church of Canada." At every stage in the sequence of expansionary union there is a concomitant commitment to the notion that Christianity is by nature revolutionary. By nature it is always enacting Hannah's Song in 1 Samuel and Mary's Song in Luke: raising up the poor and sending the rich away empty. Someone might say, "Show me this church so I can sign up for it." But the plain fact is that I cannot show it to anyone. Finding it means recognizing oneself to be a part of something that exists on the other side of the kerygmatic mode of language.[23]

Getting there, however, is not easy at all. Frye, who brings us to this point, has tremendous difficulty with the defining ideological element of the church: the sacraments. William Blake held the sacraments in contempt: they were "outward ceremony" at its most concentrated; they were the repressive energies of the Covering Cherub[24] at work in the society of Blake's time. The sacraments come too close in Frye's mind, I suspect, to the sacrifice of victims by the dreaming herd. Though Blake has absolutely no place for the sacraments, Frye is less certain.[25] The evidence of his notebooks suggests that while on the one hand he cannot see any reason to be a participating member of a sacramental church, on the other, he suspects, though he does not trust, that there could be a reasonable church in which to engage in the dialectic of belief and vision:

> Religious ritual, in itself, is a pretence of power. It may of course help to charge the batteries of power for the rest of the week—I don't know. But at least it's a community operation, not an isolated one, which is what's misleading about Blake's term 'art.' I think what's wrong with ritual, & made Blake call it Antichrist, is being informed by inorganic belief.[26]

Sacramental life has no pull for him.[27] Yet in the United Church there are two sacraments: baptism and Communion. Baptism "properly" done is the complete immersion of all the body—complete drowning of touch. Communion is the meal of bread and wine, the complete satiation of food and drink on the palate. Both sacraments are thoroughly metaphors of negation: the body and blood of the crucified Word, and death of the Word by drowning. The key point here is that every sacramental action performed is an act of the reasoning spectre of humankind, an abstraction of qualities from a substantial event—John's baptism of Jesus and humankind's crucifixion of Jesus, respectively. Frye saw the sacramental interpretations around him of the passion of Jesus in exactly these negating terms, as inorganic belief theologically performed by the reasoning, moralizing mind. It does not matter if one follows the scholastic notion of transubstantiation or the Calvinist notion of symbolic instrumentalism in understanding these dialectical/rhetorical definitions of the Eucharist. The fact is, these are negations, and Frye follows Blake in hating them. For these reasons, he could hardly have brought himself in conscience, I believe, to conduct either the sacrament of baptism or Communion.

When we follow Blake and Frye on hate, however, we turn up something else quite astounding. Blake is certain that hate is the contrary of love. Although Frye is less certain, sometimes using the word "abhorrence" and sometimes "wrath,"[28] he is certainly like-minded in thinking that hate is generally the contrary of love. The Zoa Blake identifies with hope is Tharmas, and Blake identifies Tharmas with the two senses of touch and with the western gate that will not be opened until the apocalypse. The two sacraments, then, are representative of the western gate, signs of the complete recreation of humanity, when to touch is really to touch, something Mary Magdalene was not able to do in the garden Easter morning with Jesus, yet something she could do; and something the disciples were not able to do at the breakfast of fish and bread by the Sea of Galilee some time later with Jesus, yet something they could do.[29]

Suddenly we have turned Frye's hatred of the sacraments against him and we are in a position in which we have to wonder, "How did that happen?" One of the reasons we might offer is that the stories of baptism and crucifixion are themselves negations of the sense of touch. The sacrament thus occurs as a negation of a negation. If we are able to demonstrate that within the repetitive life of an ordered religion the sacraments so conceived contribute to developing the imagination of the individual within the community, then we have a reasoned explanation for why Frye, though he did not practise pastoral ministry, never categorically rejected it. The reason we offer is not one that likely would have crossed Frye's mind, in no small part because his teaching life removed him from the practicalities of pastoral religious leadership.

Yet even here we might probe more deeply and achieve a more satisfying explanation. It is obvious that Frye found something hateful about the sacraments. What he never saw, in part because Blake was so categorically wrong, was that the contrary of love is not hate but despair. The contrary of hate is hope. We can see this in many ways in the sacraments. For example, the death of Jesus is hateful, but it is also hopeful. Similarly, the baptism of John was a hateful thing not only to Sadducees but apparently (should we be surprised?) also to followers of Jesus who after Jesus' death found themselves competing with John's followers. John's baptism of Jesus was hopeful because it was about the power humans have to repent and be forgiven and to forgive others.

This is not the time to explain in detail why the contrary of love is despair. There is a relationship between love and hate, however, and the relationship is that hate is a negation of love. Every paraphrase of love is a negation of love. Every paraphrase of love expresses a hate of love. The hatred of the sacraments and of ordered religious life fixed in the ordained conduct of those sacraments was, in fact, Frye negating love and people's love. I think despair was his motivation, the genuine contrary of love.

Only a person who is prepared not to moralize about what Frye did can really begin to appreciate the tremendous gift he gave the United Church of Canada. The sacraments in fact are the gate of the apocalypse. Frye was always interested in bringing to bear all art on the *kairos* moment of the fulfillment of all time. This meant he gave us the most thorough-going critique of religion and the habits of religion I think we have ever seen in the West. Frye's willingness to pursue the negation of love to the bottom brought him to that promised land that, like Moses, he never entered. He went deeply into hate. He went deeply into hope. As we come out near the border of that land he himself never entered in his life but to which he also came near, we do so given by Frye a language that we can use to sharpen the evangelical cutting edge of the church of which he was an ordained minister, and so continue its reformation.

ENDNOTES

1 See John Webster Grant, "The Desire for a National Church," in *The Canadian Experience of Church Union* (Richmond, VA: John Knox Press, 1967), 19–30.

2 John Ayre, *Northrop Frye: A Biography* (Toronto: Random House, 1989), 44.

3 Northrop Frye Fonds, Victoria University Archives, Pratt Library, Victoria University, Toronto, 1991/Box 12. The correspondence is indicated in the finding guide as "Toronto South Presbytery, 1963–1987" but the contents range wider than that, including records of national church action to transfer Frye's ordination from Maritime Conference to Toronto Conference in the early 1980s.

4 Northrop Frye to Rev. Bob Leland, Convener, Ministry Personnel and Education Committee, Toronto Area Presbytery, 30 October 1984, Northrop Frye Fonds, Victoria University Archives, Pratt University, Victoria University, Toronto, 1991/Box 12.

5 Frye, *LN* 621.

6 Frye, *Diaries* 105. The citation is from the 1949 diary, para. 133: "Personally, I rather like the United Church because it contains a sort of church-destroying principle within itself, having already destroyed three." Subsequent citations from the Frye unpublished material in the Collected Works will indicate the source (notebook, notes, unpublished review, etc.) and, following a period, the paragraph number given by the Collected Works editors for the cited material (e.g., Notebook 22.342).

7 "Basis of Union," Section 1.2, *The Manual of the United Church of Canada* (2007), 14.

8 "Basis of Union," Section 1.2, *The Manual of the United Church of Canada* (2007), 12.

9 "Basis of Union," Section 1.2, *The Manual of the United Church of Canada* (2007), 8.

10 George C. Pidgeon, "The Minister and the Statement of Faith," *The United Church of*

Canada: The Story of the Union (Toronto: Ryerson Press, 1950), 37–44.

11 I contrast "statement of doctrine" with "statement of faith" because the United Church of Canada has developed several statements of faith over its history, including the most recent (2006), "A Song of Faith." The United Church has also developed a catechism and, in the 1960s, an adventuresome "New Curriculum"—a Church School curriculum based on the historical-critical principles of academic biblical study.

12 Frye, Diary 1949.133, *Diaries* 105.

13 Frye writes (Notebook 21.15, *RT* 142): "The less we believe the better: the principle of Occam's razor applies to belief as well: Christian's burden of sins was not nearly as bad for him as the burden of his beliefs; William James' principle that we believe as much as we can is another way of stating the doctrine of original sin."

14 See, for example, *GC* 229–233. Frye writes as well (Notebook 21.229, *RT* 182–183): "Well, anyway, approaching the bible as myth or imgve. construct is the first step in a genuine reformation of Xy. The next step is the razor principle set down at the beginning of this notebook: the less you believe the better [par. 15]. The third step is: belief is the derivation of action from vision: no belief that isn't a visible axiom of action is a real belief. (There may be possible beliefs or hunches that are cherished but not acted on, but you aren't justified by those)."

15 Frye, Notebook 44.496, *LN* 209. In constructing his definition Frye took into account Rudolf Bultmann's popularization of the term kergyma. He writes (Notebook 50.44, *LN* 265): "Lower kergyma is the stage of law, full of prohibitions and penalties, and increasingly given to censorship in the arts – Plato is almost insane about this in the Republic. Bultmann's kergyma excluding myth is in the same tradition, as in fact is all theology."

16 Frye, Notebook 21.96, *RT* 157–158.

17 Frye, Notebook 23.22, 370.

18 Frye, Notebook 21.24, 144; Notebook 21.227, 182; Notebook 21.229, 182–183; Notebook 21.230, 183.

19 Frye, Notes for "The Dialectic of Belief and Vision." 34, *FM*.

20 The "magisterial Reformation" sought to reform the relationship of church and state rather than break the relationship. It saw itself in contention with the Roman Church for the reform of this relationship, and so held that its ordinations were as valid and effective as the Roman ones.

21 See Galatians 5:13–18. Liberty is not "license" to Frye or Paul.

22 Frye, Notebook 21.230, *RT* 183.

23 Northrop Frye, Notebook 50.430, *LN* 343: "What's on the other side of kerygma? I think that in a way it's a return to the descriptive, but not the 'literal' descriptive that postulates the non-verbal. It's rather Stevens' 'description without place,' which Stevens says is 'revelation,' referring to the biblical book [*Description without Place*, pt. 6, line 1]. Revelation itself is kerygma: beyond it is the world of words as seen by the Word. Most mystics say that this stage is beyond words: Paul still hears language, though a language that can't be repeated 'here' except in incarnational form. The descriptive-literal is the old creation, man looking at what God hath wrought; the post-kerygmatic descriptive is the new creation that follows the apocalyptic or winding-up of kerygma."

24 "Covering Cherub" in Blake's symbol system is based on the apocryphal story of angels placed at the entrance of the Garden of Eden to prevent return to the Garden after the fall of humankind. Generally in Blake it represents all sexual prudery, repression, and moralization. Blake's poetry identifies it with the zodiac and astrology and thus with all the forms of passive rationalization of fallen life that astrology represents. To Blake the administration of the sacraments in the church was imaginatively inert in the same way astrology was.

25 Frye, Notebook 23.55, 375: "All those books in the Middle Ages called Speculum indicated that nature was a secondary word of God, that is, natural 'theology,' i.e., mythology, was a mirror of Scripture. Sacrifice is an obvious example, perhaps the key to it. Perhaps too the 'outward ceremony' is not necessarily Antichrist, as Blake said, but another mirror."

26 Frye, Notebook 23.63, 376.

27 Jean O'Grady, "Frye and the Church," in *Frye and the Word: Religious Contexts in the Writings of Northrop Frye* (Toronto: University of Toronto Press, 2004), 176–177.

28 For "abhorrence" see Frye, Notebook 21.494, *RT* 231. For "wrath," see Frye, Notebook 21.468, 225.

29 The two sacraments can also be seen as a double vision in the same sense Frye employs in his last published book, *The Double Vision*. Readers of Blake will remember that Blake names four senses, the sense of touch being the same as the sense of taste—one exterior, the other interior. William Butler Yeats's poem "Those Images" (in *New Poems*, 1938)

suggests the one sense of touch and taste is both harlot and virgin. I am not sure which one Yeats thought was which, or whether both were harlot and virgin, or even that he knew. "Those Images" directs its readers to think in images and cites several of them: the lion, the harlot, the virgin, the child, the eagle:

> Seek those images
> That constitute the wild,
> The lion and the virgin,
> The harlot and the child.
>
> Find in middle air
> An eagle on the wing,
> Recognise the five
> That make the Muses sing.

The syntax of the poem suggests that "the five" are both the five images presented in the poem and the five senses of smell, touch, taste, hearing, and sight. Harlot and virgin are contrary images of one female. This one image in two aspects parallels Blake's one sense of touch in two aspects (that is, taste and touch). The two images of the one female represent hate and hope, respectively, in the Western symbol tradition. A sign of hope, for example, is the Virgin who gives birth to the Logos; a sign of hate, the Whore of John's apocalypse. Since the sacraments of baptism and Communion are constructed out of images relating to the one sense of touch and taste (water and bread and wine, respectively), harlot and virgin—symbols in Yeats of the one sense of touch and taste—point toward the contrary of hate and hope as the metaphoric basis for the sacraments.

WORKS CITED

Ayre, John. *Northrop Frye: A Biography*. Toronto: Random House, 1989.

Frye, Northrop. *Fearful Symmetry: A Study of William Blake*. Princeton: Princeton University Press, 1969.

———. *The Diaries of Northrop Frye, 1942–1955*. The Collected Works of Northrop Frye. Vol. 8. Ed. Robert D. Denham. Toronto: University of Toronto Press, 2001.

———. *The Great Code: The Bible and Literature*. Toronto: University of Toronto Press, 1982.

———. *Late Notebooks, 1982–1990: Architecture of the Spiritual World*. The Collected Works of Northrop Frye. Vol. 5. Ed. Robert D. Denham. Toronto: University of Toronto Press, 2000.

———. *Northrop Frye's Notebooks and Lectures on the Bible and Other Religious Texts*. The Collected Works of Northrop Frye. Vol. 13. Ed. Robert D. Denham. Toronto: University of Toronto Press, 2003.

Grant, John Webster. 1967. "The Desire for a National Church." *The Canadian Experience of Church Union*. Richmond, VA: John Knox Press, 19–30.

The Manual 2007: The United Church of Canada. 2007. Toronto: United Church Publishing House.

O'Grady, Jean. 2004. "Frye and the Church." In *Frye and the Word: Religious Contexts in the Writings of Northrop Frye*, ed. Jeffery Donaldson and Alan Mendelson. Toronto: University of Toronto Press, 175–186.

Pidgeon, George C. 1950. "The Minister and the Statement of Faith." In *The United Church of Canada: The Story of the Union*. Toronto: Ryerson.

Yeats, W.B. 1983. *The Poems: A New Edition*, ed. Richard J. Finneran. New York: Macmillan, 319.

Recovery of the Spiritual Other:

Martin Buber's "Thou" in Northrop Frye's Late Work

Sára Tóth

IN THE POSTHUMOUSLY published *Double Vision*, the only book in which Northrop Frye explicitly discussed the question of religion and the church as distinguished from literature, he described God as "a spiritual Other" (*DV* 20). Although Frye's engagement with religious and spiritual questions was certainly evident to careful readers of his work from the beginning, with the ongoing posthumous publication of his diaries and notebooks from 1996 onward, the religious aspect of his work has become that much more obvious. The notebooks contain uninhibited speculations on the nature of God, and they reveal how Frye's theological vision grounded and guided his views on literature, culture, and society. Apparently, Frye's earlier relegation of God to a character in a human story (see *FI* 18) turned out to be only one side of the coin. This essay proposes to investigate "the other side": how and in what stages Frye's views on the divine aspect or "otherness" of the human imagination developed in his late work.

In fact, the question of the "spiritual Other" seems to be of crucial importance as we argue for the abiding significance of Northrop Frye's work in the present cultural climate. While an ultimate theological act of trust in a "more than human" source of imaginative constructs may not be fashionable today, without it we are caught in an unending process of analyzing the hidden power relations and ideologies of texts, inevitably basing such analysis on our own tacit ideological agendas. Without Frye's Arnoldian, innocent vision of a shared imaginative heritage, culture is reduced to a battlefield of forever conflicting interest groups. Today's masters of suspicion are right in regarding the metanarrative of a unified collective imagination as just another enterprise of dominance and exclusion, *if*, and that is the crux of the question here, this imaginative heritage is *merely human*. Such suspicion condemns us to stay alienated from whoever or whatever is called "the o/Other." We can no longer expect as readers to be addressed by, much less moved by, imaginative texts. "The otherness is the text itself," writes Frye (*MM* 233), and no genuine dialogue, no encounter with any "thou" (either with or without a capital "t") seems possible if our approach is determined by suspicion that cannot be suspended. Therefore, this essay seeks primarily to examine how Frye transforms and, in fact, imaginatively redeems the concept of otherness and the kindred concept of the Father from its demonic type, the "sky-scarecrow," transforming, as it were, Lacan's narrative of alienation into a redemptive vision.[1] Most importantly, this essay will consider how the Jewish philosopher Martin Buber influenced the development of Frye's views on the spiritual Other.

Although in Frye's entire work the dialectic poles of immanence and transcendence, identity and otherness constitute an interpenetrating balance, there is more emphasis on the latter side of each, on transcendence and otherness in Frye's late writings.[2] "Without a contrary," Michael Dolzani has written in a seminal essay, the Blakean identification of the human and the divine "will result in what Jung called inflation, when the ego puffs itself up into a transcendental ego .... The only thing that can follow, in a manic-depressive cycle, is deflation" (321). Dolzani continues by referring to Frye's startlingly pessimistic description, in an interview with David Cayley published in the 1990s, of human nature as profoundly corrupt. In this interview, Frye ends up expressing his wish for "something that transcends all this" (*Northrop Frye in Conversation* 189–190; qtd. in Dolzani 321). In fact, it was probably the elderly Frye's mature perspective, with the entire 20th century behind him, that induced him to reconsider the question of God as Other who "must be thought of as the inconceivably transcendent," and to dismiss "all thoughts of that psychotic ape homo sapiens being divine" (*LN* 195). Also, a note of caution, if not of despair as in the quoted notebook entry, is discernible in the concluding sentence of Frye's essay "The Times of the Signs" (delivered as a lecture in the 1970s): "There may be an otherness of the spirit as well as of nature, and ... a *tiny part of that* too may become ourselves" (emphasis added). This explains why Frye, though otherwise reluctant to confine himself to propositional religious beliefs, makes this straightforward statement in one notebook entry (from between 1967 and 1970): "'Thou art that.' Who says so? Whoever it is, he begins with 'Thou,' so implies a communication of particulars as well as identity. I am a theist because I think the human is divisible, part of it being 'all too human' and only a part divine" (*RT* 93).

Taking this passage as a starting point, this essay argues that from the 1960s onward (the earliest notebook references to Buber date from 1967 to 1968), Frye makes increasing use of Martin Buber's dialogue principle in order to work out the notion of identity with the eternal Thou in a way that paradoxically allows God to remain Other. Rejecting the unity of being, Buber posited relation, reciprocity, and dialogue as the fundamental principle of reality:

God embraces but is not the universe; just so, God embraces but is not my self. On account of this which cannot be spoken about, I can say in my language, as all can say in theirs: You. For the sake of this there are I and You, there is dialogue, there is language, and spirit whose primal deed language is, and there is, in eternity, the word. (143)

Buber, a process thinker like Frye, describes the Spirit (or in one of Frye's terms, the "creative life") as "occurring" not "in man" but "between man and what he is not" (141), in other words, as an intermediate world of language in which the dialectic of Spirit and Word takes place neither in man nor in God but between them. In Frye's formulation, this is the case "where a Word not our own, though also our own, proclaims and a Spirit not our own, though also our own, responds" (*WP* 118). Like Frye, Buber locates "the genesis of word and form"—in other words, the origin of human creativity—in the encounter with the spiritual Other:

> Spirit word, spirit become form—whoever has been touched by the spirit and did not close himself off knows to some extent of the fundamental fact: neither germinates and grows in the human world without having been sown; both issue from encounters with the other. (176)

Frye's somewhat cryptic and speculative notebook entries on the different stages of the evolution of the religious consciousness suggest that interpenetrating dialogue rooted in the biblical tradition is a higher stage in development than the undivided unity and identity of what he calls "*tat tvam asi* mysticism." Unravelling the subtleties of Frye's speculation on the stages is beyond the scope of this paper; what is important for the purpose at hand is that the transition from the second stage (that of contemplation and speculation, ending in "Thou art That" mysticism or perennial philosophy [*RT* 100]) to the third is described as "through mysticism to dialogue—interpenetration of Word" (90). Elsewhere in the same notebook Frye writes, "The third stage is founded on this communication-community-communion triad, or the Word & its revelation, on dialogue, on the sense of the human presence of God, on the revolutionary transformation of society through the sense of divine presence" (100–101). Frye seems to have identified Buber's I-Thou principle with the paradox of identity-in-difference: "Stage 3 is what Buber calls dialogue: identical & *separate*. Even interpenetration is suspect, as it's still a formula of connexion" (109).

This complicated and never finalized speculation on the stages or levels of religion, which engaged Frye's attention for about ten years, can be considered the preliminary labour that anticipated the birth of his kerygma theory in the 1970s.[3] What seems to be a permanent element in these meditations is Frye's interest in the notion of *reversal* as closely bound up with Buber's dialogue. When the myths and metaphors of human imagination are experienced as language arriving from the other side we can talk about reversal—in other words, kerygma. Especially in notebook 21 several entries revolve around this central question: "Myth is a human language, so it isn't revelation. So what is revelation? What comes through human language the other way" (RT 154). Of course what is meant by reversal is not that the creative word suddenly reverses direction, but that it is experienced as coming from some other. Seeking to transcend secular humanism, Frye was looking for "an infinite reality that's identical with the human, & hence is personal, & yet isn't 'all too human'" (RT 93), and he seemed to have found it in kerygma: "Is it at the point of *reversal* that the genuinely human splits off from the all-too-human?" (157; emphasis added).

Although the notion of reversal is expressed by allusions to the "the other side" in Frye's published works (see WP 101, 116), it seems a particularly apt way to describe the paradoxical dynamism of Frye's ultimate experience: it is at the moment of reversal that the "explosion, or rather implosion of the ego-self into the spiritual body" takes place (WP 95). On the other hand, this is more a process than a moment: "a continuous turning inside-out" during the course of which the individual experiences herself or himself as "a whole of which Christ [or God] is part" and, conversely, that "God is a whole of which we are parts" (*LN* 427–428). The experience of becoming a spiritual body—elsewhere, "a genuine human being" (*DV* 14)—transcends "what the human subject is trying to do" and, by reversal, "we enter into a vaster operation where human personality and will are still present, but where the self-begotten activity no longer seems to be the only, or even the essentially, active power. The initiative is now usually seen to come, not from some un-reachable 'in itself' world, but from an infinitely active personality that both enters us and eludes us" (*MM* 107).

The above squares well with what Buber calls "relation," "encounter," or "dialogue." In relation, the Other has ceased to become an object or It to be transformed into word or language, Buber's world of Thou. This world "comes between a consciousness that is merely an I and a nature that is merely an 'it'" (*MM* 115). "It is both within me and outside me, it is something I speak and receive at the same time" (*WP* 118). Indeed, Frye's writings during the period in which he formulated his kerygma theory are increasingly rife with references to Buber, whom Frye calls "one of the most original thinkers" he ever read (*Northrop Frye in Conversation* 196). *Late Notebooks* contains fourteen references to Buber, and in *Words With Power* his name occurs in chapter conclusions Frye paid special attention to. But one notebook entry articulates more eloquent-ly than anything else Buber's influence on Frye concerning the paradox of God transcending and yet dwelling within us:

When God defines himself to Moses as "I am," surely one implica-tion is that he's also the I am of Moses, though still capable of dia-logue with Moses. Prayer is this kind of dialogue, and so is really, as I said, an attempt at self-knowledge that doesn't come through introspection. I suppose Buber's point is that if the possibility of this dialogue vanishes, the human being becomes merely, or all-too, human. Man's something to be surpassed, by something in-side him which is also him. Or he. (*RT* 179)

According to Buber, the antinomy of identity and difference is indissoluble and the tension must be borne by our very lives:

> Whoever affirms the thesis and repudiates the antithesis violates the sense of the situation. Whoever tries to think a synthesis destroys the sense of the situation.... Whoever would settle the conflict between antinomies by some means short of his own life transgresses against the sense of the situation. (143)

Although Frye's attitude to Hegelian synthesis is ambiguous (Denham, *Words* 11–12; Denham, "Interpenetration" 140–158), he seems to prefer a paradoxical and creative tension of thesis and antithesis rather than their resolution in a synthesis. In a notebook entry that may well have been inspired by Buber, he describes the myth-metaphor world as one in which "thesis contains and implies antithesis, but lives with it and does not transcend it" (*LN* 245). In Buber's perspective, therefore, the Hegelian absolute subject as well as the Buddhist *citta* and the Hindu "Thou art That" are "immersion doctrines" that put an end to all "You-saying" because they either eliminate or deny duality (Buber 131–132).[4] As we have seen, in some of his notes Frye contrasts dialogue and mysticism in a similar vein.

What appears contradictory at first sight is that Frye's vision of interpenetration—"the key to dialogue as well as identity" (*RT* 91)—owes much to Eastern sources; in fact, he even identifies it with the Hindu *atman* and the Buddhist *citta* (see *NFCL* 120). However, careful inspection of Frye's notes reveals that he and Buber share the same bold vision of the ultimate nature of the interpenetrative dialogue. According to Buber's daring assertion, "What the ecstatic calls unification is the rapturous dynamics of the relationship," which "in its vital unity is felt so vehemently that its members pale in the process: its life predominates so much that the I and the You between whom it is established are forgotten" (135). Similarly, when Frye speaks of mysticism as belonging to a lower awareness, he does not mean the experience itself but rather the conceptual and theological conclusion of second-stage religiosity, the end result of a process, a conclusion Frye calls the "deification of the void" (RT 103), in the course of which the One overrides the Many and is emptied of all content.[5] This is exactly what Buber describes as "the doctrine of immersion" or, metaphorically, "the deep sleep." "These are the supreme excesses of It-language," he adds, "something that can at most be an object of living experience but that cannot be lived" (137–138). Since both of them are thinkers committed to the world, this direction of mysticism, or rather its conceptualization, is unacceptable to Buber as well as Frye because it leads to a devaluation of the body and of multiplicity. In contrast, the vision of interpenetration rejects the notion of a total (male) subject swallowing all (see Buber 137); instead, it asserts a reciprocity in the course of which world, nature, and God are transformed from It to Thou, from alienated to interpenetrating Other.

In *Words With Power*, Frye's last and greatest work on human and divine creativity, he makes an implicit attempt to convert the dialogue principle into Christian terms. This is related to Frye's lifelong anxiety that if our creative products are "merely human," we are irremediably caught in the prison of Narcissus, staring at our mirror image. "There must be something other, uncreated, given," he muses in a late note (LN 712). In another one he claims that "the Buber dialogue principle is the only one that breaks out of the Narcissus prison. If Word & Spirit are human doubles, we're stuck" (394). Such speculations prepare the closure of the seventh chapter of *Words With Power*, where Frye describes Narcissus as a type of the fall of Adam, and where he depicts redemption by Christ as a delivery from the prison of Narcissus—in other words, Frye suggests, from the Lacanian mirror stage,

> Buber's I and Thou tells us that we are all imprisoned in an "It" world which is really a reflection of ourselves.... Only a 'Thou' who is both another person and the identity of ourselves, releases the

ability to love that gets us out of the world of shades and echoes ... into the world of sunlight and freedom. (*WP* 271)

Using elements of Lacan's imagery, Frye builds up his own vision on Buberian grounds. Lacan's *moi,* or the projected Narcissus, is identified with the alienated (billiard-ball-like) ego of Buber's It world, which in Frye's redemptive scheme ultimately gives place to the individual's genuine, broader identity. Frye's fascination with Buber is not the least bit surprising, as Buber seems to have provided for him a comic reversal of Lacan's narrative of alienation and misrecognition.[6] According to Buber, in the world of relation the recognition of "myself" as an integral whole is possible: "The concentration and fusion into a whole being can never be accomplished by me, can never be accomplished without me. I require a You to become; becoming I, I say you" (62).

The notion of dialectic or dialogue of Word and Spirit only implicitly finds its way into *Words With Power,* in expressions such as the "inner movement in the creative life" (118). In one sense, the Word is the descending divine principle of creation by perception—differentiating and dividing reality and so making it intelligible—whereas the Spirit is the ascending response of human creativity, participating in this intelligibility (see *WP* 89). Dialogue is the encounter or interpenetration of the two. In a note of slight Lacanian overtones, but with an unequivocally more cheerful view of language, Frye describes the encounter thus:

All human creativity drifts upward through the ivory gates from libido to ego, bringing a mixture of vision and violence, love and cruelty. A sense of articulate order comes down through the gate of horn. Creativity is a purgatory fuelled by the "blood-begotten spirits," refined into love and wisdom through words. Without words it's only the Babel of power with its confusion of tongues. (*LN* 228)

In another sense, Word and Spirit, the dividing and uniting aspects of creativity (*LN* 368), are each both human and divine (they *are and are not* our Word and our Spirit). In Frye's remark, "These dialogues of Word and Spirit constitute everything that's creative and constructive in human life" (427), the emphasis is on the human or immanent pole, but then "the Word and Spirit in man coincide into something that has its being in God" (671). Human culture as a process is not to be one-sidedly equated with the immanent dialectic of human Promethean energy or *libido* against an oppressive social order. As Dolzani puts it in his illuminating analysis of the Word-Spirit dialogue, "The end result of Frye's attempt to turn the mythologies of authority and revolution into a Yeatsian double gyre, is the dialectic of Spirit and Word that is the heart of *Words with Power*" (322).[7]

Frye's final move in the spiral of dialectic seems to be related to the question of what or who is behind the inner movement of clarifying Word and unifying Spirit, what or who is in the background of the "recognition scene of proclaiming word and responding spirit" (*LN* 395). Aware of the enduring problem of the Trinity, in the final stage of his quest Frye attempts to recover or rehabilitate with one more reversal what was lost and rejected by modernity as defined by Nietzsche, Marx, and Freud: the vision of a non-alienated Father. "After the Fall ...," Frye says, "the Father is lost and becomes otherness. At the Gospel stage the Otherness is recognized as Father" (*LN* 41). The whole of Frye's life's work can be read as converging toward this ultimate recognition scene, which we must finally examine.

In the context of alienation, the transcendent pole of otherness is overemphasized at the cost of identity and immanence. Psychologically and socially, the Father becomes a transcendent authority figure, the embodiment of Freud's superego or Lacan's Other.[8] In *The Secular Scripture*, Frye himself describes the manifestations of what he calls the otherness of the Spirit in a somewhat Lacanian vein as "the whole complex of social acceptance, with laws, rituals, customs and the authority of warriors and priests and kings":

Everything man has that seems most profoundly himself is thought of as coming to him from outside, descending from the most ancient days in time, coming down from the remotest heights in space. We belong to something before we are anything, and, just as an infant's world has an order of parents already in it, so man's first impulse is to project figures of authority, or precedence in time and space, stretching in an iron chain of command back to God. (*SeS* 182)

However, in order to rehabilitate "the inexhaustible source who is the real Father, the antitype of Satan-Nobodaddy, the sky-scarecrow" (*LN* 332), the notion of authority itself must be transformed. Supposing for a moment that the real Father as antitype of the Lacanian big Other is "spiritual authority, which is order without authority" (620),[9] the only way to reveal such authority is to renounce it, exactly as Jesus did. It was paradoxically by not wanting it that he himself as Word became *the* authority (see 356). "The paradisal vision is re-established, but without hierarchy. It's a vision of order but not of authority—except the spiritual authority that exists only in education" (395).

Talking about ultimate otherness, Frye approaches the limits of human language by means of a final paradox: finding the All in the Nothing. "In God's answer all, the All, reveals itself as language," Buber says (151), but Frye, by suggesting that at this stage the all-encompassing Word is paradoxically identical with silence or stillness, the All with Nothing, goes beyond Buber in a Christian direction, imaginatively identifying the formerly criticized "deification of the void" with New Testament kenosis.[10] Frye has suggested in his short article on Lacan that the Law in the Jewish tradition is "the codifying of Lacan's *nom du père* into a social contract," but "in the Christian perspective, where a revised revelation makes the Law a 'type' of something greater than itself, a something that culminates, as far as human history is concerned, in the Crucifixion of Christ, the *nom du père* stands first in the place of absence and then in the place of death" (*SeSCT* 393).

In other words, Jesus reveals God as Other by descending into nothingness, wiping out his own divinity, and this is re-enacted in human creative endeavours of all kinds (the genuine religious or spiritual life being
such an endeavour as well) (see *WP* 289–294). This is how "the Word,
the articulate spirit" becomes "the intelligible guide to the Otherness,"
which is "the source of our life, origin and destiny"—in other words, the
Father (*LN* 136). Part of the answer to feminist objections to this symbolism could be that out of love this Father kills his otherness in order
to become one with us: "As soon as God speaks, and transforms himself
into a Word of God, he has already condemned himself to death" (*GC*
111).[11]

Ultimately, God's otherness goes hand in hand with his hiddenness
or absence, a concept not favoured by Blake but something Frye had to
come to terms with (see Dolzani). God's ways, Frye observed, seem mysterious to us because "God's power works only with wisdom and love,
not with folly and hatred. As 99.9% of human life is folly and hatred, we
don't see much of God's power. He must work deviously, a creative trickster" (*LN* 212). Again, the elderly Frye's pungent prophetic vision of humanity is necessarily accompanied by an increased emphasis on God's
hiddenness or inscrutability. God's reality is blurred by the human mirror, and we need to clear up our picture of God by "striving" with God's
otherness addressing us through the Bible and other creative texts. And
this is in fact none other than "striving with or through oneself to obtain
a spiritual vision of God" (*DV* 79; see also 82–83).

If the confining aspect of the mirror stage consists of the inability
to love, God as love is the climax of the Frygean vision. The Father, the
power aspect of the Trinity, hides himself in order to tread the path of
Word and Spirit, of wisdom and love:

Power is concealed in nature, and when it appears in human life,
it's unimaginably evil. It has to go through wisdom, which is the
soul-body setup all right, and is dramatized by the death and bur-
ial of Christ. This is a spiritual repetition (*that* word again) of the

original embryo-birth process.[12] Once it rises into the spiritual state of love, it's safe to release power. (*LN* 714)

The story of God and Job is seen by Frye as a type of the divine kenosis, foreshadowing the paradoxical dynamics of divine power as dramatized in the New Testament. By entering the wager with Satan, God renders himself vulnerable, dependent on Job. Job, on the other hand, is renewed by overcoming evil, which is God's renewal at the same time. By enduring when in trouble, showing love for others (he prayed for his friends), and purifying his vision of God, Job manifested God's creative power in his own being, or as Buber would put it, he "actualized" God in the world (Buber 163).

Ultimately, alienation for Frye is defeated by love, which paradoxically releases its power in the state of powerlessness. Love is the creative power of the Word mediating or "turning continuously inside out" between identity and otherness. In order to love, we need the Other, but we need the Other in love. For Martin Buber, love is "between I and Thou," and it enables one "to act, help, heal, educate, raise, redeem" (66). It is this hidden power of love that nurtures Northrop Frye's vision of the innocence of culture.

ENDNOTES

1   As is apparent from several references in his later writings, Frye knew and appreciated Lacan's work; in fact, he imaginatively recycled famous Lacanian concepts and used them for his own ends, especially those concerning the mirror stage. In a short article on Lacan (titled "Lacan and the Full Word"), Frye candidly described this activity of his as a "misreading" in Harold Bloom's sense, wittily excusing himself with the help of Lacan's own dictum "that every *méconnaissance* implies a *connaissance*" (292).

2   This has been argued by Michael Dolzani in the essay "The Ashes of Stars: Northrop Frye and the Trickster God." See also Denham, *Northrop Frye: Religious Visionary*, in which the author claims that Frye's interest in the previously excluded religious initiative (or

"Spirit") marks a "radical departure" from his earlier work (64–65). In the same work, see also the discussion of the importance of the preposition "beyond" in Frye's late writings (112–116).

3 For a succinct account of Frye's kerygma theory, see Denham, *Northrop Frye: Architect of the Spiritual World* (65–69), and for a discussion of the kerygmatic breakthrough as mystical, see 172.

4 Whether Buber can be considered a mystic and, if yes, in what sense, see Martin A. Bertram's excellent article, "Buber: Mysticism without Loss of Identity."

5 For a classic description of this process see Otto 68–72.

6 Lacan denied reciprocity in the relation of the subject to the Other, describing it as circular and therefore dissymmetrical (*Four Fundamental Concepts* 206–207).

7 With this schematic outline of what Frye may have meant by the Word-Spirit dialogue I am of course far from exhausting the question. The task facing the questioner has been identified by Robert D. Denham as trying to "find a common thread running through these discontinuous speculations [i.e., on Word and Spirit]" (see Denham, *Northrop Frye: Religious Visionary*, 256–261).

8 In Lacan's formulation: "It is the *name-of-the father* that we must recognize as the support of the symbolic function, which, from the dawn of history has identified his person with the figure of the law" (Lacan, *Écrits* 67). For a useful summary of Lacan's theories of the symbolic father as Other, see Grosz 67–74.

9 See for example Žižek 39–40, 59, 98. In fact, the Lacanian "big Other" in the sense of the field of socially recognized knowledge or in the stronger sense of the agency of ideology is precisely order *with* authority. In Lacan's scheme, the entry into the symbolic order of language is synonymous with taking up one's place in the power structures of society, whereas Frye's theory distinguishes at least three or four modes of language operation. Actually, it is above all in the question of the potential of language to rise above ideology that Frye parts with post-structuralists. Frye's aspiration in *Words With Power* is to show the possibility of a "more inclusive mode of verbal communication" usually called imaginative, one that "takes us into a more open-ended world, breaking apart the solidified dogmas that ideologies seem to hanker for" (22). For Frye, imaginative language never says or asserts anything; rather, its criterion being the conceivable, not the real (22, 27), it releases the creative energy needed to transform the alienated "It-world" into a home. It is beyond the scope of this essay to do justice to Frye's distinction between

mythology and ideology (which he calls, among other things, "applied mythology"); for details see *WP* 16–62. On Frye and ideology, see Joseph Adamson, "The Treason of the Clerks: Frye, Ideology and the Authority of Imaginative Culture" in Boyd and Salusinszky 72–102, and Imre Salusinszky, "Frye and Ideology" in Lee and Denham 76–83. Frye's insistence on the innocent, non-ideological aspect of culture seems to be bound up with the paradox of self-eliminating spiritual authority or otherness.

10 In his aforementioned article, Bertram emphasizes Buber's distance from the Christian *via negativa* as exemplified by Eckhart, for whom "the self becomes one with the All which he also calls Nothing." (Bertram para. 7) For Frye's reappraisal of the "deification of the void," see Denham, *Northrop Frye: Religious Visionary*, 173–176.

11 Frye believes that it is the Father, not the Mother, that our identity is in need of, because symbolically the union with Earth Mother as an ultimate aim would in fact be a return to the Lacanian Real, to a stage prior to consciousness (See *LN* 9, 136, 164). It would simply mean that death and the earthly cycle are the final word, a suggestion that contradicts the theological act of trust suggested at the outset of this paper. The symbolic meaning of the choice of Father over Mother for Frye is that the alienation and loss ensuing with language is a necessary, though not an ultimate, stage of human experience, and in the final interpenetrative union the Word of language will become the very dialectic of I and Thou, not the medium of separation. (Describing the same tripartite process, Buber talks about the necessity of exchanging the "pure natural association" of the "prenatal life of the child" in the womb of the great Mother, through detachment, for a "spiritual association – a relationship," 76–77.) Those who grasp the mystic union on a conceptual level necessarily equate it with a pre-human, pre-linguistic state, a kind of death, but the mystics themselves experience it as a state of knowledge—to quote William James, as a passage "from a less to a more" (376). According to Buber, the mystic union is the experience of the total Word that "can only be spoken with one's whole being" (54); or to quote T. S. Eliot, "it is Word without a word," "the silent Word." Frye calls it "the real Word beyond words" (*LN* 16).

On the other hand, it should not be forgotten that this final interpenetration *is* the antitype of the primal oneness with the Mother. And so from a feminist perspective I would have welcomed more emphasis by Frye on the ancient Christian tradition of conceiving of the unifying Holy Spirit as a female principle (but see *RT* 194). What takes places here is the substitution of the notion of eternal return and cyclicity for the typological dialectic or, in Kierkegaardian terms, a "forward moving repetition." If the typological dialectic and the female symbolism of the Spirit are sufficiently taken into account, we are justified in saying that neither the Mother nor the Father is symbolically privileged for Frye: the "old Mother" is associated with the preconscious, embryonic state, and the "old Father," in turn, with the alienated, split subject (see *LN* 278)—both are cancelled *and* repeated in the new, as we will see. In the article on Lacan, this is envisioned, with amazing symbolic consistency, as "a 'second coming' of the Word" (394).

12 The "soul-body setup" is a reference to unredeemed existence or the split subject Christ identified with in his incarnational descent. The soul is metaphorically associated with the "old Father"; it is an alienated consciousness ruling over the "old Mother"-body. To quote Frye's note referred to in endnote 10: "The soul is the old Father, Adam, Joseph; the body the old mother, the *adamah*. The Spirit recreates the body-soul unit (soma psychicos) which withers away, and the soma pneumatikos, bridegroom & bride, takes its place" (*LN* 278). Spiritual repetition is the typological process in the course of which the alienated subject is lifted up into a state of love uniting body and soul, human and divine, the subject and the other.

WORKS CITED

Bertram, Martin A. 2000 (Winter). "Buber: Mysticism without Loss of Identity." *Judaism: A Quarterly Journal of Jewish Life and Thought* 1:1 [online]: bnet.com, http://findarticles.com/p/articles/mi_m0411/is_1_49/ai_61887410.

Buber, Martin. 1970. *I and Thou: A New Translation with a Prologue "I and You" and notes by Walter Kauffman*. Edinburgh: T&T Clark.

Cayley, David. 1992. *Northrop Frye in Conversation*. Interview with David Cayley. Concord, ON: Anansi.

Denham, Robert D. 2004. *Northrop Frye: Religious Visionary and Architect of the Spiritual World*. Charlottesville and London: University of Virginia Press.

———. 1999. "Interpenetration as a Key Concept in Frye's Vision." In *Rereading Frye: The Published and Unpublished Works*, ed. Imre Salusinszky and David Boyd. Toronto: University of Toronto Press, 140–163.

———. 1992. *Words With Power: Being a Second Study of "The Bible and Literature."* New York: Harcourt Brace Jovanovich.

Dolzani, Michael. 2003. "The Ashes of Stars: Northrop Frye and the Trickster God." In *Frye and the Word: Religious Contexts in the Criticism of Northrop Frye*, ed. Jeffery Donaldson and Alan Mendelson. Toronto: University of Toronto Press, 312–328.

Frye, Northrop. 2006. "Lacan and the Full Word." In *The Secular Scripture and Other Writings on Critical Theory, 1976–1991*. The Collected Works of Northrop Frye. Vol. 18. Ed. Joseph Adamson and Jean Wilson. Toronto: University of Toronto Press, 392–395.

———. 2003. *Northrop Frye's Notebooks and Lectures on the Bible and Other Religious Texts*. The Collected Works of Northrop Frye. Vol. 13. Ed. Robert D. Denham. Toronto: University of Toronto Press.

———. 2000. *Northrop Frye's Late Notebooks, 1982–1990: Architect of the Spiritual World*. The Collected Works of Northrop Frye. Vols. 5–6. Ed. Robert D. Denham. Toronto: University of Toronto Press.

———. 1992. *Words With Power: Being a Second Study of "The Bible and Literature."* New York: Harcourt Brace Jovanovich.

———. 1991. *The Double Vision: Language and Meaning in Religion*. Toronto: University of Toronto Press.

———. 1990. *Myth and Metaphor: Selected Essays, 1974–1988*. Charlottesville: University Press of Virginia.

———. 1982. *The Great Code: The Bible and Literature*. New York: Harcourt Brace Jovanovich.

———. 1978. *Northrop Frye on Culture and Literature: A Collection of Review Essays*. Chicago: University of Chicago Press.

———. 1976. *The Secular Scripture: A Study of the Structure of Romance*. Cambridge: Harvard University Press.

———. 1963. *Fables of Identity: Studies in Poetic Mythology*. New York: Harcourt.

James, William. 1987. *Writings 1902–1910*. New York: The Library of America.

Lacan, Jacques. 1977. *Écrits: A Selection*. Trans. Alan Sheridan. London: Tavistock.

———. 1977. *The Four Fundamental Concepts of Psychoanalysis*. Trans. Alan Sheridan. Harmondworth: Penguin.

Otto, Rudolf. 1962. *Mysticism East and West: A Comparative Analysis of the Nature of Mysticism.* Trans. Bertha L. Bracey and Richenda C. Payne. New York: Collier Books.

Žižek, Slavoj. 1992. *Enjoy your Symptom! Jacques Lacan in Hollywood and Out.* New York: Routledge.

Frye's "Pure Speech":

Literature and the Sacred without the Sacred

Garry Sherbert

Whatever is sacred, whatever is to remain sacred, must be clothed in mystery. All religions take shelter behind arcana which they unveil only to the predestined. Art has its own mysteries.

—Mallarmé, Art Is for All

GIVEN THE desire to write about "pure speech" (*DV* 83) in literature and the work of Northrop Frye, one might suspect that I would be precipitously thrown into a discourse on religion for, as Jacques Derrida observes, "the desire for purification in general" is "the desire for the safe and sound, for the intact or immune (*heilige*)" (*Echographies* 134). In his essay "Faith and Knowledge: The Two Sources of 'Religion' at the Limits of Reason Alone," Derrida asks, "Can a discourse on religion be dissociated from a discourse on salvation: which is to say, on the holy, the sacred, the safe and sound, the unscathed (*indemne*), the immune, (*sacer, sanctus, heilig,* holy, and their alleged equivalents in so many languages)?" (2).

However, long before his proposal of finding "pure speech" in both the Bible and literature—as early as *Fearful Symmetry,* his book on William Blake—Frye wrote about the "the word within the Word," or the relation of sacred to the secular: "While 'The Old & New Testaments are the Great Code of Art,' to regard them as forming a peculiar and exclusive Word of God is a sectarian error" (*FS* 110). Nonetheless, it would be wrong to say, as one reviewer of *The Great Code* does in an article entitled "The Secret Gospel of Northrop Frye," that "literature is religion, for Frye" (519). A more promising description of Frye's "Secret Gospel" is made by Derrida on the sacred and the secular in an interview discussing his own essay "La littérature au secret: Une filiation impossible," or, "Literature in [the] Secret: An Impossible Filiation," recently published in the second edition of *The Gift of Death* (2008).[1] Derrida states, "Secularization in literature doesn't mean anything to me. I think literature remains to us, for us, a sort of sacred space, and we have to interrogate what this sacredness, this secularized sacredness[,] may mean" ("Discussion" 20). This essay will argue that "pure speech" is Frye's way of interrogating the "secularised sacred" in literature, a sacredness that goes beyond the determined faiths, our inherited religious traditions, toward a "sacred without the sacred" (Hart 11).

Lynn Poland's review article of *The Great Code* marks an uncanny moment in the reception of Frye's work by suggesting that there is something secret about it. Significantly, Poland qualifies her statement, saying that Frye belongs to a "tradition of heretical exegeses," but his proclamation of religious truth, his "kerygma[,] is not esoteric; he intends to make priests of us all" ("Secret Gospel" 519). She concludes by declaring that "Frye's secret is universal salvation" (519). Poland's claim that Frye is "not esoteric" but that he holds a secret of universal salvation—she does not specify if "salvation" comes from religion or literature, or literature "as" religion—is tantamount to saying that Frye holds a secret that is not a secret. At times Frye appears to identify literature with religion, but there are too many examples of the contrary to oversimplify the difference between them. In *The Educated Imagination*, for example, Frye straightforwardly asserts, "Literature is not religion, and it doesn't address itself to belief" (33). Rather, and this is no secret, Frye's secret gospel lies in the structural unknowability of literature and religion, a structural unknowability that results from "pure speech," the performative nature of language.[2] Pure speech is "structurally" unknowable because it has the structure of a secret, but it has no content, like a riddle with no answer. The open secret of the performative is that literature and the religious language of kerygma, defined as "'myths to live by'" (*WP* 117), create the state of affairs to which they refer, a language that leads Frye to his most important axiom or principle, "the principle of the reality of what is created" (128).

We are now prepared to say that for Frye the "word within the Word" is a pure speech that promises to keep a secret. The secret, the fidelity to secrecy, refers to the fidelity of not just the "pure singularity of the face-to-face with God, the secret of this absolute relation," as Derrida states (*Gift of Death* 154). The secret also refers to the singularity of any face-to-face or one-on-one relationship, exemplified by a relationship with God. Frye illustrates this singular relationship that typifies "'pure speech (Zephaniah 3:9)'" (*GC* 230) in the biblical text by quoting Heraclitus's aphorism: "Every man is his own Logos" (*GC* 100). The Logos, when it is pure speech, is the out-of-body experience of a "new language" that Frye also compares to Paul's experience of the Word in 2 Corinthians 12:4 (*GC* 231). Frye cites Paul's reported experience of hearing "'unspeakable words' (*arreta rhemata*), 'not lawful for a man to utter'" (231), as a new language of structural secrecy that says the unsayable.

It is this structure of the secret that Derrida identifies as sacred in his aforementioned "Literature in [the] Secret: An Impossible Filiation." His claim of secularized sacredness for literature comes in the last essay in the second edition of *The Gift of Death* (2008), an essay excluded in the 1995 edition. For Derrida, the mysteries of the sacred text are analogous to the suspension of reference in literature, or what he calls the "secret" of literature. He argues that while literature sacrifices its filiation with the sacred in religion by going beyond the singular relation with God and regarding every singular relationship as sacred, it still bears a mark of similarity to the sacred text for the same reason, by treating the sacred singularity of every one-on-one relationship the same way it treats its relationship with God. Derrida compares the literary secret with the situation depicted in the story of Abraham, who must kill his son Isaac on Mount Moriah, but not tell his wife Sarah or the community. Derrida states (originally in parentheses), "If literature, the modern thing that legitimately bears that name, 'desacralizes' or 'secularizes' the Scriptures, the holy or sacred Scripture, it thereby repeats the sacrifice of Isaac, stripping it bare, delivering it and exposing it to the world" (*Gift of Death* 154). Literature repeats the religious sacrifice without the traditional religious significance, though not without a certain kind of sacredness, since the Latin etymology of "sacrifice," "*sacer*" and "*facere*," means "to make sacred" (*Encyclopedia* 7,997). By secularizing the sacred through the structure of the secret, literature sacrifices its filiation to the sacred text even while repeating it in a different way. Literature becomes a form of the sacred without the sacred traditions attached to it. Derrida even writes that literature must ask our pardon for sacrificing meaning, or not meaning anything in "the absence of a fully determinative context" (*Gift of Death* 130), or perhaps ask pardon for the suspension of reference, which, as Derrida carefully points out, suspends the "*thesis* or arrest, the placing or stopping of determinate sense or real referent" (*Gift of Death* 157).

To demonstrate Frye's fascination for pure speech as the secret of literature, one need only examine the frequency with which he advocates the importance of the theory of impersonality in the poet. He offers one of his usual paradoxical axioms, saying that "literature is the embodiment of a language, not of belief or thought: it will say anything, and therefore in a sense it says nothing" (*CP* 101). Furthermore, however much the poet may imitate the rhetorician's direct address, "*qua* poet he has nothing to 'say'" (*WP* 67). Frye is therefore in full accord with Stéphane Mallarmé's assertion that "the pure work implies the disappearance of the poet as speaker, yielding his initiative to words" (*Selected Poetry and Prose* 75). The purity of the work, at its origin, then begins with the performative power of language to take the "initiative." Frye even makes myth a kind of pure speech when he speaks of myth as the enabling condition of the sacred. He writes, "A mythology creates in the midst of its society the verbal equivalent of a *temenos* or sacred ground, a limited and sacro-sanct area" (*WP* 31). Frye's insistence on the autonomy of language as a condition of its purity corresponds well with what Derrida calls the "*exemplary* secret of literature, a chance of saying everything without touching upon the secret" (*On the Name* 29). As we shall see a little later, the suspension of reference is another characteristic of pure speech in Frye's theory of literature, but instead of focusing exclusively on metaphor, myth will also serve to explain how the poet yields the initiative to words and suspends reference in order to attain a purity that must be understood as a certain kind of secrecy.

Of course, myth is essential to religion and literature, but how exactly does myth, or any form of speech, become "pure" enough to create a "sacro-sanct area"? The purity, in Frye's view, comes from "a Word not our own, though also our own" (*WP* 118), a renunciation of mastery over the object of discourse by the subject of discourse. This renunciation of language, known as "*Gelassenheit*," "releasement," or "letting be," has long been a feature of the discourse in negative theology, and of course in the philosophy of Martin Heidegger, as seen in his book *Gelassenheit*, translated into English as *Discourse on Thinking* (54). Frye appeals to Heidegger's reflections on language more often than to negative theologians like Meister Eckhart, and since Heidegger repeats the Greek Platonic and Christian traditions of negative theology, he must serve as an example of the *via negativa* in the short space of this essay. Heidegger proposes, for instance, that all language is poetry because "language is the house of Being" ("Letter on Humanism" 217), where one is not the "lord of beings," but the "shepherd of Being" (245). Heidegger stresses the need for a non-appropriative way of relating to the world through language when he says, aphoristically, *"language* speaks," for "we do not merely speak *the* language—we speak *by way of* it" (*On the Way to Language* 124). Significantly, in *Words With Power* Frye alludes to this well-known passage without explicitly citing Heidegger in order to help define not only religious language but also, as I will argue, the literary language of "pure speech." Frye states,

> In poetry anything can be juxtaposed, or implicitly identified with, anything else. Kerygma takes this a step further and says: 'You are what you identify with.' We are close to the kerygmatic whenever we meet the statement, as we do surprisingly often in contemporary writing, that it seems to be language that uses man rather than man that uses language. (*WP* 116)

Frye's comment about "contemporary writing" may well refer to Derrida but also, as we shall see, to Michel Foucault, in an effort to overcome the subject-object dichotomy, an effort that Frye not only supports but needs in order to make pure speech possible.

Frye's effort to establish the autonomy of language in relation to the poet, who has "nothing" to say, constitutes one of the ways he achieves what Derrida calls a *"kenosis* of discourse" (*On the Name* 50). In Derrida's many writings on literature and religion, the kenosis of discourse, like the self-emptying by Christ of his divine nature in Philippians 2:7, empties discourse to avoid saying anything of the other so as not to reduce the other to an object subject to one's control. Such empty or pure speech that says nothing about the other keeps the other safe from the verbal abuse of instrumental language, and for this reason Derrida speaks of the *"exemplary* secret of literature," in much the same way Frye maintains the poetic theory of impersonality as the necessary recognition of the performative autonomy of language. Derrida provides a crucial context for understanding the structure of the secret in Frye's notion of pure speech in literature:

> When all hypotheses are permitted, groundless and ad infinitum, about the meaning of a text, or the final intentions of the author, whose person is no more represented than nonrepresented by a character or narrator, by a poetic or fictional sentence, which detached itself from its presumed source and thus remains locked away [*au secret*], when there is no longer even any sense in making decisions about some secret behind the surface of a textual manifestation (and it is this situation which I would call text or trace), when it is the call [*appel*] of this secret, however, which points back to the other or to something else, when it is this itself which keeps our passion aroused, and holds us to the other, then the secret impassions us. (*On the Name* 29)

Derrida's comments on the intentions of the author agree with Frye's in that the very inability of readers or the poet to know what a text means arouses us, and even arouses our desire for the author. Being in the condition of non-knowledge (or faith) with respect to the literary text is the very reason that the "secret impassions us" to want to know its meaning, not unlike our desire to know the Wholly Other, God. The "call of this secret," however, does not point to a final meaning but to something else, and holds us in a relation to the unknown. This is what Frye means when he refers to the symbolic meaning of literature as an "intrinsic mystery ... which remains unknown no matter how fully known it is" (*AC* 88), or why "*Hamlet* may contain any amount of meaning which the vast and constantly growing library of criticism on the play cannot begin to exhaust" (67).

Without launching into a comparison between Frye and a Heideggerian poetics of the holy, a poetics that is perhaps most explicitly thematized in Heidegger's book *Elucidations of Hölderlin's Poetry*, we can regard Frye's allusions to Heidegger as significant and keep the secret of pure speech before the reader so that Frye may, in his own way, accomplish a kenosis of discourse. For Derrida, the secret is a kind of kenosis of discourse extended to any language because it keeps the other, like the Wholly Other, God, for example, safe from being violated, controlled, or reduced by anything that is predicated or said about the other.

Nevertheless, Frye's version of kenosis departs from a Heideggerian poetics at the very moment of naming it, because Frye identifies kerygmatic rhetoric as a combination of "metaphor and concern" or as "a mixture of the metaphorical and the 'existential' or concerned" (GC 29). Heidegger argues in *Der Satz vom Grund* (*The Principle of Reason*) that "the metaphorical exists only within metaphysics" (48). Needless to say, Heidegger's entire philosophical enterprise is devoted to overcoming metaphysics, including its influence on religion, so it is more than a little ironic that Frye names the main metaphor of religious, or kerygmatic, language after him: "The type of identification we have been calling existential metaphor may also be called, following Heidegger, 'ecstatic'" (WP 82). "Existential" or "ecstatic" metaphor makes statements of identity and removes the subject-object split. Frye gives kerygmatic metaphor a Heideggerian name to exploit the notion of the "ecstatic." He says, "The word ecstatic means, approximately, standing outside oneself: a state in which the real self, whatever reality is and whatever the self is in this context, enters a different order of things from that of the now dispossessed ego" (WP 82). Heidegger even defines human being in ecstatic terms as *Dasein*, literally *Da-sein*, or "being there" (s. 2, 75n1). In Heidegger's *Being and Time*, the "ecstatic" means the way *Dasein* "stands out" in time, for as he puts it, "temporality is the primordial 'outside-of-itself' in and for itself" (s. 65, 377). What Frye calls the "dispossessed ego" Heidegger might describe as the ecstatic state of being with other things in the world and working toward a disposition of *Gelassenheit*, or of "letting the other things be as things." Ironically, only when we take this step back from discourse by emptying our discourse of any representation and letting things manifest themselves on their own in language can we then begin to approach the sacred, the Wholly Other, or any other, outside language.

However, the renunciation of instrumental thinking takes another turn toward language as Frye develops an analogy between the suspension of reference in both literature and religious writing through myth. Representation in language, or descriptive writing, occupies Frye for some time because the modern model of truth is correspondence, where "the criterion of truth is related to the external source of the description rather than to the inner consistency of the argument" (GC 13). As with the doctrine of mimesis that has ruled Western art since Aristotle, the more recent truth of correspondence submits language to something outside it. This phase of writing leads historians of the Bible to search for evidence of its literal truthfulness using external criteria, "demythologizing" it in order to make it more credible in relation to this modern standard. By contrast, Frye sets up an opposing criterion that, like literature, suspends the historical referentiality of the text: "What I am saying is that all explanations are an *ersatz* form of evidence, and evidence implies a criterion of truth external to the Bible which the Bible itself does not recognize" (GC 44). A little earlier in *The Great Code*, Frye characterizes the issue more dramatically: "In the next chapter I shall give my reasons for saying that myth is the linguistic vehicle of *kerygma*, and that to 'demythologize' the Bible would be the same thing as to obliterate it" (30). He goes on to argue that biblical myth is closer to the poetic than to the historical because history makes particular statements subject to the external criteria of truth and falsehood, while myth, like poetry, expresses the universal in the event. Frye then suggests what he means by pure speech:

> In our language, the universal in history is what is conveyed by the *mythos*, the shape of the historical narrative. A myth is designed not to describe a specific situation but to contain it in a way that

does not restrict its significance to the one situation. Its truth is inside its structure, not outside. (*GC* 46)

Having placed us in the house of Being to avoid instrumental language, and without giving up on truth, Frye now explicitly suspends the referentiality of mythical language to purify it of any utilitarian purpose, or avoid contaminating it with any direct representational function.

Once again, Frye's break with representational language follows Heidegger in his understanding of the truth and its structure. Frye ends the introduction of *Words With Power* using the Greek word *aletheia*, best known for its association with Heidegger, but in a context that leaves Heidegger conspicuous in his absence. Without saying that the entire book is reflected in this Heideggerian economy of truth, Frye writes, "The negative form of the Greek word for truth, *aletheia*, which means something like 'unforgetting,' suggests that at a certain point searching for the unknown gives place to trying to remove the impediments to seeing what is there already" (*WP* xxiv). In *On Time and Being*, for example, Heidegger discusses the Greek word *aletheia* as "unforgetting," interpreting the first letter, *alpha*, as the privative "a," or "un," followed by *lethe*, which means "forgetting" (71). In "The Origin of the Work of Art," Heidegger again defines *aletheia*: "Truth is un-truth, insofar as there belongs to it the reservoir of the not-yet-revealed, the uncovered, in the sense of concealment" (185). This version of truth as "unconcealment" is particularly significant for our relation to the holy, of which Heidegger observes, "even God can, for representational thinking, lose all that is exalted and holy, the mysteriousness of his distance" (*Question Concerning Technology* 26). In *Elucidations of Hölderlin*, Heidegger says, "The holy is quietly present as what is coming. That is why it is never represented and grasped as an object" (89). Obviously, these Heideggerian constructions of the truth and holiness find a place in Frye's poetic.

Since he construes pure speech as normal language emptied of its "impediments," Frye resembles Heidegger not only in his approach to the holy and sacred but also in his secularizing or emptying of the sacred. Frye and Heidegger propose that the holy cannot be represented by normal, instrumental language because it objectifies God, but both offer poetry as a way to get beyond subject and object split in language. Heidegger says, "The holy, as the unapproachable, renders every immediate intrusion of the mediated in vain" (85). Heidegger believes that by renouncing representation and the expression of meaning (which fixes the thing in a concept), the poet's word names the unnameable and thereby avoids the "intrusion of the mediated," the mediation of representational language. There is no "immediate" or direct access to God, or the holy, through any form of human mediation, including language.

Similarly, Frye argues that literature avoids objectification in language, or what he calls the "subject-object cleavage" (GC 118), though the poetic word, contrary to Heidegger, is almost always a metaphor. Frye then extends the non-objectifying discourse of the sacred to the secular, arguing that literary discourse preserves the structure of sacred discourse without being addressed exclusively to God. Frye generalizes the sacred, for instance, when he discusses the significance of kenosis in the passage already mentioned, in which Christ is said to have "emptied himself" (Philippians 2:7). Frye writes that for Paul, kenosis means that Christ has annihilated "the antitheses between a human subject and a divine object," the ultimate version of the "clumsy either-or dilemma of a choice between a religious view with a 'God' in it, and a secular or humanistic view with only man and nature in it" (WP 133, 132). Frye not only interrogates what secularized sacredness means here; he also takes up the biblical event of kenosis to deconstruct the opposition between the sacred and the secular. Derrida also resorts to metaphor to secularize, or empty, the sacred when he makes God the name, or figure, for any singular being or thing, saying, "*Tout autre est tout autre*": that every other is wholly other, because God is "the figure, or name of the wholly other" (*Gift of Death* 78).

Despite his deconstruction of the sacred and the secular, Frye keeps the literary distinct from the religious throughout the analogy he draws between these two discourses. As the epigraph at the beginning of this essay suggests, Frye's concept of pure speech corresponds with Mallarmé's conception of art in that "whatever is sacred ... must be clothed in mystery" and in that "art has its own mysteries" (*Mallarmé: Selected Prose Poems* 9). The danger that occurs whenever we "unveil" language is that we may interpret pure speech as the tradition of Western metaphysics has done, as a history of logocentrism that lifts the veil of the signifier to gain direct access to the truth. One might ask: Is Frye's pure speech merely a version of logocentrism? Derrida defines logocentrism as the "effacement of the signifier" (*Grammatology* 20), a speech that pretends to be pure because of the system of *s'entendre parler*. The phrase *s'entendre parler* possesses two meanings that logocentrism hopes will perfectly coincide: "hearing oneself speaking" and "understanding oneself speaking." The phonocentric purity of the system of *s'entendre parler* assumes that the truth, the idea, or the meaning exists in an ideal state before it is contaminated by the exteriority, the material event, of inscription (*Grammatology* 7–8). Yet, as Derrida asks, "Does not pure speech require inscription" (*Writing and Difference* 9), even an inscription in the exteriority of the voice? Frye seems to answer affirmatively, in principle, with his "fallacy of the substantial idea," which wrongly assumes that ideas are substantial and exist prior to speech, without having to be put into words, or as he writes, "the idea is substantial and ... the words which express the idea are incidental" (*WTC* 37).

Upon closer inspection, Derrida's criticism of pure speech at the origin of literary creation emerges as strikingly similar in many respects to what Frye means by pure speech. For Derrida "writing is *inaugural*" because "meaning is neither before nor after the act" (*Writing and Difference* 11).

"Only *pure absence* ... can *inspire*" (8) the creative imagination, the consciousness of nothing being the basis of all speech. Despite the anguish of writers like Antonin Artaud who complain that they have nothing to say, Derrida suggests that this anguish is an unavoidable confrontation with the consciousness of nothing as the origin and condition of every work. In order to capture the "passion" of inscription, in both its active and passive sense, Christopher Johnson notes how in the following passage Derrida exploits the Latin root of "anguish," *angustia*, as meaning "'narrowness' but also 'difficulty,' and even brevity'" (Johnson 23):

> This anguish is not an empirical modification or state of the writer, but is a responsibility of *angustia*: the necessarily restricted passageway of speech against which all possible meanings push each other, preventing each other's emergence. Preventing, but calling upon each other, provoking each other too, unforeseeably and as if despite oneself, in a kind of autonomous overassemblage of meanings, a power of pure equivocality that makes the creativity of the classical God appear all too poor. (*Writing and Difference* 9)

Inscription for Derrida is, as Johnson rightly defines it, not simply the empirical operation of graphic inscription in a given medium: "its only attribute appears to be that of actualizing the virtuality of 'pure parole,'" or pure speech (Johnson 22). The force of signification for Derrida means that the "play of meaning can overflow signification" (*Writing and Difference* 12), and neither the author nor the reader can ever completely control this overflow. The benefit of this overflow of meaning is that both author and reader must participate in the production of a text's meaning, a creative (because performative) act of interpretation that underwrites Frye's critical axiom of *verum factum*.

Far from advocating a transparent, purely representational, or logocentric language that forces the signifier to simply get out of the way of the meaning, referent, or transcendental signified, Frye has repeatedly

traced the overflow of meaning through the restricted threshold of language. He outlines the actualizing of the virtuality of pure speech in the
performative polysemy of narrative, or myth, and metaphor. He defines
pure speech precisely as the interruption of representational or descriptive language in the following:

> One of the benefits of the coming of the kingdom of the spirit,
> the prophets tell us, is the restoring of a "pure speech" (Zephaniah
> 3:9). Such purity can hardly be the abstract purity of logic or de-
> scriptive accuracy, much less the isolation of one existing language
> from others. It is rather the purity of simple speech, the parable
> or the aphorism that begins to speak only after we have heard it
> and feel that we have exhausted its explicit meaning. From that ex-
> plicit meaning it begins to ripple out into the remotest mysteries
> of what it expresses and clarifies but does not "say." (DV 83)

The renunciation of "descriptive accuracy," or the urge to say something, turns us away from the "explicit meaning" back toward the "simple speech" of parable and aphorism. The simple speech of parable and
aphorism speaks to us after the explicit meaning, or what Gerard Manley
Hopkins calls the "overthought," has been exhausted and we are turned
toward the "underthought," or the "progression of imagery and metaphor that supplies an emotional counterpoint to the surface meaning,
which it often supplements, but also often contradicts" (WP 57). If parable and aphorism use imagery and metaphor to contradict the surface
meaning of pure speech, then we can understand why they "ripple out
into the remotest mysteries." Nevertheless, there appears to be nothing
simple about why pure speech would remain without "explicit meaning"
and thus remain within the mysteries "of what it expresses but does not
'say.'" The clue to the mystery (of these remote mysteries) seems to lie in
Frye's axiom that "poetic (and kerygmatic) structures are polysemous"
(WP 118). Being fictional, as a myth or narrative, polysemous language

is "spiritually *descriptive*" in a way that "describes nothing external, but, by being a structure ... becomes a verbal something" (118). The "verbal something" in the polysemous fiction that functions "spiritually" is the performative re-description of reality.

Frye tells us that the poetic structure that describes nothing external but becomes a verbal something is "metaphorical language in which the paradox of 'is' and 'is not' is functional" (*DV* 72). He makes a direct comparison of literary discourse with the mystical writers of negative theology, whom he calls visionary, when he states, "The visionary tradition referred to in the previous chapter, the one running through Pseudo-Dionysius, laid a good deal of stress on the fact that God was a hid divinity, hidden because all language about such a being dissolves in paradox or ambiguity (*GC* 12). Thus, there is no such thing as God, because God is not a thing. All language in such areas has to carry with it the sense of its own descriptive inadequacy, and nothing but the mythical and metaphorical language that says both 'is' and 'is not' can do this" (*WP* 109). As a "hid divinity," God constitutes the ultimate secret whose very name is so sacred that it is unpronounceable and must remain unspoken. Frye contends that only paradoxical language, the "descriptive inadequacy" of myth and metaphor, makes possible a proper relation to God's sacred being by maintaining the structural secrecy, or in Heidegger's words, "the mysteriousness of his distance." Of course, to approach God by moving away is a structural feature of metaphorical, literary language that is consistent with the very definition of religion, as Derrida defines it: "*Scruple*, hesitation, indecision, reticence (hence modesty [*pudeur*], respect, restraint, before that which should remain sacred, holy or safe; unscathed, immune)—this too is what is meant by *religio*" ("Faith and Knowledge" 31).

Having written about this paradox elsewhere,[3] I will not dwell on the matter of metaphor here except to mark the importance of Mallarmé to Frye's definition of pure speech referred to below. It is Mallarmé who writes, according to Frye, that in metaphor, "The world of reality dies into nothing; the symbolic world is born from nothing, for a symbol to begin with is nothing apart from the context that forms around it and completes it" (*MM* 39). Mallarmé, whom Frye calls "the poet of the nothingness of the world" (*WP* 291), exemplifies the literary version of negative theology, or apophatic discourse, whereby we negate God, say nothing about him, to attain an experience of him. Both literature and negative theology are discourses of "apophasis," which the *Oxford English Dictionary* defines by quoting John Smith's *The Mysterie of Rhetorique Unvail'd* (1657): "Apophasis ... a kind of Irony, whereby we deny that we say or doe that which we especially say or doe." The analogy between literary metaphor and apophasis in negative theology reveals pure speech as the metaphorical "mystery in words" (*WP* 65). Like the rhetoric of mystical writings in theology, literary apophasis suggests that, paradoxically, poets have nothing to say. Poets engage in the mystery of the performative contradiction, whereby one contradicts the content of what one is saying by saying it—by saying the unsayable. Heidegger indicates something similar to Frye's statement concerning the mysteries of what pure speech "expresses and clarifies but does not 'say'" when he writes, "That which shows itself and at the same time withdraws is the essential trait of what we call the mystery" (*Discourse on Thinking* 55). Similar to Heidegger and the negative theologians, Frye believes that only in paradoxical linguistic structures like that of metaphor do we empty discourse and hold ourselves open to the mystery of "that which shows itself and at the same time withdraws"—that is to say, the sacred.

Parable and aphorism are specifically chosen as the exemplars of pure speech because of their ability to refer to a vision or "model world," namely, "the intelligible world of the philosopher and scientist, the imaginable world of the poet, and the revealed world of religion" (*CP* 32). Frye admits that while this world may not actually exist, it "is not nothing or non-existence" (31). As a "vision of possibilities" (111), literature's model world in its totality presents a "range of imaginative possibilities of belief" (128) that no one religion can match. The sense of "anguish" produced by works such as *The Satanic Verses* or *The Da Vinci Code* attests to the passion of inscription, the power literature possesses whenever its vision of possibilities exposes a determined faith to competing interpretations of a sacred text. The parable and the aphorism are, needless to say, characteristic of religious writing, but not exclusively so. Frye's purpose in privileging these examples of simple speech, "ordinary" or "demotic" speech (*WTC* 94), is to remind the reader of the ethical and participating aim that the parable and aphorism must attain if they are going to pass from "communication to community" and achieve "a vision of society" (44). Underlining this ethical or participating aim, as opposed to the aesthetic or contemplative one, Frye defines the aphorism, like the proverb, as a "council of action" (90), with the further distinction that "aphorisms are related to a total vision of life (*quo tendas*) and so become more than pragmatically moral" (91). Aphorism may be limited to a "purely human oracle" (*AC* 298), but its discontinuous form, antitheses, and paradoxes, are consistent with the structure of a mystery that shows itself and withdraws at the same time. The parable's narrative form differs from the aphorism, but Frye gives them a visionary social dimension by designating them as "myths within myths" (*GC* 33). Describing the parable as a "fable with a riddling quality" (xv) also indicates the sense of mystery that the aphorism conveys through antithesis or paradox.

Armed with the mysteries of double vision, a vision that combines the physical and the spiritual world together through the polysemy of metaphor, Frye then brings literary discourse into the realm of pure speech without distinguishing between the sacred and secular forms of language. He states,

> Not all pure speech is in the Bible: T.S. Eliot and Mallarmé tell us that purifying the speech of the 'tribe' or society around us is what gives a social function to the poet. Such purity of speech is not simply a creative element in the mind, but a power that recreates

the mind, or perhaps has actually created the mind in the first place, as though it were an autonomous force deriving from an authentic creation; as though there really were a Logos uniting mind and nature that really does mean "Word." (DV 83)

If his essay "From Poe to Valéry" is any indication, T.S. Eliot is not as enthusiastic toward the notion of "pure poetry" as Mallarmé and his admirers are. Eliot believes that "poetry is only poetry if it preserves some 'impurity'" (*To Criticize the Critic* 39), the impurity, because more common, being the instrumental language of the people. Eliot reacts against the more aristocratic aestheticism of Mallarmé's poem "The Tomb of Edgar Poe" in which the poet is said to "give a purer sense to the words of the tribe," in spite of the many-headed "Hydra's vile spasm," or the general population's rejection of the poet's "purer" language (Mallarmé, *Selected Poetry and Prose* 51). By replacing Mallarmé's "words of the tribe" with the "dialect of the tribe" as he does in "Little Gidding," the second section of *Four Quartets*, Eliot is aligning the poet more closely with the common national language as it is spoken and some more politicized version of language reform (39).

This is not the place to try situating Frye's political views of the poet's social function in relation to Eliot and Mallarmé. We can say, however, that the politics surrounding the "purity" of speech concerns the degree to which the writer is open to what Frye refers to as the "autonomous force" of the "Logos," or language. In other words, to what extent can we suspend referentiality, or what Derrida in his essay on Mallarmé, "The Double Session," describes as "reference without a referent" (*Dissemination* 206). Metaphor leaves the object indeterminate, purifying speech by opening it up so that, as Frye recounts in one of his notebooks, subject and object are swallowed up in a language that goes from being logocentric to being "logocircumferential" (LN 46). Like Derrida in his essay entitled "The *Retrait* of Metaphor," Frye believes that whenever we use metaphor, we become the content of the metaphor (103).

What is more, metaphor's polysemy ensures that we do not prejudice the arrival of the other by instrumentalizing, dominating, or determining them, by naming them in advance of their arrival. The other remains indeterminate because like God, he or she is a singularity, a singularity that arrives at the threshold of language but remains beyond our linguistic control.

Frye may be referring to this otherness outside language (which is both prior to language and the remainder left over after every event of speech) when he says, "For critical theory there seems to be a point where a change of elements from 'words' to 'Word' takes place. The Word is not the Bible or the person of Christ, for, say Mallarmé or Lacan, nor does it have to be those things for anyone. But apparently it does have to be there" (*WP* 132). He then quotes Foucault's remark that "'God is perhaps not so much a region beyond knowledge as something prior to the sentences we speak.'" Frye adds that Foucault "puts into a secular context what the opening of the Gospel of John puts into the sacred one, relating the Word that begins everything to the power behind the beginning which Jesus expresses by the metaphor of Son and Father" (*WP* 133). Frye affirms the originary power of the metaphorical word in literary and kerygmatic language whenever it is used, an originary affirmation that allows anyone to participate in the divine act of creation. The secular form of the originary power of the divine fiat is the performative speech act. Frye's appeal to Vico's axiom *verum factum* shows how humanity is a "participant" (*WP* 135) in the new creation in much the same way we use performative speech acts to create the state of affairs we refer to, as in a promise or command.

Surrendering to the "logocircumferential" might also be what Heidegger means when he says that language not only speaks but also promises itself to us and that we participate in that promise whenever we speak because "language is active as this promise" (*On the Way to Language* 76). Derrida would add that the promise of language is the trace of the call of language, a language outside language. This language that calls, as he puts it, "has started without us, in us, and before us. This is what theology calls God" ("How to Avoid Speaking" 99). It is impossible to speak the "unspeakable word" of this call of language that Frye wants to talk about in his reference to "something prior to the sentences we speak." But however much we deny being able to speak of this call of language, it is an undeniable necessity that we must respond to it in order to speak at all.

Frye's pure speech is, then, the word within the Word, saying without saying this language before language, this something prior to the sentences we speak. The secret (of) language shares in the sacred since it keeps itself pure and separate, cut off from everyday or profane language, even though it makes that profane language possible. Frye, Foucault, and Derrida identify God as the name we give to this language before language because it is a language that promises itself to us, but promises itself in secret because "its truth is inside its structure, not outside." "Myth" may well be another, more secular name for this promise of the secret, but nothing keeps the promise of the secret better than literature, for it more than anything else keeps language active as this promise. Keeping the promise of the secret gives literature a share in the sacred without belonging to a determinate religious faith, making literature a sacred without the sacred. Frye's secret gospel, therefore, his secret of universal salvation, tells us that what is said in the name of literature keeps the secret of the promise, for literature is an absolute performative, *verum factum*, the place where what is true is what we have made.

ENDNOTES

1   I have added the interpolation of the definite article to David Wills's translation of Derrida's title to convey the additional sense that the secret is a structure separate from and independent of literature, but a structure that literature necessarily shares.

2   The phrase "structurally unknowable" (101) originates, as John Caputo notes, in an interview with Derrida, in which he speaks of a "structural non-knowing" (111), but is redeployed by Caputo to explain the secret as a structure in *The Prayers and Tears of Jacques Derrida*. The connection between the secret and the performative is explicitly made by Derrida in *On the Name*, in which he states, "We testify [*témoignons*] to a secret that is without content, without a content separable from its performative experience, from its performative tracing" (24).

3   For further discussion of the paradoxical structure of literary metaphor and its relation to the sacred and religious writing, see my essay "Frye's Double Vision: Metaphor and the Two Sources of Religion."

WORKS CITED

Caputo, John. 1997. *The Prayers and Tears of Jacques Derrida: Religion without Religion*. Bloomington: Indiana University Press.

Derrida, Jacques. 2001. "A Discussion with Jacques Derrida." Interview. Paul Patton. *Theory and Event* 5:1, 1–24.

———. 1998. "Faith and Knowledge: The Two Sources of 'Religion' at the Limits of Reason Alone." In *Religion*, trans. Samuel Weber. Ed. Jacques Derrida and Gianni Vattimo. Stanford, CA: Stanford University Press, 1–78.

———. 1998. "The *Retrait* of Metaphor," trans. F. Gadsner. In *The Derrida Reader: Writing Performances*. Ed. Julian Wolfreys. Lincoln: University of Nebraska Press, 102–129.

———. 2008. *The Gift of Death*. 2nd ed. Trans. David Wills. Chicago: University of Chicago Press.

———. 1995. *On the Name*, trans. David Wood and John P. Leavey. Ed. Thomas Dutoit and Ian MacLeod. Stanford, CA: Stanford University Press.

———. 1992. "How to Avoid Speaking: Denials." In *Derrida and Negative Theology*, ed. Howard Coward and Toby Foshay. Albany: State University of New York Press, 73–142.

———. 1976. *Of Grammatology*, trans. Gayatri Chakravorty Spivak. Baltimore: Johns Hopkins University Press.

Derrida, Jacques, and Bernard Stiegler. 2002. *Echographies of Television*, trans. Jennifer Bajorek. Cambridge: Polity.

Eliot, T.S. 1965. *To Criticize the Critic and Other Writings*. London: Faber and Faber.

———. 1950. *Four Quartets*. London: Faber and Faber.

Encyclopedia of Religion. 2005. 2nd ed. Vol. 12. Ed. Lindsay Jones. Detroit: Thomson Gale.

Frye, Northrop. 2000. *Northrop Frye's Late Notebooks, 1982–1990: Architecture of the Spiritual World*. The Collected Works of Northrop Frye. Vol. 5. Ed. Robert Denham. Toronto: University of Toronto Press.

———. 1991. *The Double Vision: Language and Meaning in Religion*. Toronto: University of Toronto Press.

———. 1991. *The Educated Imagination*. Montreal: CBC Enterprises.

———. 1990. *Myth and Metaphor: Selected Essays, 1974–1988*, ed. Robert Denham. Charlottesville: University Press of Virginia.

———. 1990. *Words With Power: Being a Second Study of the Bible and Literature*. Markham, ON: Viking.

———. 1974. *Fearful Symmetry: A Study of William Blake*. Princeton, NJ: Princeton University Press.

———. 1971. *The Critical Path: Essays on the Social Context of Literary Criticism*. Bloomington: Indiana University Press.

———. 1963. *The Well-Tempered Critic*. Markham, ON: Fitzhenry and Whiteside.

———. 1957. *Anatomy of Criticism: Four Essays*. Princeton, NJ: Princeton University Press.

Hart, Kevin. 2004. *The Dark Gaze: Maurice Blanchot and the Sacred*. Chicago: University of Chicago Press.

Heidegger, Martin. 2000. *Elucidations of Hölderlin's Poetry*, trans. Keith Hoeller. Amherst, NY: Humanity Books.

———. 1993. *Basic Writings: From* Being and Time *to* The Task of Thinking. Rev. and exp. ed. Ed. David Farrell Krell. San Francisco, CA: HarperCollins.

———. 1993. "Letter on Humanism." In *Basic Writings: From* Being and Time *to* The Task of Thinking. Rev. and exp. ed. Ed. David Farrell Krell. San Francisco, CA: HarperCollins, 213–265.

———. 1993. "The Origin of the Work of Art." In *Basic Writings: From* Being and Time *to* The Task of Thinking. Rev. and exp. ed. Ed. David Farrell Krell. San Francisco, CA: HarperCollins, 139–206.

———. 1991. *The Principle of Reason*, trans. Reginald Lilly. Bloomington: Indiana University Press.

———. 1977. *The Question Concerning Technology and Other Essays*, trans. William Lovitt. New York: Harper Row.

———. 1972. *On Time and Being*, trans. Joan Stambaugh. New York: Harper and Row.

———. 1971. *On the Way to Language*, trans. Peter D. Hertz. New York: Harper and Row.

———. 1966. *Discourse on Thinking: A Translation of* Gelassenheit, trans. John M. Anderson and E. Hans Freund. New York: Harper and Row.

———. 1962. *Being and Time*, trans. John Macquarrie and Edward Robinson. New York: Harper and Row.

Lacoue-Labarthe, Philippe. 2007. *Heidegger and the Politics of Poetry*, trans. Jeff Fort. Urbana, IL: University of Chicago Press.

Mallarmé, Stéphane. 1982. *Selected Poetry and Prose*, ed. Mary Ann Caws. New York: New Directions.

———. 1956. *Mallarmé: Selected Prose Poems, Essays, and Letters*, trans. Bradford Cook. Baltimore: Johns Hopkins University Press.

Poland, Lynn. 1984. "The Secret Gospel of Northrop Frye." *Journal of Religion*, 64: 4, 513–519.

Sherbert, Garry. 2004. "Frye's Double Vision: Metaphor and the Two Sources of Religion." In *Frye and the Word: Religious Contexts in the Writings of Northrop Frye*, ed. Jeffery Donaldson and Alan Mendelson. Toronto: University of Toronto Press, 59–80.

NEW DIRECTIONS FROM OLD: RECONSIDERATIONS

PART IV

Northrop Frye and the Chart of Symbolism

John Ayre

As they prepared the *Anatomy of Criticism* for publication in the fall of 1955, Princeton University Press's senior editor Benjamin Houston and Northrop Frye knew they might be in for a rough ride. Douglas Bush, the press's major reader for the book, had given his blessing for its publication but groused about its excessive schematism. Schematism with its tables and geometric diagrams, either implied or manifest, never seems to have found a happy place in English studies. The only geometric model that has ever fully established itself is Freytag's Pyramid, which illustrates narrative resolution. Avoidance of such constructions in English studies is baffling since they are generally so common in the social sciences.

In his *Structural Anthropology*, for instance, published in 1963 and which has many affinities with the approach of the *Anatomy*, Claude Levi-Strauss unapologetically presents the reader with twenty-three tables and mandala-like diagrams showing aspects of Amazonian cultures. In *Tristes Tropiques*, Levi-Strauss goes even further in suggesting an all-encompassing single chart in which *all* behaviours and cultural expressions will find a place (160). Schematism belongs so much in structuralist territory that a Levi-Strauss follower, classicist Marcel Detienne, couldn't get through *The Gardens of Adonis* without some twenty-three tables and diagrams including a mandala showing "the cycle of the phoenix," a basic hierarchy of spice and bird symbols in Greek myths (36).

To soften the image of the *Anatomy*, Frye nevertheless suggested removing two harmless circular diagrams and a simple table of correspondences. The diagrams were two pie-like circles, one illustrating the specific forms of drama and the other showing the structures of plot and imagery. The table of correspondences is very simple, a trimmed down version of another table in *Fearful Symmetry*, showing how symbolic expressions fit into logical patterns (277–278). Frye's rejected mandalas and table were buried in his secretary's files and they didn't emerge until the Collected Works edition of the *Anatomy* came out in 2006 (364–365).

Tetradic diagram in
Byrhtferth's Manual

Certainly, killing the diagrams was tactically silly. To hide the inherent nature of the book in this manner was like trying to hide an elephant under a tea towel. The irony was that one of the most perceptive critics of the *Anatomy*, M.H. Abrams, then turned around and asked in his review: *Where* is the diagram? He confessed, "The whole is reminiscent of the medieval encyclopedic tables designed to comprehend the *omne scibile*; instinctively though in vain the reader looks for an appendix that will open out into a square yard of tabular diagram."[1]

Just as Frye once said the best thing to do with cosmological works like Dante's *The Divine Comedy* or Milton's *Paradise Lost* is to grab a pencil and start drawing, a few students did start drawing. While Frye himself had drawn many mandalas in his notebooks, he never came close to drawing the complete picture suggested in the Third Essay of the Anatomy with its circle of myths. He had to depend on others like Everett Frost, who tried to visualize the grand scheme with the six phases of each myth.[2]

However complicated these versions appeared, Frye's *Anatomy* diagram is based on a very simple structure: the cross in a circle. The vertical line represents the *axis mundi* of inspiration or spirituality and the horizontal line represents middle earth or mundane life. This basic structure is then packed, so to speak, with corresponding symbols, characters, and story types. The sorting is quite deliberate and logical and seems to follow basic psycholinguistic laws that determine that up is good and down is bad, up is bright and down is dark, up is paradisal and down is hellish, up is godly and down is satanic, up is pleasing and down is depressing, up is youthful and down is aged. One can go on suggesting many other of these dialectic positions.

Frye was simply using a form that had been around for a long time. Tables of correspondence have existed since the Roman times and in the Middle Ages; they were often turned into tidy arrangements like a tetradic diagram in *Byrhtferth's Manual*.[3] The circle combines months with astrological symbols with a quarterly division of the seasons and stages of life. Quite logically, the summer solstice is at the exact top and the winter solstice at the exact bottom. The idea was to combine parallel and contrasting aspects of life and experience in one diagram.

Another arrangement is the common medieval motif of the Wheel of Fortune, which is never less than pure geometry, and which Frye frequently used in the Third Essay of the *Anatomy*. At twelve o'clock is a king on a throne with crown and sceptre. At three o'clock is a figure in decline and at six o'clock is a wretched beggar in rags hanging on for dear life. For convenience I must confess that I am tempted to call this the Conrad Black wheel of fortune. At one time the mogul was at the top of the world. He sat in a pinstripe suit behind a massive desk in his Bay Street office. He is now wearing a dull prisoner suit in a jail in Florida. He hopes for better but Chicago judges turn down his appeals, refusing to let the wheel turn upward again.

One who used this kind of cosmological pattern was William Blake, whose well-known cruciform diagram of the mundane egg in his prophecy *Milton* presented Frye as a student with one of his first critical dilemmas about schematism.[4] It showed the Four Zoas laid out on a compass scheme with Urthona in the north and Urizen in the south. Adam is in the upper Urthona sphere and Satan in the lower Urizen sphere.[5]

Although more muted, similar geometrical shaping is obvious in other Blake paintings, including his series of the Last Judgment. The Last Judgment was a well-known motif in the Middle Ages and Renaissance, and while Christ is always at twelve o'clock in nearly all representations, Satan is sometimes absent or off to the right supervising devils torturing the sinners who are tumbling down into hell. In all his own versions, Blake put Satan at six o'clock precisely beneath Jesus, with a quite stunning *axis mundi* of enchained figures between the two. In all his versions, Blake was so interested in the up-down dialectic that he left out the usual horizontal line representing the crust on which middle earth—that's the life of you and me—exists.

Blake was an encyclopedist and like all good encyclopedists he created a wider context by packing his later Last Judgment paintings with biblical characters who don't always belong in *Revelation*. In a version Frye cites in *Fearful Symmetry* (414) and which Foster Damon charts in *A Blake Dictionary* (endpapers), Blake painted numerous biblical figures into the basic pattern. As in Dante's *Divine Comedy*, the wicked are arranged with increasing severity toward the bottom. On the left, the right hand of Christ, the good souls are either being awakened and sent on their way up or they are already there. Figures fly like wingless angels in a clockwise manner.

I should note that Tibetan Buddhists had a nearly identical motif of the Last Judgment. In place of Christ there is a youthful Buddha meditating in a pleasant landscape at twelve o'clock, while at six o'clock the black-skinned death god Yama dances in flames over a corpse. In one version, Yama's companion bull sexually violates the corpse. This form is unlikely to be the result of diffusion. It is likely the result of the way the human mind works in any culture.

I don't think that theologian Austin Farrer knew Blake's work, but in his 1949 book *A Rebirth of Images*, he devised a similar pattern to show

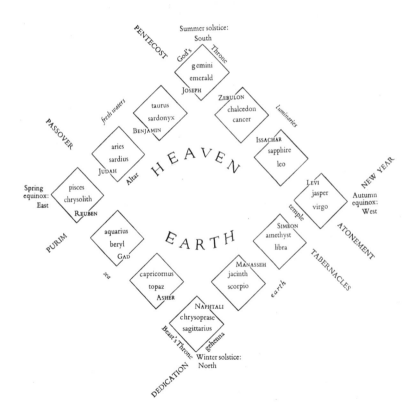

Farrer's schema

the structure of *Revelation* (unpaginated endpapers). Farrer's diamond shape is precisely divided in two, showing Heaven on top and Earth below. The zenith is God's Throne and the nadir is the Beast's Throne in the Jewish hell, gehenna. It is summer above and winter below.

Farrer noted that Gnostics who followed Valentinus regarded cosmological diagrams very seriously as spiritual charts. He guessed that St. John actually composed the Book of Revelation with a chart in front of him (185). Frye was most interested in this notion and it may have had especial appeal at the time because of his enthusiasm for the idea that such arrangements might give guidance to writers.

Frye read Farrer's book with great care and marked it up with annotations just a year before writing his most reprinted essay "The Archetypes of Literature," which offers a similar setup based on the seasons. Of course, this in turn led to the famous circle of myths of the Third Essay of the *Anatomy*, even though it entailed an embarrassing switch of seasons, in which Frye first associated spring with romance and summer with comedy, only to reverse it in the *Anatomy*.

While Blake and Farrer were dealing with only one crucial episode of the New Testament, however, a chart of the structure of the entire Bible could also be created and would appear very similar. The same could also be done with literature as a whole. The Shakespearian critic Wilson Knight, who taught at Trinity College at the University of Toronto from 1931 to 1940, was particularly sensitive to the old structure of symbolism. In the late thirties, Knight and Frye used to get together to talk shop. Frye did acknowledge that Knight's books had the effect on him that Chapman's Homer had on Keats.[6] While this is high praise, Frye never did provide many details of what he and Knight talked about. Frye once said he tried out his own early ideas about comedy on Knight but otherwise listened to Knight's monologue on all things Shakespearian.[7]

Knight had created a technique of laying out the symbolic universe. In his essay "On the Principles of Shakespearian Interpretation" in his 1930 collection *The Wheel of Fire,* Knight posited that "a Shakespearian

tragedy is set spatially as well as temporally in the mind" (3). He fully
applied his spatial method in *The Shakespearian Tempest*, published in
1932, and elsewhere quite openly and without a blush of embarrass-
ment defined spatiality as "spiritual."[8] Knight believed that the examination of symbolism, not the character analysis of the A.C. Bradley type,
was the key to understanding Shakespeare. He was quite blunt about
this: "To isolate such a [major] symbol clarifies our perception of the
whole play, whereas to isolate a 'character' distorts it" (*Shakespearean
Tempest* 17). Twice Frye endorsed the spatial method, almost parroting
Knight's view. In the *Anatomy* he says, "We begin to wonder if we cannot see literature, not only as complicating itself in time, but as spread
out in conceptual space from some kind of center that criticism could
locate" (17).

Noting the preponderance of tempest imagery in Shakespeare's
works, Knight set up a dialectic between the tempest as dark symbol
of disorder and music as the symbol of a higher world. Images and certain kinds of characters clustered together. Down below were characters
like Falstaff, Bottom, and Caliban (*Shakespearean Tempest* 105). Wolves
and bears were "recurrent tempest-beasts" (106). The "grand simplici-
ties" were the opposition of "tempests and music; night and day; summer and winter" (271). Knight went even further, explicitly associating
a kind of literary expression, tragedy, with a season, winter (273). It's a
logical association, but one can see how such an association can easily expand in a compass rose scheme, romance being the opposite of tragedy.

Although there is strongly implied structure here, Knight didn't actually sketch out a diagram until he was preparing a 1953 edition of the
Tempest book. Much more fell into place in a cruciform chart, and his
idea of "Shakespeare's Dramatic Universe" is like a trimmed down version of the Last Judgment with the top and bottom points clipped off
(xvi–xvii). The top category of "Bright Eternity" contains personalities
and qualities such as the Royal Child, Gods, Angels, Resurrection, and
Youth Eternal. At the bottom is Dark Eternity with Demonic Possession,

Hecate, Graves, and Death. Knight also added the category of Nothing. While this may be related to the theme of *Much Ado about Nothing*, its placement suggests darker contemporary connotations.

Since Knight provides space, he implies movement of characters and dramatic events within and without a sector of symbolism. For instance, he notes that the action of Hamlet operates in one dark lower corner of the chart full of ghosts, madness, death, and graves (xxi). In other words, Hamlet is trapped in darkness. With an arrow, Knight shows that romantic comedy moves the action from a lower zone to a higher one. He even provides an *axis mundi*, which he calls "Poetic Imagination," linking the nadir with the zenith.

We don't know, of course, how conscious Shakespeare was of his own cosmology. We do know, on the other hand, that Dante, Milton, Blake, and even modern novelists like Malcolm Lowry operated with a high degree of awareness. An interesting and perhaps surprising example is Charles Dickens, who published an article in 1850 about the wretched London slums in unequivocally apocalyptic terms. Presenting an image of hell, Dickens literally saw the reflection of the Prince of Darkness himself:

> I saw innumerable hosts, fore-doomed to darkness, dirt, pestilence, obscenity, misery and early death. I saw, wheresoever I looked, cunning preparations made for defacing the Creator's Image, from the moment of its appearance here on earth, and stamping over it the image of the Devil.[99]

Dickens titled the article "A December Vision." More an apocalyptic sermon than literary work, "A December Vision" does present a code for the dark characters, environments, and personal tragedies in *Oliver Twist*, which Dickens had finished just months before. In fact, *Oliver Twist* itself is saturated with dark, wintry images; the adjective "dark" is pervasive. Evil action takes place at night. It is frequently cold and raining. At least four times, Dickens explicitly makes an association between the character Fagin and the devil. Dickens is not simply describing, of course. Indirectly, he is condemning, and his condemnation automatically suggests a desire to move away from the darkness to a better world represented in the sentimental Chapter XXXII, which is set in spring and summer. *Oliver Twist* is not atypical. Novels such as *Moby Dick*, *Heart of Darkness*, and *Under the Volcano* reveal a similar preponderance of dark concentrated images with a hint of a brighter, better world above or beyond. In such works there is a cosmology, a structure of symbols, that presents both an abhorred and idyllic world, which in itself sets up a current of repudiation or acceptance. This is not necessarily conscious to the writer but it is nevertheless there doing its work, shaping symbolism and narrative in the actual work.

After the *Anatomy*, Frye himself stopped using excessively schematic thinking in his published work right up to *The Great Code*. At the same time, he continued using mandalas, diamond shapes, charts, and tables both in his private notebooks and on the blackboard in his classes. When he was Charles Eliot Norton professor for a year at Harvard in 1975, students applauded when he drew large circles on the blackboard in his mythology course early in the term. They knew they were receiving the genuine Frye.

Between 1964 and 1972, Frye had an almost secret career as he toiled away describing and sometimes sketching new schemas for a massive new 'Third Book" project he was going to call *The Critical Path* or *The Critical Comedy*. Clearly the interest and, I think, the fair success of his circle of myths was not enough for him. He really wanted to reinvent the wheel so to speak, and did so with a renewed sense of purpose:

All my critical career has been haunted by the possibility of working out a schematology, ie., a grammar of poetic language. I don't mean here just the stuff in F[earful] S[ymmetry] & A[natomy of] C[riticism] & elsewhere, but the kind of diagrammatic basis of poetry that haunts the occultists & others. (*TBN* 212)

Diagrams were as central at this stage as any he had done before the *Anatomy*. As before, he usually used the form of the cross in the circle. Despite its utility in his study *T.S. Eliot* and his major essay on Wallace Stevens, "The Realistic Oriole," Frye seemed to want to abandon the useful scheme of the cycle of the seasons. He did return to that in one instance by creating a simple "circles of images" in which four of the Greek gods were tied to seasons: Eros to summer, Adonis to autumn, Oedipus to winter, and Prometheus to spring (*TBN* 148). He weighed the usefulness of the image of Heraclitus's double gyre as central to Hopkins, Eliot, and Yeats (166). He again played with the Four Zoas cross. As he worked with these patterns, he believed there was a principle that if they were not significant they would "dry up" as he tried to wring meaning out them. Unfortunately, nearly all of them did dry up.

Frye would consider almost any other pattern, too, and in a droll entry, he pondered a schema based on the thirty-three-hole pattern of a board game he played with as a child in which it was necessary to clear off each triangular side of the board. He joked, "This game has the solution of my projected book on an I Ching model of augury. I record this because anyone reading these notes would assume that they were the work of a psychotic, so I may as well furnish the definitive proof of the fact" (*TBN* 192).

There is a dismaying irony here, because these later schemas came to little use quite possibly because their categories were not culturally resonant enough. They were the product of a neo-platonic mentality that perhaps found too much significance in bare form adorned by only a few often baffling points of identity like the names of Greek gods or Blake's Four Zoas. Nevertheless, Frye sometimes casually slipped one of his schemas into his published work perhaps hoping that it might ignite some interest. In *Fools of Time* he borrowed from Blake to define in Shakespeare the "tragedies of Urizen, tragedies of Luvah, and tragedies of Tharmas" (16). Likewise in *Words With Power*, he casually slipped in his HEAP (Hermes-Eros-Adonis-Prometheus) scheme (277).

Another factor complicating the creation of any universal pattern was the evolution of cosmologies. Frye did much work in defining how the Romantic poets, especially Blake and Shelley, had redrawn Western cosmology. Frye explored this extensively in *A Study of English Romanticism* and then in *Words With Power*, where he showed how the old pre-Romantic model was turned upside down so that the "down," the dark subterranean world with helpful Promethean figures, was now good and the "up," with an alienating God, was bad. In this model the subterranean devil is replaced by Prometheus. Frye wrote, "The real God, from Blake on, is not the descendit de coelis God of imposing order & recreation, but the Promethean God tearing loose from death & hell with smoke & grime all over his face, the mad treading-the-wine-press Messiah of Isaiah" (*RT* 111). In *Words With Power*, Frye went one step further into a third model by stripping out references to gods, high and low, and leaving the abstractions of "alienation imagery" at the top and "imaginative power ... often symbolized as under the earth or sea, like Atlantis" below (248).

In struggling to define a post-Romantic model of symbolism, Frye in fact seemed distinctly relieved at times to come across a clear representation of the old model even if ironically presented. He found it in the most unlikely of places: Paul Gallico's 1971 disaster novel *The Poseidon Adventure*, which he discovered in an airport bookshop. Frye was completely taken by the ideas that confirmed as much as Dante or Blake that there was a kind of symbolic chart all of us use in viewing the world. The novel is about an unstable ocean cruiser that is upended in a tsunami. Before it goes down forever, it floats upside down, giving a chance for a party of survivors to work their way up with great difficulty to the top of the boat, which of course is now the bottom.

In interviews Gallico always insisted that he was only a hardworking popular novelist trying to make as much money as possible. Yet in this disaster novel there is a full set of symbols, spatial references of Western mythology:

Up had always been good; down was bad. God and Heaven were up; Hell and the Devil were down. The road to damnation was the downward path. Resurrection was ascent…. Man's whole history had been an ascent … upwards, always upwards out of the ooze and slime of the sea, on to the land, higher and higher and now reaching out his arms to the planets. His mythology created the dwellers underground as misshapen dwarfs and monsters, the creatures of the upper air were exquisite, graceful, winged fantasies of light. (*Poseidon Adventure* 219–220)

Gallico tells us that the disaster happens on 26 December. The leader of the group of survivors is an obsessed Protestant minister named Frank Scott, who is an obvious Moses figure. He leads his group up through a labyrinth of wreckage, not knowing exactly where they are going but possessing a basic hunch that up is good and down is bad. He ends up giving a speech on a pile of metal wreckage called Mount Poseidon in which he calls on God to acknowledge himself knowing full well God can't, since God is an invention of man. While he knows he is hardwired with a cosmology with God on top, Scott knows there is nothing at the top. Half-crazed, he jumps to his death in an internal lake of seawater and oil explicitly called hell. Like Moses, he doesn't make it to the Promised Land. Few do. Despite their basic instinct to move upward to safety, in the end few of the characters do find safety for having followed the logic of the model. The model, in other words, was itself submerged in a destructive element and the high point wasn't high enough. The scale of the disaster was just too big.

Frye was so interested in the fact that Gallico appeared to be a novelist who knew precisely what he was doing, he planned to compare *The Poseidon Adventure* with Katharine Anne Porter's *Ship of Fools* (TBN 341). The effect may have pushed Frye toward a book on the Bible and its literary influence, since this was a clear case of the form and imagery of the Bible shaping a contemporary narrative.

Frye then did proceed to write *The Great Code* on the Bible with its pre-Romantic pattern of symbolism. It was almost an admission of defeat that the speculative patterns of the "*Third Book*" *Notebooks*, like HEAP (Hermes-Eros-Adonis-Prometheus), exhausted themselves before Frye could centrally apply them. Although *The Great Code* was viewed by critics as a complicated and even eccentric book with many themes ostensibly new to Frye, it was for Frye a return to old territory. The crux of the book, Frye admitted, was the analysis of symbolism in Chapter 6, with its Table of Apocalyptic Imagery and Table of Demonic Imagery. This is what his readers had been seeing since *Fearful Symmetry*.

Ultimately, this rather depressed Frye because of the sense that for the third time he felt he had not really progressed. In a remarkable self-denunciation he defined his three great books as not much more than a series of dumping grounds: "*The Great Code* is not volume one of anything: like the Anatomy & the Blake, it's volume zero, the book of fuck-all, the cast-skin, the excreta of dead decades (LN 62–63). Simply, he had failed to create a new diagram but no longer had great faith in working the old model.

Frye was now a critic often at war with himself. He had always wanted to define a structure based on what there was objectively in literature for the sake of education and possibly creative writers who might learn from it. When Wilson Knight built his tempest chart, he used only the symbols and points of identity that existed in Shakespeare. For the most part so did Frye in his published works. This was a process leaning more

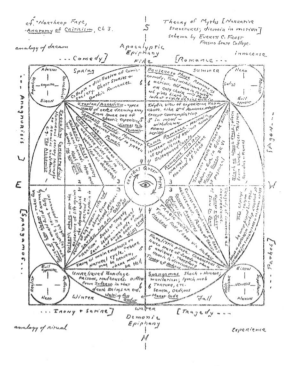

to the inductive, of seeing what there was and packing a structure with logically arranged symbols and characters.

Frye understood the dangers of what he was attempting. Any expansive pattern had an obvious tendency to take in fields around it. He firmly reminded himself, "This is a book about literature by a literary critic, using incidental & illustrative material from comparative mythology.... I'm not out to make a single construct out of mythology, but out of literature" (*TBN* 309). These personal reminders were serious but frequently violated. The evidence of the notebooks is that Frye's imagination was always yearning for the bigger picture he had seen in Blake, Spengler, and James Frazer. He'd seen it as well in Herman Hesse's novel *The Glass Bead Game*, which Frye read and annotated with great interest in the early 1970s. Hesse's vision of the Game possessed the grand sweep of a large, comprehensive chart of all there was in culture.

Of course, Frye had himself been playing the Glass Bead Game all his academic life with the same sense imparted by Hesse, that it was not just an entertaining parlour game but one devised to produce new perceptions. It was Hesse's conceit or fantasy that such a meditative game could be the core of a quasi-monastic movement, which Frye himself could neither instigate nor lead. Certainly, the question of meditation and spiritual architecture belongs more to the activities of a Kabbalah group than the needs of English Literature 101, so in the end it was an impossible task. However, there was one clear result of all his work in exploring cosmologies. As he always insisted, literature did have rules, even geometric form, which charted the areas of light and dark of our feelings, thoughts, and vision. If you start a spiritual journey you need a chart, and Frye always told us that the chart is already drawn in literature. It's full of pathways and, yes, new directions from old.

ENDNOTES

1   M.H. Abrams, "Anatomy of Criticism," Review of *Anatomy of Criticism* by Northrop Frye, *University of Toronto Quarterly* 28 (1959): 191.

2   Frost's conception of the mandala is reproduced in John Ayre, "Frye's Geometry of Thought," *University of Toronto Quarterly* 70 (2001): 836.

3   The tetradic diagram is reproduced in Stevens 71.

4   Frye's doubts are expressed in *Stubborn Structure* 176.

5   Blake's diagram appears in Keynes 523.

6   *Spiritus Mundi* 13.

7   Northrop Frye letter to John van Domelen, 6 November 1967.

8   *The Wheel of Fire* 6.

9   Dickens 21.

WORKS CITED

Damon, S. Foster. 1971. *A Blake Dictionary*. New York: E.P. Dutton.

Detienne, Marcel. 1977. *The Gardens of Adonis*. Hassocks, Sussex: Harvester Press.

Farrer, Austin. 1949. *A Rebirth of Images*. London: Dacre Press.

Frye, Northrop. 2006. *Anatomy of Criticism: Four Essays*. The Collected Works of Northrop Frye. Vol. 22. Ed. Robert D. Denham. Toronto: University of Toronto Press.

———. 2003. *Northrop Frye's Notebooks and Lectures on the Bible and other Religious Texts*. The Collected Works of Northrop Frye. Vol. 13. Ed. Robert D. Denham. Toronto: University of Toronto Press.

———. 2002. *The "Third Book" Notebooks of Northrop Frye, 1964–1972*. The Collected Works of Northrop Frye. Vol. 9. Ed. Michael Dolzani. Toronto: University of Toronto Press.

———. 2000. *Northrop Frye's Late Notebooks, 1982–1990: Architecture of the Spiritual World*. The Collected Works of Northrop Frye. Vols. 5–6. Ed. Robert D. Denham. Toronto: University of Toronto Press.

———. 1992. *Words With Power*. Toronto: Penguin Books.

———. 1976. *Spiritus Mundi*. Bloomington: Indiana University Press.

———. 1971. *Anatomy of Criticism*. Princeton: Princeton University Press.

———. 1970. *Stubborn Structure*. Ithaca: Cornell University Press.

———. 1969. *Fearful Symmetry*. Princeton: Princeton University Press.

———. 1967. *Fools of Time*. Toronto: University of Toronto Press.

Gallico, Paul. 1972. *The Poseidon Adventure*. New York: Dell.

Keynes, Geoffrey, ed. 1966. *Blake: Complete Writings*. London: Oxford University Press.

Knight, G. Wilson. 1986. *The Wheel of Fire*. London: Methuen.

———. 1953. *The Shakespearian Tempest*. London: Methuen.

Levi-Strauss, Claude. 1968. *Tristes Tropiques*. New York: Atheneum.

———. 1967. *Structural Anthropology*. Garden City, NY: Anchor Books.

Philip, Neil, and Victor Neuburg, eds. 1986. *Charles Dickens: A December Vision*. London: Collins.

Stevens, Anthony. 1991. *On Jung*. London: Penguin Books.

ACKNOWLEDGMENTS

I would like to thank Tom Willard for first alerting me to Wilson Knight's use of symbolic charts. Many thanks as well to Robert Denham and Margaret Burgess for locating references for me in Northrop Frye's vast Collected Works.

THE EARTH'S IMAGINED CORNERS:

Frye and Utopia

Michael Dolzani

A UTOPIAN tale traditionally begins by recounting how a traveller discovered utopia, usually by stumbling across it accidentally. I stumbled across "utopia" as a subject by editing two Frye texts, first the "Third Book" notebooks, and later the Collected Works edition of *Words With Power*. Somewhere around 1964, Northrop Frye began recording notes toward what he called the "Third Book"—that is, his third major work after *Fearful Symmetry* and *Anatomy of Criticism*. Since *Anatomy* was a "centripetal" approach, concerned with the formal relations of literature, the Third Book was to be about criticism and society. Its first subject was to be "contracts and utopias," and Frye's article "Varieties of Literary Utopias," published in 1965, was a preliminary study for it. With startling similarity, in notes recorded after he had finished *The Great Code* and *Words With Power*, Frye (at the other end of his career) again recorded plans for a "third book"—and again the preliminary subject was "contracts and utopias," which means it would have taken up from Chapter 8 of *Words With Power*, which speaks briefly of utopia as one of four aspects of the pattern of "creative ascent" from the depths below ordinary experience. Again there was a preliminary article, "Natural and Revealed Communities," on Thomas More's *Utopia*. Neither of these books was ever written, but the persistence of the preoccupation raises the question of why Frye should be so interested in the utopia, especially as he realized the limitations of what he called "so often a contrived and anxiety-ridden form" (*WP* 309).

Frye and utopia is a fitting subject with which to mark the fiftieth year since the publication of *Anatomy of Criticism*. In 1965, the same year as "Varieties of Literary Utopias," Angus Fletcher delivered a paper called "Utopian History and the *Anatomy of Criticism*." Its opening paragraph compares Frye to Georges-Eugène Haussmann, whom Napoleon III hired in the 1860s to modernize the city of Paris. Fletcher says, "[Like Haussmann,] Northrop Frye has cleared a 'dense confusion of houses in the center of the city' to create broad, unbroken avenues from one neighborhood to another. His *Anatomy of Criticism* is utopian city planning" (31). Frye's response, "Reflections in a Mirror," is gracious. He says, "I doubt if I can describe my ambitions for criticism more accurately than Mr. Fletcher does in his figure of the Haussmann boulevards which enabled Parisians, so to speak, to *see* Paris" (133). But a glance at any description of Haussmann's project will disclose that Fletcher's description is in fact deeply ambiguous: some admire Haussmann's design while others regard it as social engineering gone mad, the destruction of a traditional Paris that had grown up naturally and spontaneously since the Middle Ages, its winding streets not very efficient but having a crooked charm—in Blake's terms, it was the replacement of "living form" with "mathematical form." As a utopian project, Haussmann's redesign of Paris is unusual in that it was both realized, rather than merely imagined, and successful. Still, it strikingly points out how the typical criticisms of utopias are precisely the typical criticisms of the *Anatomy*:

that it achieves symmetrical design at the expense of the chaotic facts, and that it coerces individuality in the name of a collective whole.

What Fletcher does not say is that Haussmann's radial plan for the Parisian boulevards, usually taken as a bourgeois vision of rational efficiency, is actually an adaptation, conscious or not, of the most ancient of all city plans, one that is not rational but mythical. According to Joseph Campbell, the first cities were laid out according to a mandala pattern, of streets forming a cross, intersecting at the centre of a circle.[1] This plan reflected the mandala order of the cosmos: as above, so below, the temple in the central intersection forming the nexus between the heavens and the earth. *Anatomy of Criticism* is clearly laid out in a mandala pattern, as even the artist who designed the well-known purple cover of the Princeton paperback edition clearly recognized, and which Frye acknowledges in his later essay "Expanding Eyes." The horizontal timeline of Essay 1 intersects the vertically ascending phases of symbolism in Essay 2 in what Yeats would call a double gyre; the circle of mythoi in Essay 3 is followed by discussion of specific literary forms in Essay 4, each of which follows a cycle of variations comparable to the circle of fifths in music.

The first cities, with their mandala design, were *not* utopias, in the sense of humanly designed societies; rather, they were what Campbell calls "hieratic city-states," in which people lived lives ordered by a pattern given from on high. In this sense, Frye is not a modernizer but a traditionalist—and not fully a utopian either, since utopian speculation has only flourished in those eras in which humanity entertained the notion of designing its own order rather than accepting one from authority, tradition, and the gods. Yet he is not merely a traditionalist, either, not a Coleridge who sees the human "order of words" as patterned on the Christian Logos. The mandala of the *Anatomy is* a vision of the shape of human creation, not of conformity to a divine pattern, but human creation is somehow always a recreation of an order that humanity senses everywhere, yet which it did not itself create, what Wallace Stevens calls "reality" rather than "imagination." This double vision (I use the term advisedly) will become what the *Late Notebooks* and *Words With Power* refer to as the "dialectic of Word and Spirit."

But Frye's complex and qualified utopianism has another aspect. While the utopianism of the *Anatomy* is confined to the formal mandala patterns of literature in itself, the two "third books" that were to succeed it, early and late, were to be about the use of these patterns as models for the transformation of society. This involves us in looking at actual utopias, and seeing what power Frye's perspective has to clarify the whole utopian tradition. If we ask in what ways Frye's later thinking about utopia goes beyond that of the "Varieties" article, we can say that his later vocabulary gives him a more incisive way of defining utopia. A utopia is a vision of fulfilled concern, both secondary and primary. As he says in the last chapter of *Words With Power*,

> On the lower level is a vision of fulfilled secondary concerns, the sense of a political ideology that has some connection with the processes actually going on in society, or a religious community that has some relation in practice to its theoretical goals. On the higher level is a vision of fulfilled primary concerns, freedom, health, equality, happiness, love. (*WP* 309–310)

But what does it mean to fulfill a primary concern? This is not as simple a question as it may seem. If fulfilling the primary concern of food and drink were merely a matter of ensuring that everyone had a balanced diet, the enormous complex of images and stories in Chapter 7 of *Words With Power* would never have come into being. Something else is involved, as Frye partly indicates in *The Double Vision* by saying that primary concerns have a spiritual as well as physical aspect. Yet what in turn does *that* mean? In answer, let us turn to a book published in 1963, immediately before the first utopia article. *The Educated Imagination* is usually regarded as a popularization of the ideas of the *Anatomy*, but it also looks forward to Frye's next phase, in which he asks, "What good is the study of literature? What is its function in human civilization?" To answer these questions, Frye deposits us on a desert island and confronts us with the Darwinian imperative of humanity in the state of nature: survival. The task of humanity is to build a human world out of an inhuman one. The function of literature is to guide this process by providing us with model worlds: the world of realized human desire and fulfilled concern that we see in comedy and romance, and the world of thwarted desire and repressed concern in tragedy and irony. The human quest is to construct the former by deconstructing the latter.

The desert island scenario has probably been suggested by Shakespeare's *Tempest*, in which Prospero builds a new world on an island in the middle of "nowhere," bringing into being a new reality through the creative illusions of his "art," while what most of the characters think is real turns out to be illusion. *The Tempest* is something of a meditation on the possibility of utopia, as it clearly indicates through Gonzalo's speech describing the ideal commonwealth. But the narrative of creation, destruction, and recreation of a more ideal—and, in that sense, utopian society—through a meaningful ordeal is far older than *The Tempest*, and ultimately stands revealed as one modulation of the primary pattern of all mythology and literature.

On the Classical side, it begins with the *Odyssey*, in which Odysseus, who, like Prospero, is something of an artist of illusion, undergoes a transformative ordeal of wandering and rebirth out of the underworld in the first half, then rebuilds his kingdom and community in the second. Homer's plot is taken up by Virgil in the *Aeneid*, to which *The Tempest* repeatedly alludes, except that the "new world order" Aeneas builds after his own wanderings and descent to the underworld is not his private kingdom but the future Roman Empire. Dante's Christian equivalent of this is the second canto of the *Purgatorio*, in which souls after death are ferried across the waters to an island, singing a verse from the Psalms about the Exodus, where they undergo ordeals that are less punitive than recreative, and by doing so are enabled to regain both the Arcadia of the Garden of Eden and the utopia of the New Jerusalem. But Dante knows that Virgil's story is a secular type for which the antitype is the plot of the Bible itself, in which humanity falls into a desert wilderness and undergoes an Exodus to a promised land, where a holy city will later be built; the Old Testament plot is recapitulated in the career of Christ, who is tempted in the desert, descends to the underworld after his crucifixion, and who will someday return to gather us into the New Jerusalem. In the meantime, our task is to imitate Christ by building Jerusalem in England's green and pleasant land, in the words of Blake, who, as always, provides for Frye the key to the great code of art.

The theme of these works is indeed the utopian theme of realizing primary and secondary concern through the creative ordeal of constructing an ideal society, but what relation do they bear to the actual genre of utopia, whose Classical origin is in Plato's *Republic* and whose modern origin is in Sir Thomas More? Why, too, does that genre seem to be so limited? With the exception of William Morris's *News from Nowhere*, it is hard to think of another utopia that qualifies as a major work of literature. A preliminary answer is that most utopias become trapped on the level of realized secondary concern. This means that typical utopias speak the language of ideology first, and only secondarily the mythical and metaphorical language of primary concern. The reason they do so is that they accept the limits of "fallen" or desert-island reality as final and so at some point are forced into a compromise that sacrifices primary concern; that is to say, they are "realistic"—they ask: What is the best of all possible worlds that can be built within the limits of the kind of ordinary experience most of us recognize as final, the limits of what we call the human condition and earlier ages called the fall of man? Whatever the specifics of the design, the best that can be done is to impose some kind of rational, hierarchical ordering on the anarchic nature of human desire, at the cost of a certain amount of authoritarian coercion and sacrifice of the individual to the good of the collective whole. But what else can be done? For a few significantly brief moments in history, the experiment of a kind of anarchism was tried, as in the 17th century in England during the Civil War and in North America during the 1960s. The results were not encouraging, and society fell back into the safe, repressive confines of conservative order again. This oscillation between the authoritarian and the antinomian is what Blake called the Orc cycle, in which the fiery figure of desire is sacrificed by, or, worse, ages into, the figure of frozen inhibition.

What Frye is suggesting, I think, especially in his later work, is a revival of utopian thinking on a new basis, one that breaks out of the Orc cycle of the endless rise, decline, and fall of civilizations based on the "rational" and the "realistic," a new basis in the spirit of Blake's Los, the figure of creative imagination. Here, we return to our question of what it means to fulfill primary concern. The most encyclopedic of all utopian studies, *Utopian Thought in the Western World*, by Frank E. Manuel and Fritzie P. Manuel, published in 1979, includes so many utopias, founded on so many contradictory bases, that the Manuels wonder whether a typology of utopias is in fact possible.[2] Let me suggest one, based on Frye's desert island model in *The Educated Imagination*. The essential quality of that castaway situation, Frye says, is alienation: human identity consists of an isolated dot of consciousness, an ego or "I" surrounded by concentric circles of otherness or "not-I." The ego can be alienated (1) even from itself, as in various states of split consciousness; (2) from the body; (3) from the refractory instrument of language; (4) from lovers; (5) from society; (6) from nature; and (7) ultimately from God. The varieties of utopian experience tend to specialize in the healing of one of these particular modes of alienation.

For example, the humanistic psychologist Abraham Maslow, friend of the Manuels at Brandeis, spoke of creating a eupsychia, a society of mental health. Maslow shared with B.F. Skinner the idea that a science of human behaviour could be applied to the modelling of an improved society; in "Varieties of Literary Utopias," Frye contrasted Skinner's utopia, *Walden 2* (1948), with Robert Graves's *Watch the North Wind Rise* (1949), a religious utopia based on Graves's theories of the White Goddess. Since Skinner's behaviourism is one of the psychological theories that Maslow's humanistic psychology was designed to supersede, we observe here a principle that runs throughout the utopian tradition, namely, that shared concerns do not necessarily make for agreement. On the ideological level, one person's utopia is another's demonic parody. However, with the process of individuation described by the depth psychology of Jung, we move from the attunement of the ego to the social collective in a kind of vital tension, which is the concern of the utopia proper, to the integration of the ego with the unconscious, which awakens a much larger identity called the Self, which transcends opposites, including those of the individual and the collective. We notice here that as utopianism moves from secondary toward primary concern, it becomes the chrysalis of a kind of vision larger than itself.

Another acquaintance of the Manuels in the 1960s, Herbert Marcuse, along with Norman O. Brown, spoke of the renovation of society through the liberation of the body. Traditional utopias, with their stress on rational control, tend toward asceticism, the body and the senses being regarded as the seat of disruptive irrational impulse, an attitude surviving as late as George Bernard Shaw. But the idea that utopia would have to accommodate the pleasure principle as well as reason and the reality principle began to appear in the wake of the Romantic revolution. In this regard some remarkable speculations of Fourier first became widely available in time for the sexual revolution of the 1960s. But libido is not the only aspect of the body to be liberated. Aldous Huxley's utopian *Island* (1962) incorporates the results of Huxley's experiments with the expansion of the senses by hallucinogens, as recorded in his book *The Doors of Perception*. As the allusion to Blake's *Marriage of Heaven and Hell* intimates, this is no mere hedonism, like the soma habit of

Brave New World: to expand the senses is to expand the reality we live in. Once again what begins as utopianism expands beyond itself toward apocalyptic vision.

The reform of language is a project with utopian overtones. In the 17th century, a number of theorists, among them Leibniz, sought to invent a universal analytical language based on logical categories, usually those of Aristotle, the utopian dream being that if people thought in a logical language, they would be forced to think logically. Borges hilariously satirizes one of these attempts in "The Analytical Language of John Wilkins,"[3] but the hope that reform of the one would produce reform of the other because language organizes thought was an influence on the school of analytical philosophy in the early 20th century. The development of symbolic logic, with its relationship to mathematics, seemed to corroborate this hope. On a more popular level, the general semantics of Alfred Korzybski enjoyed several decades of popularity among those who wanted to improve society by improving its language, this time through the innovation of non-Aristotelian categories. The early sections on the functions of language in *The Great Code* and *Words With Power* suggest that Frye's own utopianism could be characterized as a kind of linguistic reform. Teaching people to think in the language of myth and metaphor may help people break their own "mind forg'd manacles" and thus transform society.

From the courtly love phenomenon of the Middle Ages descends a tradition of individuals whose ideal romantic love, though it alienates them from the loveless society that surrounds them, forms the potential core of a society of kindred loving spirits. The Classical ancestors of the courtly love tradition are Plato's dialogues on love, the *Symposium* and the *Phaedrus*. These are not usually thought of as belonging to the utopian tradition in the manner of the *Republic*, but in fact they do belong to it, not merely because of their content, the vision of an individual climb up the ladder of love, but also because of the *Symposium*'s social *cena* or banquet setting. A group of kindred spirits are shown bound

together by a webwork of all the varieties of love, that is, social, romantic, and spiritual—philia, Eros, and agape, to use the formal lingo—
united in those most communal of human acts: eating, drinking, and
conversation. This is itself an implicit social model and has a parallel in
the endings of Shakespearean comedies, whose happy endings include
not merely weddings but a renovated and more truly communal society. The relaxed, conversational *cena* atmosphere belongs to Frye's own
genre of the anatomy, and accounts for the geniality of his style, which
is not merely temperamental but also functional, the attempt at a non-
coercive inclusiveness: it is quite literally *inviting*.

Various economic, political, and technological utopias attempt to
reorganize the social order. This is of course the main area of the traditional utopia, and is therefore so vast that we have no time to explore it,
except to point out that, as many commentators have noticed, utopias
gravitate toward socialism, whether as a corrective to the abuses of feud-
alism, monarchy, and aristocracy, as in More, or to the abuses of capitalism, as in Bellamy's *Looking Backward*, among many others, including a
youthful Northrop Frye, member of the Co-operative Commonwealth
Federation, the early Canadian socialist party. One does not have to be a
Marxist to see that the social and political superstructure rests on a material basis. Frye shares with Marxism the idea that humanity's relation
to its physical environment comes to focus in the activity of production;
human beings are not suited to living directly in nature, like animals,
and so must produce various means of insulating themselves from that
raw environment—shelter, clothing, and so forth—which is why "property" is made a primary concern in the last chapter of *Words With Power*
in close relation to the theme of utopia. "Property" is a part of the material world that is no longer objective but instead has become "proper"
to us, a part of our identity. Technology, symbolized by the Promethean
harnessing of fire for everything from cooking to metalworking to heat-
ing our shelters, has been a central theme in utopias from Bacon's *New
Atlantis* onward.

The symbol of a material world recreated in the form of human desire is the city, and traditional utopias tend to be visions of an ideal urban life. Frye's own sensibility was urban; his early experience as a circuit rider in Saskatchewan gave him a taste of what Marx called "the idiocy of rural life," and he does not in his earlier work seem to have much temperamental affinity with the idea of "living in accord with nature," nature being to him a Canadian landscape of vast distances and harsh winters.

Still, in his first utopia article, Frye recognizes that the urban utopia may seem artificial and sterile in comparison with what he calls the Arcadia, a vision of a simplified human life as part of nature rather than in domination of it, the term "Arcadia" disclosing the tradition's roots in the pastoral tradition. Thoreau's *Walden* is one of many works that, while not actually utopias, are inescapable in any discussion of utopian ideas. Its English counterpart, William Morris's *News from Nowhere*, is the ancestor of a line of environmentalist utopias, including Ernest Callenbach's *Ecotopia* and one of the finest utopias of modern times, Kim Stanley Robinson's *Pacific Edge* (1988).

Finally, some utopias, from Campanella's *City of the Sun* onward, have been founded on religious principles. Utopias are sometimes seen as a challenge to Christianity because they view human life as perfectible, or at least improvable, by unaided human effort. There is some truth to this: instead of an earthly utopia, Dante gives us the City of Heaven in the *Paradiso*, whose citizens are bound in the *cena* intimacy of the heavenly rose of love, where Dante is invited to join in by an act of drinking the water of life. Apart from its light shows and special effects, the entire *Paradiso* (in contrast to the *Inferno*) consists of nothing but endless revelatory *cena* conversation. However, to some extent, that ideal community can be modelled on earth, not by the Church as a hierarchical institution, with its inevitable bureaucracy, but by some less compromised form of organization. More and Rabelais, in his utopian Abbey of Thelème, were attracted to an uncorrupted form of monasticism; others, like Gerard Winstanley and his 17th-century commune of Diggers, have used as a model an idealized conception of the early Christian community. Using what Frye called the royal metaphor, Paul speaks of Christians as being one in the body of Christ; conventional Christianity merely ideologically interprets the body of Christ as the institutional Church, but Inner Light Protestants like Winstanley, and Milton in *Areopagitica*, understood that human groups are always outwardly divided. The only real unity is inward, the sharing of a "common spirit," a notion secularized by Rousseau's "general will." Rational self-interest may manage to keep society from disintegrating into the war of all against all, but it knows nothing of real community, producing only an aggregate of self-seeking egos.

Of course, the more ambitious utopias incorporate more than one of these strands. Despite that, this catalogue, brief and incomplete as it is, is enough to give the impression of the utopian tradition as a hopeless jumble of conflicting visions. The common root, however, is the conquering of human alienation in its possible forms, the alienation of self from Other, of subject from object, the human condition as constituted by a split, as Lacan puts it, or by a "cloven fiction," in the words of Blake. Utopia is the attempt to mitigate this universal affliction: as it moves from secondary toward primary concern, it expands into an attempt to transcend it altogether. It is easy enough to deem such an attempt quixotic, even dangerous in its obsessive pursuit of an impossible perfection. And yet, despite Marx's contempt for utopias, it is a Marxist critic, Fredric Jameson, who counsels against too easy a dismissal of utopian speculations, not only because "the desire called utopia" is ineradicable, a part of human nature, one of "the most archaic longings of the human race," but also because, if we do so, we risk falling into a resigned passivity that human life can never be changed, that the current system is inevitable—an attitude that the powers that be encourage in every age, most definitely including that of postmodern capitalism.[4]

Insofar as they fall victim to the obsessive anxieties of ideology and secondary concern, all these types of utopia may become blueprints for tyranny. However, utopias have some more positive roles. The first, as we have just implied, is critical. By presenting an alternative, Frye says, a utopia may make us aware of the limitations of our own society and its ideology—may make us aware, at least, that there *are* alternatives, despite the inevitable attempt of every ideology to convince us that its solution, the social contract that is the embodiment of its ideology, is the only one possible. This view of utopia as critique is quite close to Paul Ricoeur's in *Lectures on Ideology and Utopia*, a title whose paired terms are comparable to Frye's "contracts and utopias." As I have also just implied, it is likewise close to the view of Fredric Jameson in one of the most important recent studies of utopia, *Archeologies of the Future*.

Jameson accepts a generic distinction between two types of utopian parody: the "critical dystopia" and the "anti-utopia." The critical dystopia "is a negative cousin of the Utopia, for it is in the light of some positive conception of human social possibilities that its effects are generated" (Jameson 198), whereas the anti-utopia is "informed by a central passion to denounce and to warn against Utopian programs" (199) of any sort whatsoever, on the grounds of the intractable corruption of human nature. Anti-utopias are thus inherently conservative, probably the greatest example in English being *Gulliver's Travels*, though Jameson cites Orwell's *1984* as a contemporary example. The critical dystopia is a negative model that implies a positive one; the utopia is a positive model that implies a negative one. Because one person's utopia is another's demonic parody, this means that utopias may come in pairs, a later utopia providing a critique of an earlier one. The famous instance is Morris's *News from Nowhere*, written as a horrified response to Bellamy's *Looking Backward*.

However, one of Jameson's major virtues as a utopian theorist is his informed knowledge of science fiction, the most important laboratory of utopian thought experiments in our time. Two science fiction utopias, Ursula LeGuin's *The Dispossessed* (1974) and Samuel Delany's *Trouble on Triton* (1976) repeat the dialectical pattern of Bellamy and Morris, but in the opposite direction. LeGuin, who makes her home in Oregon, depicts a utopia whose ideology is a synthesis of Taoism and anarchism (a later novel, *Always Coming Home* [1985], adds aspects of hunter-gatherer lifestyle as preserved in Native American societies). Delany, who as a gay male has spent most of his life in large cities like New York and San Francisco, criticized LeGuin's naïve pastoralism, as he saw it, in an essay entitled "To Read *The Dispossessed*," and then in his own novel, whose society offers the greater diversity of lifestyles possible in large cities, abetted by technology, so much so that Delany calls it a "heterotopia." Jameson is interested in such utopian conflicts—especially when they occur between two fellow members of the left rather than between radical and conservative—because, as a Marxist, he does not believe we can transcend ideology and its conflicts, and, as a post-structuralist, he does not believe we can transcend the Lacanian subject, who is constituted by a split. To him, every utopia is written against other utopias, which provides a social model that shows up the limitations of other models. As readers, then, we must read dialectically, using other utopias to show up the inevitable one-sidedness and contradictions the author has attempted to transcend or repress. All utopias deconstruct; none can provide a final solution, except in the most chilling sense: "It is not a matter of solving this dilemma or of resolving its fundamental antinomies: but rather of producing new versions of those tensions ... and make of the antinomy itself the central structure and the beating heart of Utopia as such" (Jameson 214). LeGuin's way of doing this is by honestly disclosing the limitations, tensions, and corruptions in her own utopia: the subtitle of *The Dispossessed* is *An Ambiguous Utopia*.

Delany does it by creating a pluralist utopia, a heterotopia. Jameson quotes the following passage from Robert Nozick's *Anarchy, the State and Utopia* (1974):

Utopia will consist of utopias, of many different and divergent communities in which people lead different kinds of lives under different institutions.... People will leave some for others of spend their whole lives in one; [however,] no one can *impose* his own utopian vision upon others. (qtd. in Jameson 217)

But the protagonist of *Trouble on Triton* remains perfectly miserable no matter what lifestyle change he opts for, and Delany echoes LeGuin by subtitling his book *An Ambiguous Heterotopia*.

A step further is taken by Jameson's former doctoral student, Kim Stanley Robinson:

Yet Kim Stanley Robinson's monumental Mars trilogy (1993–1996) is only one example of a new formal tendency, in which it is not the representation of Utopia, but rather the conflict of all possible Utopias, and the arguments about the nature and desirability of Utopia as such, which move to the center of attention. Here the new form seems to reach back and to incorporate within itself all the oppositions and antinomies we have identified in an earlier chapter; to reorganize itself around the increasingly palpable fact and situation of ideological multiplicity and radical difference in the field of desire. Utopia now begins to include all those bitter disputes around alternative diagnoses of social miseries and the solutions proposed to overcome them. (Jameson 216)

These "bitter disputes" are not necessarily debilitating: recreated on a higher level, they may be turned from an ideological Negation into creative Contraries, to use Blakean language, and utopia would be raised to the level of Blake's Eden or "Mental War," the creative process of the Imagination itself, whose energy is "eternal delight" and whose exuberance is beauty. What Frye adds to the utopian tradition is a sense of what makes that recreation possible. In Notebook 44 appears the following cryptic entry about the proposed book on utopias: "Mandala symbolism (I could call the book, or a chapter in it, *The Squared Circle*, or, *The*

Earth's Imagined Corners). The stuff about Solomon's temple in the first volume of Purchas" (*LN* 1:233). In the opening of *Hakluytus Posthumus, or, Purchas His Pilgrimes* (1625), Samuel Purchas notes that in order to build his temple, Solomon first sent an expedition to the land of Ophir to gather materials, including a mysterious variety of tree out of which were made both the pillars of the temple and "harps and psaltries." Purchas says that this is a type of which the voyages of the apostles are the antitype; but also that, in a higher sense, every Christian is a ship wayfaring through a stormy sea. In the margin beside the interpretation of this ordeal, Purchas cites 1 Corinthians 3:12, the passage traditionally referred to as the scriptural basis for the idea of purgatory (Purchas 6–7). One implication for utopias here is that utopia is not only a structure, a static order: it can also be seen as a purgatorial process, identical to the pattern of life itself when lived at its greatest intensity; the process of transformation, at once individual and social, that turns the desert island into paradise; the voyage to Ophir that is simultaneously the building of the temple; the unity of Yeats's two poems about "Sailing to Byzantium" and "Byzantium" itself.

But Purchas goes on to say that, on an anagogic level, Solomon's Jerusalem and temple are types of the New Jerusalem of the Book of Revelation: "This is that holy Citie figured by that of Palestina, where all is brought to Solomon, that God may bee all in all" (7). That last phrase, about God being all in all, from 1 Corinthians 15:28 (see *WP* 187), also haunts Milton in *Paradise Lost*. Purchas ends with a fireworks passage of extraordinary metaphorical identifications that elaborates on what "all in all" might really mean in the apocalypse; this is the passage I suspect Frye had in mind for his book about utopias:

> Thus in divers respects are they [the redeemed] both the Citie, and Temple, and Kings and Priests, and Instruments, and all these and none of these: For I saw no Temple herein, saith that Seer, for the Lord God Almightie, and the Lambe are the Temple of it.

Even God himselfe shall be with them, and God shall bee all in all: and as hee is incomprehensible, so Eye hath not seene, nor eare hath heard, nor can the heart of man conceive what God hath prepared for them that love him. (8)

"All in all" signifies a state not of mere collective unity, in which the individual and particular is subsumed into the whole as a drop into the sea; collective unity belongs to the lower realm of ideology. Instead, it signifies a unity that includes diversity, in which all the concentric circles of alienated otherness are reunited to the centre without loss of their own multiplicity and variety. The only language that can express such a state of "interpenetration" is the language of metaphor, the language of the spirit.

This is the fulfillment of primary concern, not merely as material or even collective social satisfaction but as the surmounting of alienation through metaphorical identification, a revelation achieved through what Frye's late work calls "ecstatic metaphor." Such a fulfillment is not possible in the world as we know it. But none of us lives entirely in the world as we know it. We also live in an otherworld, a world of imagination that is "nowhere," but to which we escape periodically with the feeling of exhilarated liberation that rejuvenates us. At one point in the *Late Notebooks*, Frye says that "every work of fiction is a Utopia, i.e., a nowhere, a description without place" (1:229). Where the world of alienation is a world of work, this otherworld is a world of play: "Work, if I'm right," Frye says, "is the basis of *contract*; play of *Utopia*" (LN 1:121). Play can be seen as the point and goal of work, the Sabbath vision at the end of six days of disciplined effort. But true work in fact *becomes* play, increasingly and cumulatively as it goes on. When we begin to acquire any new skill, from playing a musical instrument to writing poetry to interpreting literature, the process is tedious, laborious, discouraging. But the more we acquire, through practice and the right habits, the more the alienation between ourselves and the instrument, ourselves and the words or metre, is minimized, and we are released into the *sprezzatura* exuberance of play: the play of sounds, of images, of ideas; the dance of patterns. This can expand from a single skill to a whole lifestyle: Maslow says that the self-actualized person's work *is* his or her play, a notion close to William Morris's that the essence of utopia is creative work, which is not work at all by usual standards. The true utopia is the vision of life as playful expanded from the individual to the social level. A final expansion beyond that brings us to the apocalyptic vision of "all in all." To this end, in all senses, Frye quotes Blake: "'More is the cry of a mistaken soul,' said Blake: 'less than all cannot satisfy man'" (*WP* 187). What began as "nowhere" ends in an "all" the eye has not seen, the ear has not heard, the heart has not conceived, yet that love recognizes as its necessity.

ENDNOTES

1 See for example Campbell's "The Symbol without Meaning," in *The Flight of the Wild Gander: Explorations in the Mythological Dimensions of Fairy Tales, Legends, and Symbols*, 1969 (New York: HarperCollins, 1990), 151–153. In the last months of his life, Frye told Germaine Warkentin that he was eagerly reading a book she had recommended to him, Joseph Rykwert's *The Idea of a Town: The Anthropology of Urban Form in Rome, Italy and the Ancient World* (Cambridge, MA: MIT, 1988): email from Germaine Warkentin, 7 May 2007.

   Rykwert's point of departure is the fact that the Romans may have borrowed from the Etruscans a grid-like pattern of urban organization having cosmological implications. A notebook from 1946–1950 shows that Frye had been aware of that fact for almost half a century. See *Northrop Frye's Notebooks on Romance*, ed. Michael Dolzani, 32.

2 In a footnote to "Varieties of Literary Utopias," Frye indicates that his main reference was Glenn Negley and J. Max Patrick, eds., *The Quest for Utopia: An Anthology of Imaginary Societies* (Garden City, NY: Doubleday Anchor, 1962).

3 See Jorge Luis Borges, "The Analytical Language of John Wilkins," 106–110.

4 See Fredric Jameson, *Archaeologies of the Future*, 295. Utopian thinking is implicitly revolutionary and future-oriented: its social model breaks with tradition and received authority. As such, leftists are naturally attracted to it. Russell Jacoby has recently published two books about utopianism, *The End of Utopia: Politics and Culture in an Age of Apathy* (2000) and *Picture Imperfect: Utopian Thought for an Anti-Utopian Age* (2007). Conservative models of ideal societies usually involve a return to the values of the past.

WORKS CITED

Borges, Jorge Luis. 1966. "The Analytical Language of John Wilkins." In *Other Inquisitions, 1937–1952*, trans. Ruth L.C. Simms. New York: Washington Square Press, 106–110.

Campbell, Joseph. 1990. "The Symbol without Meaning." *The Flight of the Wild Gander: Explorations in the Mythological Dimensions of Fairy Tales, Legends, and Symbols.* 1969. New York: HarperCollins, 151–153.

Delany, Samuel R. 1996. *Trouble on Triton: An Ambiguous Heterotopia.* 1976. Hanover, NH: Wesleyan University Press.

———. 1977. "To Read *The Dispossessed*." *The Jewel Hinged Jaw: Notes on the Language of Science Fiction.* Elizabethtown, NY: Dragon Press, 239–308.

Fletcher, Angus. 1966. "Utopian History and the Anatomy of Criticism." In *Northrop Frye in Modern Criticism: Selected Papers from the English Institute*, ed. Murray Krieger. New York and London: Columbia University Press, 31–73.

Frye, Northrop. 2004. *Northrop Frye's Notebooks on Romance.* The Collected Works of Northrop Frye. Vol. 15. Ed. Michael Dolzani. Toronto: University of Toronto Press, 32.

———. 2000. *Northrop Frye's Late Notebooks, 1982–1990: Architecture of the Spiritual World.* The Collected Works of Northrop Frye. Vol. 5. Ed. Robert D. Denham. Toronto: University of Toronto Press.

———. 1990. "Natural and Revealed Communities." In *Myth and Metaphor: Selected Essays, 1974–1988*, ed. Robert D. Denham. Charlottesville: University Press of Virginia, 289–306.

———. 1990. *Words With Power: Being a Second Study of the Bible and Literature*. New York: Harcourt Brace Jovanovich.

———. 1970. "Varieties of Literary Utopia." *The Stubborn Structure: Essays on Criticism and Society*. Ithaca: Cornell University Press, 109–134.

———. 1966. "Reflections in a Mirror." In *Northrop Frye in Modern Criticism: Selected Papers from the English Institute*. Ed. Murray Krieger. New York: Columbia University Press, 133–146.

Jameson, Fredric. 2005. *Archaeologies of the Future: The Desire Called Utopia and Other Science Fictions*. London and New York: Verso.

LeGuin, Ursula. 1974. *The Dispossessed: An Ambiguous Utopia*. New York: Avon.

Manuel, Frank E., and Fritzie P. Manuel. 1979. *Utopian Thought in the Western World*. Cambridge, MA: Harvard University Press.

Negley, Glenn, and J. Max Patrick, eds. 1962. *The Quest for Utopia: An Anthology of Imaginary Societies*. Garden City, NY: Doubleday Anchor.

Purchas, Samuel. 1905. *Hakluytus Posthumus, or, Purchas His Pilgrimes: Containing a History of the World in Sea Voyages and Lande Travells by Englishmen and Others*. Vol. 1. Glasgow: James MacLehose and Sons.

Ricoeur, Paul. 1986. *Lectures on Ideology and Utopia*, ed. George H. Taylor. New York: Columbia University Press.

Robinson, Kim Stanley. 1996. *Blue Mars*. New York: Bantam.

———. 1994. *Green Mars*. New York: Bantam.

———. 1993. *Red Mars*. New York: Bantam.

———. 1988. *Pacific Edge*. New York: Tom Doherty Associates.

Transcending Realism:

Northrop Frye, the Victorians, and the *Anatomy of Criticism*

J. Russell Perkin

NORTHROP FRYE'S scholarly career spanned many decades, and he responded to many of the different concerns of each of them. The author of the *Anatomy of Criticism* and *The Modern Century* seems to encapsulate the mid-20th century, the era of optimism about technology and unprecedented expansion of higher education. *The Critical Path* and some of Frye's essays on education are shaped by the social protest and campus radicalism of the late 1960s. Recognizably a figure of the 1980s, the author of *The Great Code* and *Words With Power* is engaged with theoretical questions about language and culture; he also anticipates and influences the re-emergence of religion on the intellectual and political horizons of the 21st century.

But as a Victorianist, I am accustomed to reading thinkers who are obsessed with origins, and if we look at Frye with this in mind we discover that his intellectual origins, as a man who was born in 1912 into a cultural milieu that was not especially forward-looking, were solidly rooted in the 19th century.[1] In "Literature and Society," a 1968 lecture at the University of Saskatchewan and one of his more autobiographical public addresses, Frye describes the form of literary experience that he encountered in the 1920s as "Victorian—Victorian in its moral earnestness, its mixture of idealism and realism, and above all in being entirely a reading culture.... It was inevitable that my reading should be based on the great nineteenth-century novelists, to be followed, in my midteens, with some of the realists who had succeeded them" (*RW* 178). In this essay, I will concentrate on the *Anatomy of Criticism*, whose fiftieth anniversary was commemorated by the "New Directions from Old" symposium, and I will attempt to read the *Anatomy* as a response to this Victorian view of literature, and a critique of those forms of evaluative or social criticism for which Victorian realism was a pinnacle of literary achievement.

Although he is reacting against the Victorians, Frye is by no means dismissive of that period, unlike some writers of the early 20th century, such as Lytton Strachey.[2] Frye acknowledges the significance of these writers in an important essay, "The Problem of Spiritual Authority in the Nineteenth Century" (*StS* 241–256). In fact, after Blake and Milton, some of the thinkers who influenced him most were Victorian prose writers, such as Carlyle, Arnold, Mill, Newman, and especially Ruskin.[3] In them he found reference points for his discussions of humanistic education—for what in *The Critical Path* he terms the "educational contract"[4]—and in John Ruskin he found a thinker who had kept alive the tradition of biblical typology. In the *Anatomy*, Frye notes,

> Ruskin has learned his trade from the great iconological tradition which comes down through Classical and Biblical scholarship into Dante and Spenser, both of whom he had studied carefully, and which is incorporated in the medieval cathedrals he had pored over in such detail. (*AC* 10)[5]

Frye's own critical approach, like that of Ruskin, derives from Christian typological interpretation, though in both of these critics there is much more latitude than would be found in orthodox religious exegesis, so that both have something in common with cultural anthropology. Harold Bloom noted the similarity between Ruskin and Frye in the introduction to his anthology of *The Literary Criticism of John Ruskin* when he wrote,

> Ruskin is one of the first, if not indeed the first, "myth" or "arche-typal" critic, or more properly he is the linking and transitional figure between allegorical critics of the elder, Renaissance kind, and those of the newer variety, like Northrop Frye, or like W.B. Yeats in his criticism. (xvi)

Bloom's introduction to a new Princeton University Press edition of the *Anatomy* in 2000 is a revealing case study in the anxiety of influence.[6] He pays tribute to Frye and his resistance to the orthodoxies of the 1950s, but feels compelled to cut the *Anatomy* down to size, saying that he is not as fond of it as he once was (vii), and that "*Anatomy of Criticism*, in this year 2000, is not much of a guide to our current wilderness; yet, what is?" (viii). It is interesting to note in passing that Bloom alludes to Matthew Arnold in this statement; Arnold's biblical trope of "criticism in the wilderness" has had a long life, perhaps because every critic aspires to be Moses.[7] Ruskin is also mentioned in Bloom's introduction; Bloom says that Frye "is probably best thought of as Ruskin a century later" (x). One would have to qualify that by saying that Frye is characteristically far more balanced and less anxious than Ruskin ever managed to be.[8]

Though Frye may owe more to another, later Victorian, Sir James Frazer, he does indeed have many affinities with John Ruskin. For example, in *The Queen of the Air* Ruskin defines a myth as "a story with a meaning attached to it, other than it seems to have at first" (296). Frye of course uses the terms "myth" and "mythos" in several distinct senses in the *Anatomy*, but in the "Tentative Conclusion," immediately following a reference to *The Queen of the Air*, he notes that "in literary criticism myth means ultimately *mythos*, a structural organizing principle of literary form. Commentary, we remember, is allegorization, and any great work of literature may carry an infinite amount of commentary" (*AC* 341–342). Frye and Ruskin share not only this attitude to myth but also a habit, no doubt derived from their evangelical Protestant childhoods, of ending an essay with what can be called an anagogic conclusion, a visionary passage that often includes a biblical allusion and moves from the immediate topic to something of much wider significance.[9] The conclusions to the various essays in the *Anatomy* illustrate this well, as do many of Frye's other conclusions; in Ruskin the visionary imagery that concludes each of the two essays in *Sesame and Lilies* would provide a good example. It may be of related significance that for both critics the public lecture was the genre out of which most of their books evolved; they are both in effect secular preachers.

My focus on Frye and the Victorians arises from the fact that my primary area of specialization as a scholar is the literary and intellectual culture of the Victorian period: the prose writers, poets, and novelists such as Matthew Arnold, Alfred Tennyson, and George Eliot who explore the social and spiritual condition of 19th-century England. I have a strong interest in the realist tradition of English fiction, from Fielding and Richardson through Austen and the great Victorians to James, Conrad, and Forster, and among my guides to that period have been what Frye calls "public critics" (see *AC* 8), such as the humanists F.R. Leavis and Lionel Trilling, and the Marxists Raymond Williams and Terry Eagleton.

I first seriously studied Frye in a course on literary history taught by Professor Brian Corman at the University of Toronto in 1984–1985, and throughout my subsequent teaching career Frye has been the critic and theorist I have found most consistently useful as a guide when teaching literature to undergraduates (I think here especially of the *Anatomy* and of the writings on Shakespeare, Milton, and the Bible and literature). As a result, I have read Frye extensively over the last twenty years. I mention these details as background to the fact that when it came to my own period, Frye's map of literature did not present a very familiar landscape. Certainly, he talks about the major Victorian cultural prophets, but he also has a lot to say about writers who have not been central to recent trends in the field, for example, William Morris and Samuel Butler. He is far more comfortable discussing Scott as a writer of romance than writing about the Victorian realists,[10] and when he does mention major figures in the realist tradition it is often to illuminate them from a surprising perspective, as he does with his comment that "the early novels of George Eliot ... are influenced by the romance, and the later ones by the anatomy" (*AC* 312). Frye's essay on James, the favourite author of his teacher Pelham Edgar, is certainly not his best piece of criticism, and one initially feels that he misses the point of much of what James is about, but by concentrating on James's use of romance and occult elements he does draw attention to something essentially strange and significant in James's fiction, and by the end of it one comes to think that perhaps he understands James quite well after all.[11] Frye focuses on a number of James's lesser-known works, such as *The Other House* and *The Sense of the Past*, relating them thematically to the major works and suggesting that James's preoccupation with ghosts represents his desire to explore the limits of realism: "A ghostly world challenges us with the existence of a reality beyond realism which still may not be identifiable as real" (*EAC* 122).

One of Frye's more interesting and extended discussions of realist fiction comes in "Myth, Fiction, and Displacement" (1961), in which he uses as an example Anthony Trollope's *Last Chronicle of Barset*, noting that "the main story line is a kind of parody of a detective novel" (*EICT* 409). Anticipating later critics influenced by narratology, Frye shows how sophisticated are the narrative techniques employed by Trollope, the apparently artless realist. The action in a Trollope novel, Frye says, is not really the plot but rather "resides in the huge social panorama that the linear events build up" (*EICT* 409). This explains why in the whole tradition of mimetic fiction from Defoe to Arnold Bennett, the plot is a conventional, mechanical device with connections to the structure of conventionalized popular fiction.

Harold Bloom refers to Frye's "essentially irenic tendencies" (Foreword ix), and certainly in his published works, as opposed to his diaries and notebooks, Frye rarely disputes the positions of other critics. However, it is possible to read the *Anatomy* as a largely hidden polemic (a concept I derive from Bakhtin)[12] against the ethical criticism of the 20th century that regarded Victorian realism as a high point of literary achievement, thereby denigrating other literary modes that Frye valued highly. F.R. Leavis is not named in the index to the *Anatomy*, but Frye's attack on evaluative criticism takes in the judgments of the *Scrutiny* school as well as the polemics of T.S. Eliot (whom Frye does mention), and Leavis is most evident in the reference to "maturity" as an evaluative criterion. Frye writes that "it is not hard to see prejudice in Arnold, because his views have dated: it is a little harder when 'high seriousness' becomes 'maturity,' or some other powerful persuader of more recent critical rhetoric" (*AC* 22).

A.C. Hamilton points out that in saying that criticism is not a matter of value-judgments, Frye is reacting to the influence of Leavis (*Northrop* 23), although Hamilton also notes that for Leavis himself value-judgments are not prior to engagement with the text (21). But Frye did not think that it was the task of the literary critic to construct traditions, or as we might say today, canons; he often says that traditions construct themselves, by virtue of the fact that some texts are more rewarding to study than others, and some texts—his usual example is Shakespeare— just refuse to go away.[13] He concludes the "Polemical Introduction" to the *Anatomy* with a discussion of value judgments (*AC* 20–29), and returns to the issue in the "Tentative Conclusion," where he links such judgments to social anxieties, and glances again at Leavis with a reference to "great traditions":

> Culture may be employed by a social or intellectual class to increase its prestige; and in general, moral censors, selectors of great traditions, apologists of religious or political causes, aesthetes, radicals, codifiers of great books and the like, are expressions of such class tensions. (*AC* 346)

Frye explores this line of thought further in *The Critical Path*.

Frye does explicitly mention Leavis in "Criticism, Visible and Invisible":

> F.R. Leavis has always commanded a good deal of often reluctant respect because of the moral intensity he brings to his criticism, and because of his refusal to make unreal separations between moral and aesthetic values. Reading through the recent reprint of *Scrutiny*, one feels at first that this deep concern for literature, whether the individual judgements are right or wrong, is the real key to literary experience, and the real introduction that criticism can make to it. But as one goes on one has the feeling that this concern, which is there and is a very real virtue, gets deflected at some crucial point, and is prevented from fully emerging out of the shadow-battles of anxieties. (*StS* 79)

Criticism for Frye is of course a structure of knowledge, not a matter of taste or evaluation. It is interesting that he illustrates this in the introduction to the *Anatomy* by a contrast between two Victorian sages, Arnold and Ruskin. Frye compares Ruskin's analysis of the meaning of some of the names of Shakespeare's characters—what Frye calls one of the "curious, brilliant, scatter-brained footnotes to *Munera Pulveris*"—with

Matthew Arnold's condemnation of Ruskin's analysis as "a piece of extravagance" in which Ruskin, forgetting "all moderation and proportion," betrays "the note of provinciality" (*AC* 9). According to Frye, Ruskin "is attempting genuine criticism" (9), while "it is Arnold who is the provincial" (10). At the end of the *Anatomy*, Frye notes that Ruskin's *Queen of the Air* is a late example of the allegorization of myth that was so common in medieval and Renaissance criticism (341).

Frye offers his own contribution of archetypal criticism not as the one correct form of criticism but rather as the level that helps make connections among all the other approaches. From the perspective of my own teaching experience, I find this one of the most valuable enduring insights in the *Anatomy*. I advertise my first-year introduction to literature course as featuring texts "from Sophocles to Steven Spielberg," and I have found that the most helpful way to assist students to order their literary experience is to look at the archetypal patterns that link ancient texts, canonical English texts, and contemporary popular culture. This seems to me a much more valuable form of cultural studies than applying modish and tendentious theoretical models to the products of the contemporary cultural industry.[14]

It is not news to point out that Frye regards what in the second essay of the *Anatomy* he calls the "descriptive" level of meaning as of secondary importance in literary interpretation: it is preceded by the "literal" and is only a step on the way to the archetypal and anagogic phases. For Frye, literature is not primarily about knowledge of the world, and this relegates to secondary status much psychological as well as social and political criticism.[15] He discusses this issue in *The Critical Path*, where he puts the *Anatomy of Criticism* into context, explaining how it was opposed to the deterministic criticisms that sought to ground literary study in some other discipline (characteristically, Frye refers to Freudian biographical studies as the "Luther-on-the-privy" approach [*CP* 18]). This clears the way for Frye to write about how he thinks criticism can be genuinely socially engaged; one would do well to remember that *The Critical*

Path is subtitled *An Essay on the Social Context of Literary Criticism*.[16] It would be salutary if present-day students of literature could be introduced to Frye's analysis of the conceptual framework appropriate for literary study, for at the moment it seems that one's least literate student is able to critique Western patriarchal imperialism in virtually any text that is assigned, even if the text has not been read, and no self-respecting job candidate would dare give an interview talk without prominently advertising the interdisciplinary theorists on whom his or her approach was grounded.

In attacking the realist tradition, and lingering Victorian pieties, Frye had a major Victorian precursor in Oscar Wilde, as he acknowledges a number of times. In his book on the *Anatomy of Criticism*, A.C. Hamilton notes the importance of Wilde's influence on Frye.[17] In his notorious English Institute paper, W.K. Wimsatt made a glancing reference to Wilde as part of his general disparagement of Frye's critical achievement (107); Frye blandly replied that Wimsatt must have found "much more than beautifully cadenced nonsense" in his work, since Wimsatt got a number of things right, including the influence of Wilde's "Decay of Lying," "which Messrs. Ellmann and Feidelson were quite right in putting at the beginning of their collection of documents of *The Modern Tradition*" ("Reflections" 134). In "The Double Mirror," the acknowledgment of Wilde comes with more than a hint of envy, perhaps even an anxiety about belatedness: "It was Oscar Wilde who defined, in two almost unreasonably brilliant essays, the situation of criticism today" (*NFR* 87). For Frye, Wilde marks the beginning of modern criticism, as the comment in response to Wimsatt makes evident, and Frye is ahead of his time in taking Wilde seriously as the last of the Victorian cultural prophets, rather than just seeing him as an aesthete and comic dramatist.

Wilde's criticism plays a central role in *Creation and Recreation*. There Frye writes,

I find it easy to get hooked on Wilde. His style often makes him sound dated, and yet he is consistently writing from a point of view at least half a century later than his actual time. He is one of our few genuinely prophetic writers, and, as with other prophets, everything he writes seems either to lead up to his tragic confrontation with society or reflect back on it. (*NFR* 36–37)

Frye often asserted, as he does in the *Anatomy*, that the direct experience of literature is not something that can be communicated (*AC* 11–12); what is taught is knowledge about literature—that is, the criticism of literature. Frye's distinguishing between experience and knowledge explores what Wilde puts much more epigrammatically in "The Critic as Artist": "Education is an admirable thing, but it is well to remember from time to time that nothing that is worth knowing can be taught" (349). As an educator, Frye would probably not have wanted to endorse that statement, but at the same time it is clear that the scholarly study of literature is just the stage on which Frye hopes that a visionary experience will be enacted for both the student and the teacher.[18] "Reflections in a Mirror," Frye's 1966 response to the English Institute papers discussing his work, contains a very interesting comment on Lionel Trilling's "On the Teaching of Modern Literature." After summarizing Trilling's argument, Frye states,

> There is no way out of this: for better or worse, criticism is part of an educational process in which *Macbeth* is taught to children, and in which a certain insulation against emotional impact is a sign of cultivated taste. Teachers are occupationally disposed to believe in magic, and it is not surprising that many of them should cherish the illusion that they are best able to charge their students' batteries directly with the authors they teach if they do not admit, even to themselves, that all teaching is a transposition of literature

into criticism, of passion and power and anguish into pattern and craftsmanship and the following of convention. If, that is, they can keep on assuming that the direct experience of literature can somehow be, if not actually taught, at least communicated. (138)

Wilde's dialogue "The Critic as Artist" equates criticism and creativity, rejecting Arnold's notion that criticism is the activity of the desert, prior to the promised land of a creative epoch. Art should not imitate life, as does the tedious three-volume novel that "anybody can write" (358). "For," Wilde writes, "Life is terribly deficient in form," and therefore, from "the artistic point of view," it is "a failure," whereas "there is no mood or passion that Art cannot give us" (375). Similarly, the critic's task is not, as Matthew Arnold thought it to be, to see the object as it really is; in the view of Wilde's Socratic interlocutor Gilbert, "the primary aim of the critic is to see the object as in itself it really is not" (369). Art is the product of the creative imagination, not of sincere passions, or, as Wilde so memorably puts it, in a phrase beloved of Harold Bloom: "All bad poetry springs from genuine feeling" (398). Writing at the end of the 19th century, Wilde anticipated the turn of critical attention to the role of the reader that would come in the next century, with the demise of the notion of the artist as a unique and superior order of human being. Wilde's critic is the exemplary or ideal reader, or, in Frye's words in *Creation and Recreation*, "the representative reader" (*NFR* 75).

These issues are also explored in Wilde's briefer dialogue "The Decay of Lying," which is a sustained attack on the Victorian doctrine of realism and the Wordsworthian pieties about nature.[19] The speakers are named Cyril and Vivian, after Wilde's sons. "The Decay of Lying" anticipates much that Frye has to say in his critical works. As Frye sums up the dialogue in *Creation and Recreation*, its main thesis "is that man does not live directly and nakedly in nature like the animals, but within an envelope that he has constructed out of nature, the envelope usually called culture or civilization" (*NFR* 37). The verbal part of this envelope is what

Frye analyzes as mythology, the total structure of language created by human beings, with literature at its heart. Wilde laments the way that the Church of England has embraced rationalism, for it seems to him a silly concession to realism. He writes,

> As for the Church I cannot conceive anything better for the culture of a country than the presence in it of a body of men whose duty it is to believe in the supernatural, to perform daily miracles, and to keep alive that mythopoeic faculty which is so essential for the imagination. (317)

In the maxims of his new aesthetics, at the conclusion of "The Decay of Lying," Wilde says that life imitates art far more often than art imitates life, and that the proper aim of art is the telling of lies, in the sense of beautiful untrue things (what Frye less poetically will call hypothetical verbal structures). "As a method," Vivian tells Cyril, "realism is a complete failure," giving us literary works with characters so devoid of interest that "they would pass unnoticed in a third-class railway carriage" (303).

As Frye interprets Wilde, the desire for realism is a search for emotional reassurance, the desire to find something recognizable in a work of art rather than allowing oneself to be confronted with the strangeness of a truly creative vision. Wilde satirizes the tedious realism, as he sees it, of the 19th-century novel, notably Mary Augusta Ward's *Robert Elsmere*, but he reserves his most scathing language for the fiction of Zola, whose characters "have their dreary vices, and their drearier virtues. The record of their lives is absolutely without interest. Who cares what happens to them?" (296). These unreadable works all result from the mistaken idea that the artist should imitate nature, when really it is nature that imitates art. Wilde also denies that Balzac is a realist: "He created life, he did not copy it," and his "imaginative reality" is contrasted with Zola's "unimaginative realism" (299).

Frye himself is not so dismissive of Zola. He agrees with Wilde to the extent that he sees Zola, along with Dreiser, as exemplary of "the documentary naturalism" in which "literature goes about as far as a representation of life, to be judged by its accuracy of description rather than by its integrity as a structure of words, as it could go and still remain literature" (*AC* 79–80). Zola thus is largely to be identified with the descriptive phase of literary symbolism, as Frye defines it in the second essay of the *Anatomy*. On the other hand, if the critic stands back even from a novel by Zola, the "organizing design" or "archetypal organization" will become apparent: "If we 'stand back' from a realistic novel such as Tolstoy's *Resurrection* or Zola's *Germinal*, we can see the mythopoeic designs indicated by those titles" (140).

I will conclude this discussion with a more extended quotation from one of the rhapsodically poetic passages that occur frequently in Wilde's dialogues.[20] The imagery of this passage calls to mind Frye's account of the anagogic phase of symbolism, and it is interesting that Wilde even uses the word "archetypes":

> Art finds her own perfection within, and not outside of, herself.
> She is not to be judged by any external standard of resemblance.
> She is a veil, rather than a mirror. She has flowers that no forests
> know of, birds that no woodland possesses. She makes and un-
> makes many worlds, and can draw the moon from heaven with a
> scarlet thread. Hers are the 'forms more real than living man,' and
> hers the great archetypes of which things that have existence are
> but unfinished copies. Nature has, in her eyes, no laws, no uni-
> formity. She can work miracles at her will, and when she calls
> monsters from the deep they come. ("Decay" 306)

Considering that Frye was one of the first to portray Wilde as a serious thinker, perhaps the current serious interest in Wilde can serve to show a way back to Frye's criticism, even for those of an earnestly trivial turn of mind. As I have implied earlier, I think a recovery of the key points made in the *Anatomy of Criticism* offers the best hope of avoiding the mindless gulf that seems to be opening between literary studies and cultural studies, since Frye knows so much more about both of those practices, and about the connections between them, than most people currently engaged in either of them.

ENDNOTES

1   It is worth noting that Frye's parents were married in the late 19th century—John Ayre describes their marriage in a section of his book entitled "A Nineteenth-Century Home" (19–23)—and that Northrop Frye, their third child, was born when his mother was forty-one years old. In the interviews with David Cayley, Frye describes himself as in effect having been "brought up by grandparents" (*Northrop* 42).

2   One writer with whom the young Frye felt many affinities was George Bernard Shaw, and I am grateful to Germaine Warkentin for pointing this out to me. While Frye came to reject Shaw's social utopianism, preferring Spengler's "vision of cultural history" to "the onward-and-upward people ... such as Bernard Shaw and H. G. Wells, who had obviously got it wrong" (*SM* 113), he refers to Shaw frequently, and his own epigrammatic wit and trenchant style surely owe something to Shaw.

3   Ruskin is prominently mentioned in A.C. Hamilton's list of thinkers who influenced Frye (*Northrop* 213). In "Expanding Eyes," Frye says that Ruskin had "come to influence me a great deal" (*SM* 111). Frye's fascination with Victorian prose can be connected to the Nineteenth-Century Thought course he taught. See Robert Denham's Introduction to Frye's diaries (*Diaries* xxvii) and numerous references to the course throughout the diaries. Frye describes how he came to teach the course in "The Critic and the Writer" (*WE* 472). See also "Some Reflections on Life and Habit," *MM* 141.

4   See *CP*, Part Seven, 158–171. Toward the end of the book, Frye writes that "the chief mythical schemata of the twentieth century were outlined in the nineteenth, and a critic

concerned with the stereotypes of social mythology finds little that is essentially new in this field in the century since *Culture and Anarchy*" (166).

5   See Frye's review of Joan Evans's *John Ruskin* (*Canadian Forum*, 1955): "The thing that seems to me to hold Ruskin together is iconography: the sense of a vast system of design and occult correspondences manifesting itself in art and revealed by nature, which inspires alike his interest in architecture and in crystals, in the Bible and in clouds, in Greek myths and in brotherhoods of devout gardeners" (*ENC* 243).

6   Robert Denham discusses the complexities of Bloom's relationship to Frye in his own Editor's Introduction to *Anatomy*; see *AC2* xvii–xix, lxi–lxiv.

7   See my study of Arnold and Frye for the dynamics of Frye's love-hate relationship with Arnold. Bloom does not mention Arnold very frequently, especially not his work as a critic.

8   In "Literature as Possession," Frye wrote, "There have been many great critics, such as Coleridge or Ruskin, or their followers like G.K. Chesterton and others, who seem to be incapable of making an aesthetic judgment. They make no statement about literature not coloured by anxieties of some kind" (*EICT* 305).

9   This habit of Frye's is noted by Lee (Introduction to *NFR* xix) and by Pásztor (124).

10 Scott is a very frequent point of reference in *The Secular Scripture*. See in particular the autobiographical anecdote at the beginning of the book (*SeS* 4–6).

11 See "Henry James and the Comedy of the Occult" (*EAC* 109–129). James has been an author of particular interest to those critics concerned with the relationship between literature and society whom Frye terms public critics. Some examples that come to mind are F.R. Leavis, Lionel Trilling, Irving Howe, Cynthia Ozick, Joseph Epstein, and Martha Nussbaum.

12 In *Problems of Dostoevsky's Poetics*, Bakhtin writes that "in a hidden polemic the author's discourse is directed toward its own referential object, as is any other discourse, but at the same time every statement about the object is constructed in such a way that, apart from its referential meaning, a polemical blow is struck at the other's discourse on the same theme, at the other's statement about the same object" (195). David Lodge notes in *After Bakhtin* that "scholarly discourse is in fact saturated in the kind of dialogic rhetoric that Bakhtin named 'hidden polemic'" (94), but most critics cite or name their adversaries to a greater degree than does Frye. Given Leavis's fondness for controversy, one even wonders whether Frye consciously avoided naming him in the *Anatomy*.

13 The discussion of value judgments was one of the most controversial aspects of the *Anatomy*, and Frye revisits the topic in the 1965 "Letter to the English Institute," in the 1968 essay "On Value-Judgments" (*StS* 66–73), and in the 1975 essay "Expanding Eyes" (*SM* 99–122), among other places. In his foreword to the *Anatomy*, Bloom wonders whether Frye's faith that canons can construct themselves without the need for overt value judgments would have survived in an age when "Margaret Cavendish, Duchess of Newcastle, and Lady Mary Chudleigh have usurped the eminence of John Milton and Andrew Marvell." Then, realizing that he is trying to project his own anxieties onto the shade of Frye, he concedes, "His high sense of irony doubtless would sustain him" (viii).

14 As Hayden White observes, practitioners of cultural studies "have not on the whole found much of use in Frye's work" (29), in part because of the heavy Marxist influence on the field. However, both White and Wang Ning argue for the relevance of Frye's work to cultural studies. See also A.C. Hamilton's comments in "Legacy," especially 8–13. Robert Denham comments in "A Frye Centre Proposal" that Frye's cultural criticism is "a dimension of his thought that merits more attention than it has received" (3).

15 Robert Alter has taken issue with this approach as it manifests itself in Frye's manner of reading the Bible. Alter's own critical practice, before he turned to the literary analysis of the Bible, was shaped by his comparatist study of the European tradition of the novel; Frye, who was not a linguist in the way that Alter is, was formed by his study of Renaissance comedy and the traditions of romance and mythopoeic epic.

16 Similarly, it is easy to forget that the subtitle of *Culture and Anarchy* is *An Essay in Political and Social Criticism*.

17 Hamilton discusses Wilde and Frye several times. See especially 276n29. Michael Dolzani describes Wilde's "Decay of Lying" as one of Frye's "favourite works of criticism" in an interview included in the first of the three CBC programs comprising David Cayley's *The Ideas of Northrop Frye*.

18 See also the discussion of literary experience and literary scholarship in section 1 of *CP*, especially 25–33.

19 Compare this passage from Frye's essay "The Rhythms of Time": "Later in the century, Oscar Wilde remarked, in *The Decay of Lying*, which is really a manifesto of romantic and mythical writing as opposed to realism: 'M. Zola sits down to give us a picture of the Second Empire. Who cares for the Second Empire now? It is out of date. Life goes on faster than Realism, but Romanticism is always in front of Life'" (*MM* 167). Frye alludes

to the same passage from Wilde, without directly quoting it, in *Creation and Recreation* (*NFR* 39).

20 In an excellent introduction to an anthology of Wilde's prose, Linda Dowling writes of Wilde's "'poetic' prose" that "nothing has worn less well with modern-day readers, perhaps, than this sort of elaborate writing" (xxv), but she adds perceptively, "yet the point of such passages in their original contexts is always clear: they are evidence of the global change that may be wrought in individual consciousness by imaginative art. The critic speaks differently because the world has become different to him" (xxvi).

WORKS CITED

Alter, Robert. 2004. "Northrop Frye Between Archetype and Typology." In *Frye and the Word: Religious Contexts in the Writings of Northrop Frye*, ed. Jeffery Donaldson and Alan Mendelson. Toronto: University of Toronto Press, 137–150.

Ayre, John. 1989. *Northrop Frye: A Biography*. Toronto: Random House.

Bakhtin, Mikhail. 1984. *Problems of Dostoevsky's Poetics*, trans. and ed. Caryl Emerson. Minneapolis: University of Minnesota Press.

Bloom, Harold. 2000. Foreword. *Anatomy of Criticism*. By Northrop Frye. Princeton: Princeton University Press, vii–xi.

———. 1965. Introduction. *The Literary Criticism of John Ruskin*. New York: Da Capo, ix–xxvii.

Cayley, David. 1992. *Northrop Frye in Conversation*. Concord, ON: Anansi.

———. 1990. *The Ideas of Northrop Frye*. CBC Ideas Program. CBC Radio. 19 February, 26 February, and 5 March. Repeated 25, 26, 27 March 1997.

Denham, Robert. 2004 (December). "A Frye Centre Proposal." Unpublished MS.

Dowling, Linda. 2001. Introduction. *The Soul of Man Under Socialism and Selected Critical Prose*. By Oscar Wilde. London: Penguin, vii–xxvii.

Ellmann, Richard, ed. 1982. *The Artist as Critic: Critical Writings of Oscar Wilde*. 1968. Chicago: University of Chicago Press.

Frye, Northrop. 2006. *Anatomy of Criticism: Four Essays*. The Collected Works of Northrop Frye. Vol. 22. Ed. Robert D. Denham. Toronto: University of Toronto Press.

———. 2006. *The Educated Imagination and Other Writings on Critical Theory, 1933–1963*. The Collected Works of Northrop Frye. Vol. 21. Ed. Germaine Warkentin. Toronto: University of Toronto Press.

———. 2005. *Northrop Frye's Writings on the Eighteenth and Nineteenth Centuries*. The Collected Works of Northrop Frye. Vol. 17. Ed. Imre Salusinszky. Toronto: University of Toronto Press.

———. 2001. *The Diaries of Northrop Frye, 1942–1955*. The Collected Works of Northrop Frye. Vol. 8. Ed. Robert D. Denham. Toronto: University of Toronto Press.

———. 2000. *Northrop Frye on Religion Excluding The Great Code and Words with Power*. The Collected Works of Northrop Frye. Vol. 4. Ed. Alvin A. Lee and Jean O'Grady. Toronto: University of Toronto Press.

———. 2000. *Northrop Frye's Writings on Education*. The Collected Works of Northrop Frye. Vol. 7. Ed. Jean O'Grady and Goldwin French. Toronto: University of Toronto Press, 470–475.

———. 1990. *Myth and Metaphor: Selected Essays, 1974–1988*, ed. Robert D. Denham. Charlottesville and London: University Press of Virginia.

———. 1990. *Reading the World: Selected Writings, 1935–1976*, ed. Robert D. Denham. New York: Peter Lang.

———. 1976. *The Secular Scripture: A Study of the Structure of Romance*. Cambridge, MA: Harvard University Press.

———. 1976. *Spiritus Mundi: Essays on Literature, Myth, and Society*. Bloomington and London: Indiana University Press.

———. 1971. *The Critical Path: An Essay on the Social Context of Literary Criticism*. Bloomington and London: Indiana University Press.

———. 1970. *The Stubborn Structure: Essays on Criticism and Society*. London: Methuen.

———. 1966. "Letter to the English Institute, 1965." In *Northrop Frye in Modern Criticism: Selected Papers from the English Institute*, ed. Murray Krieger. New York: Columbia University Press, 27–30.

———. 1966. "Reflections in a Mirror." In *Northrop Frye in Modern Criticism: Selected Papers from the English Institute*, ed. Murray Krieger. New York: Columbia University Press, 133–146.

———. 1957. *Anatomy of Criticism: Four Essays*. Princeton: Princeton University Press.

Hamilton, A.C. 1994. "The Legacy of Frye's Criticism in Culture, Religion, and Society." In *The Legacy of Northrop Frye*, ed. Alvin A. Lee and Robert D. Denham. Toronto: University of Toronto Press, 3–14.

———. 1990. *Northrop Frye: Anatomy of His Criticism*. Toronto: University of Toronto Press.

Krieger, Murray, ed. 1966. *Northrop Frye in Modern Criticism: Selected Papers from the English Institute*. New York: Columbia University Press.

Lee, Alvin A., and Robert D. Denham, eds. 1994. *The Legacy of Northrop Frye*. Toronto: University of Toronto Press.

Lodge, David. 1990. *After Bakhtin: Essays on Fiction and Criticism*. London: Routledge.

Pásztor, Péter. 1999. "Reading Frye in Hungary: The Frustrations and Hopes of a Frye Translator." In *Rereading Frye: The Published and Unpublished Works*, ed. David Boyd and Imre Salusinszky. Toronto: University of Toronto Press, 122–139.

Perkin, J. Russell. 2005. "Northrop Frye and Matthew Arnold." *University of Toronto Quarterly* 74: 793–815.

Ruskin, John. 1905. *The Cestus of Aglaia* and *The Queen of the Air*. The Complete Works of John Ruskin. Vol. 19. Ed. E.T. Cook and Alexander Wedderburn. London: George Allen.

Wang Ning. 2003. "Northrop Frye and Cultural Studies." In *Northrop Frye: Eastern and Western Perspectives*, ed. Jean O'Grady and Wang Ning. Toronto: University of Toronto Press, 82–91.

White, Hayden. "Frye's Place in Contemporary Cultural Studies." In *The Legacy of Northrop Frye*, ed. Alvin A. Lee and Robert D. Denham. Toronto: University of Toronto Press, 28–39.

Wilde, Oscar. 1982. "The Critic as Artist." In *The Artist as Critic: Critical Writings of Oscar Wilde*, ed. Richard Ellmann. 1968. Chicago: University of Chicago Press, 340–408.

———. 1982. "The Decay of Lying." In *The Artist as Critic: Critical Writings of Oscar Wilde*, ed. Richard Ellmann. 1968. Chicago: University of Chicago Press, 290–320.

Wimsatt, W.K. 1966. "Northrop Frye: Criticism as Myth." In *Northrop Frye in Modern Criticism: Selected Papers from the English Institute*, ed. Murray Krieger. New York: Columbia University Press, 75–107.

Re-Valuing Value

Jean O'Grady

Sir Edward Elgar, that sublime and melancholy composer, found it a lasting source of wormwood and gall to be identified in the British public mind with his minor, patriotic *Pomp and Circumstance* marches. I suspect that, after the publication of his *Anatomy of Criticism* in 1957, Frye found it similarly irksome to have a reputation not as the cartographer of the literary universe but as that man who argued that critics should avoid value judgments. He certainly became tired of being asked what he meant by such an assertion. "I have nothing new to say on this question," he began somewhat testily at a special session of the MLA on the subject ("On Value" 311). Frye had emphasized in the *Anatomy* that he was talking about the academic critic or theorist of literature, not the reviewer in the local newspaper, but still his assertion had been found highly controversial. The polemical introduction had actually made two points that kept coming back to haunt Frye: first, that criticism was, or should be, a science, and second, that the critic's function was not to judge whether a work of literature was good or bad but rather to tell us what *sort* of work it was. The two points are of course related, both being part of Frye's attempt to move criticism from gifted amateur appreciation to the status of an academic discipline, a structure of knowledge that, like a coral reef, could be built up by the contributions of each scholar and taught as rationally as the sciences and social sciences. As he said in *The Well-Tempered Critic*, "Without the possibility of criticism as a structure of knowledge, culture ... would be forever condemned to a morbid antagonism between the supercilious refined and the resentful unrefined" (136).

The inclusiveness of the *Anatomy*, its openness to works of popular literature or of dubious morality, should surely endear Frye to the various postmodernist, feminist, or post-colonial critics who complain of the formation of a "canon" with its concomitant marginalization. Frye's aim in the *Anatomy* was not to rank works according to their perceived value—as had been done, for instance, by Leavis in *The Great Tradition*—but rather to study the articulation of the literary universe and the relations between literary works of all types. Moral criteria of judgment are specifically repudiated: "morally the lion lies down with the lamb. Bunyan and Rochester, Sade and Jane Austen, ... all are equally elements of a liberal education" (14). As Frye told Imre Salusinszky, "The real, genuine advance in criticism came when every work of literature, regardless of its merit, was seen to be a document of *potential* interest, or value, or insight into the culture of the age" (*INF* 754).

Critics have sometimes argued that Frye was mistaken in believing his approach in the *Anatomy* to be value free, and that the very perception of what constitutes literature is an act of judgment. When Murray Krieger developed an elaborate critique along these lines at the MLA session on value judgments in 1967 (which was prompted by Frye's notorious espousal of the question), Frye responded that he could not discuss it on this level. His subsequent remarks show that this is not what

JEAN O'GRADY

constitutes, for him, a judgment of *value*; he had all along been concerned with the more practical and commonsense notion of judgment
as praise and blame. Other critics might suggest that the *Anatomy* shows
Frye's own biases, for instance his preference for comedy and for the
Romantic period. Evidently replying to a perception by eighteenth-century scholars that their period was unfairly slighted in the work, Frye
said that "Actually I thought it was rather a compliment to the eighteenth century that I felt I could let it speak for itself" ("Response" 481).
Most critics have agreed that in spite of such variations of emphasis the
Anatomy does indeed encompass the whole field of English literature as
never before.

For Frye at this time, the value in literature is found in the ensemble,
in the imaginative structure the reader comes to possess, both of apocalyptic or demonic imagery and of the archetypal shapes of comedy, tragedy, romance, and irony. As he put it in *The Educated Imagination*,
"Whatever value there is in studying literature, cultural or practical,
comes from the total body of our reading, the castle of words we've
built, and keep adding new wings to all the time" (470). The emphasis
in teaching literature is not directly on improving the student's judgment, but on leading him or her to see patterns that link different works
together. The total pattern, "the range of articulate human imagination
as it extends from the height of imaginative heaven to the depth of imaginative hell," is what Frye calls "man's revelation to man" (474). Such a
verbal universe may be built up equally by biblical epics and lurid adventure stories; as Frye remarks, "archetypes are most easily studied in highly conventional literature," and "superficial literature ... is of great value
to archetypal criticism simply because it is conventional" (*AC* 104). It is
the archetypal pattern that provides a model or goal for humankind's
work, thus giving literature a vital role in the building up of civilization.

Does this mean, then, that we should not in fact judge between great
art and junk, or prefer one to the other? This was the question that an-
noyed Frye so. Of course we may, he would reply, but these judgments

are not really scientific, being private, personal, and unpredictable. They form part of the individual's developing maturity, but should not be incorporated into criticism as a discipline. To make the discrimination of quality one's goal would be like the direct pursuit of happiness, a chimera: happiness and good taste are a by-product of pursuing something else. Over the years, Frye elaborated his compelling reasons for distrusting or downplaying such pronouncements. In the first place, no critical work can be based on them. If you say that Shakespeare is the greatest writer who ever lived, for instance, this judgment is neither a help nor a hindrance to your analysis of the plays, and adds no new knowledge. Judgments like these are legitimate as "tentative working assumptions," indicating that a writer is likely to be worth working on, but are only provisional and heuristic (*GC* xvi).

Second, Frye argued, value judgments cannot be taught. In *The Well-Tempered Critic* he gives a typical example of an exchange between teacher and student:

(Teacher) Yeats's *Among School Children* is one of the great poems of the twentieth century. (Student) But I don't like it; it seems to me a lot of clap-trap; I get a lot more out of *The Cremation of Sam McGee*. (Teacher) The answer is simple: your taste is inferior to mine. (Student) How do you know it's inferior? (Teacher) I just know, that's all. (135)

As Frye often said, if a teacher finds that a student really enjoyed a sitcom on television last night, the best procedure is not to tell him that the Shakespeare he's studying in class is far superior and would do him more good, but rather to show how the sitcom uses the same plot shapes and character types as Shakespeare's plays. As the student's knowledge grows, so will his sense of value improve: "the more we know about literature, the better the chances that intensity of response and the greatness of the stimulus to it will coincide" (*WTC* 145). But Frye contends

that no one of the many attempts to establish what makes a work great—
or, in the terms of his youth, "swell" as opposed to "lousy" ("On Value"
317)—has been convincing enough to provide the basis for teaching literature.

Every such judgment is limited by the personal experience of the critic
or the outlook and anxieties of its own age. Should we praise perfection
of form? On these grounds Ben Jonson might well be valued more highly than Shakespeare, as indeed sometimes happened in the 18th century.
Should we prize a complex, ironic attitude as did the New Critics of the
1950s? Such a criterion would exclude melodramatic, sentimental writers like Dickens who have a towering presence. Some critics value writers
who are realistic and offer penetrating insight into their own society, but
Frye is a champion of romance, of the magic of the unlikely, the marvellous, and the happy ending, and considers realism a mere blip on the
literary radar. Or should we prize particularly the psychological realists,
with their penetrating insight into the human heart? Frye could appreciate as well as anyone a complex, well-rounded literary character, but he
saw equal value in allegorical works or anatomies, in which the characters are often abstractions or one-dimensional representatives of ideas.

As for the privileging of those writers who convey some interesting idea or enlightening theme, Frye calls this the theory of looking on
literature as "a reservoir of great thoughts which would inspire one to
meet the battle of life," and identifies it as a Victorian approach that lin-
gered on in his childhood ("Literature and Society" 178). He is adamant
that the supposed "message" of an author is not what he really means at
all; his real meaning resides in his pattern of images, and his so-called
message is the ideological part that can be snipped off—meat thrown
by the burglar to keep the dog quiet, in Eliot's image. In fact, Frye has
rather wicked fun in the *Anatomy* with Matthew Arnold's "touchstone"
theory of selected expressions that are guides to the high seriousness of
a first-rate author. Quoting Arnold's chosen line from *The Tempest*, "in
the dark backward and abysm of time," Frye remarks that the line, "Yet a

tailor might scratch her where'er she did itch," is equally essential to the same play (21).

Perhaps at the deepest level Frye was reacting against the notion of the study of literature as developing a refined, cultured elite: the mystique of the English school, as expressed by F.R. Leavis.[1] The snobbery of such a conception is described in currently fashionable idiom by Barbara Herrnstein Smith, in connection with I.A. Richards and his condescending remarks on those who enjoy an Ella Wheeler Wilcox sonnet: "the privileging of the self through the pathologizing of the Other" (*Contingencies* 38). For Frye, all negative judgments turn out to be expendable, and the critic who thinks he is showing his discrimination by condemning certain works is, finally, only judging himself ("On Value" 314). Only positive recognition of what an author was about is a contribution to knowledge.

When pressed with the objection that, for all that, *Among School Children* is generally taken as a better poem than *The Cremation of Sam McGee*, and must there not be some quality in them to account for this, Frye would agree that there might well be, but, refusing to set down any misleading criteria, usually settled for the somewhat lame-sounding conclusion that a masterpiece or classic is a work that "won't go away" (*NFR* 90), that, no matter how many times you read it, stays around to be interrogated again. This seems questionable on the individual level: for many captive students of *Paradise Lost*, for instance, the poem goes away utterly and completely soon after the final exam. But it is true enough on the social level. Good works pass the test of time, revealing new meanings to different generations, remaining sources of interest and enthusiasm, though for differing reasons. It is simply not Frye's main aim, at this stage, to single them out.

Certainly, in his private life Frye did not hesitate to make judgments. In Robert Denham's *Northrop Frye Unbuttoned*, his book of selections from Frye's notebooks, there are twenty-seven entries under "greatest," ranging from the expected praise of Plato, Bach, or *War and Peace* to the offbeat judgment that "the greatest literary genius this side of Blake is Edgar Allan Poe" (113). It is interesting to see the criteria Frye himself used. In 1975 he told interviewer Justin Kaplan that "the primary criterion of value is a certain sense of genuineness" (*INF* 314); evidently, he picked up this conception from T.S. Eliot, as he began a 1943 review by saying that

> T.S. Eliot says somewhere ... that in dealing with a contemporary poet one should not worry about whether he is great or inspired or immortal and avoid all comparisons with dead poets who admittedly are. One should, he says, look rather for some such quality as "genuineness."[2]

For ten years, 1950–1960, when Frye did act as a reviewer for the *University of Toronto Quarterly*'s annual literary survey, it was often a poet's sincerity or genuineness that he praised. In one review, he remarks that "it is the critic's job to tell [the poet] and the public that whatever his stuff means, it sounds genuine enough" (*C* 114). Sincerity, genuineness, conviction—these are not formal criteria but intuitive evaluations of the author's commitment by the experienced reader. In these reviews, Frye is of course alert to the more technical felicities of diction, sound pattern, and imagery. Sometimes he is even seduced by theme. Particularly striking is his high valuation of E.J. Pratt's poem *The Truant*, which he called in print "the greatest poem in Canadian literature" (*C* 265), and, orally in 1964, "not only the greatest of Canadian poems, but one of the almost definitive poetic statements of our time" (*C* 337). Surely it is the Blakean theme of the poem—the refusal of mankind to kowtow to a tyrannical God or a mechanical nature—that is speaking to Frye: the note of cosmic defiance.

There is another and more important criterion of judgment for the early or middle Frye. Some works, he says, are valuable because they lead to the centre of our imaginative experience. This sense of a higher level of authority is perhaps clearest when he is talking about music, where he was not a professional critic bound by his conception of his craft but rather an enthusiastic amateur. Here he draws a distinction "between listening to music, say, on the level of Tchaikovsky, where you feel that this is a very skilful, ingenious, and interesting composer, and music on the level of Mozart or Bach, where you feel that this is the voice of music [...] this is what music is all about" (*INF* 489, "Expanding" 213). In the same way, in literature, some great works are resonant; they focus our experience. The closing cantos of Dante's *Purgatorio*, for example:

> Here we are in the centre of the *Commedia*, and therefore at the centre of our whole literary experience, and so the memory of other things near the centre, late plays of Shakespeare and Sophocles, the Bible, some moments in Plato and in modern poetry, crowd into our minds, and we glimpse a mass of converging rays of significance, as though there were one great thing that the whole of literature had to say to us. (*EICT* 182)

In the seminal early essay "The Archetypes of Literature" Frye had remarked that

> the study of mediocre works of art, however energetic, obstinately remains a random and peripheral form of critical experience, whereas the profound masterpiece seems to draw us to a point at which we can see an enormous number of converging patterns of significance. (*EICT* 127)

It is this sense of the value of certain key writers that I want to pursue in the rest of my paper. I will not argue that Frye reversed himself and began to urge the critic to make conventional value judgments; that never changed. Indeed, it was probably because he believed his point had been generally accepted in the academy that he felt free to ease up on its presentation. But I do want to suggest that his later works constitute a sort of re-valuation of the value question, in that they highlight those valuable works that have a special intensity of vision and that he came to characterize as kerygmatic or prophetic. It is not precisely (as I had originally hoped to show) that Frye repented of the formalism of his earlier criticism and began smuggling in content by the back door, as it were, in emphasizing the illumination or insight generated by a supreme work of imagination. He would not make this form/content distinction: it is form, or imagery and diction, that is the vehicle for the illumination, and the insight is not equivalent to a "message." Nor is there a sharp division between this and earlier concerns; all of Frye's work unfolds from seeds one can trace back to *Fearful Symmetry*, and the kerygmatic interest grows particularly, perhaps, out of the consideration of high style in *The Well-Tempered Critic*. Nevertheless, I believe that Frye's focus shifted from literature as a whole toward valuing or celebrating the visionary insight of individual works, and that this shift is part of a natural evolution of his concerns in the latter part of his career. While never abandoning his belief in the unity of the literary universe, he became more interested in those "epiphanic ... moments of focussed consciousness" that are typical of our fragmented age.[3]

There are several ways of contextualizing this changed emphasis, which began roughly in the mid-1970s. The *Anatomy* had been criticized (somewhat unfairly) for presenting literature as a self-contained universe, and so in *The Critical Path* of 1971 Frye had stressed the social bearings of literary criticism. Increasingly thereafter he investigated the various, not necessarily literary, uses of language in society. As he told Art Cuthbert in 1978, when he was working on *The Great Code*:

I'm continually developing critical instruments and tools in order to break out of what I consider the one really hampering category, ... the category of literature.... There is a point at which the response to Shakespeare, to Milton, to Dante, to major works of literature, begins to smash through the category of literature into something much more open—the social use of words. (*INF* 420)

Unlike some modern critics, Frye did not want to abolish all distinctions in an amorphous notion of "text," but he was increasingly interested in exploring the continuum of sacred literature, literature proper, and critical or other descriptive works. In this regard the objection that the *Anatomy* arbitrarily delimits the field of literature is no longer cogent.

At the same time as Frye began to leave the purely literary critic behind and become the critic of language, he also (like many of his fellow critics) turned his attention to the reader. The *Anatomy* had considered literature objectively as structure, without concerning itself with what the writer may have put in, or what the reader might take out. The actual reading of any particular text was what Frye called precritical—a personal, varied experience where value judgments were most appropriate; criticism proper started after the reading was complete, with a simultaneous perception of the whole work. But now he began to think of reading as what he would call the excluded initiative of his *Anatomy* criticism. In *Words With Power* he admitted that "the literary work, then, does not stop with being an object of study, something confronting us: sooner or later we have to study our own experience in reading it, the results of the merging of the work with ourselves" (75). In a notebook he even talks about *Words With Power* as a book "where the recovery and incorporating of the excluded initiative of experiencing literature marked the first step from the *Anatomy* that I've taken" (*LN* 297).

A third new perspective is a preoccupation with what had always been Frye's basic concern, the expansion of consciousness: the apprehension of new realms accessible only to the imagination, rising to an intimation of infinity and eternity. I might remark here that Frye's notion that the literary universe as a whole provides the goal for humankind's work has always seemed somewhat problematical. What need of all those works to tell us we prefer vernal paradises to stony deserts, and spring awakenings to wintry deaths? Indeed, what need one?[4] Be that as it may, as Frye wrote more about literature and society, he made it clear that the literary model was not there to facilitate the construction of an actual paradisal society: in the real world utopias can only be horrible tyrannies. The literary universe rather provides an ideal in the present, a vision to guide and inspire the worker. And Frye began to describe not so much *a* model of mankind's goal as a plurality of models—hypothetical constructions for consideration, or what he calls in *The Critical Path* "the encyclopedia of visions of human life and destiny" (128). The later Frye is increasingly concerned with the way in which individual works may create this perspective in an individual mind. As he wrote in 1975, "It seems strange to overlook the possibility that arts, including literature, might just conceivably be what they have always been taken to be, possible techniques of meditation ... ways of cultivating, focussing and ordering one's mental processes" ("Expanding Eyes" 213).

The term Frye used to characterize works that addressed the imagination most powerfully was "kerygmatic." There is a certain difficulty with the application of this term, linked to the genuinely puzzling nature of Frye's distinction between sacred and secular literature. Initially it was used to characterize a mode of language peculiar to the Bible. In Frye's final formulation in *Words With Power* (developed out of a slightly different ordering in *The Great Code*), there are four general types of language: descriptive, conceptual, rhetorical or ideological, and imaginative or poetic. Frye's reading of the Bible centred on the notion that its language is mythical and metaphorical or imaginative, not to be taken as "literally true," as fundamentalists understand this term. But imaginative language was to Frye inherently hypothetical, whereas the Bible addresses its readers oratorically. However, unwilling to characterize its language as simply rhetorical, either, because of its claim to be revelation, Frye introduced in *The Great Code* the term "kerygma" (29). In *Words With Power* the biblical kerygmatic is situated "on the other side" of the poetic as a fifth type (101); unlike hypothetical imaginative literature, it proposes a total way of life or "myth to live by" (*WP* 117).

It would not be honest to ignore Frye's frequent assertions that the myths and metaphors of secular literature are always hypothetical, whereas those of the Bible are existential, having designs on the reader's consciousness and aiming to change his life. "Actual literature ... even on the highest level," Frye says in "On the Bible," "does not suggest a myth to live by, or if it does it is essentially betraying its literary function" (163). As late as *The Double Vision*, his last book, Frye was arguing that the New Testament's "myths become, as purely literary myths cannot, myths to live by; its metaphors become, as purely literary metaphors cannot, metaphors to live in" (179). He adduces Don Quixote and Emma Bovary as dreadful examples of trying to live by literary models (*LN* 695). In his last interview he explained the distinction to a puzzled Peter Yan:

> YAN: You mentioned vision. Does the vision or imagination of the writers of the Bible differ from the writers of literature?
> FRYE: There is no difference.
> YAN: I ask that because in *Words With Power* I was surprised when you wrote that in terms of a final cause or a program of action or the myths we live by, even Shakespeare didn't go as far as the Bible does in showing what we should be doing [117].
> FRYE: I'm trying to distinguish the sacred book, the Bible, from secular literature. That literature is written in the imaginative language of myth and metaphor, but it doesn't provide a model to adopt as a way of life, whereas the object of the writers of the Gospels writing about Jesus was the imitation of Christ, in the sense that they were telling a story just as the writers of literature tell a story. But the particular story they told was the one that they wanted to make a model of the life of the person reading it.[5]

Nevertheless, the thrust of much of Frye's later work is to suggest that secular literature can be a source of revelation equally with scripture. His book on romance is called *The Secular Scripture*, and about this time he noted that, now that the biblical prophecies have been absorbed into the establishment, "the power of prophecy is starting to come from the printing press rather than the pulpit, from secular rather than sacerdotal contexts" ("Responsibilities" 163). In this context he recognized that the notion of literature as hypothetical does not reflect the way people characteristically read and write. In 1984, looking back on the *Anatomy*, he remarked, "At the same time I was not happy with the merely 'let's pretend' or 'let's assume' attitude to literature. Nobody wants to eliminate the element of play from literature, but most poets clearly felt that what they were doing was more complex" (*SeSCT* 349). The difference between the intent of literature and sacred scripture becomes less absolute when we reflect that at least some writers, like D.H. Lawrence, evidently have designs on us, and that on the other hand it is possible to read and appreciate the Bible on a secular level, as the students in Frye's Bible course did. There is something of an intentional fallacy in insisting that the Bible "was clearly not intended to be a work of literature" (*INF* 657); in practice the sharp distinction based on language type is blurred.

The important fourth chapter of *Words With Power* bears this out, explaining that the second half of the book will explore "the mysterious borderlands between the poetic and the kerygmatic" (111). The "genuine kerygmatic" can be found equally "in the Sermon on the Mount, the Deer Park Sermon of Buddha, the Koran, or in a secular book that revolutionizes our consciousness" (116). But kerygmatic, Frye explains (100), is a term he had preferred hesitantly to prophetic or apocalyptic in *The Great Code*, and in the second half of *Words With Power* the term "prophetic" is generally used for literature, kerygmatic being reserved for works that set out a total "model myth" for imitation. "At this point the term prophetic falls into place as indicating both a metaliterary dimension within literature and the human medium transmitting the kerygmatic to the idiom of ordinary language" (117–118). In fact it is mostly in the more uninhibited context of his notebooks that the word "kerygma" is used in connection with secular writers.

Thus Frye began to pay more attention to those writers who reach out, like the Bible, with an involving rhetoric, and to those existential, pre-critical readings in which the individual responds with a sense of com-mitment, finding metaphors to live in. In the essay "Expanding Eyes," he talks of Blake's offering his works in this spirit, as mandalas, things for the reader to contemplate to the point at which he or she might reflect, "yes, we too could see things that way" (213). When the youthful Frye said to Helen, "Read Blake or go to hell: that's my message to the mod-ern world" (*NFHK* 426), he surely had in mind not a detached contem-plation of Blake but an active embracing of his vision. Readings of this sort may occur equally with what is normally called literature and with "literary prose" such as prophetic works of philosophy or history, works that retain their power over the mind long after their particular scien-tific scheme has been discredited.

From this point of view Arnold's touchstone theory begins to make more sense, as certain key passages stand out from their context; thus, a passage in Keats's *Ode to a Nightingale* may suddenly open a window in the mind "to suggest different orders of existence" (*WP* 66). In *Words With Power*, Frye describes the way in which the reader begins to no-tice and respond to "that's for me" details in his reading (113), beginning the process of transforming literature from an object to be admired to a power to be possessed. The failure of this step helps explain the paradox of the Nazi who loves Mozart or Goethe: the Nazi's appreciation has re-mained on the aesthetic level. Literature has a transforming power only if we approach it actively, incorporating it with ourselves by a process of what Frye called, starting with *The Secular Scripture* in 1976, recreation.

One important vehicle for such personal involvement is ecstatic metaphor. The original or primitive ecstatic metaphor identified an individual's consciousness with something in the natural world, or ex-pressed his possession by a god (*SeSCT* 346, 324–325). Literary meta-phors, though more hypothetical, still retain the power to "take us out of ourselves," as we say, to overcome our separate selfhood and link us with the rest of creation. Such is the metaphor that "not merely identifies one thing with another in words, but something of ourselves with both" (*WP* 75–76). Frye invokes Longinus's treatise *On the Sublime* in describing these dazzling moments in our response to art when the ego is dispossessed, and "all the doors of perception in the psyche, the doors of dream and fantasy as well as of waking consciousness, are thrown open" (*WP* 111, 82–83).

These peak moments of revelation can only be brief, and correspondingly Frye talks of the authors who are most kergymatic as those who tend to write in intense, oracular fragments. Speaking of the analogy between the ancient biblical prophets and the modern writer, he says,

> The creative people that we most instinctively call or think of as prophetic—Nietzsche, Rimbaud, Blake, Van Gogh, Dostoevsky, Strindberg—show the analogy very clearly. Some people pursue wholeness and integration; others get smashed up, and fragments are rescued from the smash of an intensity that the wholeness and integration people do not reach. (*WP* 82–83)

At another point he remarks, "We recognize Rimbaud or Kafka or Lawrence or Dostoevsky as great writers because of a tremendous force of passion and power and clairvoyance that comes through them" ("Reflections" 137). A value judgment of sorts is obviously being applied to such writers. Is prophetic, then, equivalent to most valuable? In a way it is, not in the sense of describing the "perfect work of art," but in the more personal sense of doing what literature should, breaking through the normal defences of the ego and allowing us to revolutionize our ordinary perception.

Shakespeare and Milton did not write prophetic, fragmentary works of this kind. But they have another quality that can be equally kerygmatic: the ability to evoke our whole literary experience. Frye himself was drawn to works whose encylopedic scope put them next door to sacred scriptures; for instance, he speaks of the writings of Homer and Shakespeare as having "passed through the stage of formal unity and come out on the other side." Here, comeliness of form is subordinated to the sense of "a world in itself ... which one can study to the end of time and still feel that one is inside an epitome of the entire literary cosmos" (*SeSCT* 481).

Words With Power studies the way certain Bible-derived clusters of imagery are used in secular literature. "This book may help one to understand," Frye writes, "why the poets whom we consider most serious and worthy of exhaustive study are invariably those who have explicitly used the kind of imagery studied here" (xxii). As we have seen, Frye had previously noted the clarity of archetypes in popular literature; evidently these greater writers employ the archetypes in a more authoritative and persuasive manner. In this sense they exhibit most clearly the grammar of the human imagination that the archetypes provide. In his notebook jottings while composing *Words With Power*, Frye remarked that he had been ducking the point that the poetic has an oracular aspect that merges into kerygma, and continued, "I can hardly say explicitly that it's the function of criticism to see a super-kerygma forming out of literature; but what else do I mean? And what else does the book mean?" (*LN* 341)

In "The Responsibilities of the Critic," an important essay of 1976 and almost a manifesto of the second half of his career, Frye had in fact suggested a role for the critic in connection with kerygma. In this address, originally given at Johns Hopkins University and twice reprinted, he focused on the prophetic authority of literature and suggested that the critic's task is to identify it. Characteristically, he emphasized that "this act, I have so often urged, is not an act of judgment but of recognition [...] The door to our Eden is still locked, but [the critic] has a key, and the key is the act of recognition" (167).

Frye will not fall back into the heresy of canon formation, even of kerygmatic works; he knows that "*no* kerygmatic canon will ever be drawn up: it would be impossible to find a committee to agree on the selections."[6] The sense of value has a subjective pole, and "anyone could make up an anthology of kerygmatic writing" meaningful to him- or herself (*WP* 117). Indeed, by the principle of interpenetration, so important for the later Frye, all works are linked to the whole and "every work of art is a possible medium for kerygma" (*LN* 643). Still, the critic has a role to play in guiding and clarifying response: his "recognition" does involve powers of discrimination. A critical consensus tends to build about which works are most worthwhile; it is partly because of social acceptance that the Bible has its status as "uniquely kergymatic in the cultural tradition of the West" (*WP* 117). What the critic recognizes is not any supposed theme but an image structure:

> What the critic tries to do is to lead us from what poets and prophets meant, or thought they meant, to the inner structure of what they said. At that point the verbal structure turns inside out, and a vortex opens out of the present moment ... into the created world. ("Responsibilities" 168)

The vortex, the turning inside out: these suggestive but untranslatable terms recall the anagogic perspective of the *Anatomy*, in which the critic sees the whole of literature as a universe of "infinite and boundless hypothesis" (*AC* 120). But whereas the austere heights of anagogy were unavailable for the ordinary practising critic, Frye now seems to open the door for him or her to celebrate insight, convey enthusiasm, and even (dare one say) guide and shape taste: a marvellous opening up of the predominantly structural approach of the *Anatomy*.[7]

Finally, if literary prose can be kerygmatic, why should criticism be excluded? One begins to see a kerygmatic impulse in the writings of Frye himself. There is an interesting passage in a late notebook: "I've so often been asked: but can't you do anything creative like writing poetry or fiction? My creative powers, I've said, have to do with professional rhetoric, on both sides of myth-metaphor"—the far side of myth-metaphor, we recall, being kerygma. "To carry this farther [*sic*]," he continues, "I'd need a distinction between specific (Biblical) and general kerygma": a distinction one wishes he had pursued (*LN* 415). As with the kerygmatic writers he most admired, his ideas came to him in aphoristic fragments, though he laboured afterward to join them into a whole. His pieces often end with a new cadence, a heightening of tone that Alvin Lee likens to preacherly "anagogic conclusions" (*NFR* xix). All four of Frye's books on Shakespeare end with *The Tempest, The Secular Scripture* ends with Spenser's *Faerie Queene*, and *Words With Power* ends with the Book of Job. It is as if he were consciously drawing on the resonance of these central works to open up a wider perspective. "Literature is seed," he wrote in a late notebook; "criticism is the kerygma of what's in literature" (*LN* 334). In "The Responsibilities of the Critic, he noted, "If the critic is to recognize the prophetic ... he needs to be prophetic too: his model is John the Baptist, the greatest prophet of his age, whose critical moment came with recognizing a still greater power than his own" (166). In his private musings Frye sometimes envisaged himself in this role, hoping for instance that a book he planned to write "may even become prophetic, a sacred book like the one it studies" (*TBN* 270).

Sir Edward Elgar may still suffer from the identification with the *Pomp and Circumstance* marches, but we owe it to Frye not to tie him down to an initial and necessary fulmination against disdainful value judgments.[8] To progress from dispassionate anatomist to fiery John the Baptist is indeed to take new directions from old.

ENDNOTES

1 On this subject there are suggestive remarks by A.C. Hamilton in *Northrop Frye: Anatomy of his Criticism*, 11–12, 23–25, and "Northrop Frye as a Cultural Theorist," 112.

2 Review of *Voices and Genesis*, 68. Eliot's remark comes from his introduction to Marianne Moore's *Selected Poems* (New York: Macmillan, 1935), vii.

3 Robert D. Denham elaborates this point in his introduction to *FM*, liv–lv.

4 Frye's later formulation, that literature addresses primary concerns, while the secondary concerns (or ideology) of individual authors can be snipped away, similarly ends in
banal generalities that scarcely need the support of great writers: that life is better than
death, health nicer than sickness, and peace preferable to war.

5 *INF* 1099. Compare a similar point made to interviewer Andrew Kaufman: "Even the
greatest writers—Dante, Shakespeare, and Homer—are still bounded by the category
of literature, whereas the Bible is not" (*INF* 678).

6 *LN* 366. Frye remarks here that his personal list would include "The Marriage of
Heaven and Hell, some fables of Dostoevsky and Kafka, the opening of Buber's I and
Thou, some Rimbaud & Holderlin": by no means the standard list of acknowledged
"masterpieces."

7 Compare the earlier essay "Criticism, Visible and Invisible" (1964), in which the criticism that is teachable is said to be confined to "knowledge *about* literature," or objective
knowledge. A higher level of "knowledge *of* literature," or possession of it, is "criticism
at once glorified and invisible" and can only be pointed toward. More and more Frye
concerned himself with the "invisible" upper limit.

8 In *Contingencies of Value* (1988), Smith focuses on the opposition to value judgments
in *AC*, partly for its influence on subsequent criticism. While Smith wholeheartedly
embraces Frye's arguments about the variability and cultural conditioning of value judgments, she argues against him that studying the dynamics of these evaluatory practices is
an important component of a systematic criticism.

WORKS CITED

Denham, Robert D., ed. 2004. *Northrop Frye Unbuttoned: Wit and Wisdom from Northrop Frye's Notebooks and Diaries*. Krankfort, KY: Gnomon.

Frye, Northrop. 2008. *Interviews with Northrop Frye*. The Collected Works of Northrop
Frye. Vol. 24. Ed. Jean O'Grady. Toronto: University of Toronto Press.

———. 2007. *Northrop Frye's Fiction and Miscellaneous Writings*. The Collected Works
of Northrop Frye. Vol. 25. Ed. Robert D. Denham and Michael Dolzani. Toronto:
University of Toronto Press.

———. 2006. "The Archetypes of Literature." In *The Educated Imagination and Other Writings on Critical Theory, 1933–1963*. The Collected Works of Northrop Frye. Vol. 21, Ed. Germaine Warkentin. Toronto: University of Toronto Press, 120–135.

———. 2006. *The Educated Imagination*. In *The Educated Imagination and Other Writings on Critical Theory, 1933–1963*. The Collected Works of Northrop Frye. Vol. 21. Ed. Germaine Warkentin. Toronto: University of Toronto Press, 436–494.

———. 2006. "The Responsibilities of the Critic." In *The Secular Scripture and Other Writings on Critical Theory, 1976–1991*. The Collected Works of Northrop Frye. Vol. 18. Ed. Joseph Adamson and Jean Wilson. Toronto: University of Toronto Press, 153–169.

———. 2003. *Northrop Frye on Canada*. The Collected Works of Northrop Frye. Vol. 12. Ed. Jean O'Grady and David Staines. Toronto: University of Toronto Press.

———. 2002. *Northrop Frye's Late Notebooks, 1982–1990: Architecture of the Spiritual World*. The Collected Works of Northrop Frye. Vols. 5–6. Ed. Robert D. Denham. Toronto: University of Toronto Press.

———. 2002. *The "Third Book" Notebooks of Northrop Frye, 1964–1972*. The Collected Works of Northrop Frye. Vol. 9. Ed. Michael Dolzani. Toronto: University of Toronto Press.

———. 1999. *The Double Vision*. In *Northrop Frye on Religion*. The Collected Works of Northrop Frye. Vol. 4. Ed. Alvin A. Lee and Jean O'Grady. Toronto: University of Toronto Press, 16–235.

———. 1999. "On the Bible." In *Northrop Frye on Religion*. The Collected Works of Northrop Frye. Vol. 4. Ed. Alvin A. Lee and Jean O'Grady. Toronto: University of Toronto Press, 158–165.

———. 1996. *The Correspondence of Northrop Frye and Helen Kemp, 1932–1939*. The Collected Works of Northrop Frye. Vols. 1–2. Ed. Robert D. Denham. Toronto: University of Toronto Press.

———. 1990. "Literature and Society." 1968. In *Reading the World: Selected Writings, 1935–1976*, ed. Robert D. Denham. New York: Lang, 177–192.

———. 1990. *Words With Power: Being a Second Study of the Bible and Literature*. New York: Harcourt Brace Jovanovich.

———. 1982. *The Great Code: The Bible and Literature*. New York: Harcourt Brace Jovanovich.

———. 1975 (Winter). "Expanding Eyes." *Critical Inquiry* 2: 199–216.

———. 1971. *The Critical Path: An Essay on the Social Context of Literary Criticism*. Bloomington: Indiana University Press.

———. 1968. "On Value Judgments." *Contemporary Literature* 9: 311–318.

———. 1966. "Reflections in a Mirror." In *Northrop Frye in Modern Criticism*, ed. Murray Krieger. New York: Columbia University Press, 133–146.

———. 1964 (October). "Criticism, Visible and Invisible.' *College English* 26: 3–12.

———. 1963. "Literary Criticism." *Aims and Methods of Literary Scholarship*, ed. James Thorpe. New York: MLA, 57–69.

———. 1963. *The Well-Tempered Critic*. Bloomington: Indiana University Press.

———. 1957. *Anatomy of Criticism*. Princeton: Princeton University Press.

———. 1947. *Fearful Symmetry: A Study of William Blake*. Princeton: Princeton University Press.

———. 1943 (June). Review of *Voices* and *Genesis*. *Canadian Forum* 23: 68–70.

Hamilton, A.C. 1990. *Northrop Frye: Anatomy of His Criticism*. Toronto: University of Toronto Press.

———. 1999. "Northrop Frye as a Cultural Theorist." In *Rereading Frye: The Published and Unpublished Works*, ed. David Boyd and Imre Salusinszky. Toronto: University of Toronto Press, 103–121.

Smith, Barbara Herrnstein. 1988. *Contingencies of Value: Alternative Perspectives for Critical Theory*. Cambridge, MA: Harvard University Press.

NEW APPROACHES

_____

PART V

The Interruption of Myth in Northrop Frye:

Toward a Revision of the "Silent Beatrice"

Troni Y. Grande

The fact that the dying and reviving character is usually female strengthens the feeling that there is something maternal about the green world, in which the new order of the comic resolution is nourished and brought to birth.
— Frye, "The Argument of Comedy" 69

A GROWING number of feminist critics are finding their own new directions from the critical path forged by Northrop Frye.[1] While his outline of literature as a "systematic structure of knowledge" (*AC* 19) has certainly been useful to feminists, Frye's myth-making, aimed at creating an integrated community, has been judged a failure insofar as it ignores the problem of gender difference—specifically, the subjugation and exclusion of the embodied woman. Yet if Frye himself showed no focused interest in the way gender inflects the reading of literature and the practice of criticism, the woman (both as a figure and an embodied being) is an insistently interrupting presence within his work. In the first chapter of *A Natural Perspective*, Frye memorably calls himself "an Odyssean critic ... attracted to comedy and romance" (2), genres that end by showing a renewed world in which every member of society can take his or her place. Frye's central myth throughout his oeuvre is indeed comic, but his vision of a united community struggles to incorporate and acknowledge the woman as a fully participating member. Though he recognizes that the woman holds a central and sacred place, Frye questions at times the power of the woman and the difference women make. Feminist critics have not attended to the ways in which the woman in Frye time and again becomes a crucial vehicle of divine inspiration and resurrection, moving society toward a new order.

Deanne Bogdan, who has provided the most comprehensive attempt to reconcile Frye's theory with feminist theory and pedagogy, argues that Frye has become "complicit with the disincarnation of women" because he has been "seduced by the breadth of his own vision" ("Re[Educated]" 93).[2] Bogdan calls for a re-examination of the embodied woman, the "excluded initiative of the educated imagination," exemplified by the "silent Beatrice" that Frye points to in *Words With Power* as existing behind and beyond the supreme anagogic vision ("Re[Educated]" 92). In her compelling account of her changing relationship with Frye (a quest myth involving "initiation, separation, and return"), Bogdan moves from being a fervent disciple of Frye to one who resists what she comes to see as his "hierarchical and androcentric" ordering of literary response (85, 88). Bogdan implies that in Frye's system Beatrice is denied subjectivity, remaining silenced and hence subjugated.

My paper takes up the challenge to re-examine the "silent Beatrice" in Frye's analysis, which Bogdan only touches upon.[3] In pointing out that the image of the silent Beatrice "might be examined within its broader context—the gendered hierarchy between subject and object" (92), Bogdan treats Beatrice as the objectified, hence disembodied woman both Dante and Frye build their mythological visions on, through, and over. However, in Frye's myth-making, Beatrice appears neither silent nor invisible as she leads Dante out of Purgatory toward the enlightenment and salvation of Paradise in *The Divine Comedy*. In the range of Frye's personal and academic writings, Beatrice occupies a central site of embodiment rather than remaining an "excluded initiative" as Bogdan has suggested. First, Frye's analyses of Beatrice give her a louder, more substantial subject position than Bogdan realizes, as well as an archetypal significance connecting her to the all-powerful dying and reviving female Frye has done so much to illuminate. Moreover, Frye's personal relation to women and the feminine bears closer examination in his *Notebooks*, *Correspondence*, and *Diaries*—all those "egodocuments"[4] that reveal Frye's private wrestling with issues of gender. While on several occasions Frye attempts to dismiss the difference generated by women, he also experiences discomfort and puzzlement over women as material beings, and falters toward an account of the difference made by women in his mythologizing of Western literature. Finally, Frye's *Late Notebooks* bear witness to his moving private attempts to refashion the figure of Beatrice while working through his grief over his wife Helen's death. Frye's ultimate rendering of Helen as Beatrice shows with poignant force how the female archetype collides with the inexorable embodiment and situatedness of human knowledge and experience. On all these levels, Beatrice is a guide to enlightenment and regeneration, a metaphor that reveals how deeply Frye's vision of an integrated and renewed community relies on the woman as other.

Bogdan suggests that in order to effect a re-vision of the educated imagination, "one must be both inside and outside anagogy at the same time, while seeing from below" (91). Bogdan is building on the work of Donna Haraway, who argues that the "view of infinite vision is an illusion, a god trick" (582), and that "seeing from below," from "the vantage points of the subjugated," is the most trustworthy means of situating and embodying knowledge (583). Yet Haraway's description of "seeing from above" does not always accurately describe the Frye of the *Diaries* and *Notebooks*. Though Frye's conceptual framework may at times give the appearance of transcendentalizing, or speaking from an unlocatable position, his writings in their broader context do not reveal him to be one of "the dominators ... self-identical, unmarked, disembodied, unmediated, transcendent, born again" (Haraway 586). Rather, Frye's writings lay bare what Haraway calls "[t]he split and contradictory self, the one who can interrogate positionings and be accountable, the one who can construct and join rational conversations and fantastic imaginings that change history" (586). As Frye reaches for a view of infinite vision, his private and public writings show him wrestling, like Jacob with the angel, to incorporate the woman as other.

The invaluable Collected Works of Northrop Frye series provides much more context for a re-examination of the ways in which the woman interrupts and informs Frye's myth-making. The Collected Works open Frye up to feminist criticism by mixing his private reflections (in the *Diaries* and *Notebooks*) with his critical books and public addresses.[5] In Frye's *Diaries*, *Notebooks*, and *Correspondence*, we gain a more open view of him that dismantles the false dichotomy between public and private, reason and feeling, mind and body, as we get the theorizing of the seasoned academic and self-declared genius alongside his most personal jottings and fretful questions. This other view of Frye—Frye "unbuttoned," as Robert D. Denham aptly puts it—opens Frye up to a consideration of the difference the woman makes in his conceptual system.

In exploring Frye's relation to the fictional construct of Woman, and to historically situated women, I hope to bring into the foreground the subject of feminist criticism, as Teresa de Lauretis has memorably formulated it: "the discrepancy, the tension, and the constant slippage between Woman as representation, as the object and the very condition of representation, and, on the other hand, women as historical beings, subjects of 'real relations'" (10). Despite his various attempts to efface the difference of gender and turn woman into an abstraction, Frye's myth inscribes the woman as an embodied being, embedded and situated in material reality. The dying and reviving woman in Frye's mythology—she who is paradoxically archetypal *and* crucially embodied—is a founding presence of the community that is such a central focus of his oeuvre. Frye's personal and academic writing reveals how woman functions as an interruption of myth, both within mythos itself and within what Jean-Luc Nancy calls the "myth of myth," that is, in the impulse toward and process of myth-making. The very function of myth, as Nancy has shown, is to found a community: "myth reveals the community to itself and founds it" (51). If, as Nancy points out, myth "is always the myth of community, that is to say, it is always the myth of a communion—the unique voice of the many—capable of inventing and sharing the myth" (51), then that myth of community is never fully or unproblematically unified. As Frye interrupts his own attempts at creating a unified mythology throughout his personal writings in the *Notebooks* and *Diaries*, he confronts with some honesty and ethical force the extent to which women as other interrupt or interrogate his efforts at articulating an open mythological system. Frye's work suggests that, as Nancy argues, ethical community building is only possible if we allow for the interruption of community through the difference of its members; that is, myth is only possible with the interruption of myth (Nancy 57).

For Frye, Beatrice is a type of maternal power, first of all in its beatific aspects. Far from constituting a simply "excluded initiative" that has no part in the higher vision Dante and Frye privilege, Beatrice provides a vital means of helping Dante achieve ultimate enlightenment. She is the divinely appointed agent of Dante's ascent, for within his Christian vision Dante must surrender his own power to that which is higher. Frye's analyses of Beatrice recognize her elevated, salvific power in *La Vita Nuova*, Dante's famous commentary and poetic sequence, and in the last two books of *The Divine Comedy*. At the end of the *Purgatorio*, Beatrice meets Dante and leads him up toward Paradise, for Virgil, Dante's guide through Hell and Purgatory, is pagan and cannot approach Paradise:

TRONI Y. GRANDE

When Dante wanted to experience states of being beyond life in thirteenth-century Italy the poet Virgil appeared as his guide. Virgil represents literature in its Arnoldian function as a 'criticism of life,' the vision of existence, detached but not withdrawn from it, that is at its most inclusive in the imaginative mode. Beyond Virgil there is Beatrice, who represents among other things a criticism or higher awareness of the limits of the Virgilian vision. (*WP* 28)

Here Frye grants Beatrice a great deal of generative power: "Dante's ascent is not directed by his own will, but by the divine grace manifested in Beatrice" (160). If there is any view from below here, it is Dante's, not Beatrice's. Indeed, Frye reflects on this view from below in the *Late Notebooks* when he makes an analogy between Virgil's inadequate vision and the Old Testament, which "is really a vision of how God looks from the human hell" (*LN* 673). Without Beatrice, Dante would be stuck in the hellish, inadequate vision.

Beatrice the heavenly guide is the site of man's primal desire. Frye notes that when Virgil leaves Dante and Beatrice enters, Dante regresses into an infant for the second time. Frye calls Dante "the greatest of Eros poets" (*TBN* 105). In the *Purgatorio*, "Eros is primarily a reversal in time, a movement toward reversal of ... childhood, ... its ultimate goal a lost Paradise" (*LN* 344). Thus "the first movement is toward the mother, or more accurately the virgin or inaccessible mother" (*LN* 344). Beatrice as paradisal mother is typologically linked to the courtly love mistress. Indeed, as Frye points out in the "*Third Book*" *Notebooks*, "[t]he Courtly Love tradition is based on the maternalizing of the mistress," for "[t]he simplest and most direct object of Eros is the mother" (105). In fact, Frye calls Beatrice "the Virgin Mother" (*TBN* 105).

In Frye's open-ended treatment of Beatrice, on one level the site of desire is the archetypal mother; on another level, however, she is significantly embodied. Frye subtly echoes Dante's own ambiguous character-

256

ization of Beatrice not just as a type of the Virgin Mary but also as a stern, more realistic mother figure. For example, in the *Purgatorio*, Dante describes himself as a small boy overwhelmed by his mother's scolding: "And even as a little boy may think / His mother formidable, I thought her so: / Stern pity is a bitter-tasting drink" (canto 30, lines 79–81). To Dante, as Frye points out, "Beatrice first appears as a scolding mamma" (*LN* 345). As she berates Dante for his faithlessness, evidenced by his many past sins, not only does Beatrice represent a higher authority that shows the limits of the Classical vision, but she is also anything but silent. Significantly, Frye's response to this event is neither theologically dogmatic nor staunchly committed to a single androcentric view; rather, it is split, contradictory, and open, seeking to incorporate the complexity of the woman into his reading: "I used to find the entrance of Beatrice rather contemptible, a selling out to the masochism of piety, but maybe it'll bear more thinking about" (*LN* 673). Frye is not alone in struggling with Dante's initial characterization of Beatrice, "who nags & scolds away like a typical Italian mother" (*TBN* 105). Maud Bodkin (whose work on archetypal patterns Frye cites)[6] is also bothered by the particular shape Beatrice takes on here. Bodkin voices "a moment of recoil" and "a feeling of revulsion" (182–183) regarding the hold that Beatrice as mother-imago appears to have over Dante. Bodkin resolves the problem by viewing Beatrice as the means by which Dante achieves a "transition from personal desire to ideal aspiration" (189). Beatrice's archetypal function aligns her with Goethe's *Ewig-Weibliche* in *Faust,* a type of the Eternal Feminine that draws us onward or upward.[7]

Yet Bodkin's ultimate effacement of the bodied, individual woman here, in favour of the sacred archetype, skews Dante's text, as Dorothy L. Sayers brilliantly points out in her introduction to the *Purgatorio*. Beatrice cannot be seen solely as a type of the *Ewig-Weibliche*, Sayers argues (38), for "she is, first of all, a person" (49). Bodkin is guilty of a "flight from the concrete, individualized, historical, and mystical into the abstract, generalized, mythical, and magical" (Sayers 39). It is precisely because Christianity is characterized by the great "scandal" of "particularity" that "Dante's encounter with an individual living woman can be made the image of the soul's encounter with a personal living God" (37). The point is that the concrete individual, in this case the very body of Beatrice as woman, is the crucial vehicle of the divine.

Dante's dependence on Beatrice for salvation involves a realization of the self in and through the other: the not-self of the woman and the divine Other, surpassing human understanding. Sayers illuminates Beatrice's duality as a woman and a type of the eternal. Frye's reading of Beatrice, though not in this kind of depth, also negotiates between the personal and the archetypal. Even when Frye stresses the archetypal significance of Beatrice, his remarks lead back to a consideration of her crucial embodiment as a woman. For example, in the *Late Notebooks*, after having emphasized Beatrice's power as a primal mother, Frye reminds himself, "Buber says (I must check) there is something maternal about his Thou" (345; cf. *TBN* 105). Frye is recalling Buber's statement that "[e]very child that is coming into being rests, like all life that is coming into being, in the womb of the great mother, the undivided primal world that precedes form" (25). Buber sets up the metaphor of the womb here by making clear that it represents spiritual oneness: "the yearning is for the cosmic connexion, and its true *Thou*, of this life that has burst forth into spirit" (25). But Buber also describes a man's relation to the womb of the *biological* mother in masculinist terms: "From her, too, we are separated, and enter into personal life, slipping free only in the dark hours to be close to her again: night by night this happens to the healthy man" (25). The description of how "the healthy man" returns to the womb is ultimately ambiguous: "night by night," this return may involve sexual union with a mother substitute, or, on another level, spiritual union, as the man connects through his dreams with the unconscious, also figured as "the womb of the great mother."

In Frye, as in Buber, we can trace a connection between the sacred and the feminine, figured both as the generalized archetype of Woman and the individualized body of the woman. Though admittedly sketchy and intermittent, Frye's attention to female sacrality anticipates feminist re-visions of the sacred and indeed current trends in *thea*logy (the study of goddess religion).[8] Unlike feminist critics, Frye refuses to cordon off a separate sphere of supreme feminine power, but he nonetheless places considerable importance on the mother archetype.[9] As late as *The Great Code*, Frye retraces his interest in the "very frequent mythical formulation" of the "earth-mother" as a paradoxical figure of beneficent, destructive, and supremely powerful nature "from whom everything is born and to whom everything returns at death. Such an earth mother is the most easily understood image of *natura naturans*, and she acquires its moral ambivalence. As the womb of all forms of life, she has a cherishing and nourishing aspect; as the tomb of all forms of life, she has a menacing and sinister aspect; as the manifestation of an unending cycle of life and death, she has an inscrutable and elusive aspect. Hence, she is often a *diva triformis*, a goddess of a threefold form of some kind, usually birth, death, and renewal in time; or heaven, earth, and hell in space" (*GC* 68). Frye's reference here recalls Robert Graves's formulation of the "Triple White Goddess" (384) who ruled the "Underworld," "Earth," and "Sky." But of course, as Graves recognizes, the archetype was invariably embodied as well:

> [I]t must never be forgotten that the Triple Goddess ... was a personification of primitive woman—woman the creatress and destructress. As the New Moon or Spring she was girl; as the Full Moon or Summer she was woman; as the Old Moon or Winter she was hag" (386).

Indeed, Frye's myth-making accounts for the presence and power of the goddess in a more extensive way than critics have noticed. For example, in her learned feminist revision of "Frye's archetypological theory" (103), Margaret Burgess faults Frye not just for some scholarly "misunderstandings" (110) regarding prebiblical myths of goddesses, but also for his neglect of the ways in which Christianity has appropriated (or "confiscated") these goddesses, along with its "confiscated gods" (118). Burgess complains that in his work Frye's "occasional speculations that the divine should contain a feminine as well as a masculine component are generally discarded" (118); she attempts to correct this oversight by offering "a new mythology ... in which God and Goddess—or divine feminine as well as divine masculine principles—are finally reconciled" (117). While Burgess offers a valuable feminist expansion, I find Frye's "speculations" on the divine feminine to be more substantial and insistent than she suggests, especially when considered in light of his focus elsewhere on the generative power of the woman.

Even Frye's early work does make reference to female goddesses alongside the dying gods who form his central myth, suggesting that the presence of the female is crucial to his mythology. For instance, in his student essay entitled "The Fertility Cults," Frye outlines the dying-god myth in a remarkably gender inclusive way while at the same time stressing the importance of the earth mother:

> [A]ll agricultural primitives develop much the same myth of a young (because flourishing and vigorous) god of vegetation slain annually in the fall and reviving in the spring. This spirit, being nourished by the soil, exists to that soil in the relation of son or daughter to mother. (*SE* 129)

While Adonis is the "most famous of all such fertility gods," Frye recognizes, "[i]n Greek mythology there are dying goddesses as well, of whom Proserpine or Persephone, beloved by Demeter (whose name, earth mother, shows most clearly her origin), Iphigenia, and Kore are the best known" (*SE* 129).

As a type of the woman who saves after her death, Beatrice is connected with the archetype of the dying and reviving female, exemplified by

Persephone and Demeter, which Frye has done so much to illuminate. His treatment of the death-rebirth mythos as a fertility rite extends from his early student essays through his *Late Notebooks*, *The Great Code*, and *Words With Power*. Moreover, as I argued in the introduction to *Northrop Frye's Writings on Shakespeare and the Renaissance*, the death-rebirth mythos forms a fundamental part of Frye's work on Shakespearean comedy and romance. Especially clear is Frye's debt to the Cambridge ritualists (Jane Ellen Harrison, Gilbert Murray, and Francis Cornford) and to Sir James Frazer's *The Golden Bough*. From these myth critics Frye expanded two key points concerning the death-rebirth archetype: that it is ultimately comic and that it is feminine or maternal. Drawing on Frazer, Frye uses the Greek myth of Demeter and Persephone as a prime example of the death-rebirth archetype. This myth figures prominently in Frye's readings of Shakespearean romance, especially *The Winter's Tale*, in which "the original nature-myth of Demeter and Proserpine is openly established," as Frye already suggests in his famous 1949 essay "The Argument of Comedy" (69).[10] Shakespeare sets up an extended analogy between Hermione and the goddess of the harvest, Demeter. The winter's tale begins for Demeter when Hades steals her beloved daughter Persephone; for Hermione, when Leontes steals (and tries to murder) their infant daughter Perdita. Demeter plunges the earth into winter, mourning the loss of Persephone. In Shakespeare's reworking of the myth, Hermione undergoes a ritual death that keeps her tyrant husband Leontes in a symbolic winter state for sixteen years until he can repent and Perdita, the lost one, can be found.

Jane Ellen Harrison sees Demeter and Persephone as two aspects of the same earth goddess, "two persons through one god" (*Prolegomena* 272). As Frye puts it, "The fact that the dying and reviving character is usually female strengthens the feeling that there is something maternal about the green world, in which the new order of the comic resolution is nourished and brought to birth" ("Argument" 69). Feminist critics and writers who have developed the Demeter-Persephone archetype have attested to its powerful resonance as a tale of shared female power (Pratt 116–120).

The renewal of the green world through a feminized force of nature becomes a central idea in Frye's later writings on romance and is set up in his remarks on "the drama of the green world" in the Third Essay of *Anatomy of Criticism*: "In the rituals and myths[,] the earth that produces the rebirth is generally a female figure, and the death and revival, or disappearance and withdrawal, of human figures in romantic comedy generally involves the heroine" (*AC* 183). Shakespearean comedy ends on the "tonic chord" of marriage ("Argument" 59), renewing society through the couple's fertile union and thereby enacting a sublime renewal of all creation, through the female resurrections of Thaisa in *Pericles*, Fidele in *Cymbeline*, and Hermione in *The Winter's Tale*. All of these female characters become redeeming guides for the male figures to lead them, and the audience, toward a vision of renewed nature. If Frye keeps circling around comedy, one of the things that comedy represents for him is a vision of female empowerment. Frye refers to Shakespearean comedy and romance as *The Myth of Deliverance* because their mythic structure ultimately emphasizes the deliverance or liberation of human forces—*including* and *led by* female forces—at least within the space of the play world.

In his writings on Shakespeare and the Renaissance, Frye's sympathy toward Shakespeare's comic heroines is shared by the woman-centred readings of Shakespeare that gained force in the 1980s and that are perhaps best exemplified by Lenz, Greene, and Neely's popular essay collection *The Woman's Part*. For example, Frye prefers Hippolyta's version of events, in *A Midsummer Night's Dream*, over Theseus's (*NP* 130). Hippolyta sees the story of the night as "something of great constancy, / But, howsoever, strange and admirable" (5.1.26–27), whereas Theseus offers a more sterile rationalizing of the events. Similarly, in *The Woman's Part*, Judith Hays echoes Hippolyta's speech while emphasizing the empowering function of Shakespeare's comic heroines:

[A]gain and again in the comedies and romances, Shakespeare seems to question the limitations of the male-instrumental experience and to suggest that the more valuable spheres of love and affiliation, the 'something of great constancy,' the "wonder" that concludes so many of the comedies and romances, require ways of behaving more characteristic of women than of men—since so often it is the play's women who lead the way into this dimension. (92)

Hays adds, "The Demeter-Persephone pattern seems to suggest the grounding in a reality larger than individual life to which human beings must cede some of their sovereignty for the sake of the greater benefits of mutuality" (92).

The dying and reviving female, as typified by the earth goddess herself, often operates as the very condition of possibility on which Frye finds that a renewed community founds itself. But so too, Frye insists, does the dying and reviving male. Frye's comic perspective envisions a human community that above all includes every one of its members and is indeed characterized by "the greater benefits of mutuality." This is a key difference between Frye's work and the early feminist readings of Shakespeare: Frye devotes his attention to the larger structure of myth underlying the plays rather than focusing solely on the woman's part. He sees the meaning of the woman in relation to her role in the community; in the world of comedy and romance he emphasizes not women's subjugation but their generative power. Frye's treatment of the woman thus avoids becoming simply an abject "view from below."

Fifty years after his student essays, Frye affirmed that the dying god can be gendered as either male or female, and that the androcentric spin usually put on it is the product of ideology, not essential to the myth at all:

[T]he traditional patriarchal emphasis, along with the dying-god (usually male) myth with the female nature in the background is ideological manipulation, not an inherent principle of myth. The Cinderella archetype is an example of the opposite development; Cinderella is quite as important an image of human purgation as Prometheus. The ewig-weibliche theme is of course male-centred too. (*LN* 223)

In fact, in a remarkably open gesture subverting the patriarchal spin that has until recently been put on Christianity, Frye presents Jesus's resurrection in female terms:

The Resurrection, then, is the marriage of a soul & body which forms the spiritual body. The body part of this marriage is female; the empty tomb is recognized solely by women.... The fact that Jesus took on flesh in the Virgin's womb has certainly been dinned into Christian ears often enough; but the fact that he took on flesh in the womb of the tomb at the Resurrection, and that there's a female principle incorporated in the spiritual body, seems to have got strangled. (*LN* 327)

Heretically (in our ideological age), Frye imagines the possibility of stripping away the ideological layer of the received Christian myth to reveal the common dying-god myth underneath, which incorporates "female" as well as "male" principles.

In a further fascinating twist, Frye links the commonality (indeed, the communism and *communion*) of myth to the human anxiety about satisfying the primary concerns (food and drink, sex, property, liberty of movement). According to Frye, Gill points out, myth is motivated by "these four bodily requirements" (Gill 186); hence, mythical discourse is grounded in and by embodied existence. Rather than accounting for differences (gender, race, religion, class) in embodied existence, Frye insists that the "axioms of primary concern" apply to "all people without significant exception" (*WP* 42). However, increasingly in the post-structuralist age, literary critics have tended to interpret literature in terms of secondary concerns (ideology) rather than primary concerns (mythology). Frye sees this tendency as fraught with problems, for it creates sects that divide and makes the interpretation of literature a matter of shifting value judgments and idiosyncratic readings that pander to ideological trends and the history of taste, rather than building up a systematic structure of knowledge:

> I see it as the essential task of the literary critic to distinguish ideology from myth, to help reconstitute a myth as a language, and to put literature in its proper cultural place as the central link of communication between society and the vision of its primary concerns. (*MM* 103)

As Frye puts it in *Words With Power*, "The central structural principles that literature derives from myth" are precisely those "principles that give literature its communicating power across the centuries through all ideological changes" (xiii). Frye's chief complaint about feminism, in fact, is that it ignores what he calls the "communism of convention" (*AC* 90, 98) in favour of advancing the interests of a special ideological camp.

In an unpublished response to Bogdan's work, an introduction he wrote for the essay collection *Beyond Communication*, Frye articulates his complaint against feminists and other ideological critics "who approach literature with the aim of annexing it to their main interest. Here every work of literature becomes a *document* for feminism or Marxism, to be examined within that point of view." Frye calls these approaches "determinisms," "imperialistic ideologies out to conquer one more field" (*WE* 614), and insists that it is possible and indeed "essential to distinguish the ideological from the mythological elements in every work of literature," for "[a]n ideology is a myth kidnapped by a power structure or a pressure group" (614–615). He laments the fact that Bogdan and the other writers in *Beyond Communication* have not "paid more attention to the study of myths and folk tales and the way in which they reflect the primary concerns of mankind, the concerns of food and sex and property and freedom" (615). These are the "concerns that the poets have inherited" and that "belong to all humanity, and are still there whatever their ideological contexts" (*WE* 615). Even feminist critics committed to the project of paying attention to women may well find Frye's plea for a common myth of concern immensely compelling, given that we are all poised on the brink of war and ecological disaster on this planet of crisis, in the dawn of what many see as our new post-post-structuralist age.[11]

Despite commonalities, however, throughout his writings Frye shows antipathy as well as sympathy for feminism, most (in)famously in the *Late Notebooks*: "I think social feminism, genuine social & intellectual equality between men & women, a centrally important issue. Feminist *literary* criticism is mostly heifer-shit" (223). Frye's chief complaint against feminism is that it attempts to change the past rather than describing the vision of society that literature presents: "Perhaps female (not feminist) writing has a great future, but that doesn't make its effort to rewrite the past any less futile" (223). Frye is not immune to the desire to change the past himself, such as when he wishes Cordelia in *King Lear* could have had a mother (490). But he believes that the critical enterprise must not "devalue the whole cultural tradition of the past in favor of a more satisfying culture to be set up in the future" (*WP* 60). The "cultural tradition" can deliver us from the burden of ideological criticism, the "art of clipping literature in order to distort it into a different shape" (60).

Despite his strong resistance to what he regards as the narcissistic self-interest of some feminist readings, Frye's focus on the contextualizing of literature and on the "communism of convention" continues to make his work useful for feminist critics and theorists. Indeed, Julia Kristeva, though admitting that she does not treat myths as "untouchable," assesses Frye's importance in terms of his "valorization of memory," which she regards as "the primordial task of literary criticism" (335):

> When we find ourselves faced with a nihilism which, after having rightly denounced the dead ends and horrors of the West, wears itself out in attacks that reject the complexity of tradition in the name of who knows what political correctness, it falls to humanists and most particularly to literary theory and criticism to defend, by elaborating, that tradition. (353)

Frye does not always serenely register the power of women within his own structural framework. Sometimes he confesses himself puzzled and caught by the difference of gender, specifically by women's powerful roles in Shakespearean comedy and romance:

> One curious feature is the way that the female is frequently the vice, either by disguise like Portia or by death & revival like Helena. As for Hermione, who vanishes from the action but returns in Antigonus' dream, that foxes me, yet I suspect that something very significant is buried in Shakespeare's entelechic females. What they accomplish I suppose is fundamentally their own will. (NRL 187–188)

Shakespeare's females represent an "entelechic"—perfecting, actualizing—power or principle, which Frye suspects is "something very significant." Here Frye deliberately leaves open the significance of the woman. On another occasion this open-ended question causes him downright perturbation: "Notice how linked the transvestite disguise & the disappearance & revival themes are: but why the hell is this theme always female?" (112).

If the female architectus in Shakespeare "foxes" Frye, so too does the female myth critic, for in *The "Third Book" Notebooks*, Frye wonders why it is *women* who have produced so much rich scholarship exploring the relation between ritual, archetype, and literature:

> [W]hy so many women? Maud Bodkin, Jessie Weston, Gertrude Levy, Helen Flanders Dunar, Madame Blavatsky, Frances Yates, Enid Welsford, Jane Harrison, Bertha Philpotts [Phillpotts], Ruth Benedict: whatever the level of scholarship a woman's book seems to meet me wherever I turn. (71)

It could be argued that what gives rise to Frye's questions here is the assumption that women (even *represented* women) should not have the power, through the assertion of their own will, to move the plot through its complication to its resolution; or that it is unusual that women should have written so many valuable scholarly books. But Frye's self-interrogations also leave open the possibility that, while myth aims at the common embodiment of primary concerns, gender *does* mark embodied experience with *difference*.

The difference that women make to the form(ul)ation of a united community becomes clear when we consider the issue of inclusive language. Up until his last works, Frye insists on using the term "man" to denote the human race, both men and women, and in so doing he reveals difficulties in negotiating a truly inclusive vision of a common humanity in our time. As the *Oxford English Dictionary* records, the inclusive sense of the word "man" has now been rendered obsolete: it is "understood to exclude women, and is therefore avoided by many people." Frye's use of the word hearkens back to its original meaning: "In Old English the word *man* meant 'person' or 'human being,' and when used of an individual was equally applicable to either sex. It was parallel to the Latin *homo*, 'a member of the human species,' not *vir*, 'an adult male of the species.'" Over time, however, "*man* has been shifting away from generality toward specificity" (Miller and Swift 12–13).

Frye's resistance to this linguistic shift apparently stems from his desire to preserve the cultural tradition, but it effectively subsumes and effaces the woman under the category of man. Although in his last works Frye begins to replace the collective noun "man" with "humanity," on more than one occasion he defends his use of exclusive language—for example, by comparing what he presents as pedantic feminists, "who refuse to pronounce the word 'chairman,'" to 17th-century "Puritans who refused to pronounce the word Christmas because the last syllable was 'mass'" (*WE* 557). Frye argues,

> [Nonetheless,] people kept on saying 'Christmas,' and Christmas did not turn Roman Catholic in consequence; it merely turned pagan. I see no reason why such words as 'chairman,' 'spokesman,' 'mankind' and the like could not fossilize in the same way. We sometimes forget how much the language has already changed in this respect. When I was growing up, in the early years of this century, men and women spoke appreciably different languages; different in vocabulary, in rhythm, in intonation. The flattening out of these differences is a sign, I think, that society has gone a long way in normalizing the relation of the sexes. (557)

Frye shows a surprising indifference to the violence inherent in language, and to the ways in which words have been used, and are still used, as weapons, to engender unequal relations—an indifference, in other words, to those members of society who interrupt his exclusive vision with a "view from below." Frye's inclusion of women in his vision of a united humanity is therefore contradictory.

Yet, though handicapped by a blind spot perhaps typical of his generation, Frye must and does include women, both as a principle of regeneration and as fundamentally embodied beings. The "female principle" continues to interrupt Frye's myth and propel it toward an inclusive comic vision of a renewed society. After all, "[t]he freer the society, the greater the variety of individuals it can tolerate, and the natural tendency of comedy is to include as many as possible in its final festival. The motto of comedy is Terence's 'Nothing human is alien to me'" ("Argument" 5). Indeed, it is this same line from Terence's play *The Self-Tormentor* that became the motto of the suffragette movement for Jane Ellen Harrison, one of the very myth critics upon whose groundbreaking work Frye built his own myth. The irony that what is seen as "human" has not always included women compelled Harrison to revise Terence's line slightly in her plea for equality between men and women during the early 1900s, when women were fighting for the vote: "On the banners of every suffrage society, one motto, and one only, should be blazoned: "*Homo sum; humani nihil* (ne suffragium quidem) *a me alienum puto.*" She translates the line: "I am a human being; nothing that is human (not even a vote) do I account alien" ("Homo" 85). Frye would no doubt agree with Harrison's plea for social equality, and might argue that the word "man" should continue to function, as it did in Old English, as a true generic like *homo*. Yet, as linguistic studies like that of Miller and Swift have documented, the use of the ambiguous word "man" in English does, in the experience of speakers and listeners, participate in the systematic absorption of the woman into an androcentric category of existence. No matter how strongly he positions "entelechic females" in his own analyses of the maternal archetype, then, Frye's social relation to embodied women is split, because it disempowers the very force he recognizes as crucially empowering. And yet the repressed other returns at the limit of Frye's own vision.

In his final notebooks Frye's mythical framework unmistakably shows a fundamental reliance on the woman, both archetypal and embodied. Frye's relation to the embodied woman first emerged most movingly in his early correspondence to Helen Kemp, the real "silent Beatrice" in and beyond Frye's work, who after her death serves as a guide to higher levels of consciousness and the vehicle by which Frye hopes to achieve a new order of existence. The personal, embodied life of Frye, which had been joined flesh and bone with that of his first wife for half a decade, interrupts the conceptual theorizing of his later notebooks, so that myth-making is seasoned with lived experience. After Helen's death in 1986, Frye's intellectual propositions and questions in Notebook 44 are interrupted for several pages by Frye's very private grief, searching for its own language of suffering. It erupts starkly: "This is not a diary, but Helen is dead" (*LN* 137). For the next several paragraphs, Frye painfully recounts the manner of Helen's death and his struggle to come to terms with her absence. He clearly reaches for a way from death back to life, to breathe life into the theoretical proposition that "tragedy is an episode in that larger scheme of redemption and resurrection to which Dante gave the name of *commedia*" ("Argument" 66). Like Dante, Frye finds the path through the figure of Beatrice, which Helen's death infuses with a new significance: "Since Helen's death I've felt my love for her growing increasingly beyond the contingencies of the human situation. I begin to understand more clearly what Beatrice and Laura are all about" (*LN* 145).

In fact, Helen, though now disembodied, becomes the centre of Frye's work, and her new role as inspiring muse to Frye seems to provoke more wonder than certainty: "I find all my ideas regrouping around her in a way I can neither understand or explain" (*LN* 150). In Notebook 44, Frye desperately uses the figure of Beatrice to try to pull the regenerative power of the woman as archetype into his own material reality:

> I may be heading for the grossest kind of illusion here, but I still wonder about Helen's functioning as a Beatrice: it may be nonsense for a man of 75 to talk about a "new life," but all I want is a new book. With God all things are possible. Beatrice was mainly

a creation of Dante's love; my love recreates Helen in the sense of recognizing that if a world exists that she's now in, she's an angel. Her human frailties, as I've said, are now nothingness: only what she really was remains. (My own weaknesses & guilt feelings, of course, have greatly increased.) She didn't read my stuff, of course, & didn't need to, but she respected what I did very deeply. So although both of us were physically infertile for many years, perhaps another Word can still be born to us, like Isaac. (*LN* 153)

Like Beatrice and the biblical Sarah, Helen is maternalized here as an agent of fertility and renewal. Helen still *is*—she is an ultimately "emancipated fellow-creature" (*LN* 148) who has become a "saint," revealing the divine (139). Frye concludes Notebook 44 by describing Helen as a dead presence and a living absence: "Helen was a pile of ashes, an absence to me, and an angel: perhaps she's a genius to me (or anyone else who loved her and is still living or not living and still confused)" (254). As with Dante and *his* Beatrice, Frye's search for renewal takes place in and through the woman whose body, now absent, still marks the site of plenitude.

In the end, then, the "silent Beatrice" has a much fuller life in Frye than an oppositional feminist reading might at first suggest. Beatrice does speak, and act, to regenerate the world in the myth of Northrop Frye. At the limits of Frye's theory of myth and community, the woman comes to occupy the centre as an absent presence. Although her embodied existence is revealed as a crucial aspect of her empowering sacred and social role, the feminist search for embodiment *in* representation must be openended and ongoing (de Lauretis 26). The real story of the "silent Beatrice"—outside representation, in the "space-off" of myth—can only just be glimpsed within the frame of Frye's vision.[12] As we end, the body is still our primary concern, engendered "elsewhere." But as we have seen, Frye's vision of an integrated humanity does crucially depend on the sacralized power of the woman, who nourishes and brings to birth a "new life" and a "new order." Through her redemptive death the woman in Frye's work both reveals the community to itself and founds it.

ENDNOTES

1 Feminist critics have respectfully used Frye's categories but have also registered their alienation from his conceptual framework. Annis Pratt builds on Frye's sense of archetypes as recurring images within literature but insists that his categories must be transformed in order to account for the marked difference between women's and men's archetypal experience. Patricia Demers offers a similar corrective to Frye, "an expanded code, and a re-vision of his literary biblical analysis to include early modern women" (99). Phyllis Galloway is more sharply antagonistic toward Frye, calling him an outright sexist because the "fundamental androcentricity of his position excludes half of humankind" (26).

2 Bogdan's work on Frye includes her 1980 doctoral dissertation on Frye's position as a 20th-century apologist for poetry, as well as several articles and books that explore her increasing ambivalence toward him. She ultimately returns to Frye by reconfiguring the educated imagination, which she argues must pay attention to what the anagogic vision passes over and effaces, as well as to what it foregrounds and empowers ("Re[Educated]" 91).

3 See Bogdan's book *Re-Educating the Imagination* for a slightly fuller use of Beatrice as a figure of both the silenced and effaced woman in male-dominated culture and criticism (283, 292, 294) and the newly empowered, speaking, or indeed singing woman (298, 304, 306). Surprisingly, Bogdan never contextualizes Beatrice as a literary character.

4 As Nancy Miller points out (26n4), the term "egodocuments" was first used by Dutch historian Jacques Presser, who defines them as "those documents in which an ego intentionally reveals or conceals itself"; feminist historians have since adopted the term.

5 As Margaretta Jolly reminds us, "It was feminism that pulled down the wall between public and private, reason and feeling, and told us that minds and bodies could not be separated" (214).

6 See *SE* 137, 343.

7 Bodkin cites the famous last lines of Goethe's *Faust*: "Das Ewig-Weibliche / Zieht uns hinan," expressing for her "that aspect of the woman archetype which we have studied in its first great embodiment in Dante's *Commedia*" (205).

WORKS CITED

Bodkin, Maud. 1934. *Archetypal Patterns in Poetry: Psychological Studies of Imagination.* London: Oxford University Press.

Bogdan, Deanne. 1994. "The (Re)Educated Imagination." *The Legacy of Northrop Frye.* Ed. Alvin A. Lee and Robert D. Denham. Toronto: University of Toronto Press, 84–96.

———. 1992. *Re-Educating the Imagination: Towards a Poetics, Politics, and Pedagogy of Literary Engagement.* Portsmouth, NH: Boynton/Cook.

———. 1990. "In and Out of Love with Literature: Response and the Aesthetics of Total Form"; "From Meditation to Mediation: Breaking Out of Total Form"; "Reading and 'The Fate of Beauty': Reclaiming Total Form." *Beyond Communication: Reading Comprehension and Criticism.* Portsmouth, NH: Boynton/Cook, 109–195.

———. 1980. "Instruction and Delight: Northrop Frye and the Educational Value of Literature." Unpublished doctoral dissertation. University of Toronto.

Buber, Martin. 1958. *I and Thou*, trans. Ronald Gregor Smith. 2nd ed. New York: Scribner's.

Burgess, Margaret. 2002. "From Archetype to Antitype: A Look at Frygian Archetypology." *Semeia* 89: 103–124.

Dante Alighieri. 1984. *The Comedy of Dante Alighieri the Florentine. Cantica II: Purgatory* [*Il Purgatorio*], trans. Dorothy L. Sayers. 1955. Harmondsworth, England: Penguin.

de Lauretis, Teresa. 1997. "The Technology of Gender." *Technologies of Gender: Essays on Theory, Film, and Fiction.* Bloomington: Indiana University Press, 1–30.

Demers, Patricia. 2002. "Early Modern Women's Words with Power: Absence and Presence." *Semeia* 89: 89–102.

Denham, Robert D., ed. 2004. *Northrop Frye Unbuttoned: Wit and Wisdom from the Notebooks and Diaries.* Toronto: Anansi.

Frye, Northrop. Forthcoming. *Northrop Frye's Writings on Shakespeare and the Renaissance.* The Collected Works of Northrop Frye. Vol. 28. Ed. Troni Y. Grande and Garry Sherbert. Toronto: University of Toronto Press.

———. 2006. *Anatomy of Criticism: Four Essays.* The Collected Works of Northrop Frye. Vol. 22. Ed. Robert D. Denham. Toronto: University of Toronto Press.

———. 2006. *Northrop Frye's Notebooks on Renaissance Literature.* The Collected Works of Northrop Frye. Vol. 20. Ed. Michael Dolzani. Toronto: University of Toronto Press.

———. 2002. *The "Third Book" Notebooks of Northrop Frye, 1964–1972: The Critical Comedy.* The Collected Works of Northrop Frye. Vol. 9. Ed. Michael Dolzani. Toronto: University of Toronto Press.

———. 2000. *Northrop Frye's Late Notebooks, 1982–1990: Architecture of the Spiritual World.* The Collected Works of Northrop Frye. Vols. 5–6. Ed. Robert D. Denham. Toronto: University of Toronto Press.

———. 2000. *Northrop Frye's Writings on Education.* The Collected Works of Northrop Frye. Vol. 7. Ed. Jean O'Grady and Goldwin French. Toronto: University of Toronto Press.

———. 1997. *Northrop Frye's Student Essays, 1932–1938.* The Collected Works of Northrop Frye. Vol. 3. Ed. Robert D. Denham. Toronto: University of Toronto Press.

———. 1995. *A Natural Perspective: The Development of Shakespearean Comedy and Romance.* 1965. New York: Columbia University Press.

———. 1990. *Myth and Metaphor: Selected Essays, 1974–1988*, ed. Robert D. Denham. Charlottesville: University Press of Virginia.

———. 1990. *Words With Power: Being a Second Study of "The Bible and Literature."* Toronto: Penguin.

———. 1983. *The Myth of Deliverance: Reflections on Shakespeare's Problem Comedies.* Toronto: University of Toronto Press.

———. 1982. *The Great Code: The Bible and Literature.* Toronto: Academic Press.

———. 1949. "The Argument of Comedy." In *English Institute Essays 1948*, ed. D.A. Robertson Jr. New York: Columbia University Press, 58–73.

Galloway, Phyllis Anne. 1977. "Sexism and the Senior English Literature Curriculum in Ontario Secondary Schools." Unpublished doctoral dissertation. University of Toronto.

Gill, Glen Robert. 2006. *Northrop Frye and the Phenomenology of Myth*. Toronto: University of Toronto Press.

Godard, Barbara. 1991. "Feminism and/as Myth: Feminist Literary Theory Between Frye and Barthes." *Atlantis: A Women's Studies Journal* 16:2, 3–21.

Graves, Robert. 1966. *The White Goddess: A Historical Grammar of Poetic Myth*. Amended and enlarged ed. New York: Farrar, Straus and Giroux.

Haraway, Donna. 1988. "Situated Knowledges: The Science Question in Feminism and the Privilege of Partial Perspective." *Feminist Studies* 14:3, 575–599.

Harrison, Jane Ellen. 1955. *Prolegomena to the Study of Greek Religion*. New York: Meridian.

———. 1915. *"Homo Sum": Being a Letter to an Anti-Suffragist from an Anthropologist*. Repr. in *Alpha and Omega*. London: Sidgwick and Jackson, 80–115.

Hart, Jonathan. 1995 (Spring). "Northrop Frye and the End/s of Ideology." *Comparative Literature* 47:2, 160–174.

Hays, Janice. 1984. "Those 'soft and delicate desires': *Much Ado* and the Distrust of Women." In *The Woman's Part: Feminist Criticism of Shakespeare*, ed. Carolyn Ruth Swift Lenz, Gayle Greene, Carol Thomas Neely. Urbana: University of Illinois Press, 79–99.

Jolly, Margaretta. 2005. "Speaking Personally, Academically" [Review of Jackie Stacey's *Teratologies: A Cultural Study of Cancer* and Ien Ang's *On Not Speaking Chinese: Living Between Asia and the West*]. *Feminist Theory* 6:2, 213–220.

Kristeva, Julia. 1994. "The Importance of Frye." In *The Legacy of Northrop Frye*, ed. Alvin A. Lee and Robert D. Denham. Toronto: University of Toronto Press, 335–337.

Miller, Casey, and Kate Swift. 1988. *The Handbook of Nonsexist Writing*. 2nd ed. New York: Harper and Row.

Miller, Nancy. 1991. *Getting Personal: Feminist Occasions and Other Autobiographical Acts*. New York: Routledge.

Nancy, Jean-Luc. 1991. *The Inoperative Community*, ed. Peter Connor. Trans. Peter Connor, Lisa Barbus, Michael Holland, and Simona Sawhney. Minneapolis: University of Minnesota Press.

Pratt, Annis. 1995. "Spinning among Fields: Jung, Frye, Lévi-Strauss and Feminist Archetypal Theory." In *Feminist Archetypal Theory*, ed. Estella Lauter and Carol Schreier Rupprecht. Knoxville: University of Tennessee Press, 93–136.

Raphael, Melissa. 1996. *Thealogy and Embodiment: The Post-Patriarchal Reconstruction of Female Sacrality*. Sheffield: Sheffield Academic Press.

Sayers, Dorothy L. 1984. Introduction. *The Comedy of Dante Alighieri the Florentine. Cantica II: Purgatory [Il Purgatorio]*, trans. Dorothy L. Sayers. 1955. Harmondsworth, England: Penguin, 9–71.

Shakespeare, William. 2003. *A Midsummer Night's Dream*. *The Complete Works of Shakespeare*, ed. David Bevington. 5th ed. New York: Longman, 150–177.

Frye and Film Studies:

Anatomy of Irony

David Jarraway

"Art, according to Plato, is a dream for awakened minds, a work of imagination withdrawn from ordinary life ... and yet giving us a perspective and dimension on reality that we don't get from any other approach to reality."
—Northrop Frye, *The Educated Imagination* (43)

"Dreams are our eggs, our larvae, and our properly psychic individuals."
—Gilles Deleuze, *Difference and Repetition* (250)

" ... all life is from the egg."
—Herman Melville, *The Confidence-Man: His Masquerade* (1098)

ON FIRST view, Northrop Frye might have been somewhat discomfited with the "new direction" that my paper proposes to rethink his critical oeuvre. After all, in a passage somewhat dismissive of Marshall McLuhan in *The Critical Path* (1971), Frye claims that it is the written document that is "the model of all teaching ... repeating the same words however often one consults it ... [hence,] a repetition of the kind that underlines all genuine education," and indeed, that "makes democracy technically possible" (150–151).[1] Yet in *Anatomy of Criticism* (1957), there are enough references to moviemaking throughout that tour de force of literary theory—"the Chaplin films" in the mythic context of John Milton, Ben Jonson, and the Old Testament, in one example (228)—to invite media pundits to view filmmaking with the same "assumption of total coherence" (*AC* 16) that, throughout his long career, Frye brought to the canons of great literature. And their efforts would not have been misplaced, according to Frye, since "the real communicating media are still, as they have always been, words, images, and rhythms [and] not the electronic gadgets that convey them" (*CP* 152). This paper, however, is not about to engage a whole system of archetypal analysis for reading film in the breathtakingly encyclopedic manner that Frye seemed to effortlessly apply to practically all of Western literature. "The purpose of criticism by genres is not so much to classify as to clarify," Frye rightly observes in the *Anatomy*'s concluding essay (*AC* 247), and to my mind, the archetypal systemization of movies, without a prodigiously gifted and agile mind at back of it, is likely to be disastrous for both Frye and film. "The basis of generic criticism in any case," continues Frye in that concluding essay, "is rhetorical, in the sense that the genre is determined by the conditions established between the poet and his public" (247).

The movie genre that interests me most in connection with Frye's work is a brand of highly unusual Hollywood filmmaking emanating from the 1940s and 1950s and retrospectively nominated "film noir." Indeed, given its exceptionally ironic relation to more mainstream[2] types of inter- and postwar Hollywood film production with its emphasis on anti-heroes and femmes fatales, obscure plot lines, weird chiaroscuro lighting, and jagged camera angles among some of its more prominent technical features, film noir is about as detached—"archetypal" rather than "allegorical" in its worried "external relation to history"—as the ideal "critic *qua* critic" ought to be (*CP* 99).³ Conceivably, such film-making might almost be the textbook example of Frye's "Mythos of Winter," in which the genres of "Irony and Satire" ineluctably recycle his archetypal criticism away from tragedy, and back to the mythoi of comedy and romance (*AC* 223–239). Mark Hamilton, for instance, in a recent PhD dissertation entitled "Northrop Frye Goes to the Movies" (2003), locates a number of well-known noir texts ranging from *The Maltese Falcon* (1941) through to *Silence of the Lambs* (1991) precisely within this critical ambit (212–249).

In this essay, I restrict my own interest in Frye and film studies to the noir film canon of Alfred Hitchcock. Fully launched by America's entry into the Second World War in 1941 with films like *Rebecca* (1940), *Foreign Correspondent* (1940), *Suspicion* (1941), and *Saboteur* (1942), Hitchcock's film noir output would almost appear to have become pro-grammatic with the addition of *Shadow of a Doubt*, made in 1943. And with its own special concatenation of dreams and eggs as in my opening epigraphs, it's perhaps possible to delineate more precisely in social and cultural terms what that program, from a considerably detached British filmmaker recently installed in David O. Selznick's breakaway in-dependent film studio, might be when the ironies of a film like *Shadow of a Doubt* are engaged from a distinctly Frygean perspective. Here, I'm thinking particularly of two scenes that occur roughly halfway through the film: the first, when Niece Charlie, the film's ostensible femme fa-tale, recounts at a family dinner her dream—a nightmare really, as she admits—of seeing her Uncle Charlie aboard the train that has recent-ly brought him to the Newton family home in Santa Rosa, California, from back east, and her recollection of him "looking so unhappy"; and the second scene, a bit earlier, when Emma Newton, Charlie's mother, finally consents to having her cake-making photographed for a feature magazine article on the typical American family sponsored by an agency called the "National Public Survey." "I'm ready for the eggs, now," she calls out to the photographer, and ruminates a short while later, "I can't go on making cakes." What might be the cultural lading of these two scenes shadowed by Hitchcock's peculiar noir mix of dreams and eggs, and shadowed further by Frye's own conception of the communicative arts' sense of critical or ironic detachment?

Interposed between the aforementioned two scenes in *Shadow of a Doubt* is a third that should make Frye's helpfulness for the study of film noir quite plain. Set in Gunner's Grill in the film's depiction of small-town life, we find in this scene another magazine reporter ostensibly on a date with Niece Charlie. In real life, the reporter is Detective Jack Graham, and he divulges to Niece Charlie that the photographing of her mother's cookery for the magazine feature has all been a ruse. The deception has allowed Graham and his camera-toting partner Fred Saunders to gain undercover access to the Newton family home in order to suss out the identity of Uncle Charlie as a possible suspect in the "Merry Widow Murderer" caper back east for which (as Niece Charlie will glean from a newspaper article tracked down in the Santa Rosa public library later) a nationwide search had been undertaken to determine the whereabouts of the killer of three rich Philadelphia women. In *The Modern Century*, Frye follows Freud in viewing contemporary society on the model of a vast "repressive anxiety-structure," and propounds the notion of a "sadist vision" rather like that of the Merry Widow Murderer as a means of cutting through "the whole structure of society itself as an anti-art, an old and worn-out creation that needs to be created anew" (79, 86). In the "cult of the holy sinner"—Chaplin's *Monsieur Verdoux* is cited as one example—"the person achieves an exceptional awareness ... from acts of cruelty," Frye contends, "or at least brings about such an awareness in us" (84).[4]

What is crucially at stake in the surrendering of Uncle Charlie's identity to the enforcement of law and to the unavoidable and fatal punishment underwriting that law is an equally unavoidable and fatal

scourging of Niece Charlie's own female identity in the film. In its nightmare conclusion, the former is enacted in Uncle Charlie being thrown
to his death, and the latter in Niece Charlie ironically provoking that
very fatality herself. For his niece, what is so compelling about a character like Uncle Charlie is his mysterious resistance to any kind of determinate nomination, a point they mutually corroborate early in Uncle
Charlie's visit when young Charlie remarks on that "something" inside
her uncle that "nobody knows about" and that therefore makes both her
and her uncle "sort of like twins." Uncle Charlie doubly reinforces the
observation with the remark that "it's not good to find out too much,"
and seals his rejoinder with the gift of what later appears to be a stolen
emerald ring. Moreover, Hitchcock's own insistence on the mysterious
fluidity of Uncle Charlie's identity throughout the film is sustained as
much by his fictitious self-naming as his inventive self-fashioning: in
the seedy crumpled attire of Mr. Spencer back in Philadelphia at the
opening, in the high-class outfit of cape and cane as Mr. Otis aboard the
train to Santa Rosa shortly after, and as the glitzy fashion-plate in leather
brogues and swish panama hat as Mr. Oakley in and out of Santa Rosa
in what follows. Even by the end of the film, despite the fact that Uncle
Charlie has thrice attempted to do away with his niece, we're not ever
really sure that he was in truth the Merry Widow Murderer, since another
purported killer had apparently done himself in, absconding from the
law back east, by running into an airplane propeller. "Cut him to pieces,"
Herbert Hawkins, the next-door neighbour, ghoulishly remarks, which
just might be the perfect metaphor for the mordantly exhilarating misordering of male identity throughout much of Hitchcock's noir canon
over the next two decades or so, right through to *Psycho* (1960).

Such a graphic misordering of symbolic identity would likely be tar-
geted by Jacques Lacan as the literal embodiment of his infamous "corps
morcelé" (see *Écrits* 4–5) and can thus set us before an ironic reading
of this whole issue via another passage from Frye that invites us to read
Emma Newton's breaking of eggs in *Shadow of a Doubt* all over again.[5]

"One of the most obvious uses [of the imagination's ironic 'power of de-tachment']," Frye observes in *The Educated Imagination* (1963), "is its encouragement of tolerance." He explains:

> In the imagination our own beliefs are also only possibilities, but we can also see the possibilities in the beliefs of others. [Moreover,] bigots and fanatics seldom have any use for the arts, because they're so preoccupied with their beliefs and actions that they can't see them as also possibilities. (32)

Thus, in *The Well-Tempered Critic* (1963), Frye avers, "Literature pro-vides a kind of reservoir of possibilities of action. It gives us wider sym-pathies and greater tolerance, and new perspectives on action; it increas-es the power of articulating convictions, whether our own or those of others" (150). And for that "reservoir of possibilities" in *The Educated Imagination*, once again, Frye resorts to the image of the egg or em-bryo, writing that "[t]he world of the imagination is a world of unborn or *embryonic* beliefs [so that] if you believe what you read in literature, you can, quite literally, believe anything" (*EI* 31, emphasis added). Or, as Herman Melville's narrator would have it in *The Confidence-Man* (1854), "[A]ll life is from the egg…" (1098).

The bigots and fanatics just alluded to by Frye would likely be set con-siderably ill at ease with the queer subtext of Hitchcock's film, an insist-ent subtext right from the significant dedication to gay playwright and novelist Thornton Wilder at the beginning (for helping Hitchcock's wife Alma with the screenplay, one supposes) to Uncle Charlie's dandi-fied leave-taking for San Francisco at the end, and variously throughout with remarks like the one Emma proffers in response to her brother's special contribution to one evening meal in particular: "Wine for din-ner? That sounds so gay!" But in light of the filmmaker's twinning of the two Charlies, I would tend to view Frye's embryology egging us on, as it were, in the direction of a notion of subjectivity in more capacious terms than any determinately straight or gay labelling of identity would inevitably fail to enclose. And it's perhaps Gilles Deleuze via his own particular sense of an emancipatory embryology (as in my second epigraph) that points us in the direction of this much larger notion of human selfhood, if in the very first instance the dreams engendered by eggs put us more liberally in touch with "our properly psychic individuals." Deleuze goes on to elaborate the reference in *Difference and Repetition*:

> In order to plumb the intensive depths or *spatium* of an egg, the directions and distances, the dynamisms and dramas, the potentials and potentialities must be multiplied. The world is an egg. Moreover, the egg in effect, provides us with a model for the order of reasons: differentiation-individuation-dramatisation-differenciation. (251)

As a dynamic of infinite potentiality, "a vision of possibilities, which expands the horizon of belief and makes it both more tolerant and more efficient," according to Frye (*EI* 55), the egg for Deleuze (like the embryo for Frye) becomes "the model of life itself," as Daniel Smith remarks, "a powerful nonorganic and intensive vitality that traverses the organism; by contrast, the organism, with its forms and functions, is not life, but rather that which imprisons life"—the egg, therefore, suggesting an intensive reality "that is 'beneath' or 'adjacent to' the organism, and continually in the process of constructing itself" (xxxvii).

As a figure for the "holy sinner" in this rather capacious sense of identity-potential, Uncle Charlie's characterization throughout Hitchcock's film is rendered more scrutable from the point of view of the social critique he insistently mounts against the "fat wheezing animals" of the world, which often seems to distil into a horrifically twisted misogyny: "... silly wives ... useless women ... Horrible, faded, fat, greedy women," and so on. If the world is "a horrible place," as Niece Charlie contends her uncle thought it might be, it was not because he "hated the whole world"; there was only one particular "organic" version of life that Uncle Charlie took violent exception to—the world "as a foul sty with swine inside." The organic reification of American culture in economic terms especially—the opening shot, for instance, of Uncle Charlie abed in a darkened claustrophobic room surrounded by cast-off ten- and twenty-dollar bills, and later the jokes at the expense of fat bank presidents and their silly sycophantic employees (Niece Charlie's bank-telling father Joe in particular)—it's this reified level of monetary form and function in society that most provokes Uncle Charlie's egregious misanthropy. Thus, it's considerably off the mark for Niece Charlie herself, outside the church door at her uncle's funeral in the film's closing scene, to conclude to her newly affianced Jack Graham that "[p]eople like us have no idea what the world is really like." After all, it's she who appears to us in an opening shot in the film identical to that of Uncle Charlie—prostrate in another darkened and enclosed room, in Santa Rosa this time rather than Philadelphia—and she who mounts an organic critique of modern culture in the presence of her father in the identical terms of her eponymous uncle-twin: "We're in a terrible rut ... mother works like a dog: dinner, dishes, bed. I don't see how she can stand it."

The portrait of Emma Newton in this revealing assessment thus returns us to Emma's cake-making, alluded to previously, in one of the film's most engagingly conflicted moments, which occurs about halfway through. From Frye's critical perspective, three things are worth remarking in this seemingly unexceptional bit of homey American domesticity dating from the Second World War years. First, I think it's important to observe for Emma's part a certain initial resistance to or perhaps detachment from the detectives qua reporters' insistent scrutiny, subjecting every last nook and cranny of the nuclear family unit, from parlour armchair to kitchen mixing bowl, to their collective probing gaze. Emma's resistance here could in part be construed as a metaphorical attempt to sustain the dynamism of the embattled subject, and so hold open that dream-like "withdrawn[ness] from ordinary life," as in the opening epigraph from Frye (EI 43), thereby maintaining an ironic detachment—the Deleuzian "spatium" previously noted—that conceivably allows for the multiplication of potentials and potentialities so threatened by their documentary containment within the constraining ideology of something *like* a typical American family. Just before this scene, we recall, it is Uncle Charlie who insists that he has never truly been photographed (even though a picture from his youth is produced for his alarmed inspection); just after, it is the elder Charlie who will insist that Fred Saunders surrender the film containing pictures of him taken against his will. More importantly, we recall much later what had been at stake in Emma's own foreclosing of those "directions and distances"of the potentially differentiated identity referenced previously by Deleuze. The curtailment manifests itself here in Emma's momentary wistful rumination about how much she might have sacrificed in yielding to an all too typical bourgeois domesticity that her present homey reunion with her younger brother obviously puts her so much in mind of: "And you know how it is," she wistfully ruminates, "how you sort of forget you're you [because] you're your husband's wife."

In the Newton household, Emma's two daughters are arguably much more insistent on maintaining their own sense of unique individuality—or, perhaps more accurately in a Deleuzian sense, "pre-personal" or "pre-individual" singularity (*Logic of Sense* 55, 107 and throughout)—in the face of a coercive middle-class domesticity. For the younger daughter Ann, who complains that her decidedly unmodern mother makes no allowance for science in her life, this recalcitrance includes turning her nose up at the proffering of cute stuffed animals and a dollhouse made of newspapers when an adventure story like *Ivanhoe* comes more easily to hand. And for Niece Charlie, in the restive style suggested by her namesake uncle, her identity flies clearly in the face of any patriarchal accommodation as she weasels past both police and detectives afoot in Santa Rosa in order to track down at the town library her uncle's purported homicidal aggression to its criminal lair mentioned earlier and, at the film's climax, take complete control of her own (and Uncle Charlie's) life. The more socially constrained Newton matriarch Emma is a mere shadow of her doubtful progeny, to go with Hitchcock's title, mustering only the gumption to extend an invitation to her hapless brother to speak about his world travels at a meeting of her Ladies Club. In the context of the cake-making scene just viewed, therefore, a second thing Emma gives expression to—at the point at which the eggs are broken— is a rather poignant urge to fold, as it were, her somewhat queerly characterized brother into the Newton family romance to which she herself has perhaps reluctantly and to an extent regrettably yielded. Indeed, by consenting to photographs after some initial hesitation, at some psychic level Emma arguably also gives expression to the need to see her own daughters ultimately folded, too, into the family batter/barter of the American recipe for domestic fulfillment circa 1943.

For a third and final significance that can be gleaned from Emma's cookery, we might do well to recall, on the subject of artistic representation, Frye's very important distinction in *The Modern Century* between "stupid realism" and "prophetic realism" (*MC* 61). For Frye, this distinction amounts to the crucial separation in Coleridge between the *natura naturata* view of experience based on the "subject-object relation of consciousness," and thus the classicist's mere imitation of nature, and the *natura naturans* view of experience whereby, as in the romanticist's view, we become "identified with the processes and powers of nature" and through such an identification embody the very "organic power of nature" itself. With the latter, Frye goes on to explain, "the realistic tendency achieves a second culmination," as in French Impressionism: "not a separated world that man contemplates, but a world of power and force and movement which is in man [and] where objects become events, and where time is a dimension of sense experience" (*MC* 59, 59–60).[6] Yet if in film theorist Raymond Bellour's unalterable and widespread view all Hollywood narratives are, as dramatizations of the male Oedipal story, about man's entry into the symbolic order (qtd. in Bergstrom 93),

Bellour's clearly reactive and ultimately disempowering scenario seems to me to provide precisely the kind of stupid realism that a noir vehicle like Hitchcock's *Shadow of a Doubt* aims to move beyond by means of the prophetic realism proactively evinced especially through the characterization of the Newtons' restively empowered female progeny. But move to where in 1943?

In her admirable *Framing History: The Rosenberg Story and the Cold War*, Virginia Carmichael alludes to the ideology of certain "perfecting myths as attempts to transcend irrational, impalatable, or unbearable social and historical realities" in the "process of making the (sublime) world cognitively apprehensible in bearable terms" (229n8). Thus, the anchoring of domestic partnerships within the later Cold War context of what Kaja Silverman, in *Male Subjectivity at the Margins*, refers to as an ideological "dominant fiction" mid-century—sovereign fathers, receptive mothers, procreative family units, and so on—is perhaps, following the Second World War, America's perfecting myth par excellence through the 1950s and early 1960s (39). And it surely comes as no accident that a correspondent belief in the "realism" of Hollywood cinema through this period, so Silverman argues at length, would become precisely the means to solidify that dominant fiction (404n70), as Hitchcock's very own successful mainstream film career following his noir period through the 1960s and early 1970s would only help corroborate.

Much of that ideological perfecting and anchoring and solidifying just described is mirrored in the development of Niece Charlie's character in the second half of *Shadow of a Doubt*, for which Emma's cakemaking/egg-breaking scene perhaps serves as the turning point: from Niece Charlie thinking that her uncle is "the most wonderful man in the world" earlier in the film to her later threat, before Uncle Charlie's Ladies Club talk later: "I don't want you to touch my mother. So go away, I'm warning you. Go away or I'll kill you myself." But in much larger historical terms, a great deal of that character reversal in Niece Charlie might be thought to be mirrored in American culture itself, as registered in Hitchcock's own wartime film. As one of that culture's own turning points, Allen Bérubé scrupulously documents how in an intensely masculinist climate of war "[e]ven heterosexual men could find themselves abandoning the norms of civilian life as they had to rely on each other for companionship and affection" (189). Thence, up to the Cold War years, and the widely accepted linkage in the decades following between sexual and political deviance, as John D'Emilio points out, "the effete men of the eastern establishment lost China and Eastern Europe to the enemy" while "'mannish' women mocked the ideals of marriage and motherhood" (60). By the end of the film, although her name belies it, Niece Charlie is hardly the mannish woman mocking the ideals of marriage and motherhood as we saw at its start. With her imminent marriage to Detective Graham at the conclusion, she has arguably come to her senses. Growing now in tandem with the rest of the world while "the other" shrinks, as Humpty Dumpty would say,[7] for all intents and purposes, she becomes like Lewis Carroll's Alice: as unrecognizable to Humpty Dumpty as Niece Charlie is perhaps unrecognizable to Uncle Charlie (and to us) at the point at which she threatens to do in her singularly nomadic uncle.

Hitchcock's noir filmmaking through the 1940s and 1950s, of which I take *Shadow of a Doubt* to be emblem, while aiming to be equally popular would appear, given the burden of social criticism outlined previously, to be proposing a view of human experience considerably more ironic—irony as a principle better understood in the context of its rhetorical rather than its generic or modal import for the study of narrative, as Frye suggests in several of his later works. Here, I'm reminded of a key passage in *The Educated Imagination* in which Frye persuasively writes about the "effect of irony" that allows us "to see over the head of a situation"—over the head of his very own *Anatomy of Criticism*, let's say—and thus is able "to detach us, at least in imagination, from the world we'd prefer not to be involved with" (*EI* 22). Film noir's brief mounted against mainstream

Hollywood moviemaking in a text like *Shadow of a Doubt* offers careful viewers imaginative detachment precisely as Frye describes: "where things are removed just out of reach of belief and action" (*EI* 32).

Holding the world in critical suspension in this rather ironically detached way has a good deal of the ambivalent about it. For instance, one thinks of Frye's ideal critic suspended between literature's allegories of "concern" and its archetypes of "freedom" as "[the critic] seeks not so much to explain a poem in terms of its external relation to history or philosophy, but to *preserve* its identity as a poem and see it in its total mythological context" (*CP* 99). If it's a case of having it *both* ways— "detached but not separated from [one's] community," as Frye would have it (*CP* 131)—to refer to Emma's cookery for a final time, with our own considerable detachment we may tend to read into Frye's critical irony not a little of the darker significance of Freud's theory of "incorporation." Tania Modleski psychoanalytically unpacks that term in the context of Hitchcock's representation of women: "[O]n the one hand, the subject wishes by devouring the object to destroy it and, on the other hand, both to preserve it within the self and to appropriate its qualities [as] truly wanting to have one's cake and eat[ing] it too" (110; see also Laplanche 19–20). Of course, Modleski is offering a highly qualified feminist reading of the Hitchcock canon in her deployment of Freudian psychoanalysis. But I would tend to see a much larger authentication of Frye's horizon of possibilities for belief and action in Emma's having her cake that speaks very much to the restive temper of wartime America.

If Emma's cake-making, like Hitchcock's filmmaking, is incorporative in Frye's ironic sense, surely it aims to safeguard that *spatium* of dynamic individuation where the Deleuzian "differenciation" of identity gains a happy berth for itself by virtue of the continuous process of self-construction beneath the intolerable weight of a too transparently known and too consciously predetermined symbolic life. Even if, as Frye elsewhere remarks, "identity ... is the one that we have failed to achieve," it is "no less a genuine ideal for not having been built" (*MC* 123). So while

Uncle Charlie may come across as merely another superficial version of the American confidence man throughout Hitchcock's filmic incorporation, it perhaps pays to remember that in Herman Melville's novel *The Confidence-Man*, the first stage of confidence is "distrust"—distrust in all forms of determinate truth whose "peculiar virtue being unguessed" requires that we "conclude nothing absolute from the human form," but instead "ponder the mystery of human subjectivity in general" since "[t] he beauty of mystery is everywhere" (928, 958, 1083, 978, 1053).

Moreover, the fact that Uncle Charlie could derive considerable pleasure in life from trashing the stultifying models of a too predetermined symbolic life just noted, albeit at the expense of distracted fathers, discomfited detectives, and perhaps even merry widows—"The whole world is a joke to me," he significantly remarks—perhaps reveals that within the genre of noir, a filmmaker like Hitchcock could have his cake, too. By focusing throughout this paper on Hitchcock's irony in its broadest sense, therefore, and by focusing in particular on those elements of counter-cultural resistance mounted against America's intra- and postwar domestic ideologies, Frye's critical theory makes it possible for us to imagine a kind of filmmaking that would appear to run defiantly counter to the Hollywood realism closeting the impalatable and unbearable presentiment of the effete man and the mannish woman ambiguously in play between the Tweedle Dee of Uncle Charlie and the Tweedle Dum of his hapless niece.

"Irony," Frye has remarked, "is not the centre of human reality, but only one of several modes of imaginative expression, and it is a function of the critic to provide some perspective for irony" (*CP* 132). I might conclude this brief anatomy of filmic irony in Hitchcock by pointing out, following Frye in his own *Anatomy*, that the mystery of human identity previously alluded to can never be merely "extrinsic"—that is to say, that kind of "mystery of the unknown or unknowable essence ... which involves art only when art is also made illustrative of something else, as religious art is to the person concerned primarily with worship"

(88). To the contrary, my take on Frye and film studies angles for a more "intrinsic" kind of mystery, that kind which, Frye astutely explains, "remains a mystery in itself no matter how fully known it is ... [because it] comes not from concealment but from revelation, not from something unknown or unknowable in the work, but from *something unlimited* in it" (*AC* 88, emphasis added). Precisely this sense of a knowledge of textuality—literary, filmic, or otherwise—infinitely engaged stands to make all the difference, it seems to me, between the merely passive critic and a more active and energetic and endlessly inspired (and inspiring) reader of communicative art on the very model of Northrop Frye himself.[8]

ENDNOTES

1 In an essay entitled "The Search for Acceptable Words" published in 1973, Frye proffers a similar reservation concerning the media in mass culture: "The book *qua* book is not linear: we follow a line while we are reading it, but the book itself is a stationary visual focus of a community. It is the electronic media that increase the amount of linear experience, of things seen and heard that are quickly forgotten. One sees the effects on students: a superficial alertness combined with increased difficulty in preserving the intellectual continuity that is the chief characteristic of education." Hence, "[t]he book ... is the technological instrument that makes democracy a working possibility" (*Spiritus Mundi* 9, 8). However, in a much later essay (1989), called "Literature as Therapy," Frye is much more convinced of the power of filmmaking. "What I am suggesting," he states, "is that we should not overlook the immense recuperative power that literature, along with the other arts, could provide in a world as crazy as ours. Poets themselves often do not realize their own potentiality in this regard. I think filmmakers, of all the producers of art, have perhaps the clearest and most consistent notion of it" (34).

2 I use "mainstream" here in the sense of what Frye would characterize as the "normal." Thus, like film noir, "What irony appeals to is a sense of normality on the part of the audience. That is, we recognize a certain action to be grotesque or absurd or evil or futile or whatever, and it is that sense of normality in the audience that enables irony to make

its point as irony. Without the sense of the normal ["mainstream" as opposed to "noir" filmmaking], irony would cease to become ironic and become simply description" ("Literature as Therapy" 29).

3   For a more thoroughgoing survey of the typical features of the noir genre, see Dickos, Introduction, esp. 6–9.

4   Several of Uncle Charlie's trenchant castigations of modern life punctuating his appearances throughout the film correspond precisely to that form of "exceptional awareness" that Frye attributes to the figure of the "holy sinner," which I am inclined to locate in the noir genre as well. To wit: "The cities are full of women, middle-aged widows, husbands dead, husbands who've spent their lives making fortunes, working and working. And then they die and leave their money to their wives, their silly wives. And what do the wives do, these useless women? You see them in the hotels, the best hotels, every day by the thousands, drinking the money, eating the money, losing the money at bridge, playing all day and all night, smelling of money, proud of their jewelry but of nothing else. Horrible, faded, fat, greedy, women ... Are they human or are they fat, wheezing animals, hmmm? And what happens to animals when they get too fat and too old?" (Screenplay dialogue here and throughout the remainder of my paper at http://www.reelclassics. com/Movies/Shadow/shadow2.htm).

    Additionally, Frye aligns the kind of awareness or "visionary" experience invoked here with the term "reality" rather than that of "realism." "That is partly what I mean," he explains, "by saying that the arts form a kind of counter-environment, setting something up which is really antipathetic to the civilization in which it exists. [Hence,] ... reality is a much more inclusive term in literature than realism. It seems to me that at certain moments of intensity what literature conveys is the sense of controlled hallucination ... where things are seen with a kind of intensity with which they are not seen in ordinary experience" ("Literature as Therapy" 33). I shall return to this whole issue of Hollywood "realism," opposing it to a noir "reality," later in the paper.

5   Here, I'm thinking of that wonderful passage in *The Four Fundamental Concepts* in which Lacan reminds us that "[w]henever the membranes of the egg in which the foetus emerges on its way to becoming a new-born are broken, [we can] imagine for a moment that something flies off, and that one can do it with an egg as easily as with a man, namely the *hommelette*, or the lamella" (197). "Doing it with a man" might suggest that Lacan's

"*hommelette*" in this passage is intended to signify the dissidence of the queer subject fly-ing off in the face of the more normative reproductive one signed by the egg, an observa-tion my subsequent argument will elaborate more fully.

6   In a subsequent passage, Frye elaborates this tendency as a kind of "revolutionary realism"—that is, "a questioning, exploring, searching, disturbing force [that] cannot go over to established authority and defend the fictions which may be essential to au-thority" since this "new kind of energy"—"the revolt of the brain behind the eye against sensation"—is "without reference to representation" (*MC* 62). In an essay entitled "Au-guries of Experience" from 1987, this revolutionary tendency is aligned with what Frye (following Freud, once again) refers to as "the essential 'reality principle,'" which "con-sists in what human beings have made," and therefore what "they can remake," as op-posed to reality *tour court* where "'reality' can only be what does not change or changes entirely on its own terms: as far as we are concerned, its future has already occurred" (8).

7   Here, I allude to another egg-headed passage in Deleuze, this time from *The Logic of Sense*, where the figure of Humpty Dumpty as a kind of shadow for what Uncle Charlie comes to represent in Hitchcock's noir canon provides the sternest of warnings about the killing constraints of "Commonplace" ideologies, and the price we pay for allowing "consciousness" to become completely overtaken by them. Thus, in Deleuze, "[Humpty Dumpty] is uniquely made of shifting and 'disconcerting' singularities, [and] will not recognize Alice, for each of Alice's singularities seems to him assimilated in the ordinary arrangement of an organ (eye, nose, mouth) and to belong to the Commonplace of an all too regular face, arranged just like everyone else's ... As Humpty Dumpty says, it is always possible to prevent that we grow in tandem. One does not grow without the other shrinking. [Hence,] there is nothing astonishing in the fact the paradox is the force of the unconscious: it occurs always in the space between consciousnesses, con-trary to good sense or, behind the back of consciousness, contrary to common sense (80)." In mythic terms, of course, we're only too well aware of Humpty Dumpty's great fall from the wall, and now in filmic terms, Uncle Charlie's horrific fall before a speeding locomotive. In a parallel rumination concerning the fall to madness of Friedrich Nietz-sche, Deleuze imagines such destruction as the loss of the subject's "free, anonymous, and nomadic singularity ... independent of the matter of their individuation and [as in

Melville] the forms of their personality"—in a word, the death of "'Overman' ... [as]
the superior type of *everything that is*" (107). "This is strange discourse," Deleuze wistfully concludes (107), and thus puts us in mind of Uncle Charlie once again in his first
encounter with his niece, when he remarks, "You're a strange girl, Charlie."

8   And all the difference, finally, between the merely passive and the more active student
in our very own classrooms, Frye further reminds us, where "[l]iterary education should
lead not merely to the admiration of great [works], but to some possession of [their]
power of utterance [whose] ultimate aim is an ethical and participating aim, not an
aesthetic or contemplative one ..." (*WTC* 47).

WORKS CITED

Bergstrom, Janet. 1979. "Alternation, Segmentation, Hypnosis: An Interview with Raymond Bellour." *Camera Obscura* 3–4: 71–104.

Bérubé, Allen. 1991. *Coming Out Under Fire: The History of Gay Men and Women in
World War Two*. New York: Plume.

Carmichael, Virginia. 1993. *Framing History: The Rosenberg Story and the Cold War*.
American Culture 6. Minneapolis: University of Minnesota Press.

D'Emilio, John. 1992. "The Homosexual Menace: The Politics of Sexuality in Cold War
America." *Making Trouble: Essays on Gay History, Politics, and the University*. New
York: Routledge, 57–73.

Deleuze, Gilles. 1994. *Difference and Repetition*, trans. Paul Patton. New York: Columbia University Press.

———. 1990. *The Logic of Sense*, trans. Mark Lester and Charles Stivale. Ed. Constantin
V. Boundas. New York: Columbia University Press.

Dickos, Andrew. 2002. *Street with No Name: A History of the Classic American Film
Noir*. Lexington: University of Kentucky Press.

Frye, Northrop. 1993. "Auguries of Experience." In *Northrop Frye, The Eternal Act of
Creation: Essays, 1979–1990*, ed. Robert D. Denham. Bloomington: Indiana University Press, 3–8.

———. 1993. "Literature as Therapy." *Northrop Frye, The Eternal Act of Creation:*

Essays, 1979–1990, ed. Robert D. Denham. Bloomington: Indiana University Press, 21–34.

———. 1976. *Spiritus Mundi: Essays on Literature, Myth, and Society*. Bloomington: Indiana University Press.

———. 1973. *The Critical Path: An Essay on the Social Context of Literary Criticism*. 1971. Bloomington: Midland-Indiana University Press.

———. 1969. *Anatomy of Criticism: Four Essays*. New York: Atheneum.

———. 1967. *The Well-Tempered Critic*. Bloomington: Indiana University Press.

———. 1963. *The Educated Imagination*. The Massey Lectures, Second Series. Toronto: Canadian Broadcasting Corporation.

Hamilton, Mark. 2003. "Northrop Frye Goes to the Movies." PhD dissertation. Florida State University.

Hitchcock, Alfred, dir. *Shadow of a Doubt*. Perf. Joseph Cotton and Theresa Wright. David O. Selznick, 1943. Original screenplay online, http://www.reelclassics.com/Movies/Shadow/shadow2.htm.

Lacan, Jacques. 1977. *Écrits: A Selection*, trans. Alan Sheridan. New York: W.W. Norton.

Laplanche, Jean. 1976. *Life and Death in Psychoanalysis*, trans and intro by Jeffrey Mehlman. Baltimore and London: Johns Hopkins University Press.

Melville, Herman. 1984. *The Confidence-Man: His Masquerade*. New York: Library of America.

Modleski, Tania. 1988. *The Women Who Knew Too Much: Hitchcock and Feminist Theory*. New York: Routledge.

Silverman, Kaja. 1992. *Male Subjectivity at the Margins*. New York: Routledge.

Smith, Daniel W. 1997. "'A Life of Pure Immanence': Deleuze's 'Critique and Clinique' Project." Introduction. In *Gilles Deleuze: Essays Critical and Clinical*, trans. Daniel W. Smith and Michael A. Greco. Minneapolis: University of Minnesota Press, xi–liii.

Reframing Frye:

Bridging Culture and Cognition

Michael Sinding

OPINION IS divided on Northrop Frye's relation to ruling schools of thought in literary and cultural scholarship—that is, cultural studies and new historicism. Some in these schools have drawn deeply on Frye's literary thought while condemning a perceived anti-historical, formalist, and religious bias (e.g., Jameson—see White, "Frye's" and "Ideology" for other critics). Others (Hamilton, Salusinszky, Adamson, Wang) have strongly argued Frye's importance as both contributor and challenger to these schools. Hayden White calls him the "greatest natural cultural historian of our time" ("Frye's" 28). However, such contextualizations, even when favourable, risk leaving Frye obscured in the shadow of the present: superseded as contributor or doomed as challenger. I think we should instead develop Frye's core ideas by putting them into play with current debates. I shall do so by making them talk to two lively intellectual undertakings, cultural studies and cognitive linguistics.

In *The Critical Path*, Frye speaks of his long preoccupation with the question, "What is the total subject of study of which criticism forms part?" (14). Literary criticism "seemed to be part of two larger but undeveloped subjects. One was the unified criticism of all the arts"—that is, "aesthetics"; the other was "some area of verbal expression which had not yet been defined," which he calls "mythology" (14). Toward a definition, he takes up Vico's account of "how a society, in its earliest phase, sets up a framework of mythology, out of which all its verbal culture grows, including its literature" (34). Early verbal culture includes a group of stories, some of which take on educational functions and canonical importance, sticking together to produce stable personal gods and heroes. Mythology "tends to become encyclopaedic, expanding into a total myth covering a society's view of its past, present and future, its relation to its gods and its neighbours, its traditions, its social and religious duties, and its ultimate destiny"; it "comprises everything that it most concerns its society to know" (36). Images of accretion give way to an arboreal metaphor of gradual diversification:

> In origin, a myth of concern is largely undifferentiated: it has its roots in religion, but religion has also at that stage the function of *religio*, the binding together of the community in common acts and assumptions. Later, a myth of concern develops different social, political, legal, and literary branches. (36)

"Mythology" thus grows to mean "verbal culture" in general, and the modern critic's remit is consequently broadened:

> [H]is total subject embraces not merely literature, but the areas of concern which the mythical language of construction and belief enters and informs. These areas constitute the mythological subjects, and they include large parts of religion, philosophy, political theory, and the social sciences. (98)

Disciplinary partitions still discourage this kind of daunting and exhilarating charge, but interdisciplinary passages have opened up in places. Both cognitive linguistics and cultural studies have some jurisdiction here, with their overlapping themes or topics: imagination, language, literature, culture, society, ideology. When it comes to approach, these two have little common ground. However, in the spirit of finding new directions from old, I propose that Frye has enough in common with both to help us bring them into productive alignment: that a mixed framework is possible, and probably necessary, if we're to pursue the "impossible project" of "the study of all the relations between all the elements in a whole way of life" (Nelson et al. 15). Cultural studies and new historicism produce compelling analyses of "applied mythology," the ways in which culture and language are mobilized for "concerned" social purposes. But they lean on shaky assumptions about how meaning works. Cognitive linguistics produces powerful analyses of how metaphor, narrative, and models shape everyday language and thought. But it needs a richer view of the relation of language and ideology to literature and culture.

Frye can bridge these analyses because his account of meaning in language and literature is interwoven with an account of their role in society and history, both centring on an evolving overall mythology, or model of the human situation and destiny, built out of myth and metaphor. We can compare these frameworks where their overlaps converge on a common question: "social mythology," or, *how cultural meaning creates political common sense*. Our example will be the metaphors and myths behind concepts of liberalism and conservatism.

Introductions to cultural studies tend to observe that it grows out of "both a broad, anthropological and a more narrowly humanistic conception of culture." But it departs from traditional forms of these in arising from "analyses of modern industrial societies," and in rejecting "the exclusive equation of culture with high culture"; in fact, "all forms of cultural production need to be studied in relation to other cultural practices and to social and historical structures" (Nelson et al. 4). Cultural studies continues to rethink the relation of culture to society, beyond the Marxist dogma that an economic/material base "ultimately determines" a mental superstructure or ideology.[1] Three principles recur:

1. Ideology (of dominant vs. subordinate groups) is still the main issue in interpretation, although it is seen as neither wholly determined nor all-encompassing.[2]

2. Meaning is in the first place literal, and cultural meaning is therefore the representation or coding of literal concepts in symbols, myths, and images.

3. The effect of this coding is to make the "meaning"—which is a debatable product of the dominance of a particular culture, class, or group at this point in history—appear as normal, natural, universal, and eternal, as common sense, or "just a fact" (Barthes 124).[3]

Critics claim that these ideas are overenthusiastic extensions of structuralist and semiological ideas about language, applied to literature and culture:

· Meaning is arbitrary (i.e., our names for things are conventional, not natural).

· Meaning is defined by binary oppositions (originally a point about sounds and phonemes, extended to words and concepts).

· Meaning is sign-like: a use of symbol X to stand for concept Y.[4]

All of these points are undermined in modern linguistics.[5]

Roland Barthes[6] treats myth as "a type of speech" (109): on a magazine cover, "a young Negro in a French uniform is saluting, with his eyes uplifted, probably fixed on a fold of the tricolour" (116). The whole situation depicted "is the *meaning* of the picture," the signifier. The signified is "French imperiality" (118ff.), or, more fully, "that France is a great Empire, that all her sons, without any colour discrimination, faithfully serve under her flag, and that there is no better answer to the detractors of an alleged colonialism than the zeal shown by this Negro in serving his so-called oppressors" (116). The "presence of the signified through the signifier" is "signification" (116–117). In its own context, the signifier has a genuine meaning, value, and history: "The meaning is already complete, it postulates a kind of knowledge, a past, a memory, a comparative order of facts, ideas, decisions" (117). Thus, "a *complete* image would exclude myth … myth prefers to work with poor, incomplete images, where the meaning is already relieved of its fat, and ready for a signification, such as caricatures, pastiches, symbols, etc." (127). Myth alienates that meaning by tearing the signifier out of its own context in a complex reality, making us forget that context by placing it in another, hollowing it out and turning it to other purposes (such as propaganda, advertising, entertainment)—those of the myth's producers and consumers:

> In the case of the soldier-Negro, for instance, what is got rid of is
> … the contingent, historical, in one word: *fabricated*, quality of
> colonialism … If I *state the fact* of French imperiality without ex-
> plaining it, I am very near to finding that it is natural and *goes with-
> out saying*: I am reassured. (143)

In Frye's view, that Barthes treats myth as *ordinary* discourse is a basic mistake. The principle context for literary texts is literature, and literary discourse assumes and invites a kind of attention distinct from ordinary discourse: "centripetal" or coherence oriented, as opposed to "centrifugal" or reference oriented (*CP* Chap. 1).[7] Barthes's "mythology" is Frye's "social" or "secondary" mythology (as we will see below). His example is not literature, but his analysis is off target anyway because his view of ordinary discourse is also off target, overlooking its literary dimensions. Semiology exaggerates the sense that meaning is a literal assertion,

MICHAEL SINDING

contained in a "sign" or "code," packed up and sent by a speaker and un-
packed by an addressee. This carries the potential for significant distor-
tion, as when the implications are taken up, that the sender aims solely
at persuasion or dictation. Thus, the recipient should agree or disagree,
submit or resist; and so verbal culture is all "ideological struggle," propaganda, or even, because it's all around us as a "way of life," blanket mental
obfuscation and oppression, omnipresent but mysteriously sourceless,
like gravity. In reaction to this, cultural studies developed a recognition
of creative "resistance" by cultural consumers; this in turn snowballed
into visions of omnipresent resistance (as one critic complained, "the
discovery that washing your car on Sunday is a revolutionary event"
[Morris 312]).

However, the Barthesian legacy includes fascinating sociology and
anthropology of high culture, pop culture, and everyday life, and acute
studies of the uses of cultural forms to frame moral and political situations and arguments.[8]

Cognitive linguistics is also highly interdisciplinary and claims a very
broad scope, examining metaphor, figures, and narrative in many areas,
including literature, philosophy, religion, anthropology, politics, mathematics, and particularly world view and common sense.[9]

Frye and George Lakoff agree that metaphor and myth are schematic, pervasive in language and thought, and grounded in bodily experience. Discussing the literary basis of non-literary discourse, Frye speaks
of a "conceptual rhetoric" (*AC* 331ff.), famously suggesting that "the nature and conditions of *ratio*, so far as *ratio* is verbal, are contained by
oratio" (337).[10] For Lakoff, metaphors are in the first place conceptual
mappings, ways of understanding one thing in terms of another. Hence,
meanings are also *motivated* rather than arbitrary, often widespread or
universal, and there are limits to the explanatory reach of ideology and
social construction.[11]

In recent years, Lakoff has set up a progressive think-tank and written
four remarkably influential cognitive studies of politics to alleviate his

frustration at how liberals were being manoeuvred into accepting conservative framing assumptions instead of arguing from their own turf.[12] Frames are knowledge structures; they shape the way we see and act in the world. Words are defined relative to frames, and evoke those frames. Since negating a frame also evokes it, which reinforces it, Lakoff's advice is to "respond by reframing" (*Don't* 119). Consider the recent Republican mantra of "tax relief." In the frame for *relief*, there must be an affliction, an afflicted party, and a reliever who removes the affliction and is therefore a hero. Anyone trying to stop the hero is a villain (*Don't* 3). When this is connected to "tax," it becomes a *metaphorical* frame (4): Republicans will rescue the electorate from financial torment. To oppose the idea in these terms is to side with the villain. You may have all the facts and figures in the world on your side; if you accept the wrong frame, you hide them all under your big black hat. As Lakoff puts it, "Frames trump facts" (*Don't* 115). This is not to say that facts don't exist or matter. Indeed, the key difference from the cultural studies model of discourse is the insistence on the possibility and importance of *honest* and *accurate* framing.[13]

There are interconnected levels of framing: "tax relief" and other slogans are *surface frames*. To work, they must hang on *deep frames* that constitute moral or political world views and "define one's overall 'common sense'" (*Thinking* 28).[14] Lakoff's analysis of conservative and liberal deep frames begins with several puzzles. First, their language "seemed to use virtually the same metaphors for morality but with different—almost opposite—priorities"; hence, they "could seem to be talking about the same thing and yet reach opposite conclusions" (*Moral* 11–12). Also, typical sets of opinions seem at first glance random: "What does opposition to abortion have to do with opposition to environmentalism? What does either have to do with opposition to affirmative action or gun control or the minimum wage?" (12). The same goes for the liberal "cluster of opposing political stands" (12). They are also split on what they like to talk about: discipline and toughness versus need and help social causes versus direct causes (13). The question is: How must liberals and conservatives think, to produce these effects? Lakoff's explanation is that the coherence of political world views is based on coherent moral world views, which in turn are based on two opposing models of what family life should be: they are about "strictness and nurturance as ideals at all levels—from the family to morality to religion and, ultimately, to politics" (x).

The Strict Father model is a traditional nuclear family. The father is responsible for supporting and protecting and has authority to set and enforce rules for the children. The mother cares for the house and children, and supports the father. By respecting and obeying their parents children build character (self-discipline and self-reliance) (33). In the Nurturant Parent model, parents share responsibility equally. Love, empathy, and nurturance are primary, and children become responsible, self-disciplined, and self-reliant through being cared for and caring for others. Parents therefore support and protect, which requires strength and courage. Children's obedience comes from respect, not fear (33–34). These are *idealized* models of family life (and in abbreviated form here), so most people have some version of both models, they may have variations and combinations, and may apply them in different domains (156–161).

Strict Father priorities include moral strength, respect for authority, and strict behavioural norms; Nurturant Parent priorities are empathy and helping those in need (34–35; see Chaps. 5 and 6). The principles of each model appear in the other but with opposing priorities, which drastically changes their effects (35). So in the Nurturant model, strength functions in the service of nurturance; and in the Strict model, empathy and nurturance are means to the end of moral strength (e.g., as "a reward for obedience" [35, 101]). Lakoff goes on to analyze the models' contrasting reasoning on a wide range of policy issues (Chaps. 10–16).

But other or further explanations for the political division are possible. For example, Steven Pinker sees views of human nature as key.[15] He names the conservative versus liberal visions after literary genres—that is, "tragic" versus "utopian." However, what Pinker downplays—the metaphoric and narrative aspects of these "visions"—Frye delves into directly.

The Critical Path presents conservatism and liberalism first as elements of society constituted by myths of concern and freedom and then as social views based on polarizing social myths: the social contract and the utopia.

Frye begins with a dialectic of concern and freedom. Freedom grows out of concern but conflicts with it; the myth of freedom is "part of the myth of concern, but is a part that stresses the importance of the non-mythical elements in culture," those supporting "truth of correspondence" (such as logic and evidence) (44). Such mental attitudes become social: objectivity, suspension of judgment, tolerance, and respect for the individual (44). Frye states, "The myth of freedom thus constitutes the 'liberal' element in society, as the myth of concern constitutes the conservative one" (45).

Literature is a totality or great code of all possibilities of concern, and thus provides a context for myths of concern rather than being one itself. Social mythology is a poor substitute for the genuine mythology of literature, stealing its forms. At times Frye writes as if it is junk mythology, wholly irredeemable:

> All around us is a society which demands that we adjust or come to terms with it, and what that society presents to us is a social mythology. Advertising, propaganda, the speeches of politicians, popular books and magazines, the clichés of rumour, all have their own kind of pastoral myths, quest myths, hero myths, sacrificial myths, and nothing will drive these shoddy constructs out of the mind except the genuine forms of the same thing. (*StS* 105)

So Barthes's saluting soldier suggests a perverted myth of loyalty and sacrifice to a colonial occupier, demystifiable only by literary myths of devotion to some genuine (spiritual) authority. In *The Critical Path*, a mythology need not be closed but may be open. An open mythology allows a progressive education in forms of social mythology, from early clichés geared toward civil obedience to later forms that may confirm, question, or outgrow the initial ones (for example, we may come to see democracy rather than capitalism as the real American myth of concern) (136–138).

Conservatism and liberalism as social views are based on concerned versions of the two myths that polarize social mythology, the social contract and utopia (158):[16]

> There are two social conceptions so deeply rooted in our experience that they can be presented only as myths. One is the social contract, the myth which attempts to explain the nature of the conditioning we accept by getting born. The other is the Utopia, the myth of an ideal social contract. Both these myths have religious affiliations: the contract is connected with the alienation myth of the Fall of Man, and the Utopia with the transcendence myth of the City of God. The overtones of the social contract myth are ironic, sometimes tragic. (*SM* 36)

Conservative and liberal views side with social contract and utopia respectively and understand personal development in relation to them. The conservative's "development is a matter of growing organically out of the roots of his social context," whose fundamental institutions civilize and give significance to life, whereas "[t]o try to reject what one is already committed to can only lead to confusion and chaos, both in one's own life and in society" (*SM* 36). The radical feels that "[m]aturity and development ... are a matter of becoming aware of our conditioning, and, in becoming aware, of making a choice between presented and discovered loyalties" (37). The conservative favours commitment and the radical detachment followed by new commitment: "The end of commitment and engagement is the community: the end of detachment, then, is clearly the individual" (39). Both tend to rationalize rather than recognize anomalies and absurdities in their chosen society (*CP* 160–162).

But how exactly do these myths induce moral and political values? Interestingly, Lakoff examines how arguments and stories can interpenetrate, since "arguments have implicit story elements—heroes, victims, villains, crimes, rewards, punishments" (*Thinking* 137) (and vice versa). They guide understanding by bringing along inferences about moral values and principles. Thus, a common background in political arguments is a kind of fairy-tale story or, Frye would say, Romance myth.[17]

Indeed, frames have a narrative structure. The concept was developed in part from sociologist Erving Goffman's analysis of how we grasp social situations and institutions in terms of the "life is a play" metaphor: we know how to act in hospitals, restaurants, banks, courts, parties, and so forth, because we know all of their conventional *roles, settings, props*, and *scenes*, and their *internal logic and order*.[18] So there appear to be seeds of major genres (or myths) in various arguments, and even within that little phrase "tax relief," which as we've seen also evokes a conventional scenario with roles of victim, villain, and hero.

In Lakoff's terms, the basic story/argument elements of Frye's models are the abstract "characters" of society and the individual and their relations. Specifically, Frye presents contrasting narrative models of the individual developing or maturing as a function of her attachment to and/or detachment from existing or ideal societies. These models have role-defining moral values. The conservative sees existing society as good: to break from it to pursue a utopian mirage would be a crime, and would be punishable by social and personal chaos (making them both victims as well as villains). Heroism means defending social institutions and is rewarded with order and fulfillment. The liberal sees existing institutions as partly or potentially unjust, defined by villains harming victims. It is heroic to try to redress such crimes by rejecting the social status quo to build the ideal or improved society, which is the hero's reward.

There is much more to be said about how these narrative models create inferences that transfer to other forms of discourse, and about how the two frameworks relate in general. But the main point is that Frye shows that other conceptual structures must be considered: conservatism and liberalism must be understood in terms of conventional narrative patterns—myths—in addition to metaphors. Lakoff's studies paint an important part, but not the whole picture of the political contrast.[19]

We should also note that Lakoff's investment in family metaphors may need correction or supplementation.[20] For example, he never examines his concepts of strictness and nurturance beyond their manifestation in his family models. I think they apply even more broadly than he indicates (as psychological types, for example) and I have a hunch that they may be metaphorically based on the contrast between muscular tension and relaxation. We all experience this contrast every day, but the rigidity associated with tension and the flexibility associated with relaxation can translate into entire bodily postures, and concepts of "posture," "stance," "attitude," and "disposition" also apply metaphorically to whole world views. Moreover, in the classic political texts of Hobbes and Rousseau, the "body politic" metaphor is far more important than any family model, and in fact the social contract is the act that creates the body. Hobbes's *Leviathan* opens with an account of the body-state mapping, which ends with a reference to this mythical act: "Lastly, the *Pacts* and *Covenants*, by which the parts of this Body Politique were at first made, set together, and united" (81–82). The family metaphor, on the other hand, appears only in a brief aside: "Cities and Kingdomes ... are but greater Families" (224).

In Rousseau's *Social Contract* the family metaphor gets better billing. Chapter 11, "The First Societies," begins,

The oldest of all societies, and the only natural one, is that of the family.... It can thus be said that the family is the first model of political societies: The father corresponds to the ruler, the children to the people; and all, having been born free and equal, give up their freedom only for their own advantage. (9)

Thus, the family also participates in the social contract. But Rousseau notes the limits of this metaphor, and it fades from view by the time we reach the story of the contract in Chapter VI, which, as in Hobbes, culminates in the metaphorical body's creation: "In place of the individual persons of the contracting parties, the act of association immediately creates a collective, artificial body ... and the same act gives this body its unity, its collective self, its life, and its will" (17–18). As these examples show, in actual discourse, metaphor generally interacts with narrative and conceptual reasoning. It will be a further question just how and how far all these structures fit and work together.

Nonetheless, this way of linking common-sense social knowledge, linguistic knowledge, and cultural knowledge is, I think, far more supple, powerful, and true to experience than that suggested by Barthes. And I think it will refine rather than dislodge the kind of cultural critique of rhetoric and symbolism done in all of our frameworks: it indicates that these are structures we see by but that hide certain things from us as they reveal others. *Anatomy of Criticism* and Frye's other studies are pre-eminently rich and suggestive analyses of these structures in literature, culture, and society. He recognized that "myths of concern, democratic, Marxist, or what not, are ... founded on visions of human life with a generic literary shape" (*CP* 128). And he recognized that these myths are descended from scriptural and ritual forms, where they are often integrated in an overall form. If we want to understand how culture, society, literature, language, and common sense interconnect, we will have to make a place at the table for Frye and take a fresh look at his work.

There remain large questions about the details of this interconnection, and just where mixing frameworks might take us. Given Frye's commitment to the autonomy of culture and the detachment of criticism and the university from any myth of concern, it is difficult to imagine him putting his grasp of mythology to work for a party or a movement. Frye proposes reintegrating conservative and liberal myths at the imaginative level, to envision people assimilating their social traditions in order to grow through them toward social progress via disciplined individuality (*SM* 39–40). But while Lakoff and cultural critics may be more openly partisan than Frye, their studies too help alert us to our social-mythological conditioning, and so also "liberate the language of concern" (*CP* 166) and return us to literature—the "laboratory of myths" (*SM* 44) and the "great code of concern" (*CP* 128)—having won some of the imaginative freedom that gives glimpses of a "concern behind concern" (103).

I thank the Alexander von Humboldt Foundation for supporting my research through a Post-doctoral Fellowship.

ENDNOTES

1   See for example Williams's revisions of base and superstructure (*Culture* 31–49), and his concept of "structures of feeling" (22–27); Stuart Hall's "articulation," and "preferred/ negotiated/ oppositional" kinds of readings (see Nelson et al. 8; Storey, Introduction ix); Althusser's "relative autonomy" of Ideological State Apparatuses; Gramsci's "hegemony" as dominance of provisional social alliances by popular consent (see also Hebdige 357–367; Williams, *Culture* 37–40, and "Hegemony" in *Keywords*). Also significant is Volosinov/Bakhtin's view of ideological struggle within language by re-accentuating signs. Useful overviews of this post-Marxism are found in Hebdige; Hall, "Cultural Studies"; and McRobbie. The original formulations of Marx and Engels are briefly extracted in Storey (196–201).

2   Despite revisions, "ideology is the central concept in cultural studies" (Storey, Introduction viii–ix). For Storey, Hall's formulation from the early 1980s is "generally accepted as the dominant working definition within cultural studies. ... meaning is always the result of an act of 'articulation' (an active process of production in use within specific social

relations). ... The cultural field is defined by this struggle to articulate, disarticulate and rearticulate cultural texts and practices for particular ideologies, particular politics" (ix).

3   Ideology "saturates everyday discourse in the form of common sense" so it "cannot be bracketed off from everyday life as a self-contained set of 'political opinions' or 'biased views'" (Hebdige 363).

4   For the use of structuralism and semiology in cultural analysis, Barthes's *Mythologies* and Hall's "Encoding, Decoding" are central. For discussion of "the theoretical advances which were made by the encounters with structuralist, semiotic, and poststructuralist work," see Hall, "Cultural Studies" (283–284).

5   Cognitive critics have identified Saussurean linguistics as a source of post-structuralism's theoretical weakness. See Turner (*Death, Reading*), McConachie and Hart. Pinker, Norris, Holland, and others have critiqued the linguistics of Derrida and Lacan. Reddy critiques the "conduit metaphor" for language.

6   I focus on Barthes for several reasons. *Mythologies* came out in the same year as Frye's *Anatomy* (1957), was a major influence on cultural studies, and continues to be extracted and discussed. Frye refers to Barthes in his published works, and privately associates him with the post-structuralist "Holy Family" with its "sacred cow" of "the omnipresence of ideology, & the impossibility of ever getting past it" (Notebook 27.276, qtd. in Adamson, "Treason" 77). Also, I believe Barthes's view of ideology in culture is more representative than Althusser's more famous and extreme view, which has met with some criticism.

7   Here Frye speaks of the "two mental operations" of all media experience, pre-critically following a linear narrative and then studying its structure as a "simultaneous unity" (25–27); he uses "centrifugal" and "centripetal" only as the names of fallacies (32–33). See the discussions of centrifugal and centripetal attention elsewhere (*AC* 73–74ff.; *GC* 56–63, *WP* 3ff.).

8   On the topic of genre, for example, see Montrose on political uses of pastoral, Radway's sociology of romance, and Williams's materialist account of drama (*Culture* 125–147).

9   It is said to be "all-inclusive or all-embracing" (Dirven et al., ed. 3), and "heading for its own built-in final destination, that of cognitive semiotics" (2). It is very interested in "worldview, that is, with everyday conceptualization, reasoning, and language," and common sense (Lakoff, *Moral* 3–4). New subfields include cognitive versions of

sociolinguistics, discourse analysis, poetics, stylistics, rhetoric, anthropology, and religious studies. For cognitive studies of ideology, see Dirven et al., ed.

10 Frye later speaks of the need to train people to "think rhetorically, to visualize ... abstractions, to subordinate logic and sequence to the insights of metaphor and simile, to realize that figures of speech are not the ornaments of language, but the elements of both language and thought" (*StS* 93–94). Lakoff calls for a "higher" or "real" rationality that recognizes the imaginative dimension of thought and language (*Whose* 15–17, 249–259; *Thinking* 39–41). Turner calls for a "cognitive rhetoric" that would link everyday thought and language to literature and criticism (*Reading* Chap. 11). The classic text of conceptual metaphor theory is Lakoff and Johnson's *Metaphors We Live By*. For metaphor in reasoning and philosophy, see their *Philosophy*. For literature, see Lakoff and Turner, and Turner, *Death*, *Literary*, and *Reading*. Spatial schemas are especially important for both Frye and the cognitive linguists. Frye's ideas about metaphor are most fully set out in *Anatomy*, "Theory of Symbols," and importantly developed elsewhere.

11 In fact, both Barthes and Hall recognize limits to "arbitrariness." Barthes qualifies that signs and myths are partially motivated by forms of *analogy*—with other signs, by fitting into a structure (e.g., grammar: subject-predicate agreement), and with reality (the black soldier's salute with that of the French soldier) (126). But such formal analogies are created by history and are always partial, and motivations are chosen among other possible ones: "I can very well give to French imperiality many other signifiers" (127). Compare Lakoff and Johnson on the motion of semantic motivation in cognitive linguistics (*Philosophy* 464–466).

12 In 2000, Lakoff and colleagues established the Rockridge Institute to counter the decades-long think-tanking of the right (see www.rockridgeinstitute.org; it closed in April 2008). His work soon came into the political spotlight. Prominent democrats (including the Clintons) heard, read, and recommended his work and consulted with him. *Don't Think of an Elephant!* was praised by progressive luminaries, became a *New York Times* bestseller, and got Lakoff publishing, appearing, and talked about in major opinion journals, and on radio and television. The story of Lakoff's rise is told in Matt Bai's *New York Times Magazine* cover story, "The Framing Wars."

13 "Framing is normal. Every sentence we say is framed in some way. When we say what we believe, we are using frames that we think are relatively accurate" (*Don't* 100). Thus,

Lakoff can contrast honest and truthful framing with "spin" and "propaganda" (*Don't* 100–101). In cultural studies these often seem distinctions without a difference—for example, in Althusser's model of the construction of all subjectivity by ideological apparatuses. Hall is less extreme: "The cultural industries do have the power constantly to rework and reshape what they represent; and, by repetition and selection, to impose and implant such definitions of ourselves as fit more easily the descriptions of the dominant or preferred culture. ... These definitions don't have the power to occupy our minds; they don't function on us as if we are blank screens. .... [These effects] are neither all-powerful nor all-inclusive" ("Notes" 460). Social constructionism favours simply framing in support of the right values and politics (i.e., progressive or emancipatory) and against the wrong ones (i.e., conservative or reactionary).

14 For more on types of frames, including lexical, surface, issue-defining, and deep frames, see *Thinking*, Chap. 3 (25–48).

15 Pinker's scathing review prompted an angry exchange of letters (noted in my citations). His full account of liberal and conservative visions is in *The Blank Slate*, Chap. 16.

16 The following account from *Spiritus Mundi* appears in a slightly different form in *The Critical Path*, Chap. 7. Note that he speaks of "radical" rather than liberal views. Frye later develops his view of the relation of culture and ideology, especially in *Words With Power*.

17 For discussions of "fairy-tale" structures in political discourse, see Lakoff, "Metaphor in Politics"; *Don't* 71–72; and *Whose* 151–154. Smith critiques the over-reliance on nuance-less "melodrama" structures in American discourse. Chapter 8 of *Thinking Points* discusses the relation of stories to arguments.

18 Goffman is an intellectual link between cognitive linguistics and cultural studies. He is cited by Foucault ("Space" 164), Bourdieu ("How" 343, 348), de Certeau ("Practice" 478, 484n9), and Radway ("Reading" 286), as well as Lakoff (*Thinking* 25–28).

19 Lakoff says the models assume "backgrounds," but does not discuss the narrative qualities of these backgrounds. For example, the Strict model's "view that life is difficult and that the world is fundamentally dangerous" (*Moral* 65) is neither a metaphor nor a model, but we could say it is, or is part of, a very broad and abstract narrative frame. It specifies qualities of a large-scale action (life) and situation (the world), and so seems to imply or constrain scenes and settings.

20 This may be due to the American political context, in which powerful radical conservatives are fixated on "traditional family values," including forceful discipline. Conservatives in Canada and elsewhere seem more concerned with the kind of values Frye and Pinker describe. See Lakoff's discussion of James Dobson's "Focus on the Family" group as evidence for his Strict Father model (*Don't* 6, *Moral* 182–183, 339–348).

WORKS CITED

Adamson, Joseph. 1999. "The Treason of the Clerks: Frye, Ideology, and the Authority of Imaginative Culture." In *Rereading Frye: The Published and Unpublished Works*, ed. David Boyd and Imre Salusinszky. Toronto: University of Toronto Press, 72–102.

Althusser, Louis. 1994. "Ideology and Ideological State Apparatuses." In *Cultural Theory and Popular Culture: A Reader*, ed. John Storey. New York: Harvester Wheatsheaf, 151–162.

Bai, Matt. 2005 (17 July). "The Framing Wars." *The New York Times Magazine*, 38+.

Barthes, Roland. 1973. *Mythologies*, trans. Annette Lavers. 1957. Frogmore: Paladin.

Bourdieu, Pierre. 1995. "How Can One Be a Sports Fan?" In *The Cultural Studies Reader*, ed. Simon During. 1993. London: Routledge, 339–356.

De Certeau, Michel. 1994. "The Practice of Everyday Life." In *Cultural Theory and Popular Culture: A Reader*, ed. John Storey. New York: Harvester Wheatsheaf, 474–485.

Dirven, René, Roslyn Frank, and Martin Pütz, eds. 2003. *Cognitive Models in Language and Thought: Ideology, Metaphors and Meanings*. Cognitive Linguistics Research 24. Berlin: Mouton de Gruyter.

During, Simon, ed. 1995. *The Cultural Studies Reader*. 1993. London: Routledge.

Foucault, Michel. 1995. "Space, Power and Knowledge." In *The Cultural Studies Reader*, ed. Simon During. 1993. London: Routledge, 161–169.

———. 1994. "Method." In *Cultural Theory and Popular Culture: A Reader*, ed. John Storey. New York: Harvester Wheatsheaf, 163–169.

Frye, Northrop. 1991. *Spiritus Mundi: Essays on Literature, Myth and Society*. 1976. Richmond Hill: Fitzhenry and Whiteside.

———. 1990. *Words With Power: Being a Second Study of "The Bible and Literature."* Orlando: Harcourt Brace Jovanovich.

———. 1981. *The Great Code: The Bible and Literature.* Orlando: Harcourt Brace Jovanovich.

———. 1971. *Anatomy of Criticism: Four Essays.* Princeton: Princeton University Press.

———.1971. *The Critical Path: An Essay on the Social Context of Literary Criticism.* Bloomington: Indiana University Press.

———. 1970. *The Stubborn Structure: Essays on Criticism and Society.* Ithaca: Cornell University Press.

Gramsci, Antonio. 1994. "Hegemony, Intellectuals and the State." In *Cultural Theory and Popular Culture: A Reader*, ed. John Storey. New York: Harvester Wheatsheaf, 215–221.

Grossberg, Lawrence, Cary Nelson, Paula A. Treichler, eds. 1992. *Cultural Studies.* New York: Routledge.

Hall, Stuart. 1995. "Encoding, Decoding." In *The Cultural Studies Reader*, ed. Simon During. 1993. London: Routledge, 90–103.

———. 1994. "Notes on Deconstructing 'the Popular.'" In *Cultural Theory and Popular Culture: A Reader*, ed. John Storey. New York: Harvester Wheatsheaf, 455–466.

———. 1992. "Cultural Studies and Its Theoretical Legacies." In *Cultural Studies*, ed. Lawrence Grossberg, Cary Nelson, Paula A. Treichler. New York: Routledge. 277–294.

Hamilton, A.C. 1999. "Northrop Frye as Cultural Theorist." In *Rereading Frye: The Published and Unpublished Works*, ed. David Boyd and Imre Salusinszky. Toronto: University of Toronto Press, 103–121.

———. 1993. "Northrop Frye and the New Historicism." Northrop Frye and Contemporary Literary Theory. Special issue, *Recherches sémiotiques/Semiotic Inquiry* 13:3, 73–83.

———. 1994. "The Legacy of Frye's Criticism in Culture, Religion, and Society." In *The Legacy of Northrop Frye*, ed. Alvin Lee and Robert D. Denham. Toronto: University of Toronto Press, 3–14.

Hebdige, Dick. 1995. "From Culture to Hegemony." In *The Cultural Studies Reader*, ed. Simon During. 1993. London: Routledge, 357–367.

Hobbes, Thomas. 1968. *Leviathan*, ed. and introd. C.B. Macpherson. 1651. Harmonds-worth, England: Penguin Books.

Holland, Norman. 1991. "The Trouble(s) with Lacan." In *Literature and Psychology: Proceedings of the Seventh International Conference on Literature and Psychology*, Urbino, 6–9 July 1990. Lisbon: Instituto Superior de Psicologia Aplicada, 3–10 [online]: http://web.clas.ufl.edu/users/nnh/lacan.htm.

Jameson, Fredric. 1981. *The Political Unconscious: Narrative as a Socially Symbolic Act*. Ithaca: Cornell University Press.

Lakoff, George. 2006 (30 October). "Beyond Beauty and Wonder: Understanding the Mind Is Necessary to Understanding Politics." The Rockridge Institute [online]: http://www.rockridgeinstitute.org/research/lakoff/beyondbeautyandwonder.

———. 2006 (12 October). "When Cognitive Science Enters Politics by George Lakoff: A Response to Steven Pinker's Review of Whose Freedom? in The New Republic." The Rockridge Institute [online]: http://www.rockridgeinstitute.org/research/lakoff/whencognitivescienceenterspolitics.

———. 2006. *Whose Freedom? The Battle over America's Most Important Idea*. New York: Farrar, Strauss and Giroux.

———. 2004. *Don't Think of an Elephant!: Know Your Values and Frame the Debate*. White River Junction, VT: Chelsea Green.

———. 2002. *Moral Politics: How Liberals and Conservatives Think*. 2nd ed. Chicago: University of Chicago Press.

———. 1991. "Metaphor in Politics: An Open Letter to the Internet from George Lakoff" [online]: http://philosophy.uoregon.edu/metaphor/lakoff-l.htm.

Lakoff, George, and Mark Johnson. 2003. *Metaphors We Live By*. 2nd ed. Chicago: University of Chicago Press.

———. 1999. *Philosophy in the Flesh: The Embodied Mind and Its Challenge to Western Thought*. New York: Basic Books.

Lakoff, George, and Mark Turner. 1989. *More Than Cool Reason: A Field Guide to Poetic Metaphor*. Chicago: University of Chicago Press.

Lakoff, George, and the Rockridge Institute. 2006. *Thinking Points: Communicating Our American Values and Vision*. New York: Farrar, Straus and Giroux.

McConachie, Bruce, and F. Elizabeth Hart, eds. 2006. *Performance and Cognition:*

Theatre Studies and the Cognitive Turn. Advances in Theatre and Performance Studies. London: Routledge.

McRobbie, Angela. 1992. "Post-Marxism and Cultural Studies: A Post-script." In *Cultural Studies*, ed. Lawrence Grossberg, Cary Nelson, Paula A. Treichler. New York: Routledge, 719–730.

Montrose, Louis Adrian. 1994. "'Eliza, Queen of Shepheardes,' and the Pastoral of Power." In *The New Historicism Reader*, ed. H. Aram Veeser. New York: Routledge, 88–115.

Morris, Meaghan. 1995. "Things to Do with Shopping Centres." In *The Cultural Studies Reader*, ed. Simon During. 1993. London: Routledge, 295–319.

Nelson, Cary, Paula A. Treichler, and Lawrence Grossberg. 1992. "Cultural Studies: An Introduction." In *Cultural Studies*, ed. Lawrence Grossberg, Cary Nelson, Paula A. Treichler. New York: Routledge, 1–22.

Norris, Christopher. 1998. "On Noam Chomsky: Language, Truth and Politics." *Theoria: A Journal of Social and Political Theory* 91: 45–52.

Pinker, Steven. 2006 (3 November). "Metaphorical Limits: George Lakoff's Tendentious Theory of Everything." *The New Republic* [online]: http://www.tnr.com/.

———. 2006 (19 October). "Angels and Demons: A Response to George Lakoff." *The New Republic* [online]: http://www.tnr.com/.

———. 2006 (2 October). "Block That Metaphor! A Review." *Whose Freedom? The Battle Over America's Most Important Idea. The New Republic* [online]: http://www.tnr.com/.

———. 2002. *The Blank Slate: The Modern Denial of Human Nature.* New York: Viking Penguin.

Radway, Janice. 1995. "The Institutional Matrix of Romance." In *The Cultural Studies Reader*, ed. Simon During. 1993. London: Routledge, 438–454.

———. 1994. "Reading *Reading the Romance.*" *Cultural Theory and Popular Culture: A Reader*, ed. John Storey. New York: Harvester Wheatsheaf, 284–301.

Reddy, Michael. 1981. "The Conduit Metaphor: A Case of Frame Conflict in Our Language about Language." In *Metaphor and Thought*, ed. Andrew Ortony. Cambridge: Cambridge University Press, 284–324.

Rousseau, Jean-Jacques. 1975. *The Social Contract: The Essential Rousseau*, trans. Lowell Bair. 1762. New York: Penguin Books.

Salusinszky, Imre. 1994. "Frye and Ideology." In *The Legacy of Northrop Frye*, ed. Alvin Lee and Robert D. Denham. Toronto: University of Toronto Press, 76–83.

Smith, Glenn W. 2007 (18 June). "Snidely, Saddam and Melodramocracy." The Rockridge Institute [online]: http://www.rockridgeinstitute.org/research/rockridge/snidely-saddam-melodramocracy/.

Storey, John, ed. *Cultural Theory and Popular Culture: A Reader*. New York: Harvester Wheatsheaf, 1994.

———. 1994. "The Study of Popular Culture within Cultural Studies." Introduction. In *Cultural Theory and Popular Culture: A Reader*. New York: Harvester Wheatsheaf, vii–xii.

Turner, Mark. 1996. *The Literary Mind: The Origins of Thought and Language*. New York: Oxford University Press.

———. 1991. *Reading Minds: The Study of English in the Age of Cognitive Science*. Princeton: Princeton University Press

———. 1987. *Death is the Mother of Beauty: Mind, Metaphor, Criticism*. Chicago: University of Chicago Press.

Veeser, H. Aram, ed. 1994. *The New Historicism Reader*. New York: Routledge.

Wang Ning. 2003. "Northrop Frye and Cultural Studies." In *Northrop Frye: Eastern and Western Perspectives*, ed. Jean O'Grady and Wang Ning. Toronto: University of Toronto Press, 82–91.

White, Hayden. 1994. "Frye's Place in Contemporary Cultural Studies." In *The Legacy of Northrop Frye*, ed. Alvin Lee and Robert D. Denham. Toronto: University of Toronto Press, 28–39.

———. 1991. "Ideology and Counterideology in the *Anatomy*." In *Visionary Poetics: Essays on Northrop Frye's Criticism*, ed. Robert D. Denham and Thomas Willard. New York: Peter Lang, 101–111.

Williams, Raymond. 2005. *Culture and Materialism: Selected Essays*. 1980. Radical Thinkers. London: Verso.

———. 1994. "The Analysis of Culture." In *Cultural Theory and Popular Culture: A Reader*, ed. John Storey. New York: Harvester Wheatsheaf, 56–64.

———. 1976. *Keywords: A Vocabulary of Culture and Society*. Fontana Communications Series. Ed. Raymond Williams. Glasgow: Fontana.

An Access of Power:

Job, Evolution, and the Spirit of Consciousness in Northrop Frye and Daniel C. Dennett

---

Jeffery Donaldson

MY SUBJECT here, simply put, is the relationship between spirit and the neurological brain. I hope to translate what would normally (and dismissively) be called an "analogous" relationship between a brain's synapses and an individual's spirit—in Frye, so closely linked to if not synonymous with powers of the imagination—into a contiguous narrative that shows how one may be related to the other (that is, spirit to brain cell) as a blossom is to its seed, and not as a painting of a flower is to the real flower. In *Words With Power*, Frye himself comes near to reflecting on these matters when he briefly considers the relationship one might discern between imaginative "emblems of eternity" (like the *ouroboros*) and the "designs" of modern science: "I am aware that Kekulé's discovery of the circular structure of the benzene molecule was inspired by a dream of the *ouroboros*, just as I am aware that the DNA molecule has affinities with a double spiral. But I am not sure what to do with these analogies" (*WP* 164). If you trace this passage back to Frye's ruminations in the corresponding notebook, you find him completing the thought thus: "Nothing is discovered out there that isn't in some sense already here" (*LN* 1:286. This sentence actually stands in place of the one that begins "But I am not sure what to do"). This gives us one side of the puzzle—that is, that the myths and metaphors of science can only show us what is already a part of the mind's mental machinery.

At other times in the late notebooks, Frye appears to reflect on the other side of the puzzle—that is, the degree to which those powers of the mind are themselves evolved in terms that we might come better to understand. He writes,

> [M]an is born using his consciousness in the service of the selfish gene.... The purgatorial process transfers power to the instrument of consciousness: the word. The relevance of machinery is that our behaviour is mechanical now: purgatory reverses this to the control of mechanism. (*WP* 247)

His point here is that a mechanical process is set in motion that has its roots in our evolving genes (our "selfish" ones, Frye allows, in deference to Richard Dawkins' theory).[1] Elsewhere, he makes this implication more or less explicit: "There is ... a human and moral order that has developed out of the process of natural evolution" (*WP* 142). This is a mechanical process, one that might entrap us (and condemn us to the potential horrors of a misconceived social Darwinism)[2] if it were not also true that we can and must rise above our own roots via what Nietzsche called a Will to Power (*WP* 174), a transcending power of mind that gives us control of our own natural machinery. The evolutionary process itself is a purgatorial one, this being the principle myth that governed Darwin's own work: the long arduous process by which human being climbs clear of its own roots in nature on its way to some fuller promise.

I hope to fill in the picture of how, in evolutionary terms, we might think of spirit as arising from physical nature. Understanding spirit as a condition of evolved brain habits, *while* understanding those brain habits as themselves a function of spirit, or metaphoric mind, can produce the kind of interpenetrative vision that Frye himself might have countenanced. I offer a small example of how this contiguity between brain chemistry and spirit might manifest itself in our imaginative and scientific thinking. Even more specifically, I want to draw a line between Daniel Dennett's theory of how intelligent consciousness has evolved to the advantage of homo sapiens and Frye's theory of how the Bible's Job gains an "access of power" when he first and at long last gains an apperception of the *conscious* orders of experience granted to him by God. Both writers have their sights fixed on the particular features of human experience that relate words with potency and that reveal, as Wallace Stevens says, the precious portents of our own powers.

In his long processional of rhetorical questions near the end of the story of Job, one of the things God does *not* ask his wounded patriarch is: "Where were you when I created symbolic thinking," or even, and more to the point, "who told you you could think?" In his account in *Words With Power* of this apocalyptic exchange between God and Job, Frye shows that the question is implicit in God's entire speech, where the advantages of being able to think consciously are obvious to any reader. The question of when a person *becomes* conscious seems to be the actual focus of this particular discussion of Job among Frye's published many.[3] Job, we might say, evolves toward an understanding of the world in symbolic terms after enduring a series of trials, both at the hands of Satan, who takes much away from him, and from his accusing friends, who tempt him with what we come to see as more primitive ways of responding to his situation. We might say that he lurches or leaps to this understanding in a manner very unreminiscent of evolutionary crawl—that is, as soon as God speaks and lays all clear. But surely the earlier parts of the experience—the loss, the desperate and failing attempts to come to terms—were equally necessary to Job's being able finally to 'see' the cosmic orders in their proper context. The process by which Job comes to be redeemed can be seen on the one hand as an evolution in the understanding of his place and purpose—that is, a change in how he thinks about things (I return to this point shortly). Something evolves in the story. At the same time, the story of Job's growth of mind may offer us a unique perspective on the story of human evolution itself, our species' own growth of mind, if you like, or consciousness. This is something the Bible and other literary works are seen to do: offer insights, metaphoric or otherwise, into what we have come to understand as secular or scientific processes (as for instance where Frye himself argues that the story of creation in Genesis provides us with an allegory of how in psychological terms we think of ourselves as waking up from dream states; see *GC* 108). Critics, then, have found ways of relating literature's handling of experience in myth and metaphor to science's descriptive modellings of experience. I'm hoping it will be clear that the method I am working with here, while somewhat similar, leans in the direction of something beyond mere analogy.

We need, then, a brief account of how intelligent consciousness has evolved to the advantage of its host, and so we turn to Daniel C. Dennett's always exciting and controversial work in evolutionary biology, the neurosciences, and cognitive philosophy. Director of the Centre for Cognitive Studies at Tufts University in Boston, Dennett is one of America's leading philosophers of mind and cognition. In his books *Darwin's Dangerous Idea* and *Kinds of Minds*, Dennett investigates, among a variety of issues relating to biological and human evolution, the question of when human being became human. He attempts to isolate and investigate the blurry line that separates those like us who are part of the consciously mindful orders and those of the animal kingdom who for one reason or another do not, on a behavioural level, manifest the same mental states or powers.

We begin by noting that evolution, for Dennett, is an entirely unconscious, unintentionally directed phenomenon. There is no divine agent handling the puppet strings from above, in Dennett's picture, no greybeard in any guise drawing species upward toward a desired or ideal state. There is only the arduous and millenniums-slow labour of trial and error (a purgatorial process, as Frye conceived of it), survival of the fittest, where the "errors," the mutations that are less well adapted to their conditions, get knocked off and the fitter forms live to mutate another day. In *Darwin's Dangerous Idea*, Dennett characterizes these two conceptions of agency in evolution by way of what he calls the "Sky Hook" and the "Crane" model, respectively. A sky-hook scenario, as you may guess, is one in which some external influence (mythopoeically from "above") participates in the evolutionary process either to initiate it or purposefully direct it in such a way that it concludes with us at the top of the evolutionary pile, resplendent in our biological complexity. Alternatively, the crane model is one in which the evolutionary process pulls itself up, as it were, by its own bootstraps, grounded in a process that requires nothing more than good old-fashioned cell-by-cell mutation and regular reproductive variation.

This principle of crane-style evolution—as opposed to sky-hook— is the calling card of strictly materialist scientists and evolutionary thinkers and is a central axiom in Dennett's work. The main objective of *Darwin's Dangerous Idea* is to put to rest any notion that a vestige of sky-hook evolution may be preserved in our understanding of how we got here. It seems no accident to me that Dennett's two conceptions of evolution align with Frye's mythopoeic *axis mundi* and his theory of the Four Variations.[4] Elements of the mountain variation align rather well with the notion of a top-down power descending from above to change or influence creation below. Just so, elements of the furnace variation align with the crane model, where the world that "evolves" must be built from the ground up by purgatorial hard labours, bootstrap refining processes, and sheer grunting "unconscious" ingenuity. In a while, I will be venturing another example of how Frye's model of the *axis mundi* may be mapped onto the models of Dennett's science as a way of revealing their initiatives and orientation; to be sure, it is a rich and suggestive activity.

Suffice it to observe here, as Frye himself did, that Darwin's model of evolution, as one might expect of a 19th-century thinker, with its from-the-ground-up orientation, betrays a manifestly post-Romantic bias, in terms of where the creative "power" we find all about us is seen to originate.[5]

We move now from the concept of crane-style evolution to the issue of how consciousness itself has evolved in this bootstrapping fashion, without divine intervention. I say again that Job is made to be conscious in more ways than one, though the lines between those ways blur. God bestows consciousness on Job, as he does on any human soul, by simply giving it to him in a sky-hook fashion ("Who has put wisdom in the inward parts, or given understanding to the mind?" Job 38:36). Job also passes through a series of experiences that in the end make him, alone, "conscious" of his place in the created cosmos, in a way that he had never been before; his having the "right" thoughts at last, now that he can "see" (Job 42:5), has much to do with what he has survived. As Frye writes, "[W]hat is restored to Job at the end of the poem is in a considerable measure the world of what Job has recreated by his own endurance" (*NLBR* 577). Job evolves. Dennett's evolving genotype (this term for the genetic constitution of the individual can be used as a metonymic shorthand for the individual itself) is also conscious in these ways. Homo sapiens' experience of *being* conscious has everything to do with the evolution of conscious thinking and the gradually evolved ability to have certain kinds of thoughts in certain contexts. That is what, for Dennett, is the assurance of this particular genotype's election, if you like, among the earth's creatures.

Somewhere along the line of human evolution, something must have happened to the brain to incarnate whatever neurological processes we associate with a having of consciousness. Dennett has stood in opposition to a host of cognitive philosophers, among them John Searle, David Chalmers, Joseph Levine (see *Sweet Dreams* 8–13), who with individual nuances argue that there must be a seat of consciousness in the mind, a place where the "youness" of you is housed, a central meaner, a homunculus or observing agent that in your brain acts as a kind of audience for all the thoughts and sensations you are having, where the experience of "what it is like to be you" is existentially grounded. Without such a property of mind, we would all be zombies, they argue.[6] I think it is worth noting here that the idea of a central meaner in the brain is not that different from the notion of a Jobian, cosmological central meaner, the holder of creation's puppet strings, who sets things in motion but seems for the most part to stand back and watch how it all unfolds. That is, what cognitive philosophers describe as the seat of consciousness may in metaphoric terms be a version of the watchmaker god, certainly as far as the notion of being an audience is concerned. And there is an interesting corollary here. We feel driven to describe the workings of a cosmos whose mythic maker, as such, variously controls or observes what goes on inside the space it has created. But what ends up getting embodied in those descriptions, Frye always showed, are the workings of our own minds, whose conditions and limits are in essence what we are trying to grasp.

While Dennett's own descriptions of the nature of consciousness have themselves evolved over thirty years, he has never swayed from his conviction that there is no central meaner in the brain, no homunculus or "little you" manipulating all the strings inside you. There are only the infinitely complex activities of neurons, whose synapses make up what we think of as our consciousness. We could even say that those synapses make up the "illusion" of consciousness, so long as we remember not to lose sight of Frye's belief in the potential reality of illusion (*WP* 129, 131). What Dennett *has* modified over the years are the metaphors he uses to try to describe the phenomenon of consciousness.

For most of the time between the publication of *Consciousness Explained* and his most recent volume on the subject, *Sweet Dreams*, he has worked with what he calls "the multiple drafts theory" of consciousness:

> Mental contents become conscious not by entering some special chamber in the brain, not by being transduced into some privileged and mysterious medium, but by winning the competitions against other mental contents for domination in the control of behaviour.... One of the most effective ways for a mental content to become influential is for it to get into position to drive the language-using parts of the controls. (*Kinds of Minds* 155)

In *Sweet Dreams*, Dennett refines his theory of consciousness in response to his critics of the past twenty years. He describes the experience of consciousness as "fame in the brain." In comparing his multiple-drafts theory to his "fame in the brain" idea, one difference that occurs to me is that Dennett has steered slightly away from the idea that language is related, in a precisely determinative way, to what is most conscious in us. Doing so opens up consciousness to states beyond those in which you are primarily just "talking to yourself," or preparing to. One reason he might have steered away from such a notion is that it may appear to favour the idea of a goal in consciousness—that consciousness, in order to be consciousness, is trying to get somewhere, that is, into the language controlling areas of the brain. This would be but a hair's breadth from the notion that consciousness is not consciousness until it enters a "special chamber." What Dennett wants is a metaphor that doesn't suggest our mental contents are *trying* to get into any position whatsoever. The theory he now calls "fame in the brain," alternatively, speaks to what is in essence an echoing property, a self-reflexive looping mechanism in the brain that "beefs up" the conscious-seemingness, or "clout," of certain neurons as they fire with greater and greater frequency "above" those neurons of other thoughts, emotions, and physical sensations that are firing less frequently or intensely.

If you think of neurons firing with increased frequency as generating a kind of heat, then consciousness, Dennett argues, is the heat so generated. The experience, or *experiencer*, of the heat, Dennett believes, does not stand over and against or opposite to the generation of the heat itself. Trying another trope, if all firing neurons in your brain made a noise, consciousness would be those sounds that are heard above the crowd, as it were. But if you go with this metaphor, you would need to take care not to think that there is a distinct sound maker and a distinct sound hearer. Dennett writes, "[W]e need to explain away this seductive metaphor ... the searchlight of attention, by explaining the *functional* powers of attention-*grabbing* without presupposing a single attention-*giving* source" (*Sweet Dreams* 161–162). There is a kind of metaphoric unity between a network of neurons firing and that network's experience of itself *as firing*. The paradox may come clear when you try to think of what it feels like when you touch the skin on your index finger to the skin on your thumb. Which is feeling which? Impossible to say. There is only the "feeling" of skin. One neuron can connect to or "rub against" another neuron, and each will feel, or "realize," the other's friction. (Look up M.C. Escher's drawing of "Drawing Hands" [1948] and you'll get the picture.) Visualize the still larger context. If whole populations of neuron networks chugged away in relation to one another, each in a sense experiencing or registering the impacts of others, it would be very difficult, if not impossible, to say how precisely the totality of their experiences were gathered together or where precisely it was centred. Frye can help us here: it is everywhere and nowhere at once, a vast array of centres whose circumference is infinite.

Let us stay with this idea for a moment. The human brain is made up of neurons that fire connections to other neurons across gaps called synapses. These synapses and their behaviours vis-à-vis the stimulation of brain cells are of three general kinds, serving three different purposes. There are what we would call unconscious neurological inputs and outputs that drive and regulate the heart, the lungs, and many other, though not all, of our physical processes. There are also those inputs and outputs that have to do with emotional responses and physical states, such as pain, hunger, the appetites, our sexual drives, signals that still do

· not appear to think about themselves *as such*, that may fall short of our being aware of them, but which "struggle" or "compete" with other inputs to rise into consciousness—that is, to the point at which you will find yourself consciously thinking "I am in pain," or "I need to eat something." (Freud's theory of the subconscious obviously becomes relevant here.) And finally there are those inputs and outputs that we call our conscious thinking states, and they include the thoughts and feelings we have and that we *know* we are having (i.e., whose *having* we experience), our rational thinking, our active impressions and feelings, our imaginative powers of mind, and the further, though not necessary, association of all of these with their potential or actual representation in language. These latter neurological events, Dennett argues—and this is one of his most controversial claims—are not different in kind from the other brain functions, only in degree. The degree of our awareness of them has to do with how much "clout" the synapses associated with them have in the brain at any one particular moment. "Clout" is a function of the degree to which synapses, or networks of them, repeat. The more they fire repeatedly—that is, the more they are stimulated—the more they come to "dominate" the other synapses that are, as we might describe it, competing for the same right to determine action and response. This is precisely *how* they are conscious to us, or rather how there *is* consciousness.

I would like to venture another aside here, as promised earlier, to note how effectively this theory of levels of consciousness can be mapped, once more, onto Frye's *axis mundi*. With a bottom-up, post-Romantic orientation, the unconscious neurological inputs/outputs that drive the body's organs align with the furnace variation. Remember especially that, in Frye's thinking, buried mythopoeic worlds, such as Atlantis (symbolized as under the sea), are conceptualized as a *source* of creative power, not a manifestation of it. It inaugurates that subconscious that we do in fact "visit" when we can (as in the cave variation), but is not itself a place that we are conscious of (we know our brains are telling our hearts something, we will just never hear what it is). Next are those neurological inputs, which, as they grow stronger and stronger, *approach* a being-conscious, like pain and hunger. These align with the cave variation, the "something subordinated, neglected, or underestimated in power which is excluded from the thought ... yet is dangerous to ignore" (*WP* 248). When such inputs become strong enough—that is, resisting our powers to ignore them—they rise up into our conscious thoughts: "I'm getting hungry, I need to eat something." Next come our actual conscious thoughts, the networks of neurons that fire with sufficient frequency or intensity that they dominate the landscape, have more "clout" in relation to the inputs that are not quite so loud. These align with the garden variation (where in the post-Romantic orientation we do most of our living), our conscious rational and metaphoric thinking, where thoughts mingle and identify, circulate about one another as in a dance. As for the final mountain variation, this is the "area" that Dennett comes to terms with when he works to describe "consciousness itself," the consciousness of consciousness, the experience of being sentient, the "what it is like to be you."[7] Dennett sees this level of consciousness as the haunted part—at least as it would have to be, he would say, in the minds of his adversaries—where the elusive bugaboo of that homunculus wanders about in your brain thinking about you, or rather thinking *for* you (a pretty fair definition of paranoia, when you think about it). It is no surprise that Dennett would portray this "highest" state as essentially alien or remote when thought of as a homunculus, quite specifically the illusion of what is in reality a solely mechanical operation (note that Frye portrays such alienation imagery as mechanical in *WP* 248). For Dennett, such higher states are not different in kind from the "lower" states of everyday conscious thinking, and therefore in a sense don't exist, at least not as a separate level or medium of mind. There is, then, no obvious distinction between garden and mountain variations in Dennett, between your conscious thoughts and your sentient experience of those conscious thoughts as such. The higher thoughts are merely those lower thoughts thinking about each other (see the trick of index finger and thumb above). Though he may not distinguish these higher thoughts of consciousness from the mechanisms that constitute them, Dennett nonetheless finds himself trying to account for the "hallucination" of consciousness—that is, why it is that we should experience consciousness at all as a "special medium" inside us (*Sweet Dreams* 162). The attempt to account for it at all suggests that there is an *experiential* distinction to make. There is ink to be spilled in accounting for even just the *illusion* of a real experience that won't go away. This puts us in the territory of distinctions we *put there*, as opposed to distinctions we objectively find.

We should remember, with Frye, that an "all-seeing" cognitive power—the kind Job hears from in the end—*appears* to come from both within and without in the same way that "consciousness" appears to come from a *youness* that is both yourself and not yourself, at once both a here and a nowhere in particular. Thus, a phrase like "consciousness of consciousness" very nearly collapses into a phrase like "consciousness of God" in both the suggestive valences of this phrase. There is the scientific sense, in the partitive construction "consciousness *of* god," where god is the *object* of conscious thought, suitably undressed and dissected as such, and shown to be an illusion. The other is the onto-phenomenological sense, "the consciousness of god" in the subjective genitive, the consciousness that god *is*. While the phrase points in the first instance to our need to limit objective analysis to observable facts, it also reminds us, in the second instance, that the spirit we seek may not be in the observable facts but in the act of conscious thinking and observation itself. It is nice to imagine that such a simple phrase might hold a clue to how science and spirit are fundamentally related.

Consciousness, as both Dennett and Frye would agree, is a handy thing to have. The brain is that part of a creature that controls its actions and responses to the environment. Job's brain, given his physical destitution, is just about all he has left to help him cope with his new tragic reality. When our environment is relatively stable, responses can be simplified, and the living creature's equipment for response may also be kept relatively simple, for efficiency's sake. The daisy responds to its mostly unchanging environment of alternating light and dark with photosynthesis. As the environment becomes more complicated, however, the responses must themselves become more complex and versatile in order for that species to do well. No squirrel is going to survive long on the evolutionary tree if it uses only a daisy's ability to respond to light when it senses a fox nearby. It must have more options at its disposal, and to have more options it must have some computing equipment on board that will allow it to construe the variables and respond accordingly.

Dennett breaks down into four types of creature the degrees of conscious responsive power that living things have. They are the "Darwinian" creature, the "Skinnerian" creature, the "Popperian" creature, and the "Gregorian" creature.[8] The Darwinian creature is the unthinking species, like the daisy. The daisy's progeny survives not because each particular daisy can respond effectively to changes in the environment but because some daisies evolve in such a way that favours them. No thinking is done here, but as the environment changes those daisies that are lucky enough to change in step with its conditions will persist. (Note that if we were to look in prospect at a whole field of daisies over a thousand years (using stop-frame animation), it would appear to us that the field was thinking, trying out this and that response to the environment with its many potential daisy options, until it found the "right" option and "went" with it, so to speak.)

The Skinnerian model—named after B.F. Skinner's theories of behaviourism—is similar to the Darwinian model in that its phenotype is essentially unthinking. Like a computer that runs through a series of potential algorithms until it finds one that fits the data that has been input and then responds according to a set of programmed instructions, a Skinnerian creature will randomly try out a variety of potential responses in succession until it receives a reinforcing or negating signal from the environment. No mind is required. Different options are tested, but the creature is not thinking about those options, it merely runs through them. Dennett goes on to the next stage:

Skinnerian conditioning is a good thing as long as you are not killed by one of your early errors. A better system involved *preselection* among all the possible behaviours or actions, so that the truly stupid moves are weeded out before they're hazarded in "real life." We human beings are creatures capable of this particular refinement, but we are not alone. We may call the beneficiaries of this [adaptation] "Popperian Creatures," since as the philosopher Sir Karl Popper once elegantly put it, this design enhancement "permits our hypotheses to die in our stead." (*Kinds of Minds* 88)

For this preselection function to work, Dennett argues, there must be "a filter" in the brain, a sort of "inner environment," not especially sophisticated at this stage, in which potential responses may be tested against the likelihood that they would be favoured if they were actually performed. One such example of this more primitive inner environment is the nausea that an animal might experience when it smells rotten food. Something in its inner makeup is telling it that it might not be a good idea to proceed further with the "contemplated" action. At a higher level of this adaptation, memory becomes important: a creature may record the undesirable consequences of an action and use them as warning representations to itself when similar circumstances arise again.

What happens, then, when we make the final step to human consciousness? We are "Gregorian creatures," Dennett argues (naming our condition after the pre-eminent British information theorist Richard Gregory), because an inner environment evolves that can be informed not just by sensory data and memory, for instance, but by other elements in the world that *are themselves products of design*. Those *designed elements* may range from what the creature sees other creatures doing (succeeding or failing: "there but for the grace of God go I"), to the use of tools that are themselves designed or that have otherwise fallen into our hands as useable. "Tool use is a two-way sign of intelligence," Dennett writes. "Not only does it *require* intelligence to recognize or maintain a tool ... but a tool *confers* intelligence on those lucky enough to be given one.... Among the pre-eminent tools, Gregory reminds us, are what he calls mind tools: words."

Dennett comes at last to Frye's territory: the introduction to the human individual of words and symbolic thinking, and the advantages that such tools confer on human being in its struggle for survival. Dennett continues:

> Words and other mind tools give a Gregorian creature an inner environment that permits it to construct ever more subtle move generators and move testers.... Gregorian creatures take a big step towards a human level of mental adroitness, benefiting from the experience of others by exploiting the wisdom embodied in the mind tools that those others have invented, improved, and transmitted; thereby they learn to think better about what they should think about next—and so forth, creating a tower of further internal reflections with no fixed or discernable limit. (*Kinds of Minds* 100–101)

Notice how similar Dennett's world has become to Frye's concept of the critical reader when he writes of "the wisdom embodied in the mind tools that those others have invented, improved, and transmitted" and "a tower of further internal reflections with no fixed or discernable limit." Such a world in which there is no discernable limit to our internal reflections seems well on its way to Frye's vision of a manmade cultural cosmos (the mind tools "out there") available to any reader doing any reading, where everything is potentially related to everything else, and where the god in the midst of it would be the perceiving agent that puts it there and holds it all together as a unity.

Frye's account of Job has to do double duty for him at the end of *Words With Power*. He must on the one hand conclude his discussion of the furnace variation (the last of the four), represent its elements of

purgatorial journey and descent to nothingness as creative and potentially revolutionary experiences. On the other hand, he needs a story
whose structure and context may illustrate something of his theory of
the reading experience itself, particularly of the Bible and the aspect of
the kerygmatic he discerns there and seeks to illuminate.

Frye speaks of Job's "purgatorial trial" as "a testing and refining
operation ... directed toward what one can still be" (*WP* 310–311). As
we noted earlier, the evolution of a genotype over millennia may also
be seen as a form of purgatorial trial, a testing and certainly a refining
operation, where the genotype is transformed over time by its environmental encounters, its failures and successes in relation to them, and is
ultimately (however unconsciously) directed toward "what it can still
be." Like a genotype struggling for survival, Job faces the hardships and
challenges of his environment and is looking for the best way to move
forward. As Frye writes in *The Great Code* (196), the important thing
now is not how he got into his situation but how he plans to get out of
it. Picture our four brain types facing the obstacles of their environment
and responding in whatever ways their powers of mind make possible.
In his cloud of unknowing, for most of the story Job would probably fall
somewhere between a Skinnerian and a Popperian creature. He doesn't
understand what sort of situation he is in, and he certainly doesn't have
much of a sense of how to move forward from where he is. He might,
like a Skinnerian creature, simply try on as many possible responses he
can think of, hoping like a gambler that one of them will work. And indeed, this is certainly what his accusers tempt him to do, each crying out
to be heard over the others, "Think of it this way, Job, and respond as I
tell you." Job passes up on each haphazard offer, knows enough that he
shouldn't be scrambling about looking for anything that only "might
possibly" work. He wants the bigger picture, the power of mind that
will help him respond to his situation with better than a mere gambler's
chance of getting beyond his nightmare.

What then does God offer Job that gives him more power? God, Frye
writes, "answers Job by recapitulating his original creation in the form

of a vision which is held in front of Job in the present.... He has reached the end of his narrative in his present situation, and must now look up and down" (*WP* 311). In effect, Job is given a book of the created cosmos, one that is "held out in front of him" for him to read. Readers familiar with Frye's other writings will recognize this account of Job's experience as characteristic of our reading experience in general. We start at the beginning of a book with no, or next to no, knowledge of the world we are passing through, and read on without a definite sense of where we are headed; when we are finished, though, we can look back at the work finally as a fixed structure, in which any point may be related to any other point, from start to finish. We no longer experience the narrative *in* time, but from *above*, as it were. We become metaphorical gods at that point, because all of the created experience is encompassed in our minds. We possess it, and that possession gives us more power to determine the relations among all its parts and between the parts and the whole. We gain control, thanks to the vision supplied by a power that can see in all directions at once. We become increasingly able to perceive the world we inhabit from a metaphorically omniscient perspective.

Paul Ricoeur writes in *The Rule of Metaphor* that "language possesses the reflective capacity to place itself at a distance and to consider itself ... as related to the totality of what is" (304). Frye states,

> When the infinitely remote creation is re-presented to [Job], he becomes a participant in it: that is, he becomes creative himself, as heaven and earth are made new for him. He is given no new discovery, but gains a deeper apprehension of what is already there. This deeper apprehension is not simply more wisdom, but an access of power. (*WP* 312)

So Dennett might say as well, with the advent of our Popperian and then Gregorian creature: he does not discover anything new about what is in front of him in the environment, but he does gain a deeper apprehension and understanding of what is already there, because he "sees" and encounters it now in the form of a symbolic tool that he has created and/or discovered—that is, he possesses a symbolic picture of it in his mind. This deeper apprehension is not simply more wisdom but an access of power. He is now more likely to make decisions that are not merely mechanical. Remember that in Frye it is the merely mechanical agent, the unthinking machine in the brain, that is most feared in the post-Romantic *axis mundi*.

What God gives to Job, Frye says, are the tools he needs to move forward: "The answer of God [puts] Job's primary concerns into a larger context of what Paul Tillich calls ultimate concern" (*WP* 312). By placing Job's primary concerns into the context of ultimate concern, God is effectively ordering and structuring them, giving them a place in a larger context, showing how they are related to one another and to the kinds of creative power that are available to Job. What God puts into Job's head, then, is the vision of the *axis mundi*, a picture of the imaginative cosmos that human beings themselves have put there simply by being the creators they are. That is, what God offers Job is a vision of the world we ourselves have designed, a picture of our creative apprehension of the cosmos, and his most important act is to make that designed world intelligible to us by spinning it into patterns and orders.

And this is the crucial point. For Dennett and Frye, it is not just any knowledge that will do to advance the potential of its user. For both, it is knowledge of the *already designed* element, the world we have already put out there or discovered and recorded as otherwise meaningful to us, that gives us particular evolutionary lift. "We learn," Dennett writes, "to spread our minds out in the world, where we can put our beautifully designed innate tracking and pattern-recognizing talents to optimal use" (*Kinds of Minds* 139). We offload the contents of our minds into the world by thinking symbolically and acting upon our symbolic thoughts. The external world thus comes clear, at least to the extent that we *recognize* it as a projection of our internal operations of mind, one that we can then perceive from our detached perspective and so manage and choreograph as best suits us. The more we see that this *there* is where we are, the more the subject/object divide in the world falls away and we become possessors and inhabiters of a universe that is both very real *and* very symbolic at the same time.

For Dennett the designed world that dwells in the Gregorian's mind is made up of "elaborate systems of mnemonic association—pointers, labels, chutes and ladders, hooks and chains. We refine our resources by incessant rehearsal and tinkering, turning our brains (and all the associated peripheral gear we acquire) into a huge structured network of competences" (*Kinds of Minds* 152). For Dennett's "pointers, chutes and ladders, hooks and chains," think of Frye's mountains, ladders, caves, and all the descent and ascent motifs of his Four Variations. These are part of a system of mnemonic association that assembles the contents of our brains into a structured network of competences that becomes, along with the world, increasingly intelligible to us the more we go over it. Dennett's Gregorian creature and Frye's Job are both advantaged because, unlike those who came before them, they can finally "see," *as such*, those offloaded, symbolic pointers, chutes and ladders, hooks and chains of the designed world.

So Dennett writes,

> As we improve, our labels become more refined, more perspicuous, ever better articulated, and the point is finally reached when we approximate the near-magical prowess we began with: the *mere contemplation* of a representation is sufficient to call to mind all the appropriate lessons. We have become *understanders* of the objects we have created. (*Kinds of Minds* 151)

The same might be said of Job, that he enjoys in the end a near-magical prowess, and that the mere contemplation of the vision God has put before him is sufficient to call to mind all the appropriate lessons; he becomes an *understander* of the world he has endured. Dennett's findings in the biological and evolutionary sciences corroborate Frye's theory that it is our meditations on the designed world, as it enters and re-enters our minds, that bestow on us increased mental power. And just as the advent of consciousness represents the beginning of community in Dennett's evolutionary theory, so Job's newly conscious experience represents, as Frye argues, the restoration of a lost world, one that is reborn in rather the same manner that enabled human society to evolve in the first place.

I've spent a fair amount of time in this essay talking about what, in current cognitive philosophy, consciousness is seen to be, washing away all the illusions and bugaboos of the homunculus that used to live there. Job too is purged in the end of whatever illusions he had harboured: "I have heard of thee by the hearing of the ear: but now mine eye seeth thee. / Wherefore I abhor myself and repent in dust and ashes" (Job 42:5–6). Frye argues that what Job is letting go of here is the idea of himself as a stable identity, and that what he is plausibly saying is, "I no longer consider what I call myself, an ego, as any reality at all, and I am withdrawing from it" (*NLBR* 573). We may believe in the self, in identities that belong to us as our own, in a spirit of consciousness that we feel dwells inside us as ourselves. But for both Dennett and Frye, an apperception of the reality that lies behind that conscious disposition, illusory or otherwise, would be highly conscious indeed.

ENDNOTES

1   See Richard Dawkins, *The Selfish Gene* (Oxford University Press, 30th Anniversary Edition, 2006).

2   See *WP* 174.

3   Two other of Frye's important discussions of Job are "Blake's Reading of the Book of Job" in *Spiritus Mundi: Essays on Literature, Myth, and Society* (Bloomington: Indiana University Press, 1976), 228–244, and several lectures included in a series that Frye gave in 1981–1982 called "The Mythological Framework of Western Culture," now published in

Northrop Frye's Notebooks and Lectures on the Bible and Other Religious Texts, The Collected Works of Northrop Frye, Vol. 13 (Toronto: University of Toronto Press, 2003), 553–577.

4   For the purposes of saving space, and given the fact that this is a volume of essays that assumes at least some familiarity with Frye's thinking, I will elide any lengthy paraphrase of this aspect of Frye's late *theoria*. Readers can of course go to the source, the entire last half of *Words With Power*. In addition, Glen Gill offers a very fine synopsis of the Four Variations and their corresponding primary concerns in his essay "Beyond Anagogy: Northrop Frye's Existential (Re)visions" in *Northrop Frye: Eastern and Western Perspectives*, eds. Jean O'Grady and Wang Ning (Toronto: University of Toronto Press, 2003), 42–53.

5   I also make the association between the *axis mundi* and Dennett's notions of "Sky-hook" and "Crane" evolutionary models by way of drawing attention to what some might see as a revealing irony in this approach to Frye's thought. Frye himself sees imaginative creation as coming from both metaphoric "directions," above and below. The voice calling us to our promise is both not our own and *also* our own, he coined memorably in *Words With Power* (118). Readers who are less familiar with Frye's nuanced characterization of creative power in both its secular and spiritual dimension might be surprised to learn that his study of the Bible should be so commensurate with a strictly materialist conception of evolution—in all its "godless" momentum—and indeed that it may offer that conception a clarifying account of its enabling mythopoeic power.

6   See the fuller argument in *Sweet Dreams* 1–23.

7   "The interests of modern poets in ladders and spirals is not nostalgia for outmoded images of creation, but a realization that because such images stand for the intensifying of consciousness through words, they represent the concern of concerns, so to speak, the consciousness of consciousness" (*WP* 165).

8   Dennett offers a series of very helpful illustrations of these levels of consciousness in *Kinds of Minds* (see 84, 86, 89, 100).

WORKS CITED

Dennett, Daniel C. 2006. *Breaking the Spell: Religion as a Natural Phenomenon*. New York: Viking.

———. 2005. *Sweet Dreams: Philosophical Obstacles to a Science of Consciousness*. Cambridge, MA: MIT.

———. 1996. *Kinds of Minds: Towards an Understanding of Consciousness*. New York: Basic Books.

———. 1995. *Darwin's Dangerous Idea: Evolution and the Meanings of Life*. New York: Simon and Schuster.

———. 1991. *Consciousness Explained*. Boston: Little Brown.

Ricoeur, Paul. 1981. *The Rule of Metaphor: Multi-disciplinary Studies of the Creation of Meaning in Language*. Toronto: University of Toronto Press.

Biographies

John Ayre is a journalist who is author of *Northrop Frye: A Biography* published by Random House of Canada in 1989. On many occasions he has lectured on Northrop Frye's thinking and published several articles, notably "Frye's Geometry of Thought" in the *University of Toronto Quarterly* in Fall 2001.

D. M. R. Bentley is Carl F. Klinck Professor in Canadian Literature at the University of Western Ontario. His recent publications include the Norton Critical Edition of Stephen Leacock's *Sunshine Sketches of a Little Town*, "Tradition on Location: Ted Goodden's Ridgeway Windows," and essays on the poetry and painting of William Morris, Dante Gabriel Rossetti, and other Pre-Raphaelites.

Robert Denham is the world's greatest expert on the work of Northrop Frye. He was John P. Fishwick Professor of English at Roanoke

College in Salem, Virginia, until he recently retired. His books on Frye include *Northrop Frye on Literature and Society, 1936-1989*, *Northrop Frye's Notebooks and Lectures on the Bible and Other Religious Texts*, and *Northrop Frye's Notebooks for "Anatomy of Criticism."*

MICHAEL DOLZANI was Frye's graduate student from 1978 to 1982; his research assistant from 1980 to 1991; the co-editor, with Robert Denham, of his unpublished work for the Collected Works project; and the editor of *Words With Power*, forthcoming in the CW. He has taught at Baldwin-Wallace College, in Berea, Ohio (a suburb of Cleveland), since 1989, and is currently chair of the English Department.

JEFFERY DONALDSON is professor at McMaster University and is co-editor of *Frye and the Word: Religious Contexts in the Writings of Northrop Frye* (2004) as well as of *Introduction to Frye and the Word: Religious Contexts in the Writings of Northrop Frye* (2004).

TRONI GRANDE is associate professor of English at the University of Regina, where she teaches Shakespeare, early modern drama, and theory. She is author of *Marlovian Tragedy: The Play of Dilation* (1999). She is also co-editor of Frye's writings on Shakespeare and the Renaissance for the Collected Works series.

DAVID JARRAWAY is professor of American Literature at the University of Ottawa. He is the author of *Wallace Stevens and the Question of Belief: "Metaphysician in the Dark"* (1993), *Going the Distance: Dissident Subjectivity in Modernist American Literature* (2003), and many essays on American literature and culture, most recently a chapter inclusion in *"The Cambridge Companion to Wallace Stevens"* (2006).

ALVIN LEE is the general editor of the thirty-volume *Collected Works of Northrop Frye* project; he has edited two volumes himself, including an edition of Frye's *The Great Code*. He also wrote the introduction to the Penguin Modern Classics editions of *The Great Code* and *Words With Power*. He is also an internationally renowned scholar of Old English and served with great distinction as the president and vice-chancellor of McMaster University from 1980 to 1990.

JEAN O'GRADY is associate editor of the *Collected Works of Northrop Frye*. She has two forthcoming publications relating to Frye: one, "Interviews with Northrop Frye" and two, as co-editor, "Northrop Frye, The Critical Path and Other Writings on Critical Theory, 1963–75." Dr. O'Grady also had the pleasure of being a student of Frye's at Queen's College.

J. RUSSELL PERKIN is professor of English at Saint Mary's University. He published *A Reception-History of George Eliot's Fiction* in 1990, and he is the author of several pieces on Frye, including studies of Frye and Catholicism and Frye and Matthew Arnold. He teaches the Bible and Literature, and is primarily a Victorianist. His current research includes the interrelationship of masculinity and religion in Victorian literature.

GARRY SHERBERT is an associate professor in the Department of English at the University of Regina. He is co-editor of volume 28 in The Collected Works of Northrop Frye entitled *Northrop Frye's Writings on Shakespeare and The Renaissance*. He is the author of *Menippean Satire and the Poetics of Wit* (Lang 1996) and has recently co-edited *Canadian Cultural Poesis: Essays on Canadian Culture* (Wilfrid Laurier Press, 2006). He has published essays on Northrop Frye and Jacques Derrida and also has an essay on culture in the July issue of *Mosaic*.

MICHAEL SINDING's McMaster University dissertation reconsiders Northrop Frye's and Mikhail Bakhtin's views of genre and Menippean satire. He was granted a SSHRCC postdoctoral fellowship to study genre mixture as "conceptual blending" and is now entering a Humboldt Fellowship year at Justus-Liebig University in Giessen, Germany, to further research genre in terms of cognitive psychology and linguistics. He has published in *New Literary History, Genre, Semiotica, Style, Postmodern Culture* and other journals.

IAN SLOAN is a minister of the United Church of Canada in Sudbury, Ontario. He has presented papers on Frye and theology at various conferences. He organized and chaired the symposium Creation and Recreation: Northrop Frye and United Church Ministry as part of his appointment as a research associate at the Northrop Frye Centre, Victoria University, in 2000 and 2001. A fellow of the Centre for Reformation and Renaissance Studies at Toronto since 2001, he has lectured in English Literature at Guelph, Madonna University in Detroit, and Laurentian University in Sudbury.

ROBERT STACEY is member of the Department of English at the University of Ottawa, where he teaches Canadian literature. He has published articles on Leonard Cohen, John Steffler, William Kirby, Anne Hebert, Hugh MacLennan, and Al Purdy. His recent work has focussed on genre and the historical imagination in Canadian poetry and fiction.

SÁRA TÓTH teaches at Károli Gáspár University of the Hungarian Reformed Church in Budapest, Hungary. Her main area of interest is the interplay between Christianity and the arts, more particularly literature and Christian belief, literature and the Bible. She completed her doctorate in 2003 with a dissertation on the religious aspects of the work of Northrop Frye.

THOMAS WILLARD teaches courses in English and Religious Studies at the University of Arizona. His essays on Frye include contributions to *Centre and Labyrinth: Essays in Honour of Northrop Frye* (1982), *Visionary Poetics: Essays on Northrop Frye's Criticism* (co-edited with Robert D. Denham, 1991), *The Legacy of Northrop Frye* (1994), and *Northrop Frye: Eastern and Western Perspectives* (2003). He is now writing a book on Frye's literary pedagogy. In addition he has written on alchemy and literature and has edited the works of Jean d'Espagne (2000).

Index

on the "difference" of Canadian literature, 85–89

and displacement, 88–89, 91, 93

Frye as author of, 57–58

and garrison mentality, 56, 67–70, 75n18, 87, 88

influence of, 80–81

and myth, 65–67, 94–99

and the natural world, 59–62

and romance, 81–82, 84

and self-plagiarism, 58–59

and the sentimental, 93–94

stark terror and, 55–56, 62, 64–65, 67, 69–70, 85

and the tension between Frye's Canadian and international work, 82–85

The Confidence-Man (Melville), 278, 283, 291

Congregationalists, 108, 109, 110

Conrad, Joseph, 209

consciousness, 319–338

evolution of, 322–325, 332–333, 336–338

and the four brain types, 331–333, 334, 335–336, 337

Frye on, 320, 330, 336–337

Job and, 321–322, 324, 330, 334–338

levels of, 328–330

metaphors of, 326–328

multiple-drafts theory of, 325–326

See also Dennett, Daniel C.

Consciousness Explained (Dennett), 325

conservatism, 303–307

contraries, theory of, XX, 115–116, 118–120, 200

Co-operative Commonwealth Federation, XXIII, 195

Corman, Brian, 209

The Correspondence of Northrop Frye and Helen Kemp 1932-1939, 1–2

crane-style evolution, 323–324

Creation and Recreation (Frye), 214–215, 216

creative power, 137, 242–243, 324, 328, 336

creatures and conscious power, 331–333

Creighton, Donald, 65–66

The Cremation of Sam McGee (Service), 229, 231

The Critical Path (Frye), XXI, XXVII, 20, 83, 93, 107, 177–178, 206, 207, 212, 213–214, 234, 236, 279, 298, 305

"Critical Theory: Structure, Archetypes, and the Order of Words" (Frye), 27

"The Critic as Artist" (Wilde), 214–215, 216

Criticism. See Literary Criticism

"Criticism, Visible and Invisible" (Frye), XXVIII–XXIX, 211–212

critics on

The Anatomy of Criticism, 17–21, 65, 169, 170, 234–235

The Great Code, 181

Culler, Jonathan, 26

cultural history, Canadian Criticism as, 85, 88

cultural studies, XXVII, 213, 219, 299–302, 303

Culture and Anarchy (Arnold), 28

Current Contents, 26–27

Cuthbert, Art, 234–235

Cymbeline (Shakespeare), 262

Daedalus: Journal of the American Academy of Arts and Sciences, 37–38

Damon, Foster, 172

Dante, XII, XIII, XXV, 176, 179–181, 191, 255–258, 271–272

The Divine Comedy, 171, 172, 253

Inferno, XII

La Vita Nuova, 255

Paradiso, 196

Purgatorio, 190

Darwin, Charles, 324

Darwinian creature (Dennett), 331

Darwin's Dangerous Idea (Dennett), 322, 323

The Da Vinci Code (Brown), 159

"The Decay of Lying" (Wilde), 214, 216–217

"A December Vision" (Dickens), 176

deconstruction, 22

DeGroote, Michael G., 12, 13

Delany, Samuel, 198–199

de Lauretis, Teresa, 254

Deleuze, Gilles, XXVI, 278, 284, 286, 290

Demeter, 260–261

D'Emilio, John, 289

Denham, Robert D.

and the coda to Northrop Frye's Late Notebooks, 35–36

and the Collected Works project, XV–XVI, 4–5, 6, 7, 8, 9, 11, 12

The Correspondence of Northrop Frye and Helen Kemp 1932-1939, 1–2

influence of the Anatomy on, 15–17

Northrop Frye Unbuttoned, 231

Dennett, Daniel, C., XXVII–XXVIII, 321–338

Derrida, Jacques, XXI, 19, 143–150, 153–155, 157, 160–162

Der Satz vom Grund (Heidegger), 150

detachment, ironic, 281, 282, 283–284, 286, 289–290

"The Dialectics of Poetic Tradition" (Bloom), 41, 43

Dickens, Charles, XXII, 176–177, 230

Difference and Repetition (Deleuze), 278, 284

Discourse on Thinking (Heidegger), 147

displacement, 22, 88–89, 89, 91

The Dispossed (LeGuin), 198–199

Dissertation Abstracts International, 23

The Divine Comedy (Dante), 171, 172, 253, 255

REAPPRAISALS: CANADIAN WRITERS

REAPPRAISALS: CANADIAN WRITERS was begun in 1973 in response to a need for single volumes of essays on Canadian authors who had not received the critical attention they deserved or who warranted extensive and intensive reconsideration. It is the longest running series dedicated to the study of Canadian literary subjects. The annual symposium, hosted by the Department of English at the University of Ottawa, began in 1972 and the following year University of Ottawa Press published the first title in the series, The Grove Symposium. Since then our editorial policy has remained straightforward: each year to make permanently available in a single volume the best of the criticism and evaluation presented at our symposia on Canadian literature, thereby creating a body of work on and a critical base for the study of Canadian writers and literary subjects.

Gerald Lynch
GENERAL EDITOR

THE THOMAS CHANDLER HALIBURTON SYMPOSIUM, edited and with an introduction by Frank M. Tierney

STEPHEN LEACOCK: A REAPPRAISAL, edited and with an introduction by David Staines

FUTURE INDICATIVE: LITERARY THEORY AND CANADIAN LITERATURE, edited and with an introduction by John Moss

REFLECTIONS: AUTOBIOGRAPHY AND CANADIAN LITERATURE, edited and with an introduction by K.P. Stich

RE(DIS)COVERING OUR FOREMOTHERS: NINETEENTH CENTURY CANADIAN WOMEN WRITERS, edited and with an introduction by Lorraine McMullen

BLISS CARMAN: A REAPPRAISAL, edited and with an introduction by Gerald Lynch

FROM THE HEART OF THE HEARTLAND: THE FICTION OF SINCLAIR ROSS, edited by John Moss

CONTEXT NORTH AMERICA: CANADIAN/U.S. LITERARY RELATIONS, edited by Camille R. La Bossière

HUGH MACLENNAN, edited by Frank M. Tierney

ECHOING SILENCE: ESSAYS ON ARCTIC NARRATIVE, edited and with a preface by John Moss

BOLDER FLIGHTS: ESSAYS ON THE CANADIAN LONG POEM, edited and with a preface by Frank M. Tierney and Angela Robbeson

DOMINANT IMPRESSIONS: ESSAYS ON THE CANADIAN SHORT STORY, edited by Gerald Lynch and Angela Robbeson

MARGARET LAURENCE: CRITICAL REFLECTIONS, edited and with an introduction by David Staines

ROBERTSON DAVIES: A MINGLING OF CONTRARIETIES, edited by Camille R. La Bossière and Linda M. Morra

WINDOWS AND WORDS: A LOOK AT CANADIAN CHILDREN'S LITERATURE IN ENGLISH, edited by Aïda Hudson and Susan-Ann Cooper

WORLDS OF WONDER: READINGS IN CANADIAN SCIENCE FICTION AND FANTASY LITERATURE, edited by Jean-François Leroux and Camille R. La Bossière

AT THE SPEED OF LIGHT THERE IS ONLY ILLUMINATION: A REAPPRAISAL OF MARSHALL MCLUHAN, edited by John Moss and Linda M. Morra

HOME-WORK: POSTCOLONIALISM, PEDAGOGY, AND CANADIAN LITERATURE, edited and with an introduction by Cynthia Sugars

THE CANADIAN MODERNISTS MEET, edited and with an introduction by Dean Irvine

MARGARET ATWOOD: THE OPEN EYE, edited and with introductions by John Moss and Tobi Kozakewich

OTHER SELVES: ANIMALS IN THE CANADIAN LITERARY IMAGINATION, edited and with an introduction by Janice Fiamengo.

THE IVORY THOUGHT: ESSAYS ON AL PURDY, edited by Gerald Lynch, Shoshannah Ganz and Josephene Kealey.

This book is set in Adobe Garamond Premier. Designed by Robert Slimbach in 1988, it is based on the original metal punches of Claude Garamond, a French punch cutter, who produced an array of book types in the mid-1500s. The italics are based on the metal punches of Garamond's contemporary Robert Granjon.